The Art of
Conducting Technique

a New Perspective

By Harold Farberman

President/COO: Sandy Feldstein
Project Editor: Thom Proctor
Production Coordinator: Diane Laucirica
Technical Editor: Dale Sloman
Interior Art: Demara Duffy
Typesetting: Maria Chenique
Cover Design: Ken Rehm

© 1997 WARNER BROS. PUBLICATIONS
All Rights Reserved

Any duplication, adaptation or arrangement of the compositions
contained in this collection requires the written consent of the Publisher.
No part of this book may be photocopied or reproduced in any way without permission.
Unauthorized uses are an infringement of the U.S. Copyright Act and are punishable by law.

DEDICATION

To all my students from whom I've learned so much.

ACKNOWLEDGEMENTS

To Ms. Joni Steshko, my thanks for helping me organize the scattered basic materials for *The Art Of Conducting Technique* into a coherent whole.

To Dan Lewis, friend and wonderful conductor/teacher, my thanks for his positive comments and welcome suggestions.

Finally, the care and attention every page of this book received from Ms. Corinne Curry defies mere words. She read, pointed out obscurities, typed, reread, joined phrases and typed again until it was *clear*. Her effort was nothing less than superb.

Is it any wonder why I've been married to her for so long?

© 1997 BELWIN-MILLS PUBLISHING CORPORATION
All Rights Administered by WARNER BROS. PUBLICATIONS U.S. INC.
All Rights Reserved.
No part of this book may be reproduced, in any form or means, without permission in writing from the publisher.

PREFACE

When a conductor is ready to perform publicly, his or her preparation is generally the culmination of a three-step process:

(1) Learning the score
(2) **Devising a technique to convey that knowledge to the orchestra**
(3) Conducting the music in rehearsal

The Art of Conducting Technique focuses on step two and is written for beginning conductors as well as practicing professionals. It challenges accepted technical views by supplying a complete and detailed analysis of the physical production of sound within a new set of concepts for baton movement.

From its inception *The Art of Conducting Technique* has been based on a single source -- the composer's score. It is my belief that the composer's needs generate the following conducting necessities:

The Conductor's Space
Visual Score Study
Baton Placement
Pitch Registration Levels
Dynamic Registration Zones
Spatial Registration

A new, three-dimensional system for charting baton movement called The PatternCube incorporates all of the above and represents a radical departure from standard two-dimensional pattern diagrams. Using the baton accurately requires an understanding of the three components of the conducting arm and their natural strokes, including the wrist-induced 'Click' Family.

Before the baton is grasped, every movable part of the conductor's body that might impact negatively on the stroke is investigated. This is especially critical for the beginning conductor. The feet, the knees, the nose, eyes and even the hair on top of the head can, and often do, have a negative impact on the clarity of the baton stroke. A chapter entitled Body Technique is devoted to these potential problems.

Selecting the 'right' baton and securing a basic baton grip is given special attention. The straight line and curved strokes and their variations are fully covered. Exercises for all strokes are designed for both hands.

Strokes form patterns, but **repetitive patterns cannot make music**. Formula patterns must be broken and replaced by pattern shapes which **grow from the music**. Numerous examples of new patterns are drawn and explained in the multi-dimensional system called the PatternCube.

Current conducting techniques are carefully examined. Detailed analysis of holds, beginning a piece on different beats within a measure, cut-offs, and mixed-meters are provided. While these subjects have been amply covered in other texts, **A New Perspective** offers alternative technical solutions for the conductor's consideration. Exercises, charts, and illustrations for all the newly proposed techniques appear throughout the text.

The Repertoire Section includes the three works that appear most often in conducting competitions. Scores for relevant sections of Mozart's *Magic Flute Overture,* Beethoven's *Fifth Symphony,* and Stravinsky's *Rite of Spring* are reproduced, along with complete PatternCubes for each of the sections discussed.

Careful study of *The Art of Conducting Technique* provides a literate, physical architecture to creatively reflect the conductor's comprehension of the score.

TABLE OF CONTENTS

Acknowledgements and Dedication ii

Preface iii

Table of Contents iv

Introduction vii

Foreword xi

Chapter One—<u>The Conductor's Space</u>..1
Identifying the areas in which the conductor works.
Summary.

Chapter Two—<u>Body Technique-Part One</u>..3
The first of two chapters that deal with the elimination of physical movements that impact negatively on the motions of the baton. This chapter addresses the feet, torso, waist and the blocks.
Summary.

Chapter Three—<u>Body Technique-Part Two</u> 8
The use of the conductor's head as a baton, the hair, eyes, eyeglasses, nose, mouth and body response to unfulfilled strokes are examined.
Summary.

Chapter Four—<u>The Conductor's Arm and The Baton</u> 13
The components of the conductor's arm: the upper arm, the forearm, the wrist, the fingers and the palm. Independence of hands. The baton, an extension of the arm, and the basic baton grip. Baton length and balance point.
Summary.

Chapter Five—<u>Baton Technique: Part One</u>..23
Straight Line Strokes and Curved Line Strokes. The 'Click' family: 'clicks,' 'flicks' and parts of each 'click' family stroke.
Not-To-Be-Used-Strokes.
Summary.

Chapter Six—<u>Baton Technique: Part Two</u> 28
Use of the mirror, metronome and video machine. Connection to the tip of the baton, the extension of the arm. Exercises for vertical and horizontal straight line strokes and their variations.
Summary.

Chapter Seven—<u>Baton Technique: Part Three</u> 34
Exercises for Curved Line Strokes and their variations.
Summary.

Chapter Eight—<u>Patterns</u> 39
Present day patterns, a two dimensional view. Basic arm positions when forming strokes. General rule for forming patterns. Diagrams supplied for patterns in two, three, four, five, six, seven, nine, and twelve beats.
Summary.

Chapter Nine—*Legato* and *Staccato* Patterns 49
Diagrams of various patterns employing *legato* and *staccato* strokes.
Summary.

Chapter Ten—Mixed-Meters 55
The Extended Stroke: the height, the speed, and the delivery of mixed meters.
Examples of patterns in 5/8 and 7/8.
Summary.

Chapter Eleven—The Upbeat 59
The Golden Rule. Making upbeats to the first beat. Positions of preparatory beats on all beats
in duple, triple, and meters in four. Examples in meters in five and six on all beats plus divisions:
3 + 2, 2 + 3 and 3 + 3, 2 + 2 + 2. Examples in meters in seven, and in one.
Starting mixed meters in five and in seven.
Summary.

Chapter Twelve —The Elements Of A New Technique..72
The PatternCube, Part One - The Pattern
The Score, Visual Score Study/Baton Placement.
The PatternCube-Part One, the Pattern. Symbols in the Pattern and the Pitch Line.
Summary.

Chapter Thirteen—New Beat Patterns..83
Examples of new beat patterns with diagrams and pitch lines.
Summary.

Chapter Fourteen- The PatternCube - Part Two
The Cube - Columns One and Two..87
The Cube contains 5 Columns which describe the physical movements that create the patterns.
This chapter introduces Column One which indicates the meter, and Column Two which contains
the four Pitch Registration Levels. A glossary of stroke, arm, and left hand symbols is included.
Summary.

Chapter Fifteen—Part Two of the PatternCube, Continued 93
The Cube - Column Three: indicates Dynamic Registration. The three Zones.
Summary.

Chapter Sixteen—Part Two of the PatternCube, Continued..99
The Cube - Columns Four, Five and the Information Box: shows Spatial Registration within the
entire Conductor's Space, left hand movements and special physical moves within the Cube.
Summary.

Chapter Seventeen—Visual Score Study/Baton Placement 103
Examples.
Summary.

Chapter Eighteen—The Left Arm/Hand 109
The role of the left hand. The Palm: left hand indications for *forte, crescendo,* and *diminuendo.*
Various opportunities for the use of the left hand. Eighteenth and Nineteenth Century string
seating can be used to expand the use of the left hand.
Summary.

Chapter Nineteen—Cueing 117
The two parts of a cue, and how to make a cue. Exercises.
Summary.

Chapter Twenty—The *Fermata* or Hold, with Cut-Off Motion 124
The two parts of the hold. The right and left hand duties for making the hold and the cut-off.
Forearm and open palm movements in the cut-off. Examples with holds on different beats
within a measure. The concluding hold, and holds with *diminuendi,* and *crescendi.*
The final upward cut-off, and holds without cut-offs.
Summary.

Chapter Twenty One—Rests 134
Rest in opening and final measures. Pauses, and moving toward and away from a rest.
Examples of attacks after rests.
Summary.

Chapter Twenty Two—Accents, Syncopation 139
Preparing accents, and use of the wrist. Size of the preparatory stroke. Preparing a *fortissimo* accent in a *pianissimo* sonority, and a *piano* accent in a *fortissimo* sonority. Syncopation, and accents within syncopation.
Summary.

Chapter Twenty Three—Tempo 146
What is tempo? Choosing a tempo. The unit of rhythmic propulsion, and its effect on tempo. Changing the
time value of a rhythmic unit.
Summary.

Chapter Twenty Four—Tempo, Part Two 153
Tempo modification, *accelerando* and *rallentando*. The effect of momentum in tempo transitions. Metric
Modulation and unprepared changes of tempo, with examples.
Summary.

Chapter Twenty Five—Accompaniments, Instrumental 161
The soloist/conductor partnership, prior to orchestral rehearsals. Accompanying a soloist, in concert when
problems arise. Solutions. Conclusion of *cadenzas*. Who leads, who follows? Examples.
Summary.

Chapter Twenty Six— Accompaniments, Vocal 168
The importance of syllables, vocal freedom, and baton motion in the elongated stroke. Accompanying
Recitative, with examples.
Summary.

Chapter Twenty Seven—Speaking To An Orchestra 174
In rehearsal: six points. General advice and the rehearsal order. Bowings, building a library.
The Negative face.
Summary.

Chapter Twenty Eight—Repertoire 178
Is there a 'correct' physical response to a musical problem? Visual Score Study/Baton Placement and complete PatternCubes for excerpts from:
Mozart - *Magic Flute Overture* 179
Beethoven - *Symphony No. 5* 184
Stravinsky - *Rite of Spring* 239

Bibliography 289

INTRODUCTION

A century ago, in 1894, the great theorist Heinrich Schenker (1868-1935) predicted (with characteristic pre-science) that the future would require a new kind of orchestra conductor, not the proverbial "time-beater" (the so-called *Kapellmeister*) to which late nineteenth century concert audiences had become accustomed. Musicians and listeners would increasingly demand someone who could "breathe with the spirit" of music; who excelled in a sort of "painting" that derived from the "work itself" and that transformed mere "sound" into "line."[1] Harold Farberman's book will help vindicate Schenker's optimistic prophecy. The kind of conducting Schenker hoped would materialize in the future is still in short supply. Farberman's treatise is the first of its kind in the sense that it offers a practical and theoretical guide for developing those "painterly" skills that can make the difference between a routine performance and an insightful and memorable one.

This book is at once unlike any other text on conducting and also a worthy successor to the handful of classic treatises on conducting. It is perhaps closest in spirit to Hermann Scherchen's *Handbook of Conducting*, which first appeared in 1929 and was translated into English in 1933. Like Scherchen (a great conductor and fiery iconoclast), Farberman brings to his task not only the benefit of a distinguished international career on the podium but also the perspective of a tireless advocate of contemporary music. For him, the making of music is not merely bringing to life the treasures of a musical museum in an antiquarian spirit. It was Farberman's set of recordings of the music of Charles Ives that first placed the full breadth of Ives' achievement -- in superb renditions -- before the public.

But unlike Scherchen, Farberman is also a composer of distinction. The interpretation of a score -- in fact the entire task of performing the work of others -- should be, to some considerable degree, an act of re-composing. The performer must be able to think like a composer. The failure of performers to have tried their hand at composition and to have learned the craft of writing music (even if the results are not memorable) is among the most severe shortcomings encountered in otherwise superbly trained aspiring performers today. The great names of the past -- Fürtwangler, Weingartner, Szell, and even Toscanini (not to speak of instrumentalists such as Paderewski, Heifetz and Casals) all wrote music of their own. On practically every page of this book one senses the analytic and interpretive habits of a composer with a consummate mastery of the elements of music.

If that were not enough, Farberman spent more than a decade as a percussionist in the Boston Symphony Orchestra. From the vantage point of membership in one of the world's greatest orchestras, he witnessed the finest (and worst) conductors of the day. He saw what worked and what did not. He was the beneficiary and victim of both spellbinding and tragicomic conductorial behavior. Most important, he learned the difference a conductor can make with the best of ensembles playing repertoire totally familiar to them. When there was no need for time beating, and little need for cues, the capacity of a conductor (or the inability) to make music, to shape time, and to cultivate sound became crystal clear.

Through this book both the aspiring and the experienced conductor will benefit from Farberman's experience and ideas. Each reader can take from Farberman's recasting of the technique of conducting and his systematization of gesture and the space the conductor uses something that allows him or her to take the next step to getting inside a score and realizing one's ideas on stage.

---

[1] Heinrich Schenker, "Konzertdirigenten" in *Die Zukunft* Vol. 7 (Berlin 1894) reprinted in Hellmut Federhofer, editor, *Heinrich Schenker als Essayist und Kritiker* (Olms Hildesheim 1990) pp. 81-82.

Last but not least, what lends this book its authority is the fact that it derives from years of teaching conducting. Harold Farberman created the famed *Conductor's Institute*, now located at the Hartt School of the University of Hartford in Connecticut. Farberman has spent summer after summer working with conductors at all levels of proficiency. He has integrated into the curriculum orchestra players, professional conductors from all schools of training, and leading composers and their music. Novices and accomplished instrumentalists eager to begin to conduct, as well as conductors in mid-career have benefited from Farberman's ability to instill basic technique and to augment and alter existing styles. Although Farberman has evolved his own vocabulary and strategy, his intent is that each conductor develop his/her distinct approach. His ambition as a teacher is that conductors assimilate his teaching and then shape the elements of conducting technique to fit their ideas, their aspirations, and the opportunities and limitations of the circumstances in which they practice the art of conducting. There are many who would agree that he is the preeminent conducting pedagogue in the United States. He is a great teacher.

The history of conducting is unlike the history of any other form of musical performance art.[2] As Rudolf Cahn Speyer (who studied with Nikisch, taught in Berlin and conducted in Budapest) noted in 1919 (at the very beginnings of the age of modern technology of the mechanical reproduction of music), conducting has been and will continue to be the hardest aspect of music making to evaluate. In 1919 the problem was that most of the audience never could know a score well enough to judge or evaluate an interpretation.[3] Today, the situation is quite the opposite. Musical literacy of the traditional sort within the audience, and therefore the score, has disappeared. Instead, the standard repertory has been recorded nearly to death. Audiences are not dependent on miniature scores, piano reductions, or their own cultivated musical memories. They have in their ears repeated hearings of letter-perfect renditions of the work they are about to hear in concert. They know the repertoire in a new way.

In 1919 it may have been relatively easy to impress an audience with the ability to get through a work of music, to accomplish the rudimentary task of directing traffic (so to speak). Today that is not enough. Furthermore, the group of people whom every conductor has to convince -- if not impress -- has only gotten more discerning: the musicians in the orchestra. In 1919 musicians could tell the difference between someone who knew what he or she was doing and a charlatan. Today, that is even more the case. Today's orchestra musicians are not only fabulously adept technically but also have a good deal of the repertoire in their ears, if not in their fingers, through recordings.

The burden on the conductor is then to lead both the orchestra and audience into a deeper or perhaps novel and challenging understanding and appreciation of very familiar works of music. In some cases, conductors will choose to concentrate on new and unfamiliar music. But insofar as they also confront the canonic set of musical works that provide the musical examples in this book and the basic repertory of every orchestra, they must develop a technique that goes beyond the elementary aspects of time-beating and the demonstration of the essential elements of dynamics and articulation.

Therefore Schenker's prediction of the need for a "painterly" dimension for conducting was on the mark. The technique of conducting, in its least metaphysical sense, concerns the ability to create sound, line, and meaning with physical motion. The baton, the hand, the body, and the eyes -- all without words and

---

2 See Georg Schünemann's *Geschichte des Dirigierens* (Breitkopf und Hartel Leipzig 1913) and Eliott W. Galkin, *A History of Orchestral Conducting In Theory and Practice* (Pendragon Press: New York, 1988). The writings of the late Norman del Mar are also highly recommended.
3 Rudolf Cahn Speyer, *Handbuch des Dirigierens* (Breitkopf und Hartel: Leipzig, 1919) p. 271ff.

explanation -- must achieve a subtle and differentiated result. Conducting is an elaborate ritual of pantomime, whose underlying grammar is recognized by musicians the world over. The moves made by the conductor are complex and traditional, and at the same time universal and entirely susceptible to personalization. What Farberman teaches will work on a podium in South America, Asia, Europe, or America; with orchestras that do not share a common ordinary language with the conductor.

Conducting, like any other performing art, is contingent on the command of technique. But like playing an instrument, that technique must be linked with and adapted to musical ideas and specific musical contours. Transferable dimensions of technique are molded to fit the piece of music one is about to learn and conduct. Analysis and preparation before a rehearsal and ultimately a performance are about using technique to realize interpretation based on musical texts. As one teacher properly asked when an enthusiastic and ambitious beginner announced that he wanted to conduct: "I know you want to conduct, but what do you want to conduct?" The adaptation of technique to answer that challenge is what Farberman teaches, not the indiscriminate application of formulas. Technique and musicianship are intertwined in his treatise, which is as it should be.

In his preface to *Capriccio*, Richard Strauss (who was a great conductor in his own right) admonished (in his usual provocatively ambiguous manner) all future conductors about to prepare and perform the work that conducting was a balance between faithful adherence to the notes of the score and congenial improvisation.[4] Indeed, what the command of conducting technique permits is the capacity to realize and shape music and therefore to go beyond what any text can indicate and to improvise, even in performance. No matter what has happened in rehearsal, every performance is and should be unique. The capacity to seize the moment and deliver a memorable performance; to do the unexpected, to respond to inspired playing; to be transported in the act of performance requires the most secure and second-nature command of conducting technique. No orchestra -- even of amateurs and students -- will fail to follow a new idea communicated through the baton and physical gesture if it is properly executed.

What makes *The Art of Conducting Technique* a truly exceptional contribution is its recognition of the historical moment facing the art of conducting. We are in the midst of a seemingly never-ending era of nostalgia in our culture. We speak of the past as if it will never be equaled, much less surpassed. This is a dangerous and crippling illusion. The conductors of the past, their tricks, foibles, idiosyncrasies, and styles have become the stuff of legend.

Furtwangler's jagged and shaky downbeats, Reiner's lack of motion, Strauss' detached manner (left hand tucked into his pants pocket), and Toscanini's mesmerizing and fluid baton all have become familiar to us. We have the benefit not only of a recorded legacy but of a visual documentary library as well. We are reminded, somewhat annoyingly, of so-called great traditions that have been lost.

The blunt fact is that, as Mahler once pointed out, the appeal to "tradition" by a new generation of performers is a bad excuse and a form of sloppy thinking. Performance is the art of communicating with the audience of one's own time and place. What worked with players and audiences in Strauss' day, or even Leonard Bernstein's, may be irrelevant. No videotape and no CD will recreate what happened in a hall; what was heard and felt by the audience at a moment in time that has passed exclusively into memory. Memoirs by players and audience members can articulate how moved and touched they were, but despite this, the moment has passed beyond retrieval. No record will recreate it. Our task therefore, is to offer our

---

[4] Richard Strauss, *Capriccio* (Oertel: Berlin, 1942).

own audiences the same level of engagement -- an equal intensity of response that allows listeners a comparably unforgettable experience of being moved and transported by a live concert. To help achieve this end, Mahler even reorchestrated Beethoven and Schumann. Like many others, he transcribed older music. We in our own time are too insecure to follow in their footsteps. As a performer, Mahler (like all other great conductors of the past) was "true" to the spirit of the music of Wagner, Beethoven, and Mozart by interpreting it in a manner that effectively reached and convinced his audience. That task of interpretation -- the rendering of music so that it seems indispensable and actual to one's contemporaries -- is what the great conductors of the past understood and put into practice brilliantly.

Conductors of today need to emulate this achievement. They need not imitate older styles or copy ideas from yesteryear. No doubt some things do not change. For example, a young conductor will invariably show too much, and provide more physical motion than is required. The young Mahler did. A young conductor may intrude on sound, especially in highly charged and lush and loud passages. Restraint and economy are hard to learn. They are not necessarily signs of indifference and detachment. And this type of technical discipline can be taught and learned.

But whether the conductor's style is highly expressive visually or naturally restrained, the strategies and techniques carefully and clearly presented by Harold Farberman in this book can make the difference between routine conducting and distinguished conducting in our own historical era. This is why a new first-rate book on conducting technique has been sorely needed. Farberman's approach will help a contemporary conductor reach the highest plane of interpretive accomplishment. Years of experience on the podium and in the classroom have shown this to be the case. The publication of this book therefore opens up the possibility that musicians, students, and even enthusiastic music lovers can gain the benefits of a unique, analytic and practical perspective through reading and the use of this book in the classroom.

Many fields are literally inundated with textbooks and handbooks. Very few of these are ever original or truly useful. Conducting is an art that has been shortchanged. What books have been published are few in number and have appeared only intermittently. And among those only a handful have been either interesting or practical. It is to Farberman's credit that a gap finally has been filled with a modern book on conducting that is original, enlightening, and helpful in a refreshing, affectionate, and disarming manner.

Leon Botstein
Music Director, American Symphony Orchestra
President, Bard College
Editor, *The Musical Quarterly*
Annandale-on-Hudson, NY 12504
January 2, 1996

FOREWORD

Art Form is "the more or less established structure, pattern, or scheme, followed in shaping an artistic work." [1]

The art of conducting requires a technique that should be considered an Art Form. The rationale for that technique is derived from a highly developed, complex, and wondrously individual art form: Music.

Music is defined as "the art of sound in time which expresses ideas and emotions in significant forms through the elements of rhythm, melody, harmony and color." [2]

Music, ever changing, is the initiator of the technique that reflects its content. Simply put: **MUSIC CREATES TECHNIQUE**. A conductor committed to a clear presentation of a score must utilize a technique that can serve as the varying visual representation of the printed page, the frozen textural kaleidoscope of the composer's voice.

More often than not, the same repetitive physical gestures are imposed upon measure after measure of the score regardless of the changing content of the music. Leading an orchestra is frequently reduced to a proficient, 'correct' down-sides-up series of movements. Those movements, first codified in 1701 by Thomas Janowka (1660-1741) under the heading of "Tactus" in his *Clavis as Thesaurum Magna Artis Musicae*,[3] were designed for one purpose -- to keep performing musicians together by indicating a constant pulse.

Janowka's hand signals answered the technical needs of the music of the late 17th, early 18th centuries by providing an excellent mechanism for indicating time without intruding on the music. Since then, composers have reshaped the size and technical expectations of performing ensembles and in the process have justified the presence of a vastly different kind of signal-giver. Despite the enormous changes the signal-giver, now called the conductor, finds that for the most part the signals themselves have remained the same. Surely the continued use of simplistic 300 year old formulas for indicating pulse must be questioned, and conducting technique, the physical tools of our profession, should be reexamined and redefined.

What is conducting technique?

Conducting technique is the conductor's response to the realities of the composer's score. That response is tempered by mental and physical factors, each dependent on the other for the fullest realization of the composer's intent.

Factor One: The chances for a full realization of the composer's language depends upon the conductor's musical and extra-musical knowledge, factors directly influencing the performance plan.

Factor Two: The conductor's performing skills convey the performance plan (factor one) to the players. The equation is simple. The greater the conductor's physical flexibility, the broader the control she/he can exercise over the orchestra. The concert hall result is the presentation of music with a sharply defined, clear profile.

The reason for this text is Factor Two, the summation of the conductor's mental process as reflected in the conductors **physical** performing skills, **the art of conducting** technique. It will command all our attention.

Without a clear vision of a composer's musical rationale, a conductor is divorced from the changing realities of the music. Even superb musical minds, with focused views of a work, falter and fail if a **compositionally derived conducting technique** is not in place. Brilliant musicians and barely competent journeymen are reduced to time-beating equals.

---

[1] Random House Unabridged Dictionary, Second Edition, (1987) p. 118
[2] Random House Unabridged Dictionary, Second Edition, (1987) p. 1268
[3] Elliot W. Galkin, *A History of Orchestral Conducting* (New York: Pendragon Press, 1988) p. 198

TIME-BEATING MUST BE REGARDED AS PHYSICAL ILLITERACY. It is simplistic, boring, and totally destructive of the composer's intentions. Lacking musical and creative distinction, the present technical status-quo remains mired in the past.

With one notable exception, those closest to the conducting profession have neither questioned the continued use of our antiquated technical tools nor offered help.

CONDUCTORS

Conductors generally do not talk or write enough about the technical nuts and bolts of the profession. Indeed, until rather recently [4] conductors hardly spoke to one another. Some aspects of the profession remain shrouded in myth and mystery. Unquestioned, misguided 'wisdom' persists; "conducting cannot be taught" or "conductors are born, not made," and "women are not meant to be conductors."

All young untutored musicians bring varying degrees of talent, imagination and intuition to their hoped-for profession. The process that teaches and lifts the musically gifted hopefuls out of the pack and creates the potential for a conducting career is barely acknowledged in our profession. The myth of the fully formed "born conductor," the universally adapted European model *obermensch*, remains in place. The journey to earn the right to be called a conductor is made step by step over time. It is not a title bestowed overnight to an aspiring applicant.

Discovering how to study a composition, how to listen, how to **work** sound and **work with** sound while connecting shapes and building phrases into a cohesive musical structure is a complex learning process. Each element is a separate skill, an individual, intricate part of a larger working craft that must be experienced and ingested, layer by varying layer. Each skill needs a source, a master musician/teacher willing to share his or her years of experience and knowledge. As each new musical/technical challenge is encountered and conquered, enduring a heavy work load is a factor in achieving success.

While gaining the necessary experience needed to discover the various physical gestures that generate different musical responses, the fledgling conductor must also learn to deal with his/her instrument, the gifted individuals who make the sounds.

The learning process takes time. The probable truth is that the most famous and revered maestri went through the same kinds of long term working/growth processes, made the same kinds of mistakes, and experienced the same kinds of learning calamities BEFORE they could be lauded as "....*a born conductor!*"

"Born conductors?" Hardly. With the rarest of exceptions, it is a myth.

COMPOSERS

Generally speaking, composers have disengaged themselves from the recreative process. This was not always the case. One has only to think of Berlioz, Mendelssohn, Wagner, Mahler, Strauss and notable exceptions in our own times: Bernstein, Boulez, Foss, and Schuller. For most present day composers, the task of trying to conduct their own scores has proven to be a genuinely alarming experience. An almost total lack of understanding about the conductor's physical connection to the orchestra makes it virtually impossible for the composer to offer technical help to the conductor involved in the process of recreation.

---

[4] The Conductor's Guild was founded in 1975 and became a member of the American Symphony Orchestra League in 1976. Its major aims were enumerated in its charter;
A-To share and exchange relevant musical and professional information
B-To support the development and training of conductors
C-To publish periodicals and newsletters dealing with the conducting profession
　　The author was the founder of the Conductor's Guild and its first President, serving for two terms. In 1985 the Guild became an independent organization. Its membership is well over two thousand and growing. It is an organization worthy of every conductor's support.

ORCHESTRAL MUSICIANS

Orchestral musicians are the voice of the conductor, and are a source of constant and unfailing help to the podium occupant. A conductor and an orchestra at work are a partnership. In the best of all possible worlds it is an equal partnership, each of the components bringing to the other matching levels of musical excellence. The help the orchestral musician offers to the conductor is full compliance, a willingness to realize a respected partner's musical vision.

When the equality of partnership is in question, the orchestral musician will 'help' the conductor but in a strikingly different manner. They will NOT comply with the conductor's directions.

How is this done? Orchestras at all performing levels know the basic symphonic/concerto repertoire and the music of their national composers very well, and are often better informed than the conductors who stand before them. When an orchestra's natural performing level is musically superior to the conductor's, it creates a fascinating paradox.

If a conductor's technique, supposedly the outward manifestation of his/her inner musical impulses is deficient, the outcome should be a poor performance. In many instances the **opposite** will occur. Thanks to the musicians, the orchestra **willingly supplies the missing ingredients** for the conductor and shapes a performance well beyond the conductor's capabilities. The 'help' the players offer inept conductors not only carries the podium pretenders through the music, but perhaps more importantly, helps the orchestra preserve its own artistic standard. [5]

And the paradox?

The conductor does not understand what is taking place. Experiencing what she/he hears, the conductor believes s**he/he** is responsible for the performance the **orchestra** creates. Totally ignorant of the reality, this species of conductor is doomed to embrace its ineptitude endlessly. They are destined to survive because of the kindness of strangers -- the orchestral musicians who help save their careers.

Unless one is acutely aware of the technical realities that envelop conductor and orchestra, it is difficult to comprehend who is actually responsible for what is occurring onstage.

QUESTIONS

How can we expect others to comprehend what many in our own profession fail to understand? The answer is that we must first reeducate ourselves about the **complex mental act of creating a performance via physical motions, the true art of conducting.**

Is it possible to peel away the protective mystique of conducting? Perhaps. Tradition resists change and fresh insight.

Is it possible to put into place a set of technical criteria which would identify a conductor as a true artist rather than a journeyman time beater?

The answer in an unqualified yes.

---

[5] Before the 1957 season Charles Munch, Music Director of the Boston Symphony Orchestra, fell ill. I was then a member of the orchestra. A series of guest conductors were invited to replace Munch; the orchestra's reaction to the various guests could be gauged by the sound the orchestra produced. If the orchestra was not persuaded by the abilities of the guest, they sounded exactly like the BSO under Munch. When a guest was able to impose his musical will upon the players, the sound of the orchestra changed. The qualities manifested by the guest matched the musical expectations of the orchestra. They were quite willing to submit themselves to music-making on their own level.

CHAPTER ONE

THE CONDUCTOR'S SPACE

A conductor's technique is fully displayed in the area I call the **CONDUCTOR'S SPACE**, where baton and orchestra unite to create sound.

The Conductor's Space is divided into the **Immediate** and the **Extended** Conductor's Space and has evolved with one basic characteristic -- an unhampered sight line between orchestra and conductor to accommodate constant baton movement. The complete Conductor's Space **allows for every conceivable technical gesture to be delivered to the orchestra players with clarity.**

The Immediate Conductor's Space

The **podium** is the conductor's working area in the **Immediate Conductor's Space,** as outlined in Figures 1 and 2. The dimensions of an Immediate Conductor's Space are determined by the length of the arms at full extension. Because the human form is contoured in an infinite variety of shapes, every Immediate Conductor's Space will be filled and used differently.

Defining the Work Area of the Immediate Conductor's Space

Sideways Up, Sideways Down

The following movements define the natural outer limits of the **sideways up, sideways down working area** of the Immediate Conductor's Space.

- Raise both arms, close to the ears as high above the head as they can reach.
- Slowly drop the arms **sideways** until they are
- shoulder high and parallel to the floor. Again slowly drop the arms and
- lower them until they rest at the sides of the body.

Fig. 1

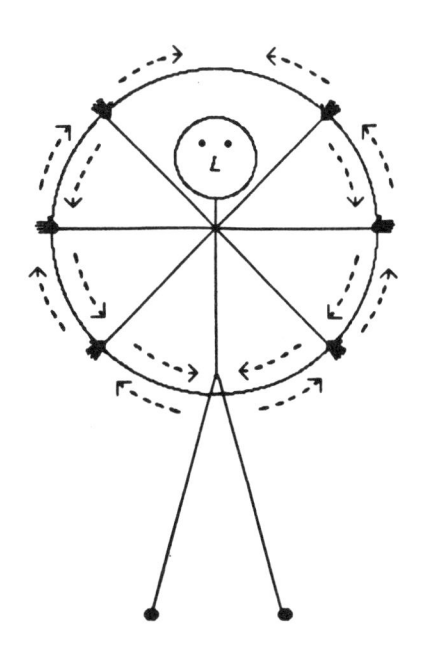

Frontward Up and Frontward Down

This exercise defines the natural limits of the **Frontward Up, Frontward Down work area** in the Immediate Conductor's Space.

- Raise both arms as before. At full extension, lower the arms **in front** of the body until they are
- shoulder high and parallel to the floor in front of the body. Slowly drop the arms and
- let them rest at the sides of the body.

Fig. 2

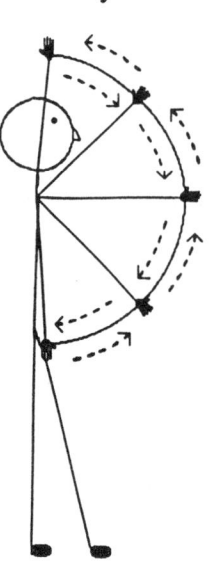

The Extended Conductor's Space

Is there more to the Conductor's Space than the immediate working area? Yes. The space beyond the podium has not been clearly defined; it is the natural extension of the Immediate Conductor's Space, the **connective tissue which binds orchestra to conductor.** It is an area "wired" for sound. Imagine the space beyond the podium as a source of potential energy, containing a precise network of lanes and circuits running from the podium (the energy source of the Conductor's Space) to every player on the stage. The lanes and circuits are the conduits that transfer silent physical energy (baton movements) into audible sound. Performance is the response.

The complete Conductor's Space is a **combination of the Immediate and the Extended Conductor's Space.** It is the entire stage area, because every performer on the stage is, or should be, an extension of the mind, heart, and will of the conductor who serves as the mind, heart and will of the composer.

CHAPTER ONE SUMMARY

The Conductor's Space is a work area divided into the **Immediate and Extended Conductor's Space.** The complete Conductor's Space makes it possible for every conceivable technical gesture to be delivered to the orchestra players with extreme clarity.

The Art of Conducting Technique explores and uses every area of the Conductor's Space. The **Immediate Conductor's Space** is the podium area and is outlined by the limits of the conductor's reach. Since the human form is contoured in a variety of sizes and shapes, every Immediate Conductor's Space is filled and used differently.

The **Extended Conductor's Space** is the area beyond the podium, the connective tissue that binds the orchestra and every player to the conductor. The addition of the Extended Conductor's Space to the Immediate Conductor's Space creates the **Complete Conductor's Space** -- the entire stage.

CHAPTER TWO

BODY TECHNIQUE -- PART ONE

Physical Motion

The Eyes/The Ears
Conducting technique begins with **body control**, the elimination of all physical movement that impacts negatively on the carefully conceived motions of the baton.

Consider the following:

"....for the first time, I saw him direct. Although I had heard much of his leading, yet it surprised me in a high degree. He had accustomed himself to give signs of expression to his orchestra by all manner of extraordinary motion of his body. So often as a strong *sforzando* occurred, he tore his arms, which he had previously crossed upon his breast, with great vehemence asunder. At a *piano* he bent himself down, and the lower, the softer he wished to have it. Then when a *crescendo* came, he raised himself again by degrees, and upon the commencement of the *forte* sprang bolt upright. To increase the *forte* yet more, he would sometimes also join in with a shout to the orchestra without being aware of it.[6]" The concert Louis Spohr witnessed in Vienna in 1814, was conducted by the composer, Ludwig van Beethoven.

Beethoven as conductor is not under serious discussion; Spohr's description leads one to conclude that Beethoven's deafness exaggerated his style of leading the orchestra. The word picture raises an important question, however: are there physical motions that intrude upon and harm the progress of the music? The answer is yes. When the conductor's unexpected physical movements violate the **Conductor's Space** the eyes become more important than the ears **and movement cancels sound.** The audience is torn between listening to the music and watching a spectacle.

How much physical movement is appropriate? As little as possible. I was fortunate to have heard Maestro Herbert von Karajan in his final New York concert with the Vienna Philharmonic. A frail Karajan was helped on stage and rested his body on the railing that framed the back of the podium. He never left that position throughout the concert and conducted with only the upper portion of his body. **His feet never moved.** Yet all the hallmarks of a major Karajan performance were intact. His presence and use of the Conductor's Space were totally focused.

On another occasion, I had the pleasure of hearing Maestro James DePreist conduct the Oregon Symphony. Once on the podium, DePreist sat on a chair, laid down his crutch, and went to work. From a seated position DePreist had the orchestra on the tip of his baton. His conducting space was apparent and fully utilized. His upper body flow reflected the excellent music he and his orchestra produced; it was a whole evening in every respect. In both cases, little or no mobility in the lower half of the body had no effect on the process of recreating the music.

It is appropriate to conclude this segment with an observation about a musician who was this generation's most brilliant, and perhaps most physically volatile, conductor -- Maestro Leonard Bernstein.

Thirty years ago, I heard Bernstein conduct Mahler's *First Symphony*. The final triumphant return to D major (rehearsal No. 54 in the last movement) made a lasting impression. A split second before the D major, a lean Bernstein leapt high into the air and landed on the podium at the precise arrival of the home key. He transformed his entire body into an energetic, airborne baton. It was startling, and at that time a typical Bernstein gesture. It was a moment to be savored, but that one physical moment is all I remember about my first Mahler/Bernstein encounter.

[6] Elliott W. Galkin, *A History of Orchestral Conducting,* (New York: Pendragon Press, 1988)

Many years later, my wife and I were invited to a New York Philharmonic Benefit Concert. Mahler's *First Symphony,* with Bernstein conducting, was on the program. The glory of the Mahler/ Bernstein connection had been universally confirmed and I knew that Bernstein, then approaching seventy, had matured into a recreative force that seemed a far cry from the unlicensed pilot of yesteryear. I awaited the D major arrival at rehearsal No. 54. When he got there his physical movements were confined to his arms. He thrust them, fully extended, high above his head (the jump) and marked the D major arrival with a solid right-arm downward motion (the landing). His left arm remained fully extended, high above his head. A brilliant technical/musical use of space, it not only confirmed the D major arrival, but sustained the D pedal -- an exact reflection of the music. And, like Karajan and DePreist, **his feet never moved.**

The line between physical motion that helps the music and a physicality that obstructs its flow is a fine one. Can the movements which inhibit the progress of the music be identified? The answer is yes.

The Feet

Perhaps it is too much to claim that a conductor's feet are as important as the hands, but it's a closer call than one might imagine. The influence of the feet upon the baton is direct and the musical consequences are often destructive.

The **Immediate Conductor's Space** has a **fixed place**. It is the orchestra's point of reference for 'reading' baton motions. When the feet move and carry the body beyond the players' reference point, the fixed place is violated and the baton's movements are compromised. Body-generated movements result in **secondary rhythmic pulses** which often conflict with the hand (right or left) responsible for indicating the primary pulse.

The principles are simple. Unexpected movement (movement of the feet) added to precise movement (baton strokes) disrupts predictability (formation of patterns).

What follows is a detailed, slow-motion analysis of a seemingly minor, but often encountered physical motion. That motion is a quick move to the left, to face the first violins, **a movement led by the feet.** The result is a momentary creation of four deviations of the original tempo, resulting in two new, but differing, tempi.

The deviations:
1. The **feet move ahead of the basic pulse** to face the first violins. The feet are followed by the upper body.
2. The body movement causes a **strong head-accent motion**, also **ahead** of the basic pulse.
3. **The baton is now marginally ahead** of the original tempo because of the abrupt left pull of the body. The baton now faces the first violins and is hidden from half the orchestra.
4. **The right elbow**, now facing the orchestra where the baton used to be, is a bit **behind** the original beat.

The two new tempi resulting from the abrupt movement of the feet are:
1. For the first violins and the orchestra members seated to the left of the conductor, the baton continues in the **new and slightly faster tempo.**
2. For the rest of the orchestra the **elbow** has displaced the baton as the pulse point. While the elbow is in rhythm with the baton, it is slightly **behind the tempo** of the baton, like the return of an echo: the same but late.

And the musical consequence? On the surface, a very slight rhythmic disruption is quickly repaired because the orchestra 'goes' with the rhythm of the first violins. But within the orchestra the sonority is out of sync. Balance, color and phrasing suffer with little chance of recovery as the orchestration changes while the music goes forward. Two solutions for leftside movement appear in the section titled **The Waist**. It is worth repeating: movement of the baton is easier to read if the feet and body are **stationary,** and is more difficult to follow if the feet and body are in **motion.**

The Position of the Feet-The Root/The Blocks

A conductor whose feet move constantly fosters a sense of restlessness. In contrast, a firmly anchored stance has a focused presence and projects a look of authority. The elimination of restless feet is an urgent technical and musical priority.

Just as no two conductors fill the Immediate Conductor's Space identically due to differences in height, weight, and physical characteristics, a single "correct" stance does not exist. Body balance, lack of tension and overall physical comfort are basics that must be considered.

Two common stances have wide appeal:

1. Feet aligned, but slightly apart.

Fig. 3

left foot   right foot

The distance between the feet may vary from four to seven inches. The gap depends on comfort and how the body balances its height and weight. Experiment with **the space of the gap**. Use the stance shown in Fig. 3 if it 'feels' right. If not, try the following:

2. Place one foot, generally the left one, slightly in front of the other foot.

Fig. 4

left foot   right foot

Find a comfortable gap and check the body for balance. This is the firmest and most comfortable root position for many conductors. If it 'feels' good, use it. If neither position is comfortable, keep experimenting until your body finds a working position that fulfills the basic needs defined above.

I would not recommend a currently favored position of conducting while standing on the balls of the feet, leaning forward and rocking between toes and heels. The constant up-down motion is distracting to the audience.

Once the body finds a natural, tension-free podium stance, the young conductor might imagine the body as the trunk of a tree, and the feet as the **roots of the tree,** riveted into the soil of the podium. A stationary foot stance makes it possible for the upper body to articulate the most complex baton patterns with absolute clarity.

If you have an inclination to move about when conducting, use **two blocks of wood**, each one inch thick and approximately 6" x 12" wide, as a corrective tool. Place them on the floor in the exact position of your stance. Do all exercises and all physical score preparation while standing on the blocks and discard them only when your foot movement decreases. You will still 'feel' the space restriction and your feet will not move.

When you can honestly say that your feet are ready to supply solid, unmoving support for your conducting motions, make the following resolutions :

1. **Not to move your feet once the music is in progress.**
2. **Not to bend your knees once the music is in progress.**
   Not only is the baton in danger of disappearing beneath the music stand, but the audience will be treated to an outward extension of a part of your anatomy that is best kept hidden in the folds of your tails.
3. **Not to jump upward once the music is in progress.**

From a fixed root position the **upper body, the torso, functions as a delivery system for the baton.** It is constantly preparing and placing both hands in the Conductor's Space.

The Torso

Almost without exception the torso should face the orchestra. Assuming the celli are to the right of the podium, the first violins should not stare into the conductor's back for the beginning of Wagner's "Liebestod," from *Tristan und Isolde*. Not only will the baton be hidden from the first violins, but after the opening bars, the conductor will have to **shift** the position of the feet to face the orchestra. That unnecessary movement can break the mood and the line, and will certainly disrupt the movement of the baton.

The torso is not meant to quiver, heave, turn abruptly, bend rapidly, or shake, rattle and roll. It is meant to "breathe" with the flow of the music, a **subtle** movement that enhances the progress of the line. Please note the word subtle. The torso can swivel to the right and to the left, but it should move in those directions **from the hips, not the feet.**

The Waist

Useful conducting movements from the mid-body pivot point are restricted to the swivel, a forward bend, a backward lean and a sideways lean. Avoid the quick, **steep** forward motion from the waist, which is meant to signify a *piano* dynamic. The movement itself is a *forte* gesture and is overused and musically abusive. Spohr's description of Beethoven's *piano* kneebend is still encountered in concert halls the world over.

Two solutions for **left side movement, without foot movement** are:
1. Turn slightly or swivel from the waist and hips in one motion toward the first violins. Within that motion to the left you may add a slight, further left turn of the head to engage the back stands. This entire left movement should be a one-motion flow. Do **not** move your right hand to the left. Keep it stationary or move it slightly forward, toward the orchestra. From either position the baton will be visible to the entire orchestra.

2. Use a full left hand extension to the left side of the podium. The left hand assumes the function of **primary time beater.** The right hand and torso remain in place. The open left hand may be in a variety of positions: palm up, facing the first violins, with fingers pointing toward the floor; palm turned over facing the floor; or for rhythmic, forceful music the left hand can move to a closed-fist. Along with the extended left hand gesture, add a **slight** left movement of the head toward the violins. (The movement to the left does not disrupt the line and flow of the music in either solution.) The right hand 'marks' time until it is ready to assume its normal duties. (A conductor 'marks' time by making a small up-down 'click' beat from the wrist which defines the pulse, but does not initiate musical movement.)

For a **right side movement, without foot movement,** try the following:
1. If the baton is in your right hand, movement to the right of the podium does not involve the waist. Make a full right arm extension to the right, along with slight head turn to the right. No other movement is necessary.

CHAPTER TWO SUMMARY

This chapter, **BODY TECHNIQUE -- PART ONE,** dealt with the elimination of physical movement that impacts negatively on the motions of the baton. While both hands have the freedom to use every area of the Conductor's Space, adding excessive body motion during a performance should be avoided. When the eyes of an audience become more important than their ears, the concert loses its musical rationale and becomes visual entertainment.

A firm, comfortable, tension-free podium stance allows the baton to form strokes with precision and clarity. Do not move the feet, bend the knees, or jump during a performance. The principle is simple: unexpected movement of the feet, added to precise movement (baton strokes), disrupts predictability (formation of patterns). Remember the following:

1. A moving baton is in **controlled** motion when a body is firmly rooted.
2. Foot movement can cause body movement, disrupting the placement of the baton.
3. Disrupting the placement of the baton **adds extra movement** to the baton and results in **uncontrolled** motion.
4. A baton in **uncontrolled** motion loses its authority.

The **upper body** functions as a delivery system, preparing and placing both hands in the Conductor's Space. If the delivery system is to work well avoid the following movements:

- **The torso:** Do not quiver, heave, twist, shake, rattle and roll.
- **The waist:** Resist the steep bend to produce a *piano*. The bend is a *forte* gesture.

CHAPTER THREE

BODY TECHNIQUE -- PART TWO

The Head

The amount of musical information needed to structure a performance is mind-boggling. As a source of inquiry you can imagine the recreative process that goes on **inside** the head of the conductor. However, we will investigate how a conductor's head is used as a **physical object for technical purposes,** rather than as a mental machine.

The components of the head -- the eyes, nose, mouth, hair, and the head itself -- are a series of accidents waiting to happen. They are a conductor's minefield. Let us count the detonators.

The Head as Timekeeper

Every word written about eliminating unnecessary motion in other parts of the body applies to a conductor's head. Almost every movement of the head may be accomplished more musically, more efficiently, and more effortlessly with the baton.

Many beginning conductors are guilty of indicating pulse with their head. It is a **disruptive gesture that disarms** the baton of authority by supplying an **alternative** beat within the Conductor's Space. A head pulse, or beat, most likely will **not correspond** with the baton beat. Thus, at the point of attack, the conductor offers the orchestra a choice of **two pulses.** Most often the result is a weak, imprecise orchestral entrance.

Head beats usually occur at the beginning of movements, on accented downbeats, before and after holds, at meter changes and at abrupt changes of tempo. **All are musically sensitive contact points between orchestra and conductor.** Conductors in the early stages of development must be especially wary. Without a reliable baton technique in place, alternative **physical** means are sought to secure orchestral attacks. Be patient. Trust the baton and learn to use it properly. It is the conductor's most reliable technical tool for achieving exact attacks, rhythmic cohesion, melodic shaping and overall pacing.

Exercises for the Head

Place a book on the top of the head. Do not use a baton. Vigorously beat the measures in both exercises that follow. It is not important that the strokes form clear patterns of two, three and four beats. It is important that each stroke be *forte* or *fortissimo* in character. Begin with the right arm extended slightly forward, the elbow forming an L shape. During the repeats of the exercises gradually move the arm forward until it is fully extended. Begin slowly and get faster. **Choose a different tempo each time the exercise is repeated.**

Vary tempi between 60 and 110 to the quarter note.

Ex. 1

Vary tempi between 96 to 138 to the dotted quarter. One beat per measure.

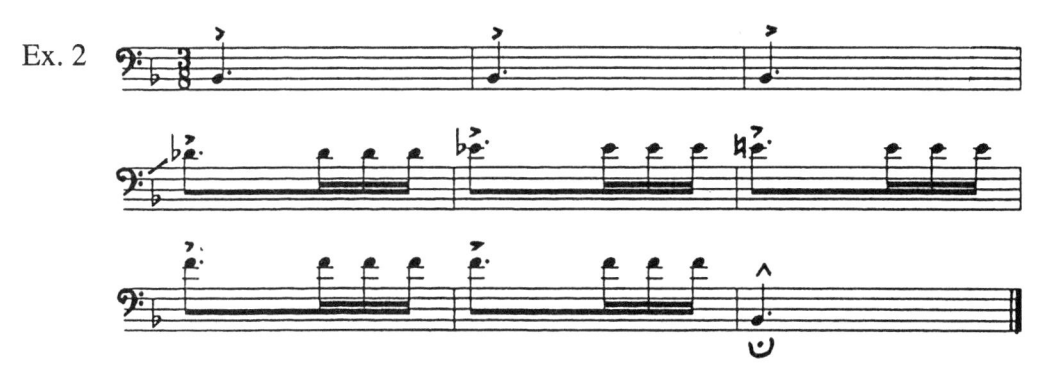

Ex. 2

If the book falls off while the baton is in motion, a head pulse has been added. Repeat the exercise until the book remains in place.

The Head as Cue-Giver

Cueing with the head is risky and often ineffective. The head cannot pinpoint exact locations, but cues may be **precisely** indicated by right or left hand extensions, direct eye contact, or a combination of both. A subtle nod of the head and raised eyebrow are welcomed by a player in need of special attention. Cueing will be discussed in greater detail in a later chapter.

Head as Surveillance Instrument

Have you ever encountered the toy whose head is mounted on a metal spring over its body? The spring keeps the head in constant motion, bobbing it up and down and moving it from side to side.

The constantly gyrating head-in-motion conductor is what I call a surveillance head -- looking right, left, cueing to the center, snapping left, swiveling right, etc. She/he **does** command the audience's attention, but the cost is dear. The surveillance head conductor proves that the eyes do cancel sound.

The Hidden Head

The opposite of the hyper or surveillance head is the chin-to-the-chest, head-in-the-score conductor. I don't know who said it or when it was said, but no one has ever given a better piece of advice to conductors: **have the score in your head and not your head in the score!**

The Hair

Hair can be treated like a garden, well kept and carefully trimmed or left to grow wild. Whatever stylistic statement conductors choose to make with hair, two points should be kept in mind:

1. Hair **must** be contained or it is distracting. Conductors with long hair must be doubly careful not to constantly move their heads, or a great amount of time will be spent brushing free flying hair from the face. The conductor's hands ought to concentrate on the music's architecture, not on the hair. If hair ornaments are used, avoid large, distracting, brightly colored pins or jewelry with reflecting surfaces.
2. Hair should never cover the eyes. Choose a hair style that **preserves the 'openness' of the face**. Covering the forehead and sides of the face diminishes the players' sight line to the conductor's eyes.

Conductors with beards must be be careful not to cover the bottom half of the face with a large beard if the top already sports lots of hair. The face will be in danger of becoming an accessory to the hair. (Think of the famous picture of Brahms playing the piano.)

The Eyes

I have already alluded to the importance of the eyes. Many musicians believe that a performance may be 'conducted' with the eyes. The most powerful contact a conductor has with a performer is eye to eye contact. Some conductors have a problem with direct eye contact and stare **above** the orchestra, or at the ceiling or walls when on the podium. Some flit from player to player like a restless bird, moving **away from** contact with the performer. Other conductors prepare cues very well, then **abandon** the performer as soon as she/he begins to play. In every case, the conductor must overcome personal or psychological barriers and look directly into the eyes of the players.

Is there a cure for conductors who knowingly choose and acquire affectations and then consciously graft them onto their own personalities? Probably not. Consider the vogue of conducting-with-eyes-closed. During a performance there may be a moment of utter serenity, or utter chaos, that prompts a withdrawal into one's inner spirit. Closing the eyes may even enhance the music, depending on the reaction of the orchestra. But why negate one of the conductor's most powerful assets, the eyes? The answer cannot be because a film was made in which a great conductor created a great performance and did it while his eyes were closed. That is a specific conductor, in a specific instance, involved in an art form that is not purely musical. A film imposes a set of visual criteria for performance that has little, or nothing, to do with the realities of the concert hall.

A conductor's eyes can be wonderfully evocative; they make magic happen. Eyes not only see, they "speak" to an orchestra, and make it easier to "hear" an orchestra. **Illuminate your work, keep your eyes open.**

Glasses

Seeing the score or the faces of the players as clearly as possible is essential. If your eyes need help, get contact lenses or wear glasses! If you wear glasses on stage choose **glasses without frames, clear frames,** or **thin, silver colored frames.** Avoid thick and/or dark frames that diminish the players' access to the eyes. Choose frames that preserve the openness of the face. Don't wear dark glasses that conceal the eyes.

The Nose

It appears that some conductors feel obligated to help oncoming, dramatic upbeats or important entrances with **loud** nasal preparatory sniffs. Fleshy nostrils squeezed together emit a frightening sonority and the 'sniff,' or inhalation through the nose, is **heard** in the texture of the music. It can be a noisy, distracting habit and needs to be controlled.

The Mouth

- **Avoid sing-a-longs.** Do not hum or sing while conducting. The sounds created within the head blocks out the sound on the stage.
- **Avoid the dropped jaw.** This looks like a fly trap awaiting its prey, or creates the impression that the conductor is amazed by unfolding events.
- **Avoid the open-close fish-mouth position.** Does the mouth open and close as the music unfolds? If it does, the orchestra will think the conductor is impersonating a fish.
- **Avoid the pucker position.** I urge all conductors, especially those who play brass instruments, to stand in front of a mirror. 'Conduct' anything. If the lips constantly form a pucker while the baton is in motion, do everything in your power to dismantle the pucker, lip by lip.

Body Response to Unequal Distance Between Beats

The unnecessary movement of various body parts in response to unfulfilled movement in baton patterns is a major cause of poor music making. In a basic four beat pattern, outlined in Chapter Eight, the distance covered when moving from beats 1 to 2, from 3 to 4, and from 4 to 1, is more or less equal. **However, the distance covered when moving from beat 2 to beat 3 is longer than the others.**

When beat 2 moves to beat 3 from left to right correctly, the conclusion of the across-the-body stroke should move the baton well **beyond** the right side of the body. Instead, beat 3 generally **stops** at mid-point of the stroke, or well **within** the frame of the body. **The longer distance needed to complete the movement from beat 2 to beat 3 has not been completed, not fulfilled.** The result of that unfulfilled third beat stroke has many unintended physical consequences and justifies its inclusion in this chapter.

The **body** senses the need to complete the stroke and keep the pulse intact, so various parts of the body act as **independent** agents on behalf of the conductor. **When the baton stops, one or more of the following body movements completes the unfulfilled stroke:**

- The arm, led by the elbow, **swings** out.
- The wrist **turns** inward and up and loops directly into beat 4.
- The entire body ever-so-slightly **sways** to the left.
- The body **comes forward** - the backside moves outward.
- The chin **tilts** upward.

This is just a partial list. The extra movements are within the pulse frame but are a series of musical hiccups constantly intruding on the musical line, especially in sonorities that unfold slowly. It is important to recognize the inherent dangers of not fulfilling the left to right, **across-the-body stroke** in four beat patterns or other patterns discussed in Chapter Eight.

CHAPTER THREE SUMMARY

The **head** of the conductor should not be used as a **technical object**. It should not beat time, be in constant motion, hide in the score, or be used as a cueing instrument.

Hair, especially long hair, should not be left unattended to fly around, or be adorned with large, shiny objects. Hair should not cover the face, especially the eyes.

The **eyes** should maintain contact with the player or sections of the orchestra responsible for creating the music's momentum. The conductor's eyes should not be fixed on the ceiling, flitting about and above the players.

If **glasses** are worn on stage the conductor must be careful not to destroy the openness of the face. Choose eyeglass frames that will not conceal the eyes.

The **nose** is not a musical instrument -- avoid loud sniffing.

The **mouth** must be under control. The conductor should not sing-a-long with the music or become a caricature by dropping the jaw, puckering the lips, or making a fish-mouth.

Do not emulate an admired **conductor's musical style** without understanding the musical impulses that motivate the style. Do not mimic another conductor's **physical mannerisms** for the sake of effect, especially when the eyes are involved. Do not hide behind someone else's personality. If you do, you will never discover your own.

If the conductor does not fulfill baton strokes, especially the movement from beat 2 to beat 3 in a four beat pattern, **various parts of the body will** add movement to complete the stroke. Each bodily intrusion is like an unwanted musical hiccup and impacts negatively on the flow of the music.

CHAPTER FOUR

THE CONDUCTOR'S ARM AND THE BATON

Young conductors are taught that the function of the right arm, or baton hand, is to indicate time clearly and precisely, and that the left arm is to be used to indicate dynamics or expressive content. Some conductors believe that the left hand is not needed at all and that entire performances may be conducted and controlled by the right hand (arm). A noted Austrian conductor, the late Kurt Wöss, told me the following story:

When he attended the Vienna Hochschule, Maestro Wöss frequented a cafe that was a meeting place for Vienna's most noted musicians. One day, he was seated at a table enjoying a coffee when Richard Strauss, who was conducting *Salome* at the Opera House, entered with Wöss' conducting teacher, Felix Weingartner. The two sat in a corner booth across from Wöss.

Strauss, who was noted for a conducting style that featured wrist movement and a lack of perspiration, said rather loudly to Weingartner that he could conduct all of *Salome* with one hand, from beginning to end! Weingartner disagreed, doubting that even the composer could conduct *Salome* with one hand. After a heated debate, Strauss proposed a wager and Weingartner accepted.

That evening Kurt Wöss sat with the second violins as Strauss entered the pit. The maestro bowed to the audience and looked up at Weingartner sitting in a box overlooking the stage. Staring at Weingartner, Strauss stuck his left hand in his left pants pocket, sat down on his stool, and began the performance.

As the opera progressed, Strauss conducted with his right hand while the left rested comfortably in his pocket. Before the head of Jokanaan was presented to Salome, Wöss noted that Strauss had risen from his stool. When the plate bearing the grisly package made its appearance, Strauss was on his feet and in the midst of that horrifying moment, his left elbow began flapping at his side. Strauss suddenly turned and looked up at Weingartner leaning expectantly over the rail. Strauss immediately sat down and continued conducting with his right hand and motioned, with his head, to his left hand, still in his pocket where it remained until the end of the performance. Strauss collected his wager. It is worth noting that Strauss had a reputation as a fine poker player.

Unless a reader of this text feels she/he is the reincarnation of Strauss, I strongly urge the use of both hands when conducting.

The Components of the Arm

The arm is a superbly designed conducting tool with three major **movable** components: the shoulder, the elbow and the wrist. Fingers have limited technical value to the conductor, while the palm of the left hand is a major asset.

When baton technique is evaluated, it is the movement of the conductor's arm that is under discussion. Why? **Because the baton is an extension of the arm.** When a baton is added to the hand, one of the arm's components **delivers** it to pre-determined points in the Conductor's Space. That delivery uses one or more of the arm's **natural strokes**. Every baton stroke **begins** with the natural stroke of one component of the arm.

Natural Strokes

The Upper Arm

The natural stroke of the upper arm comes from the **shoulder**. The weight of a stroke delivered from the upraised or fully extended arm is most efficient in *forte* or *fortissimo* passages. Upper arm movement is most useful when the arm is fully extended or when slightly less than fully extended.

The Forearm

The natural stroke of the forearm comes from the **elbow.** The forearm is particularly geared to *piano* through *forte* dynamic ranges. It is most effective when the arm is partially extended or close to the body.

The Wrist

It could be said that the natural stroke of the wrist is initiated by the hand. However, this text considers the conducting stroke **delivered** by the wrist as the natural stroke of the wrist.

The wrist is extremely supple and may be the most valuable part of a conductor's arm. The wrist functions effectively in all areas and at all dynamic levels. It is especially useful in *piano* to *pianissimo,* for fast tempi and *staccato* articulations. The wrist can elicit articulations with a variety of gestures that spinoff of its natural strokes.

Because clarity of stroke must be a constant concern to the conductor, do not violate the following rules:
- When the **wrist** is in motion, **do not move the forearm.**
- When the **forearm** is in motion, **do not move the wrist.**

The rare exceptions that combine wrist and forearm movement within a stroke will be discussed in later chapters.

Figure 5. When the baton is moved by **wrist motion,** no other part of the arm should be in motion. *As a result an unbroken line is created between the tip of the baton and the wrist.*

Movement here   No movement beyond wrist

Fig. 5

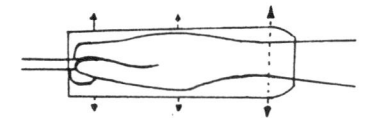

baton motion is created from the movement of the wrist only

Figure 6. When the baton is moved by forearm motion, no other part of the arm should be in motion. The wrist is 'locked' (does not move) and rises and falls with the movement of the forearm. *An unbroken line is created between the tip of the baton and the forearm.*

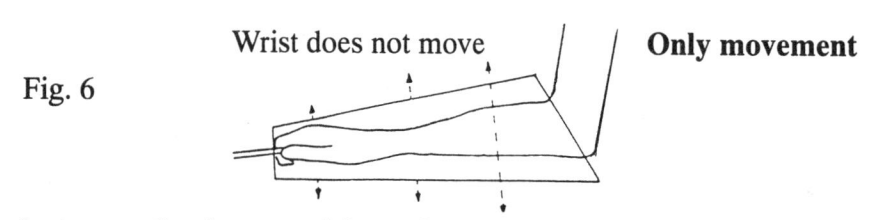

Wrist does not move   **Only movement**

Fig. 6

baton motion is created from the movement of the forearm only

Simultaneous, but differing, wrist and forearm movements create hard-to-read loops at the conclusion of the strokes. Despite its ambiguities, loop patterns continue to be taught and favored for slow tempi and music that is perceived to have highly emotional content. **The loop acts as an ornament, disguising the most critical part of the baton stroke,** *the pulse point.*

Figure 7. The loops, or curves, in the 4/4 pattern are a result of **using wrist and forearm motions at the same time. The pulse points,** the circles next to the numbers in Figure 7, **are ambiguous.**

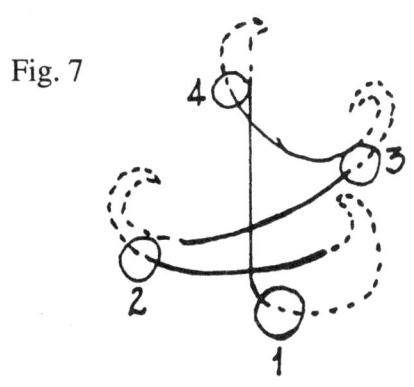

Fig. 7

Figure 8. The same 4/4 pattern **using only wrist motion or only forearm motion.** The pulse points are absolutely *clear*.

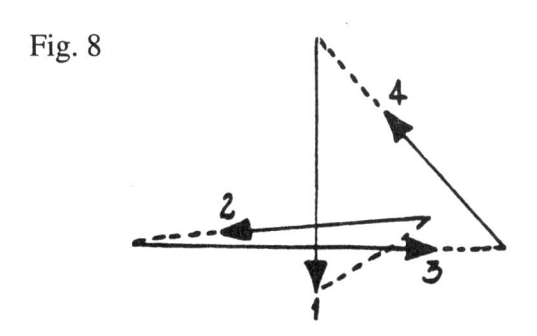

Fig. 8

The Hand

The Fingers

Many conductors use fingers in a rolling motion that manipulates the baton to shape phrases or refine articulations. Sir Adrian Boult was an outstanding exponent of the technique, but constant finger movement is problematical. The baton grip is violated; instead of being in a horizontal position, facing the orchestra, the baton is held vertically, pointing to the ceiling with the knuckles of the hand facing the orchestra. In that position the subtle characteristics of the conductor's rolling motions are not easily read by the orchestra. The range of articulations generated by the fingers can be accomplished by the wrist or the forearm with more clarity and precision.

Independence of the Hands - Mirroring

Many conductors make the same motion with both hands for long periods of time. This duplication of effort is called **mirroring;** a great waste of time and energy, since neither hand lends anything of musical value to the other. Mirroring removes the possibility of independent hand movement during a performance. The option must always exist to use either hand for **any** purpose, or to use both hands simultaneously in **differing** contexts. Both hands should rarely do the same thing. Exceptions are discussed in subsequent chapters.

THE BATON

It is time to examine the only object the conductor carries onto the stage: the baton. Concertgoers mistakenly refer to the baton as the conductor's instrument (it is not, the orchestra is), but correctly identify its inexpensive nature. It can be long, short, thick, thin, with or without bulb handles, made of wood, plastic or aluminum. It is invariably straight, weighs little and has a long history.

The baton as a symbol of authority can be traced to 709 B.C. A description of a performance under the leader "Pherekydes of Patrae, Giver of Rhythm"[7] indicates that he used a golden staff to start, and presumably stop, 800 performers. What we now identify as a baton has undergone some severe permutations since the golden staff. Long wooden rods have thumped the floor, large and small colored paper scrolls have been waved in the air, and violin bows have led ensembles. Finally, the small wooden or plastic shaft has emerged as the modern baton. Throughout its history the object in question was meant to do one thing: indicate a tempo to a group of musicians in order to keep them together.

It may come as a shock to a male dominated profession to learn that in 1594, the first documented use of a baton in the modern manner was by the **Maestra** (name unknown) of a group of nuns at the convent of St. Vito,[8] well known for their musical skills.

The Basic Baton Grip

The importance of a sound baton grip cannot be overemphasized. The dazzling array of exotic baton grips one encounters are a source of constant amazement: batons clutched like a hammer, held with two fingers, three fingers, stuck between fingers, held sideways, in the middle of a long shaft, at the tip of a short shaft and shifted from hand to hand, to name just a few. The musical realities that make a secure stance a necessity also hold true for the baton grip. While the feet are furthest from the action, **the baton IS the action!**

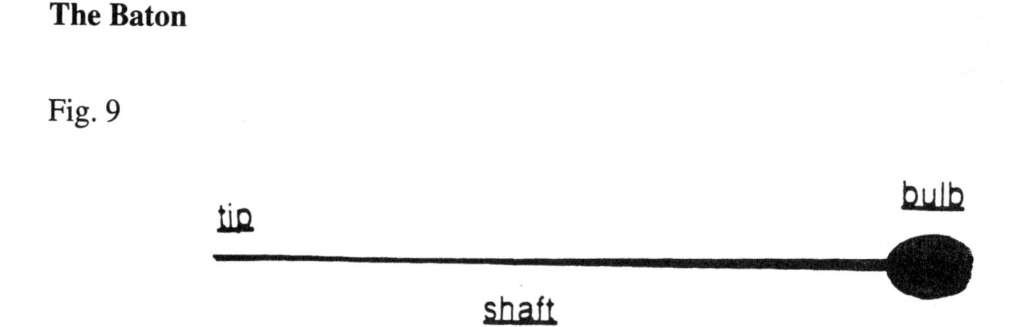

The Baton

Fig. 9

---

[7] Elliott W. Galkin, *A History of Orchestral Conducting,* (New York: Pendragon Press, 1988) p.487
[8] Galkin, p.491

1 - Turn the right hand palm over.

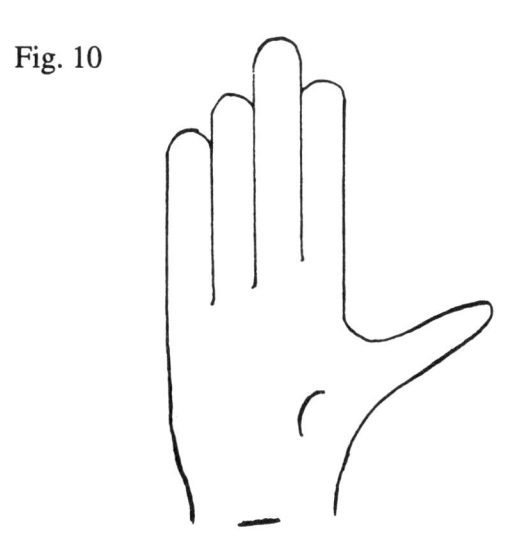

Fig. 10

2 - Place the bulb of the baton toward the back part of the center of the palm. The shaft of the baton should be angled to the right, about 30 degrees, crossing the bottom of the second finger and the top of the forefinger.

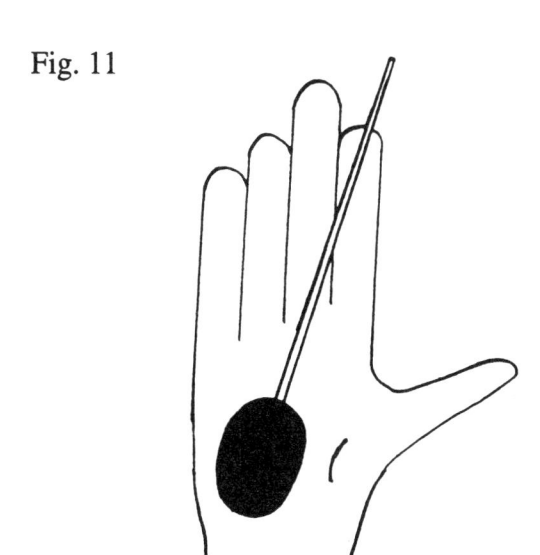

Fig. 11

3 - Wrap the second, third and little fingers lightly around the bulb of the baton.
(This is called the wraparound).

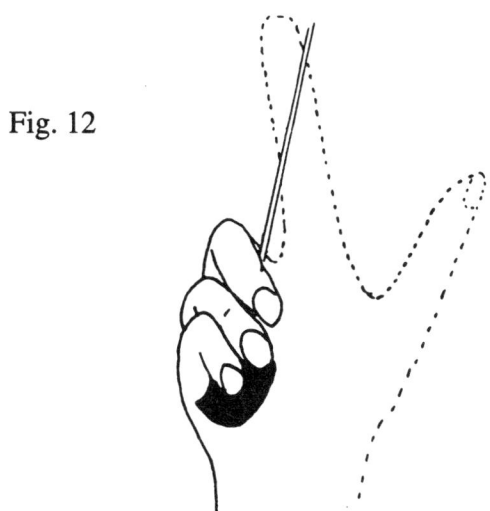

Fig. 12

17

4 - Place the thumb on the shaft above the second finger.

Fig. 13

5 - Wrap the forefinger around the shaft and lock it underneath the thumb. The point of contact between the thumb and the forefinger is the actual **bonding point**.

The baton is firmly gripped and remains in the hand even if the other three fingers are removed from the bulb.

Fig. 14

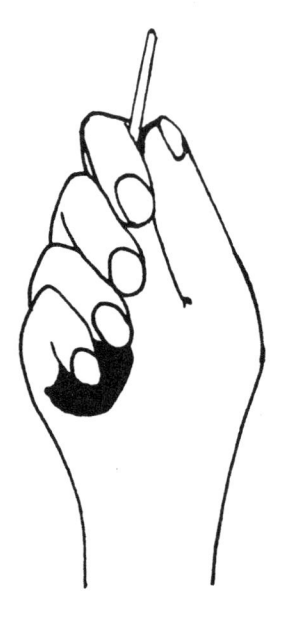

6 - Turn the hand over. The conductor is now looking at the top (also called the back of the hand but always referred to as the top in this text) of the hand. The fingers are wrapped around the bulb and the bottom of the shaft of the baton.

Fig. 15

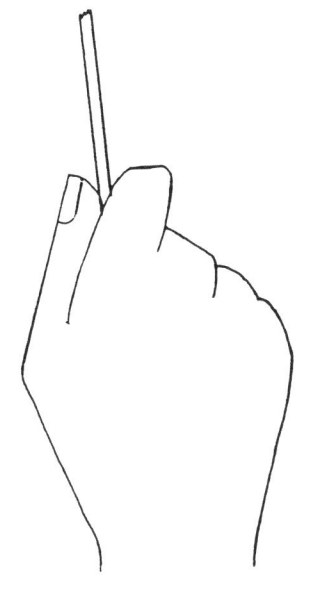

This is the basic baton grip. Obviously, this is not the only possible baton grip, but it is the one I strongly advocate. It has proven to be the one grip that truly connects the arm to the baton, and unfailingly provides the tip of the baton the most effective entry into the Extended Conduoctor's Space. I consider it the basic baton grip.

Checkpoints for the Basic Baton Grip

1. **The baton is an extension of the arm.** Make sure the baton is in a horizontal position, facing the orchestra, straight out or veering left at **no more** than a thirty degree angle. Do not force the wrist to the right to make a straight line. It is an unnatural position and may cause muscle pull and tightness. Do not hold the baton with its tip pointing to the first violin section. If that happens, the bulb of the baton is no longer in the center of the palm and the pulse point for the orchestra ceases to be the baton; **the knuckles or the side of the forearm become the pulse indicator.** That particular baton position also raises the awful possibility of stabbing the left hand palm with the tip of the baton.

2. Make certain the second, third, and little fingers **remain lightly wrapped around the bulb of the baton.** Make the hand grip a solid unit, without spaces between the fingers and without fingers off the shaft extended into space. Orchestral sound seems more concentrated when the unit that produces the sound (the hand and the baton) is a single, focused entity. Extended second, third and little fingers offer three more points of reference to the orchestra, diluting the effectiveness of the baton. If the fingers are hard to control, **tape them together or use a rubber-band to keep them together.** Do not discard the remedy until you feel certain your fingers will remain on the bulb of the baton.

3. Once the grip has been established, **DO NOT MOVE ANY PART OF THE GRIP BELOW THE WRIST! THE HAND HOLDING THE BATON SHOULD BE CONSIDERED A SINGLE, SOLID UNIT.** THEREFORE, KEEP THE **FINGERS** STILL AND ON THE SHAFT. DO NOT PULSE THEM ALONG WITH THE BATON STROKE, OR USE AND MOVE ANY, SOME OR ALL OF THE FINGERS TO INDICATE THE TEMPO.

Finger movement on the shaft negates the movement of the baton, and robs the baton of its pulse points. Orchestral attacks and articulations suffer, and the music loses its focus.

4. Do not turn the baton hand over to the right. **The thumb replaces the top of the hand which can no longer be seen.** This is a baton position favored by many conductors but it lessens the effectiveness of the conductor's strongest natural stroke, the up-down wrist stroke, essential for fast tempi and *staccato* articulations. If the hand insists on turning to the right, practice the following exercise:

- Place a coin on top of the hand and conduct a series of patterns. If the coin falls, the hand is turning. Repeat until the hand maintains the correct position.

Differences in the lengths and shapes of hands make it impossible for one baton grip to fit all needs. Small hands need a small bulb so the wraparound is easily accomplished. Larger fingers need a substantial bulb. The size of the fingers and the curve of the thumb affect the comfort of the grip.

Modify the basic grip to fit your hand but bear in mind all the basics described above.

Baton Length

The key to finding the right grip may be in finding the right baton. Choosing the 'right' baton is a subjective procedure, but it is essential that the baton **'feel' good** and that it is **well balanced.** Both relate to the length and weight of the stick.

Since we are not replicas of one another there is no sure way of deciding on a single, **correct**, baton length. If you have trouble finding a length that feels right in your hand, try measuring the distance from the elbow to the tip of the middle finger. Choose a baton length which does not vary from that measurement by more than an inch, longer or shorter. This method works for many, but not all conductors. Let us assume that after experimenting, the conductor has found a baton length that feels 'good' in the hand. Now the stick must be checked for balance.

Baton Balance

Every baton has a balance point. It is the spot on the shaft where the baton can be laid across an extended finger and balanced. The balance point is usually a short distance from the bulb. If the balance point coincides with the thumb and forefinger position on the shaft, the baton is perfectly balanced. **The baton feels weightless** since perfect balance cancels the baton's weight. Light as it is, the baton must not feel like an addition to the hand.

The circle in the diagrams indicate the thumb-forefinger grip point, the point at which the thumb and forefinger meet on the shaft of the baton.

Balance-Testing Point
Thumb-forefinger grip point
Fig. 16

Thumb-forefinger grip point
Fig. 17

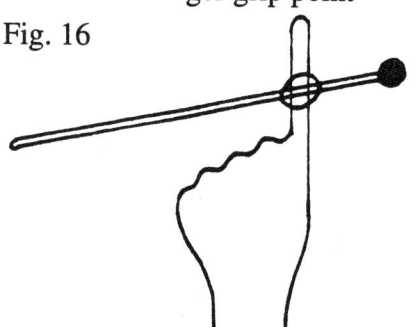

Tip points downward: Not balanced

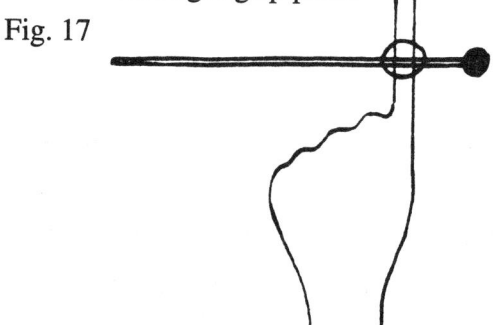

Tip remains horizontal: Perfectly balanced

CONDUCTING WITHOUT A BATON

Some conductors choose not to use a baton. While a minority, they include some world renowned present day maestri, including Kurt Masur and Pierre Boulez. In the recent past, Leopold Stokowski, and for a short period, Leonard Bernstein, conducted batonless. Some conductors do not use a baton because of physical constraints, others **choose** not to add a baton to the conducting arm.

In the latter group the predominant reason is the belief that the baton is physically and musically inhibiting. If a conductor has honestly deliberated the issue and concludes that she/he is a more efficient conductor without a baton, the decision must be respected. In defense of that position, remember that many who use a baton often conduct large sections of music without the stick. Sometimes the left hand acts as the only conveyor of pulse and shape, and the right hand may shift the baton to the left hand and continue to conduct batonless.

My own belief is that a baton, **properly used and musically driven,** adds clarity, form and shape to every single gesture. It is the conductor's greatest ally.

CHAPTER FOUR SUMMARY

The Arm and its components are a superbly designed conducting tool, placing the baton within the Conductor's Space and making the baton an extension of the arm.

The arm has three major movable components, the shoulder, elbow and wrist (or hand). Each one has a natural stroke.

The natural stroke of the upper arm comes from the **shoulder.** It is most useful at full extension and most efficient in *forte* to *fortississimo* passages.

The natural stroke of the forearm moves from the **elbow.** It is most effective in partial extension or with the forearm closer to the body. It covers *forte* to *piano* levels effectively.

The natural stroke of the **wrist** comes from the wrist; perhaps the most valuable part of the conductor's arm. The wrist functions in all areas and at all dynamic levels. It is especially useful in *piano* to *pianississimo* dynamics, as well as for fast tempi and *staccato* articulations.

The fingers used as 'rolling fingers' by some conductors destroy the basic baton grip along with the position of the baton. The technical efficiency of the wrist and the arm can duplicate the achievements of rolling the fingers with even more clarity and preserve the baton grip as well.

Important Rules:

When the forearm is in motion **do not move the wrist.**

When the wrist is in motion **do not move the forearm.** When both are in motion at the same time the baton **creates a loop stroke.** The loop stroke obscures the beat (pulse point) and the baton stroke lacks clarity. Rare exceptions to these rules are covered in later chapters.

The arms should not be restricted to predetermined roles. The right hand can do more than beat time and the left hand is capable of indicating more than an '*espressivo*' gesture. In the Conductor's Space both hands can be fully involved and used independently. Each hand should perform multiple tasks simultaneously to accomplish differing musical agendas without **mirroring** one another. Doing the same thing is a duplication of time, a waste of energy, and forecloses the possibility of independent hand usage.

The baton grip influences the sound, the shape and the flow of the music. The basic grip should be modified to fit the hand. Review the six-step process outlined in the text that leads to a comfortable baton grip, and carefully check the following points:

- The baton is an extension of the arm and should face the orchestra. The baton may move to the left, but by no more than 30 degrees.
- Do not force the wrist to the right in an effort to have the baton facing the orchestra. It is an unnatural position for the wrist and may cause muscle tension. Instead, move the forearm to the right, away from the body until the baton faces the orchestra.
- Do not hold the baton parallel to the body -- the knuckles or the elbow become the pulse point, and the conductor may be in danger of stabbing the left hand palm with the point of the baton.
- Keep the fingers lightly wrapped around the baton.
- Once the grip is in place, keep the fingers motionless and on the shaft!
- Do not pulse or indicate tempo with the fingers.

Keep the baton hand flat! When the hand is turned to the right, the thumb moves to the top of the hand position. A thumb-on-top baton grip limits the use of the wrist, one of the conductor's chief technical assets.

Finding a baton to fit the hand is subjective and requires experimentation. If a baton fits the hand, check its balance (the area on the shaft where the baton can be laid across an extended finger and balanced). If that balance point is where the thumb and forefinger meet on the shaft, it should be a perfectly balanced baton and feel weightless in the hand.

We are ready to put the baton to work.

CHAPTER FIVE

BATON TECHNIQUE -- PART ONE

Baton Strokes

Baton strokes define and shape music. They are organized into patterns which orchestra players 'read' and translate into sound. The strokes of the baton must be clear **and** musically meaningful. There is no room for error.

We know that a baton stroke starts from, and is delivered by, a component of the arm. As the arm/baton generates a stroke it generally travels from pulse point to pulse point in a **straight** or **slightly curved** line. The straight or curved line stroke can move in an up, down, in, out, diagonal or sideways direction. The proper use of either the straight or curved stroke guarantees maximum clarity when moving from beat to beat within a pattern. It remains fundamental that all strokes be delivered by a single component of the arm to avoid strokes that loop.

Straight Line Baton Strokes

Basic Straight Up-Down Stroke

The straight line stroke **moves in a direct line** from pulse point to pulse point. The stroke can be used in any tempo.

Fig. 18

Check the baton grip. Move the baton slowly and smoothly in straight up and straight down strokes in any part of the Conductor's Space. Use a variety of slowly moving pulses and practice the motions over and over again without varying the speed of the strokes.

Basic Straight Line Across-The-Body Stroke

Strokes move straight across-the-body to the left and to the right.

Fig.19

Check the baton grip. Move the baton slowly and smoothly in a straight line across-the-body to the left and to the right in any part of the Conductor's Space. Use a variety of slowly moving pulses and practice without varying the speed of the strokes. Remember that the conductor must always see **the top of the hand -- not the thumb --** when straight line across-the-body strokes are being made.

Curved or Round Strokes

Instead of a straight line stroke, the use of a curved line stroke allows the conductor to vary gestures within patterns to accommodate phrase markings. This is especially helpful in tempi that move slowly, but the curved or round stroke may be used in quick tempi as well. Curved strokes are particularly effective when the Conductor's Space and Registration (explained in an upcoming chapter) are fully utilized.

The curved stroke contains either **a dip or a crest in the middle of the motion.** The dip or crest in the stroke forms the curve. Just as the loop must be avoided in the straight line stroke, the delivery of the curved line stroke must be made with a single component of the arm.

The Upward Curve stroke can start from any position in the Conductor's Space and **move upward in any direction,** outward, inward, or to the sides.

Fig. 20

Check the baton grip and practice upward curved line strokes just as straight line strokes were practiced. Make certain the stroke begins in the lower part of the Conductor's Space to allow enough room for comfortable upward baton movement. Explore different parts of the Conductor's Space, and vary the length of the stroke and the size of the curve.

The Downward Curve can start from any position in the Conductor's Space, **moving downward in any direction,** outward, inward or to the sides.

Fig. 21

Check the baton grip and practice the downward curve line stroke. Make certain the stroke begins in the upper part of the Conductor's Space so that there is enough room for comfortable downward baton movement.

THE 'CLICK' FAMILY

What is a 'click?' A 'click' emphasizes and affirms the **pulse point** within baton strokes. The pulse points outline the beat. (If you count one, two, three in a 3/4 pattern, the pulse points are the one, two, and three in the count.) The 'click' is **a part of the stroke,** not an event **separated** from the stroke, and is made **within the flow** of the stroke. Because the 'click' moves in the flow, or direction of the stroke, it divides into variants based on **direction.** The up and down movements are called **'clicks.'** The side to side movements are called **'flicks'** (author's terminology). The 'click' and the 'flick' are produced by movements of the wrist.

How to make a 'click'

Imagine standing in front of a closed door. Raise your forearm, close your hand into a fist, pull your wrist back (or up) and knock on the door. The rap-on-the-door movement, the quick, short, down/up snap of the wrist creates a 'click.' (The quick upward rebound after the 'click' is a part of the stroke, and serves as the preparation for the next movement of the baton). The 'click' may be made in any part of the Conductor's Space and other than placing the wrist in the proper area of the Conductor's Space, the **forearm and shoulder are not** involved in 'click' or 'flick' strokes.

'Clicks' are only used in vertical (up-down) motions. Do not use 'clicks' in horizontal (side to side) motions. Adding a vertical motion to a horizontal gesture interrupts the flow of the stroke. The upward and downward motions of the 'click' can be **short, stopped strokes** (to indicate short notes or *staccato* articulations). They can also be the initial attack point of a continuing *legato* **'click'** stroke. In the latter case, the 'click' and its *legato* rebound could indicate an accented note of long duration in a slow moving tempo.

Check the baton grip, especially the fingers on the shaft, and practice the basic quick up and down 'click' strokes. Place the strokes in various parts of the Conductor's Space.

Making a 'click'

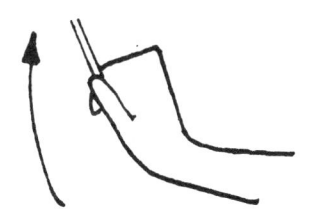

Fig. 22
quick upward wrist motion

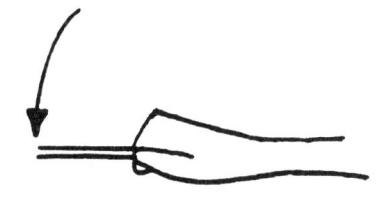

Fig. 23
quick downward wrist motion

Consecutive 'click' Strokes

Consecutive 'click' strokes contain 'clicks' on **both** the upward movement as well as the downward movement, e.g. beat 4 to beat 1 in a 4/4 measure, (or both sideways 'flick' movements, e.g. beat 2 to beat 3 in a 4/4 measure).

Repeat Figures 22 and 23 and add a 'click' to the **upward** motion in Fig. 22.

Parts of the 'click' stroke

- **Upward Half 'click'** is the upward movement in the consecutive 'click' stroke. (see Fig. 22). **The 'click' is placed at the beginning of the upward motion,** and should be used for all preparations and cut-off gestures. (Preparations and cut-offs are covered in detail in upcoming chapters.)
- **Downward Half 'click'** is the downward movement of the consecutive 'click' stroke. (see Fig. 23). **The 'click' is placed at the conclusion of the downward stroke** and is an excellent indicator of pulse points.

THE 'FLICK'

The 'flick' is made by a sharp sideways movement of the wrist **in the direction of the stroke.** **'Flicks' are only used in horizontal strokes;** never in vertical strokes. Adding a horizontal movement to a vertical line causes a break in the flow of the line. The same forearm and shoulder restrictions that apply to the 'click' also apply to the 'flick.'

'Flicks' move to the right or to the left in a straight or curved line. The 'flick' cannot be correctly articulated unless the conductor is looking at the top of the hand, not the thumb. 'Flick' strokes make the same **short articulations** described previously for 'clicks,' as well as a *legato* **'flick'** stroke. Like the 'click,' wrist 'flicks' are guaranteed technical solutions for strokes meant to have clear **pulse points**.

Check the baton grip, and practice the 'flick' stroke to the right and to the left. Place the stroke in various parts of the Conductor's Space.

Making a 'flick'

Fig. 24 — basic position

Fig. 25 — left 'flick'

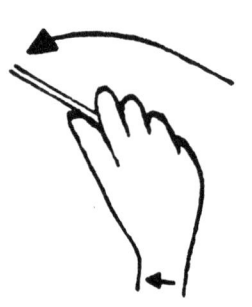

Fig. 26 — right 'flick'

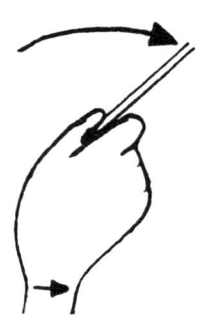

quick wrist horizontal motion to the <u>left</u>   and to the <u>right</u>

Do not use the 'flick' stroke in vertical (up, down, motions).

Parts of the 'flick' stroke
- **Left 'flick'** is the left motion placed **at the beginning of a stroke that moves to the left.** (see Fig. 25)
- **Right 'flick'** is the right movement placed **at the beginning of a stroke that moves to the right.** (see Fig. 26)

'Click' family strokes are used in all tempi, but are especially suitable for *allegros*, to articulate *staccato* figures, to initiate orchestral sound and to help clarify complex rhythmic figures.

However, 'click' family strokes cannot and should not be attached to every stroke, especially in very *legato* passages. 'Clicks' or 'flicks' can chop an already singing *legato* line into small, unmusical segments. A judicious use of the wrist 'click'/'flick' pays enormous musical dividends.

OTHER STROKES

There are several strokes that can be placed in a **not-to-be-used** category but have been seen so often they deserve to be catalogued.

The Shakers shake the baton throughout a beat pattern or in the direction of individual players. They are especially addicted to prolonged shaking on holds. (Why don't the players reciprocate by shaking their instruments at the conductor?) The sound scatters as a result of the very wide vibrato employed by the observant orchestra, a direct result of the shaking baton.

The Jabbers, like fencers, thrust and jab strokes at the orchestra. Players sitting in front of the podium cannot read the stroke since the pulse point is actually in the elbow which winds up behind the conductor. The result is a line that sounds punctured, lacking secure, uninterrupted motion.

The Baseball Pitchers begin this numbing stroke with a behind-the-head wind-up, then let fly with a mighty right hand *fortissimo* heave. The response of the orchestra is a sound best compared to a loud thud.

There are lots of baton strokes that can be used sparingly and effectively and still other musical strokes that will be invented by the creative conductor to meet the demands of a special musical text. However, the two basic strokes, their variations, plus the family of 'click' strokes will meet the needs of most composers.

CHAPTER FIVE SUMMARY

Baton strokes define and shape music. They must be clear and musically meaningful. Baton strokes generally travel from pulse point to pulse point in straight or curved lines. Strokes may move up or down, in and out, sideways and diagonally and occur in any and all parts of the Conductor's Space. All strokes are delivered by a single component of the arm. If two components are used the stroke will loop. A loop within a stroke disguises the clarity of the pulse point.

The **straight line stroke moves in a direct line** from pulse point to pulse point, or 'click' to 'click.' The stroke is used in any tempo, and moves up or down, from side to side across-the-body or away from and toward the body.

The **curved, or round, stroke has either a dip or crest in the middle of the stroke** that forms the curve. As with the straight line stroke, the loop is to be avoided. The curved stroke can move up, down, out, in, away from and toward the body and is used in all tempi and throughout the Conductor's Space.

'Clicks' and 'flicks' are quick movements of the wrist. The 'click' is made by a quick **down/up** movement of the wrist, and the 'flick' is produced by sharp **sideways** movement of the wrist. 'Clicks' and 'flicks' form a family of strokes, including upward and downward half-'clicks,' and right and left 'flicks.'

A 'click' is only used in **vertical strokes,** and not in horizontal strokes. 'Clicks' emphasize pulse points and are especially suitable for fast tempi and for articulating *staccato* and rhythmic figures.

A 'flick' is only used in **horizontal strokes** and not in vertical strokes. The hand must be in a flat position or the 'flick' cannot be articulated. 'Flicks' are capable of the same articulations as 'clicks' and both are sure-fire technical solutions for strokes meant to have clear pulse points.

A variety of strokes should not be used as they rupture the sound of the orchestra. They are best defined as the Shaker, Jabber, and the Baseball Pitchers strokes. Avoid them.

CHAPTER SIX

BATON TECHNIQUE--PART TWO

STRAIGHT LINE STROKES

The space in which the conductor works has been defined, and the baton, the extension of the arm and its components, has been equipped with the basic technical strokes to generate and control orchestral sound. *The Art of Conducting Technique* is predicated on the principle that the conductor's baton strokes take advantage of the **entire** Conductor's Space, just as the composer uses the entire range of instrumental sound. The exercises in this Chapter are designed to begin the **spatial exploration of baton movement.**

The Tip of The Baton

When knowledgeable conductors refer to "the baton" they are really speaking about **the tip of the baton,** the ignition point for generating orchestral sound. It creates and dictates movement or pace and is responsible for the articulation of the overall shape of the performance.

The mind and heart of the conductor may conceive how and why the music should be heard in a particular way, but it is the tip of the baton, placed by a component of the arm that conveys the conductor's musical images to the orchestra. Therefore, as the tip of the baton moves through the Conductor's Space, its clarity and flexibility must be maintained. As we begin to explore designed baton movements, all other motions that infringe upon the clarity of the baton must be eliminated or the conductor's vision will be compromised. (Re-read the chapters on Body Technique.)

The Conductor's Connection to the Tip of The Baton, the extension of the Conductor's Arm

Once a conductor embarks on the specially designed exercises in this Chapter, she/he must feel directly connected to the movements of the tip of the baton, which functions as the extension of the conducting arm.

For example, in Exercise One, lifting the arm from the shoulder is a natural movement that automatically raises the baton. However, the initial shoulder movement negates the baton as a true extension of the arm. Consider the opposite, that it is **the tip of the baton which must first move,** and in so doing, lifts the entire arm.

As an illustration, imagine a heavy lead weight sitting on top of the end of the baton. To move the lead weight upward, the baton must first be moved. As the lead weight is pushed upward by the tip of the baton, it lifts the entire arm. **Shoulder movement is a result of baton movement.** The downward motion of the tip of the baton should be thought of in the same way, but moving in the opposite direction. A resisting object, e.g. a sprung Jack-In-The-Box, is pushed down with a movement that begins from the tip of the baton and leads the entire arm throughout its downward descent. Again the shoulder follows the movement of the baton.

After a short period of trial and error, the conductor can sense, and thus control movements in the extension of the arm, the tip of the baton.

General Instructions

Practice exercises in front of a **mirror** and with the help of a **metronome,** since the exercises are designed to move through space at varying speeds, to a fixed measure of time. The most critical point in forming a baton technique is the moment the conductor begins to experience **designed** baton movement. Body control, arm movement, baton placement and a proper baton grip are essential new elements in building conducting technique and cannot be properly experienced unless they are **witnessed** by the practitioner. A mirror is the answer, as it reflects physical reality rather than the conductor's imagined physical movements. A step beyond the mirror is the video machine. Tapes are extremely helpful as an immediate corrective teaching tool, as well as a catalog of daily, weekly and monthly progress. Perhaps most importantly, **video** tapes can be viewed by others to review the technical flaws the young conductor overlooks.

Beginning conductors ought to think of baton stroke exercises as the equivalent of scales and arpeggios. They are designed to provide mobility for the components of the conducting arm. Before beginning the exercises **check the baton grip.** The baton must feel comfortable and secure in the hand. A poor grip generally forces the hand into an awkward position and may create tension in the forearm, the shoulder or the lower back. If the wrist is used, 'lock' and do not move the forearm. If the forearm is used, 'lock' and do not move the wrist. Add **'clicks'** to pulse points where indicated. Fulfill all baton movements in clear, uncluttered motions (no loops) and in **uninterrupted, unbroken motions.** Repeat each exercise a minimum of ten times or until the physical mechanics of the strokes feel comfortable.

The Vertical Straight Line Stroke
(And Exercises for the Right Hand)

The vertical straight line stroke moves in a direct line from pulse point to pulse point, or 'click' to 'click,' and is used in all tempi. It can move in a number of directions and angles, toward and away from the front and the sides of the body, and can start and finish in any area of the Conductor's Space.

Basic Movements-The Vertical straight line Stroke

Exercise 1: Allow the right arm to rest freely at full extension at the side of the body, locking the wrist and forearm. The shoulder joint is the only part of the arm that moves, *forming an unbroken line from the tip of the baton to the shoulder. Think of and sense the tip of the baton.* Set the metronome at 68 and begin the pulse when you are ready to start the exercise. Make one stroke per pulse. Begin the stroke with the baton pointing to the floor. Use a consecutive downward/up 'click' to initiate motion, raise the arm forward and upward in a straight unbroken motion until the baton tip is at eye level. Stop. **The baton is now parallel to the floor.** Make a small downward/upward 'click' on the 'and' of the last upward pulse and move downward until the original starting position is reached. Add a downward 'click' at the completion of the stroke. **The arm remains at full extension throughout the exercise and the following variations.**

While the metronome pulse for this exercise remains constant at 68, **the speed of the baton stroke varies** between the point of departure and the arrival point (eye level). Count the number of metronome pulses in each variation aloud.

Exercise 1

Variation 1A. As described in Exercise 1, move the baton upward to the **eye level arrival point** in **3 metronome pulses,** initiating the count with a (downward/upward) 'click.' From the eye level position, make an upward/half-'click' on the and of three (3) and return to the starting position in **3 metronome pulses.** The wrist, now in the upward half-'click' configuration is in a position to make a downward 'click' on count one. to repeat the exercise.

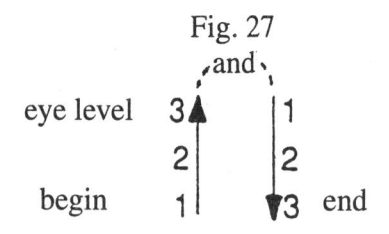

Fig. 27

```
                    ‚and‚
eye level    3▲      |1
              2|     |2
begin        1|      ▼3  end
```

Variation 1B. Repeat the upward and downward movement in **5 metronome pulses** for each direction.
Variation 1C. Repeat the upward and downward movement in **7 metronome pulses** for each direction.
Variation 1D. Repeat the upward and downward movement in **8 metronome pulses** for each direction.
Variation 1E. Repeat the upward and downward movement in **9 metronome pulses** for each direction.

As the number of **metronome pulses increases, the speed of the baton stroke decreases**. The amount of space covered by the baton stroke remains the same, therefore **control of the stroke is of utmost importance**. Once the baton is in motion **the speed of the stroke must not vary.** Strive for a stroke that is smooth, constant, and uninterrupted by jerks and starts.

Straight Line Strokes from the open "L" position

Exercise 2: Allow the right arm to rest freely against the side of the body. Raise the forearm with the elbow close to the body; the arm forms an open letter 'L' shape, with the bottom of the letter 'L,' the forearm, sloping slightly downward. The open letter 'L' configuration of the forearm positions the baton hand at or below waist level, depending on the length of the conductor's arm. Lock the wrist. The forearm is the only part of the arm that moves, *forming an unbroken line from the tip of the baton to the elbow. Connect to the tip of the baton.*

Set the metronome at 80 and begin the pulse when you are ready to start the exercise. Make one stroke per pulse. Begin the stroke at or below waist level with a down/up 'click' to initiate motion. Raise the forearm upward in a continuous motion until the baton reaches eye level. When eye level height is reached, stop. **The tip of the baton points toward the ceiling.** As before, make an upward half-'click' on the and of the last upward pulse and move downward to the original starting position. The baton is at or below waist level in the original open letter 'L' position. The wrist, now in the upward half-'click' configuration is in a position to make a consecutive down/up 'click' on count one (1) to repeat the exercise

Exercise 2

Variation 2A. Move the baton upward from at or below the waist, to eye level height in **2 metronome pulses.** Return to the original starting position in **2 metronome pulses.**
Variation 2B. Repeat the upward and downward movement in **3 metronome pulses** for each direction; slightly slower baton stroke.

Variation 2C. Repeat the upward and the downward movement in **4 metronome pulses** for each direction; less speed in the baton stroke.

Variation 2D. Repeat the upward and downward movement in **5 metronome pulses** for each direction; getting even slower.

Variation 2E. Repeat the upward movement in **6 metronome pulses** for each direction; slowest baton stroke.

Straight Line Strokes with 'Clicks' from the "V" Position

Exercise 3: This exercise is restricted to repeated upward and downward half 'click' movements. The wrist will be in constant motion in a very small, compact space. The forearm and shoulder do not move and there is an *unbroken line from the tip of the baton to the wrist.* In this exercise the connection to the tip of the baton is easier to make because of the short distance between the wrist and the end of the baton.

The arm is bent at the elbow and close to the right side of the body. The bent elbow forms a letter "V" configuration, and the baton hand is underneath the chin, to the right of the mid-chest area. The tip of the baton is pointing upward because of the letter "V" position. Since the half 'clicks' are made within a very small area, the tip of the baton covers no more than three to seven inches in its overall movement. All wrist movement in these exercises is made quickly and **with a stop after each 'click'** articulation. **Do not move the forearm!**

The speed of the 'clicks' increases as the number of strokes increases within the metronome pulse and the **space needed for the 'clicks' varies.** The pulse remains **constant.**

Set the metronome at 58. **Before beginning the exercises let the metronome pulse two times.** Establishing the pulse allows the conductor to place the first 'click' accurately.

After two metronome pulses, place **the first of 2 upward half-'clicks'** within the next metronome pulse, and **2 downward half-'clicks'** within the following metronome pulse. Repeat ten times and do not move the forearm or shoulder.

Exercise 3

Variation 3A. After two metronome pulses, place **3 upward half-'clicks'** and **3 downward half-'clicks'** within one metronome pulse.

Variation 3B. After two metronome pulses, place **4 upward half-'clicks'** and **4 downward half-'clicks'** within one metronome pulse.

Variation 3C. After two metronome pulses, place **5 upward half-'clicks'** and **5 downward half-'clicks'** within one metronome pulse.

Variation 3D. After two metronome pulses, place **6 upward half-'clicks'** and **6 downward half-'clicks'** within one metronome pulse.

The three vertical straight line exercises and their variations use the arm in three different positions -- at full extension, in the open 'L' configuration, and in the 'V' shape. Each arm position causes the vertical single line stroke to travel through **different** areas of the Conductor's Space. Restricting movements of the baton to a **single** area of the Conductor's Space promotes **time beating.**

Horizontal straight line strokes-Basic Movement

Exercise 4: Start with the fingers of the baton hand resting on **top** of the left shoulder. The tip of the baton is across and behind the left shoulder. The elbow forms the letter 'V' configuration.

Set the metronome at 72 and begin the pulse when you are ready to begin the exercise. Make one stroke per pulse. Begin the stroke with a right-side 'flick.' Move the baton to the right in a straight line, across and away from the right side of the body to a comfortable full arm extension. Throughout the stroke the straight line motion of **the baton remains parallel to the floor.** Do not raise or lower the baton - maintain the shoulder height level. At the conclusion of the stroke be careful **not to pull the arm behind the back.** If someone of similar height stood next to the conductor, at arms length, the baton would rest on their shoulder. From the full arm extension position, move the **wrist** further to the right (the 'and' count after the last pulse). Make a left-side 'flick' and move the baton to the left across the body until it returns to the starting point. The wrist is now in position to make a right side 'flick' and begin the exercise again. **All the variations begin with the baton hand resting on top of the left shoulder.**

Exercise 4

Variation 4A. Move the baton across the body to full arm extension to the right in a straight line in **2 metronome pulses**. Return to the original position in **2 metronome pulses**.

Variation 4B. Repeat the variation in **3 metronome pulses** for each direction.

Variation 4C. Repeat the variation in **5 metronome pulses** for each direction.

Variation 4D. Repeat the variation in **6 metronome pulses** for each direction.

Variation 4E. Repeat the variation in **8 metronome pulses** for each direction.

Diagonal straight line stroke-away from and back towards the body

Exercise 5: Raise the right arm in front of the body to shoulder height and extend fully. From this position move the forearm to the left until it is on the left side of the body at shoulder height; the distance between the forearm and the body is about 9 to 12 inches. Keep the arm parallel to the floor. The movement to the left forms the letter 'L,' and the tip of the baton is beyond the body, pointing to an imagined first violin section. Raise the forearm upward until the hand is at or near eye level. The baton is now being tilted diagonally toward the ceiling. Lock the wrist. *There is now an unbroken line from the tip of the baton to the elbow.* This is the starting position for Exercise 5 and the following variations.

Set the metronome at 84 and begin the pulse when ready to start the exercise. Make one stroke per pulse. Begin the stroke with a right 'flick' and move in **a downward and outward diagonal motion, away from the body, in a straight, unbroken line.** The stroke finishes at full extension at or below the waistline in the space **beyond** the right side of the body. Return to the original letter 'L' position from the full extension with a left 'flick' on the upward stroke. Keep the top of the hand visible throughout the stroke.

Exercise 5

Variation 5A. Make the downward and outward diagonal motion from the shoulder to the waist area in **2 metronome pulses**. Return to the original position in **3 metronome pulses**.

Variation 5B. Downward motion in **3 metronome pulses**. Return in **4 metronome pulses**.

Variation 5C. Downward motion in **4 metronome pulses**. Return in **5 metronome pulses**.

Variation 5D. Downward motion in **5 metronome pulses**. Return in **6 metronome pulses**.

Variation 5E. Downward motion in **6 metronome pulses**. Return in **7 metronome pulses**.

All strokes should remain fluid and smooth through the changes of speed in the baton movement.

EXERCISES FOR THE LEFT HAND

Do not use a baton. Keep all **fingers and the thumb** fully extended and close together, eliminating any spaces between the fingers. For some hands the space between the thumb and fingers cannot be closed. If that is the case, do not force the thumb and fingers together.

Repeat each of the right hand exercises with the left hand. Follow all instructions but **reverse the direction** of the strokes. Strokes **beginning** on the left side begin on the right, strokes **moving** from left to right instead move from right to left. Upward and downward movements remain the same. Outward movements remain the **same.** All starting position areas remain the same but begin on the **opposite** side of the body.

All other instructions should be honored. Strokes must be fluid and smooth and the speed maintained from start to conclusion. **The technical training of the left hand is as important as the training of the right hand. Either hand should be able to duplicate the technical accomplishments of the other.**

CHAPTER SIX SUMMARY

All exercises in this chapter were designed to begin the exploration of **baton movement within the Conductor's Space.** When the conductor begins to experience designed baton movement, a **mirror** and a **metronome** are necessary training tools. A **video** is even more valuable if used consistently and correctly, especially with another viewer to point out what the student may have missed.

The tip of the baton is the extension of the arm and the ignition point for orchestral sound. When knowledgeable conductors speak of "the baton" they are really referring to the tip of the baton. Keep it clear and eliminate all other motions that can disrupt its clarity. Learn to connect with, and sense the tip of the baton, and to make strokes that begin from the tip of the baton.

The exercises and their variations move into and out of various areas of the Conductor's Space **at different rates of baton speed,** emphasizing straight line vertical, horizontal and diagonal strokes. All components of the arm are used -- at full extension, in the letter "L" shape, and the letter "V" shape.

All strokes are to be made in uninterrupted, unbroken lines, and in clear, uncluttered motions. Avoid loops, and check the baton grip regularly.

The left hand, without the baton, should duplicate all the technical strokes of the right hand. **It is extremely important for the beginning conductor to spend as much time training the left hand in these exercises as is allowed for the right hand.**

CHAPTER SEVEN

BATON TECHNIQUE -- PART THREE

CURVED-LINE STROKES

Right Hand -- Basic Movement

The curved line stroke provides the conductor with one of the simplest solutions for diversifying physical motion to meet changes in the musical text. You may recall that the curved-line stroke contains a dip (the downward curve) or a crest (the upward curve) in the middle of the movement between pulses. As with the straight-line stroke, avoid the loop, and deliver all strokes with smooth unbroken motions using a single component of the arm.

The following exercises prepare the conductor for a variety of curved strokes to be used in the Conductor's Space.

Use the mirror and the metronome. If a video machine is available do not hesitate to use it. Continue to check the baton grip! Repeat each exercise a minimum of ten times or until the procedure that produces the various curves in the strokes feels comfortable.

The Upward/Inside and Downward/Inside Curve Stroke: Within-The-Body-Frame

Exercise 1: Allow the arm to rest freely at the side of the body and lock the wrist and forearm. The shoulder joint is the only part of the arm that moves, *forming an unbroken line from the tip of the baton to the shoulder. As in the previous exercises, connect with the tip of the baton throughout the stroke.*

Set the metronome at 72 and make one stroke per pulse. Begin with the baton pointing to the floor, the arm at full extension. Initiate the stroke with an upward-left 'flick.' Curve the stroke upward, within the frame of the body, completing a half-circle at eye level with a 'flick' to the right. The middle of the curve is about waist level on the left side of the body. At the end of the stroke the arm remains fully extended, in front of the body.

After the stop, make an upward 'flick' to the right and on the 'and' of the next pulse **downward** with a left hand 'flick' in the path of the original half-circle until the starting position is reached, the baton pointing to the floor. Finish the stroke with a 'flick' to the right. **The arm remains at full extension throughout the exercise and in the following variations.**

Exercise 1 - -Variations

The first count initiates movement of the baton. The speed of the baton stroke between the point of departure and the arrival point varies, but the metronome pulse remains constant.

    Variation 1A. Make an **upward/inside** stroke from the right side of the body to eye level height in **3 metronome pulses.** Return to the starting position with a **downward/inside** stroke in **3 metronome pulses.**

    Variation 1B. Make an **upward/inside** stroke from the right side of the body to eye level height in **7 metronome pulses,** and the downward movement in **7 metronome pulses.**

The Upward/Outside and Downward/Outside Curve Stroke

Exercise 2: The starting position of an **upward/outside** curve stroke is the same as in Exercise 1, forming a half-circle that stops at eye level. The difference is that all baton motion is **outside**-the-body-frame to the right. Allow the arm to rest freely at the side of the body and lock the wrist and forearm. The shoulder joint is the only part of the arm that moves, *forming an unbroken line from the tip of the baton to the shoulder. Sense the tip of the baton.*

Set the metronome at 86 and make one stroke per pulse. Begin with the baton pointing to the floor, the arm at full extension. Initiate the stroke with an upward 'flick' to the right and curve the stroke, outside the body's frame. When the middle of the stroke is above waist level, move the curve to the left completing a half-circle at eye level. At the end of the stroke the arm remains fully extended at the right side of the body.

After the stop, make an upward 'flick' to the left and on the 'and' of the next pulse move **downward** with a rightward 'flick' in the path of the original half-circle motion until the starting position is reached -- the baton pointing to the floor. The arm remains at full extension throughout the exercise, as well as during the following variations. Use 'flicks' at beginnings and conclusions of curved strokes in all the exercises.

Exercise 2 -- Variations

    Variation 2A. Make an **upward/outside** curved stroke from in front of the body to eye level height in **5 metronome pulses** and the downward/outside curve movement in **5 metronome pulses.**

    Variation 2B. Make an **upward/outside** stroke from in front of the body to eye level height in **8 metronome pulses** and the downward movement in **8 metronome pulses.**

Exercise A and B -- Circle Variation

Make a left **upward/inside curved** stroke from the **middle** of the body to eye level height in **4 metronome pulses** and the rightside **downward/outward** movement to the **middle** of the body in **6 metronome pulses.**

Note: Try to complete a circle in this exercise by finishing the downward stroke in the **original position** of the upward stroke.

The Across the Body/Upward Curve: Left to Right and Right to Left.

Exercise 3 (for the Right Hand-Basic Movement): Allow the arm to rest freely against the side of the body. Raise the forearm so that the elbow remains close to the body and forms a letter 'L' shape. The open letter 'L' positions the baton at or below waist level. Move the baton to the left side of the body and about twelve inches away from the body. The baton is tilted in the direction of the floor. Lock the wrist and keep the top of the hand visible throughout the stroke. The forearm is the only part of the arm that moves, *forming an unbroken line from the tip of the baton to the elbow. Continue to think of connecting to the movements of the tip of the baton.*

Set the metronome at 98 and make one stroke per pulse. Without 'flicks,' begin the stroke from the **left** side of the body and curve the stroke **upward** to the right in one smooth continous motion. The height of the curve is near or at eye level. Continue curving the stroke, concluding **beyond the right side of the**

body at or below waist level, twelve inches away from the body. The baton is tilted in the direction of the floor. Return the stroke by retracing the curve to the starting position on the **left** side of the body, at waist level. Try to maintain the twelve-inch distance from the body throughout the stroke, and in the following variations as well. Do not use 'flicks' in the variations.

Please note that some conductors find it necessary to move the upper arm to complete the stroke. Do not resist that extra movement if it helps create a clear, smooth curved stroke.

Exercise 3 -- Variations

Variation 3A. Make a **left to right** across-the-body/upward curve stroke from or below the waist level in **2 metronome pulses.** Return to the original starting position in **2 metronome pulses.**

Variation 3B. Make a **right to left** across-the-body/upward curve stroke from or above the waist level in **4** metronome pulses, finishing the stroke beyond the left side of the body. Return to the original starting position in **4** metronome pulses.

The Across-the-Body/Downward Curve: Left to Right and Right to Left

Exercise 4 (for the Right-Hand-Basic Movement):

The technique for creating the **across-the-body/downward** curve stroke is exactly the same as for the across-the-body/upward curve stroke. The difference is that the curve, the half-circle, moves downward rather than upward.

Set the metronome at 112 and make one stroke per pulse. Begin the curved stroke from the **left** side of the body above waist level, twelve inches from the body with a **downward** and right 'click.' The curved stroke concludes **beyond the right side of the body** above waist level, still twelve inches away from the body. The middle of the stroke is at or above the knee level of the right leg. Begin the return stroke from the exact spot of the conclusion of the initial stroke on the 'and' of the next pulse with a right 'flick.' Make a left 'flick' on the following pulse and retrace the curve to the original starting position on the **left** side of the body.

Exercise 4 -- Variations

Maintain the twelve-inch distance from the body and use 'flicks' in both variations.

Variation 4A. Make a **left to right** across-the-body/downward curve stroke from the waist **3 metronome pulses.** Return to the original starting position in **3 metronome pulses.**

Variation 4B. Make a **right to left** across the body/downward curve stroke from the waist level in **5** metronome pulses, finishing the stroke beyond the left side of of the body. Return to the original starting position in **5** metronome pulses.

Exercise C and D -- Circle Variation

Make a left to right across-the-body/**upward** curve stroke from or above the waist level in **6 metronome pulses and stop.** Begin an across-the-body/**downward** curve stroke from right to left back to the starting position of the upward curve stroke in **8 metronome pulses.** The combined strokes form a circle.

The Outward Curve Stroke-Basic Movement

Exercise 5: This outward curved stroke moves **away** from the body, in **any** and in **all** directions. Begin with the elbow in a letter 'V' configuration, the baton hand close to mid-chest. Vary the metronome settings between 56 - 126.

Variation 5A. Move the baton slowly **upward,** away from the body with a curved stroke, to eye level in all spaces. Use 'V' configuration to full extension. Use either hand.

Variation 5B. Practice curved strokes moving **downward,** away from the body to all spaces until the baton hand is at waist level. Use either hand to full extension.

Inward Curve Stroke -- Basic Movement

When the outward curve stroke moves back to its starting position, **the return stroke forms the inward curve stroke.** Like the outward curve stroke, the inward curve stroke can move upward, downward, sideways, diagonally and in any and all parts of the Conductor's Space.

Exercises for the Left Hand

Do not use a baton. Keep the fingers and the thumb of the left hand fully extended and close together, eliminating all spaces.

Repeat all Curved Stroke Exercises with the Left Hand

Follow all movement instructions for the right hand, but **reverse the direction** of the strokes. Strokes **beginning** on the left side will start from the right side, strokes **moving** from left to right will move from right to left. However, upward, downward and **starting position areas remain the same.** Maintain the speed of the stroke, and maintain the shape of the curve as the "baton" travels from left to right or up and down.

Create exercises for each of the Outward/Inward Curved Strokes for Both Hands

Curved line strokes may move in any direction and into any part of the Conductor's Space. Use the previous stroke exercises as models. Set your own tempi and the number of pulses needed to complete the strokes. Lock various components of the arm in each of the exercises **and think and feel the tip of the baton as an extension of the arm.** Use the entire Conductor's Space. Count aloud and remember to make each stroke a smooth, uninterrupted line from start to finish. **This is the foundation of a singing** *legato* **stroke!**

Every one of the curved strokes described can be used in a variety of ways. They are especially helpful in slow to moderate tempi. The physical beauty of a well-placed curved stroke, after a series of straight line strokes is clearly seen when Registration is an integral part of the stroke. (Registration is introduced in Chapter Twelve -- "The Elements Of A New Technique").

Physical discomfort in any part of the conducting arm or back is usually the result of a faulty baton grip. Persistent discomfort is a warning to check the grip and seek advice from a conducting teacher.

CHAPTER SEVEN SUMMARY

The curved-line stroke provides the conductor with one of the simplest means of diversifying motion to meet changes in the musical text. The curved-line stroke must contain a dip (the downward curve) or a crest (the upward curve) in the middle of the **movement between pulses.** Avoid the loop and deliver all curved line strokes with smooth, unbroken motions.

Continue to use the mirror, the metronome and the video machine if one is available to check the progress of the strokes.

The exercises in this chapter explore several variations of the curved stroke **delivered from various starting positions in the Conductor's Space and using all the components of the conducting arm:**

1. The Upward/Inside and Downward/Inside Curve
2. The Upward/Outside and Downward/Outside Curve
3. The Across-the-Body/Upward Curve
4. The Across-the-Body/Downward Curve
5. The Outward Curve
6. The Inward Curve

The exercises in this chapter are to be **repeated by the left hand.**

Continue to practice all the exercises until the strokes can be made in smooth, uninterrupted motions, the foundation for a singing *legato* stroke.

CHAPTER EIGHT

PATTERNS

Present Day Patterns -- A Two-Dimensional View

The new principles of arm/baton movement that drive the *Art of Conducting Technique* lie ahead. The Conductor's Space will be divided into Zones and areas that accommodate movement based on **Visual Score Study** and **Baton Placement** techniques. Every motion made by the conductor derives its rationale from the composer's text and will be notated in **PatternCubes,** a new concept that charts baton movement in a three-dimensional system. However, the point of departure for the new is the old, so we must first understand present-day conducting patterns.

Music might be thought of as a compilation of measures, and the flow of the music accounted for by movements of the baton. These movements are organized into patterns, the physical index of how well a conductor understands a composer's intent.

BEAT PATTERNS

What is a beat pattern? It is a physical articulation employed by the conductor to measure pace (tempo), and the number of pulses (beats) within a measure. That much is clear. The virtues attached to beat patterns as we know and presently use them are less clear.

The generally held view is that current use of repetitive patterns delivered with rhythmic accuracy is a coveted technical achievement, and that the conductor who attains that sought-after technical level has a greater chance of realizing the full potential of the music. Neither of these assumptions is totally true. The fault lies not with the conductor who strives for these goals, but rather with the limitations of the 300-year-old patterns and their application. **Constant repetition of patterns has no musical value and must be rejected**. A repeated formula pattern imposed upon music that is **constantly changing** quickly divorces itself from the content of the music. The repeated pattern becomes, at best, an efficient but non-musical mechanical/technical tool. **In contrast, a musically driven pattern reforms and reshapes itself constantly, changing and breathing with the varied contours of the ongoing music.**

Two-Dimensional Patterns: *Break Them*

The traditional two-dimensional beat patterns have their origins in the eighteenth century. While music has changed radically since 1701, patterns remain intact, even sanctified. Most children or non-musical adults quickly learn to beat patterns because a basic pattern has **no inherent musical value** other than to indicate pulse. The frightening aspect of this innocent physical endeavor is its unquestioned acceptance as *conducting* by the unknowing observer!

The blame for this simplistic view of our craft rests within our profession. Standards for creating physical motion to interpret the genius of Mozart and Beethoven are so primitive, it is actually possible for a child to 'conduct' after scant minutes of time-beating instruction. Are we willing to acknowledge and tacitly sponsor the monotonous motions of repetitive time-beating as musically valid conducting technique? Perhaps, because continued and unquestioned use of constant repetition of a pattern confirms the view that simple time-beating **is** conducting.

To change that view, an essential first step is **the restructuring and breaking of basic two-dimensional patterns.** The distinctiveness of a series of motions tailored to conform to and shape the progress of music are never to be mistaken for simple time-beating. A directory of informed intelligence is needed to explain why waving a stick in a repetitive series of motions is **not** conducting.

The mechanical apparatus that has served to convey the message for 300 years must not be completely discarded. Learn the traditional patterns and beat them correctly. In this text it is only the **first** step in pattern use, but not the **final** technical step. After studying the concept of Baton Analysis (Chapter Sixteen), the conductor will have a firm idea of how to employ and transform pattern shapes in the Conductor's Space.

Basic Arm Position when Forming Pattern Strokes

Some confusion exists about the spatial placement of patterns. Many conductors believe that patterns are made exclusively in the area directly in front of the body. The basic position of the conducting arm should **not** be pushed to the left toward the middle of the body because the elbow gets jammed into the rib cage and restricts left forearm movement.

The diagrams indicate the basic arm position. Let the right arm drop freely at the side and bend the elbow, forming the letter 'L' shape. This is one of the basic arm positions from which to form baton strokes. It allows the orchestra to 'read' patterns easily and the conductor to modify and move strokes unhampered and in all directions in the Conductor's Space.

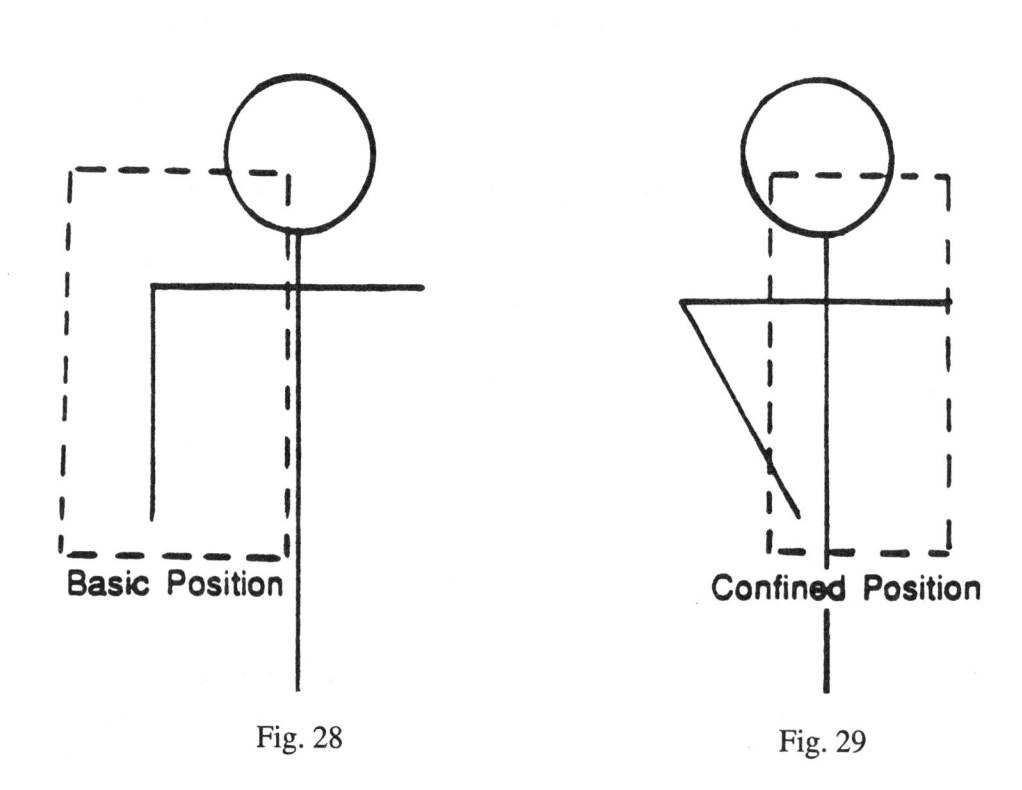

Basic Position

Confined Position

Fig. 28

Fig. 29

General Rule for Learning to Beat a Pattern

The baton arrives at every beat (or pulse point) **from the opposite direction.** For example, in a four-beat pattern the preparation for the downbeat is an upward motion; the arm **moves up in order to move down.** The rebound of the downbeat is slightly to the right so the second beat in the pattern is able to move left; the arm must **move right in order to move left.** The third beat moves across the body to the right (the arm moves **from the left to the right).** The rebound of the third beat moves further out to the right so the fourth beat can be made inward, up to the left, the original starting point (the arm must **move right in order to move upward left).**

This principle holds for the basic two-, three- and four-beat patterns, as well as for patterns that are a combination of twos, threes and fours.

For example, a six-beat pattern can be 3+3; a large two with inner beats, containing **two** structural points -- beats 1 and 4. These beats have to be approached from the **opposite** direction, while the **inner beats** move in the **same direction** from point to point, except for the upbeat. Drawings for this pattern appear in the six-beat section. A six-beat pattern can also be 2+2+2; considered a large three with inner beats, containing **three** structural points -- beats 1, 3 and 5. These beats are approached from **opposite** directions, while the **inner beats** move in the **same direction,** except for the upbeat. Drawings for this pattern also appear in the six-beat section.

The same principle holds for meters containing 7, 8, 9, 11 or 12 beats and are discussed later in this chapter.

When practicing the outlines of the basic patterns that follow (Figures 30-52), keep the forearm in the letter 'L' position. Use simple straight line motions--up, down or sideways. Lock the wrist and use forearm motion, or occasionally trace the patterns with wrist 'clicks' only from the letter 'L' position. Use a metronome and vary the settings, starting with faster pulses before moving to slower ones. Complete each beat in a continuous motion and do not stop the movement in mid-stroke. Make patterns with the right **and** the left hand. Practice each of the examples regularly. Check the baton grip and connect to the tip of the baton!

OUTLINES OF THE BASIC PATTERNS -- WITHOUT REBOUNDS

Two-Beat Pattern

This is the simplest of all the stroke patterns; a straight down, straight up movement.

Fig. 30

Three-Beat Pattern

Draw a line through a triangle from its top. The right side of the dissected triangle is a perfect diagram for the three-beat pattern. It is a straight down, sideways to the right, and upward to the left movement.

Fig. 31

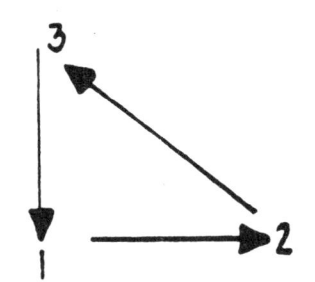

Four-Beat Pattern

In this pattern the across-the-body stroke between beats 2 and 3 **covers more space** than between the other beats. That **unequal** distance was alluded to in Chapter Three. The **across-the-body** stroke from beat 2 to 3 **must be fulfilled,** otherwise **some part of the body will move when the baton motion stops.** The outline of the pattern is straight down, sideways to the left, straight across-the-body to the right **(the unequal stroke),** and upward to the left. (An across-the-body stroke is one that moves from right to left, or left to right, in a straight horizontal motion across the body.)

Fig. 32

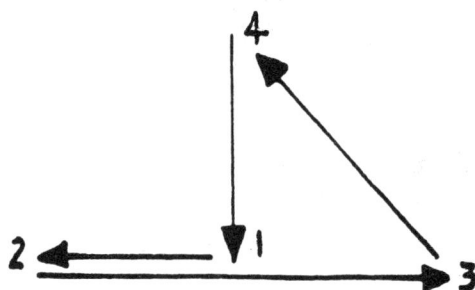

Five-Beat Pattern

A 5/4 measure should have **one** downbeat. If a 2/4 measure and a 3/4 measure are combined to make a 5/4 measure, the combination measure will contain **two** downbeats, and the intent of a single 5/4 signature is corrupted. A true five-beat pattern contains one downbeat and one **across-the-body stroke** on beat 3 (2+3) or on beat 4 (3+2).

Five-Beat pattern: 2 + 3

To outline the first two beats of the pattern, begin with the forearm raised, move straight down, then sideways to the left. Next make a short across-the-body stroke to the right (**not** an unequal stroke), a further stroke to the right (both strokes more or less make up the length of the longer unequal stroke) and an upward stroke to the left to complete the pattern.

Fig. 33

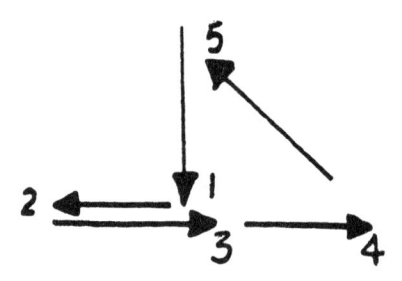

Five-Beat pattern: 3 + 2

To outline the first three beats in the pattern begin with forearm raised, move straight down, then sideways to the left, and make a further left movement. Next, make a long across-the-body stroke to the right (the unequal stroke), and an upward stroke to the left completing the pattern.

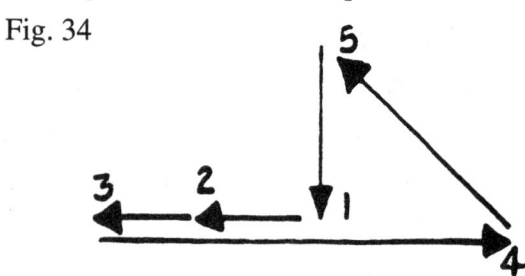

Fig. 34

Six-Beat Pattern

Six-Beat patterns usually divide themselves in half (3+3), or in three (2+2+2).

Six-Beat Pattern: 3+3

There are two versions of this pattern; the so-called German and/or the Italian pattern. The German pattern begins with a straight downward stroke, a sideways stroke to the left, and a further left movement to form the first three beats. Next, a short across-the-body movement to the right (**not** an unequal stroke), a further movement to the right, and a final upward stroke to the left completes the final three beats.

Fig. 35   Fig. 36

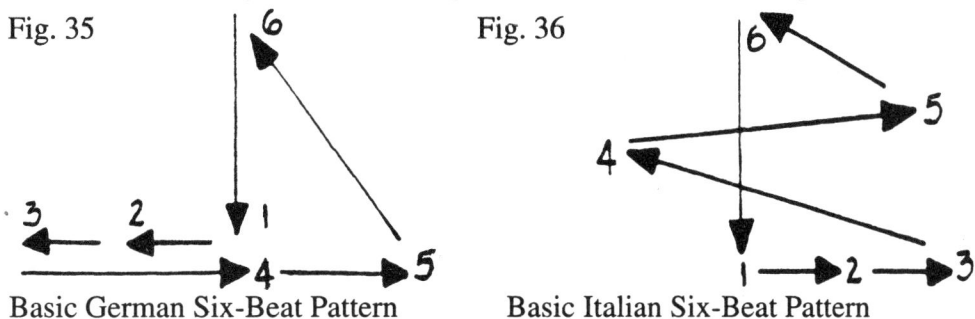

Basic German Six-Beat Pattern   Basic Italian Six-Beat Pattern

The Italian six-beat pattern is very different from the German. After the first downward stroke the short second and third strokes move to the right to complete the first three beats. The fourth beat moves upward to the left, the fifth beat moves slightly higher to the right and a final upward and inward sixth stroke completes the pattern. There are numerous variations.

Six-Beat Pattern: 2+2+2

This pattern is a subdivided three. It begins with a straight downward stroke and a left movement for the first two beats, an across-the-body stroke to the right and a further movement to the right for beats three and four. Finally an upward movement to the left, and after the rebound, a straight up movement concludes the pattern.

Fig. 37

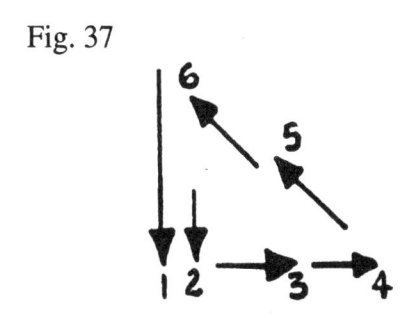

Seven-Beat Pattern

In many instances the composer divides a seven-beat measure into fractions of three and four beats. A clearly divided seven-beat measure can contain **two** downbeats; beats one and four (3+4) or beats one and five (4+3). However, if the composer writes a measure in seven with but **one** downbeat, the conductor is obliged to conduct what is written. The following seven-beat patterns have a **single** downbeat.

Seven-Beat Pattern: 3+4

Begin with a straight downward stroke, then move to the left and make a further left movement to complete the first **three beats.** Then move to the right and make an **extended,** longer stroke for the fourth beat and add a further right movement. Next, an upward and left movement, and an additional upward stroke completes the last **four beats** in the seven-beat pattern. (See Fig. 38.)

Fig. 38

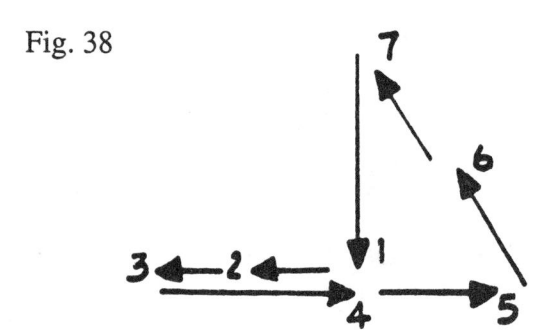

Seven-Beat Pattern: 3+4, another version:

The first three strokes are the same as in the pattern above; then follow with a full across-the-body stroke to the right, a slightly higher left, inward movement, a slightly higher right, outward movement, and finally a slightly higher upward, left stroke for the final four beats to complete the pattern.

The last four strokes are referred to as a **Christmas tree pattern,** and occur on the **right side of the downbeat.**

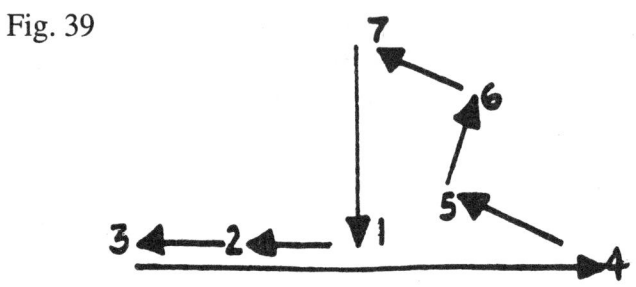

Fig. 39

Seven-Beat Pattern: 4+3

The first **four strokes** in this version are the Christmas tree pattern, and they are made on the **left side of the downbeat.** After the first downward stroke, move upward and to the left in an outward, inward, outward, upward pattern for beats 2, 3 and 4. All strokes are on the left side of the pattern. Make a straight downward diagonal stroke to the right, a further right, downward movement and a final extended upward stroke to the left to complete the final **three beats** in the pattern.

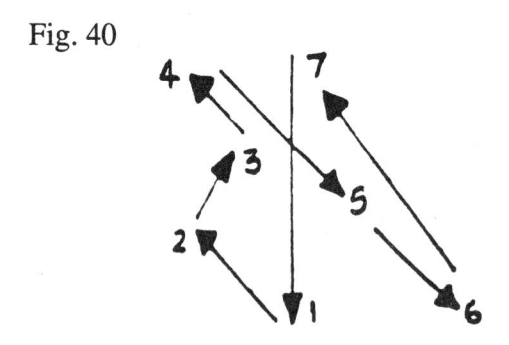

Fig. 40

Other Seven-Beat pattern variations within the Three-Beat Pattern
Seven-Beat Pattern: 2+3+2

This version of a seven-beat pattern is not uncommon. It is a **three-beat pattern with inner beats:**

The first stroke is straight down, the second stroke moves to the left to complete the first **two inner beats** (the **first overall beat** in the three pattern). Make a short stroke to the right, a further short stroke to the right, and yet another short stroke to the right to complete the **three inner beats** (the **second overall beat** in the three pattern). Move up and inward to the left and straight up and to the left for the final **two inner beats** and the **third large overall beat** in the pattern. (See Fig. 41)

44

Fig. 41

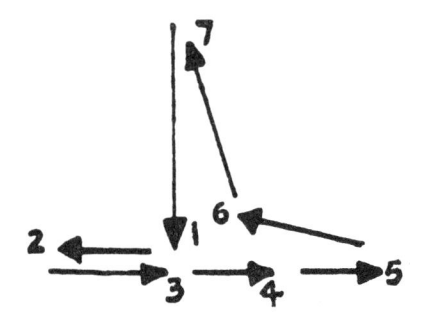

Seven-Beat Pattern: 2+2+3

Another version of the three-beat pattern in a seven-stroke structure:

The first two strokes are the same as the pattern above. The **second large overall beat** begins with a stroke to the right followed by another stroke to the right to complete the **two inner beats.** The final **three inner beats** in the pattern are an inward, upward, left movement, an upward, outward, right movement, and another inward, upward, left movement. These strokes form the Christmas tree pattern, as well as the **third large overall beat.**

Fig. 42

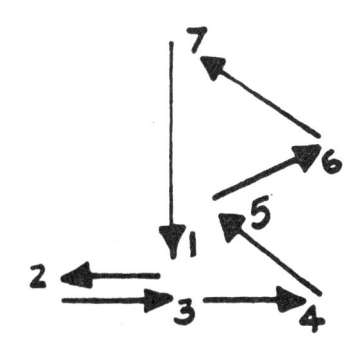

Seven-Beat Pattern: 3+2+2

And yet another version of the three-beat pattern in a seven-stroke structure:

The first stroke moves downward as before, the second and third strokes move to the left to form the **three inner beats** and the **first large overall beat** in the pattern. Make two strokes to the right for beats 4 and 5, forming the **second pair of inner beats** and the **second large overall beat.** Move upward and to the left and upward again for beat 7 to complete the final **two inner beats;** the **third large overall beat** in the pattern.

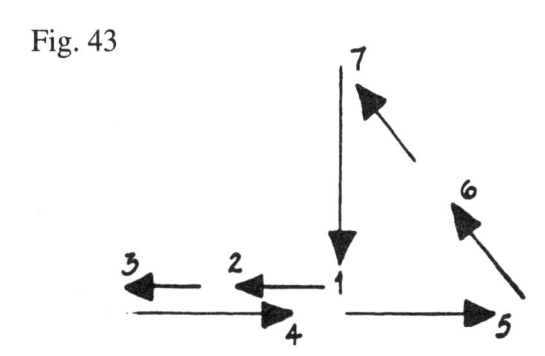

Fig. 43

45

Nine-Beat Pattern: 3+3+3

The nine-beat pattern can be considered a **three-beat pattern with inner beats**:

The basic nine-beat pattern begins with a straight downward stroke, a sideways move to the left and another left stroke. These three strokes are the **three inner beats** and the **first large overall beat.** Make three more short continuous strokes across the body to the right, creating the second set of **three inner beats** and the **second large overall beat.** Move inward and upward to the left, outward and slightly higher to the right, inward and upward to the left for the final movement. These last strokes are the final **three inner beats**; the **third large overall beat** in the pattern.

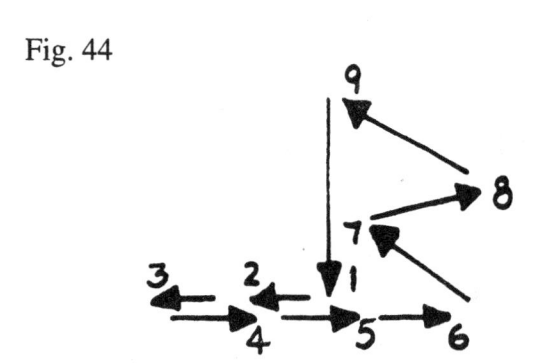

Fig. 44

A nine-beat pattern can also be conducted in a basic **four pattern.** Any combination of **three 2s** plus **one 3** to create nine beats in a measure can be conducted in four:

1. 2+2+2+3: **beat 4** in the four-pattern is beat 7, 8, 9.
2. 2+2+3+2: **beat 3** in the four-pattern is beat 5, 6, 7.
3. 2+3+2+2: **beat 2** in the four-pattern is beat 3, 4, 5.
4. 3+2+2+2: **beat 1** in the four-pattern is beat 1, 2, 3.

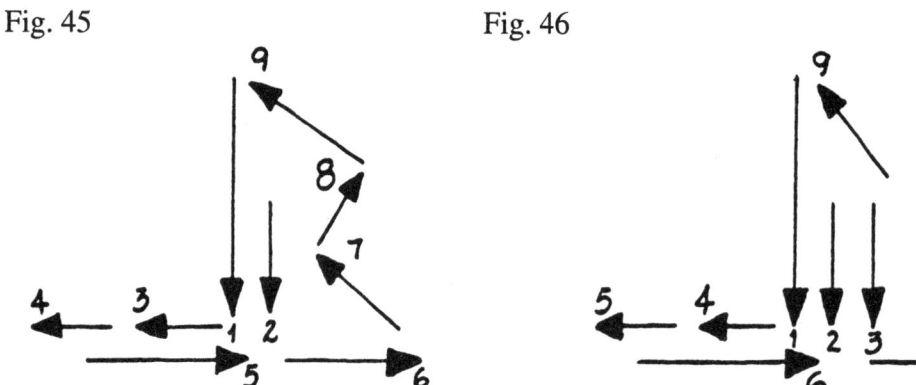

2+2+2+3   3+2+2+2

Fig. 45   Fig. 46

Twelve-Beat Pattern: 3+3+3+3

The twelve-beat pattern is a **four-beat pattern with inner beats**:

Begin with a straight, downward stroke, a much shorter downward stroke to the right and a similar downward stroke further to the right. These are the first **three inner strokes**; the **first large overall stroke.** Make three short strokes across the body to the left. These are the second set of **three inner beats** within the **second large overall stroke.** Then move to the right, across the body, with three short strokes. These are the third set of **three inner strokes** within the **third large overall beat.** Make the upward Christmas tree pattern for the final **three inner strokes** in the **fourth large overall beat** in the twelve-beat pattern.

Fig. 47

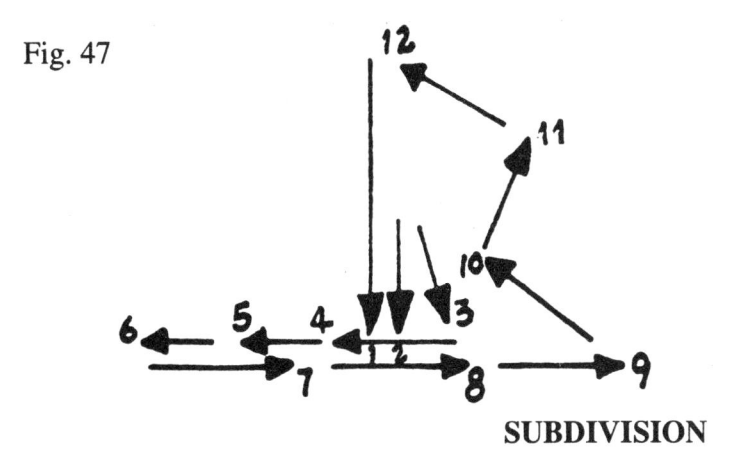

SUBDIVISION

Subdivision is used if the basic tempo is slow enough to accommodate a divided pulse, a large *rallentando* is in progress, or the articulation of difficult rhythmic figures are problematical for the orchestra. Subdivision should **not** be imposed on moderate tempi because the extra beats make it easier to keep time. **Subdivision is not about keeping time, it is about carrying time, sustaining line and maintaining the flow of the structure.**

Once the patterns have been learned, the mechanical/physical act of subdivision is rather simple: **each beat receives two pulse points instead of one.** The second pulse in the subdivision is generally smaller than the primary pulse and moves away from the direction of the next stroke.

Examples of Subdivided 2/4, 3/4, 4/4

The basic patterns have been discussed. The primary beat and all subdivision strokes flow in the same direction, and the subdivision stroke is in the immediate vicinity of the primary stroke. The plus sign (+) in the diagrams indicate the 'and' of each beat, **the subdivision point.**

Fig. 48   Fig. 49 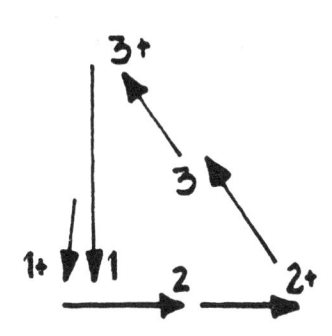   Fig. 50

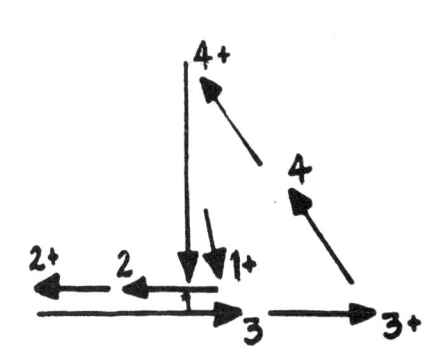

Subdivided 6/8, 9/8, 12/8

Meters in 6, 9, and 12 may be thought of as subdivisions of primary pulse units. (The 6/8 meter is a large divided two or three, the 9/8 meter is already a subdivided three and on occasion subdivided in four, and the 12/8 meter is a large subdivided four.) Therefore, a **further** subdivision of any of these meters is an enormous amount of baton movement within a measure: Twenty-four strokes for a subdivided 12/8! **Avoid polluting the stage environment with lots of arm waving if possible,** but if it is necessary the patterns would read as follows:

The conductor will be called upon to subdivide these two common meters. Keep each of the subdivided beats small and close to the larger basic pulse which clearly outlines the basic structure of the patterns for the player.

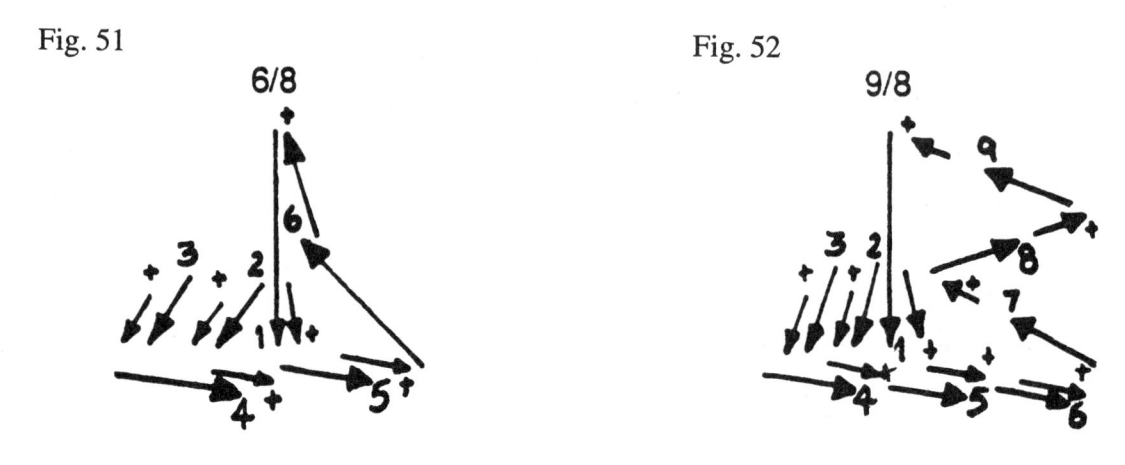

Fig. 51 6/8

Fig. 52 9/8

CHAPTER EIGHT SUMMARY

This chapter covers the formation of beat patterns. A pattern is a physical articulation that determines pace (tempo), and the number of pulses (beats) within a measure. Rhythmic accuracy and exactness in beating patterns are qualities to be encouraged, but **constant repetition of a single beat pattern must be rejected.** Patterns ought to be constantly reshaped to fit the changing contours of the music.

The Basic Two-Dimensional Beat Patterns have been with us since the eighteenth century and remain essentially unchanged and intact. They are so simple children can learn the mechanics of beating patterns without difficulty. That is not surprising since **a pattern has no inherent musical value other than to indicate pulse.**

Basic patterns are valuable and should be studied, learned, and practiced by all conductors. Remember an important rule for forming patterns: **the baton arrives at every beat, or pulse point, from the OPPOSITE direction.** In a 4/4 pattern the **downbeat** is prepared by an **upward stroke,** the left side second beat is approached from the **right,** the right side third beat is approached from the **left,** and the left upstroke is approached from the **right.**

Diagrams have been supplied for all the patterns. Stroke directions for patterns in 2, 3, 4, 5, 6, 7, 9, and 12 beats, including variations in dividing patterns in 5, 7, and 9 beats have been provided.

The physical act of **subdividing** is simple. Each beat receives two pulse points instead of one. The second pulse is generally smaller than the primary one and flows in the same direction as the primary pulse. The technique of **subdivision should not be used to simply keep time, it is used to <u>sustain line</u> and <u>maintain the flow</u> of the structure of the music.** It is very helpful in slow tempi and in large *rallentandi*, and especially helpful for players articulating difficult rhythmic figures.

CHAPTER NINE

LEGATO AND STACCATO PATTERNS

Once the shapes of basic patterns have been learned, the strokes that form the patterns must take on the character of the musical text. *Legato* lines are generally made with smooth, flowing baton motions, and *staccato* or *marcato* passages are articulated with short, stopped strokes.

Symbol Chart for *Legato* and *Staccato* Patterns

Fig. 53

↓ = The arrow attached to a solid line indicates the pulse point in the pattern and the direction of the stroke. A line under the arrow indicates a *legato* stroke.

↓⊙ = A **dot** underneath the arrow indicates a stopped, *staccato* stroke.

- - - - - = A broken line indicates the **rebound** of the stroke (the continuation of the stroke after the pulse point) and the direction of the stroke to the next pulse point (the solid line with the arrow).

Exercises: General Instructions

Tempi for *legato* patterns range from the quarter note equals 54 to 80. Tempi for the *staccato* patterns range from the quarter note equals 60 to 96.

Begin all patterns with the baton hand in the letter 'L' configuration. Make all first beats on the right side of the body. Practice each of the drawn patterns a minimum of ten times or until the hand moves the baton easily and confidently through each of the patterns. Then **vary the shapes of the patterns.** Experiment by making each of the patterns taller, wider, shorter or more compact. Each change in the outward shape of a pattern affects the **size and speed of the baton stroke.** Continue to check the baton grip and make the tip of the baton an extension of the arm..

The distance between beats in the drawings is not meant to be exact. Although the curved stroke is used in all the patterns there are **no loops.** Make all strokes with a single component of the arm!

Legato Two Pattern

Fig. 54

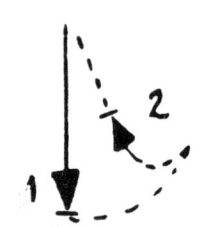

Add a downward 'click' on the first pulse point (beat 1), and an upward 'click' on beat 2. **Do not stop the stroke on the 'click!'** Keep the stroke moving throughout the pattern or the *legato* movement will be broken.

Legato Three Pattern

Fig. 55

Do not add 'clicks' to this pattern. Keep it smooth and flowing. Remember to approach each stroke in the pattern from the opposite direction. Note the upward/inside and outside curve rebounds after beats 1 and 2.

Legato Four Pattern

Fig. 56

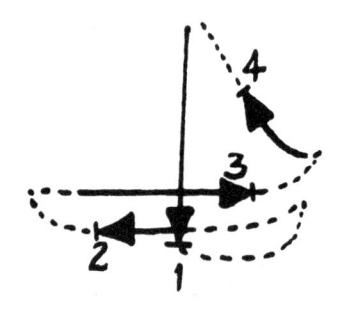

Add a left 'flick' on beat 2 and a right 'flick' on beat 3. Note the downward curve rebound after beat 1, and the upward curve stroke on beat 4.

Legato **Five Pattern: 2+3**

Fig. 57

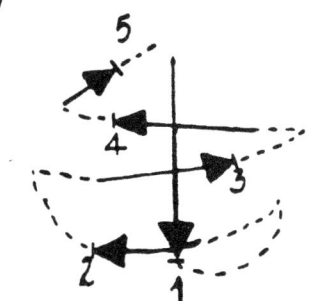

In this 2+3, five- beat pattern, beats 2, 3, 4, and 5 form the Christmas tree pattern. The extended stroke on beat 3 makes it easy for the orchestra player to read the division of the five pattern as a two plus three measure. Beats 3, 4, and 5 can be made in rising straight line strokes. Add the appropriate 'flicks' to beats 3, 4 and 5.

Legato **Five Pattern: 3+2**

Fig. 58

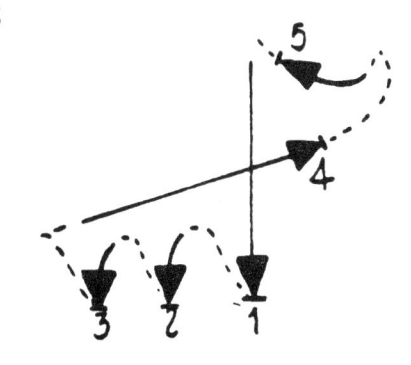

Add 'clicks' to beats 1, 2 and 3 moving into the rebounds without a pause after the 'clicks.' Note that the extended stroke comes on beat 4 and divides the measure into a three plus two structure.

Legato **Six Pattern: German Six, 3+3**

Fig. 59

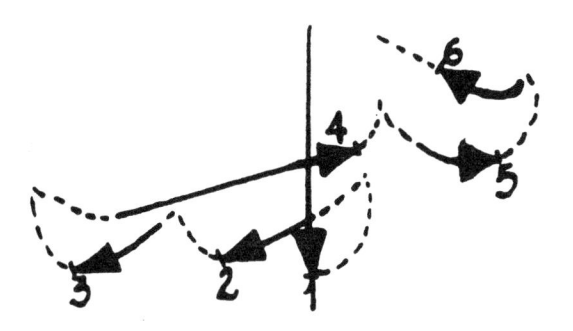

The German six is a large two-beat pattern containing three inner beats in the first half of the pattern and three inner beats in the second half of the pattern. The extended fourth beat stroke divides the pattern into equal halves. Keep the curved rebounds in this pattern flowing evenly from pulse point to pulse point. Avoid looping the curved strokes, and do not add 'clicks' to any beats in this pattern.

Legato Six Pattern: Italian Six, 3+3

Fig. 60

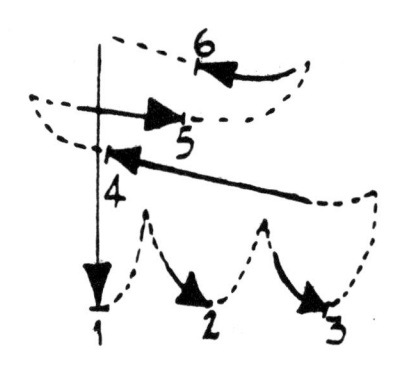

The Italian Six pattern is also a large two pattern with an extended fourth beat that divides the pattern in equal halves. Beats 4, 5 and 6 are the Christmas tree pattern. Add 'clicks' to beats 1, 2, and 3 and move all the strokes through each beat smoothly and evenly.

Legato Six Pattern: 2+2+2

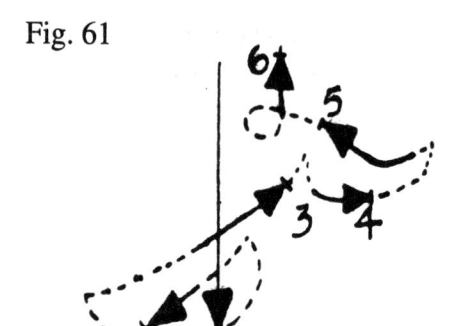

Fig. 61

This six-beat pattern is a large three. In this drawing **beat 6 is made from the wrist with an upward circular movement of the wrist. No other part of the arm moves on the pulse point!** *This small circular wrist stroke is extremely valuable because the tip of the baton rebound lifts the forearm upward and positions the arm and wrist for a variety of downward gestures.*

Legato Seven Pattern: 3+4

Fig. 62

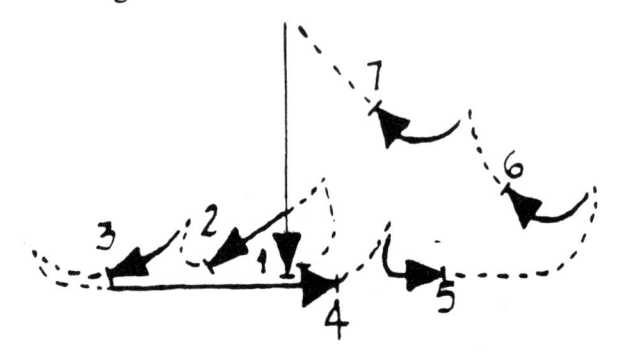

In this pattern the extended stroke is beat four and it divides the pattern into 3+4. Add a 'click' on beat one and 'flicks' on beats two and three. Keep all strokes flowing.

***Legato* Seven Pattern: 4+3**

Fig. 63

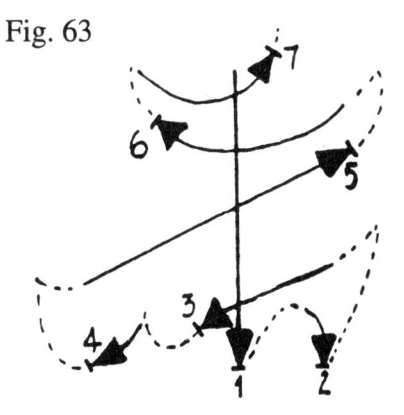

Stroke five is extended in this pattern and divides the seven beats into a 4+3 alignment. Add 'clicks' on beats 1 and 2, and a right 'flick' on beat 5, the extended stroke.

Patterns in 9, 10, 11, 12 and beyond, are multiple combinations of 2+3 beat units. **Ten beats** can be units of 3+3+2+2 in any order and in an overall four-beat structure. **Eleven beats** can be 3+3+3+2 in any order in an overall four-beat structure, or 2+2+2+2+3 in any order in an overall five-beat structure. The combination of beat units that make a pattern is not a haphazard undertaking. **The score creates the patterns.**

***Staccato* Two-Beat Pattern**

Fig. 64

The dot under the pulse points indicates that **the baton stops momentarily** before moving in the direction of the next pulse point, or beat, in the pattern. Check the baton grip and concentrate on the clarity of the baton tip.

***Staccato* Patterns for Three Beats and Four Beats**

Fig. 65   Fig. 66

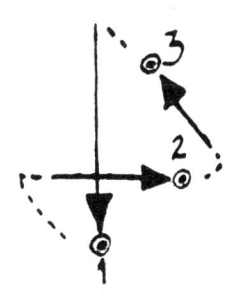

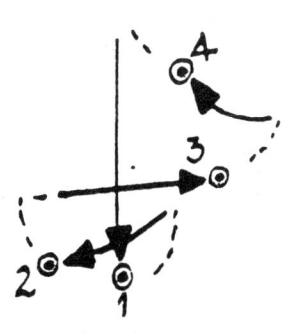

Outlines for all patterns remain the same. Because of the stopped motion of the baton in *staccato* patterns, the outer contours of the patterns may be somewhat smaller in size than *legato* patterns with the same numbers of beats.

Staccato Patterns for Five beats and Six beats

Fig. 67

Fig. 68

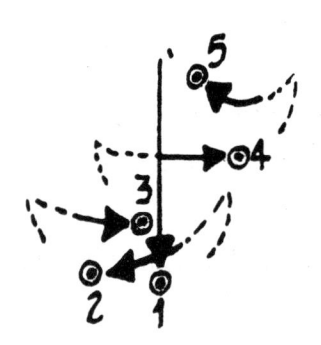

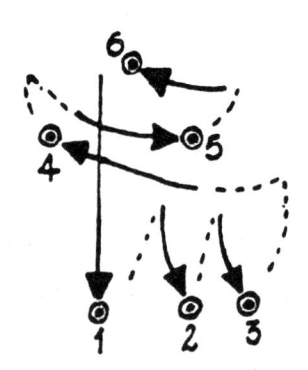

CHAPTER NINE SUMMARY

The conductor's response to the musical text determines the ultimate form of the patterns in 2, 3, 4, 5, 6, 7, 9, etc. A variety of basic pattern shapes are covered as well as two articulation devices: the *legato* stroke and the *staccato* stroke.

In *legato* passages the strokes in the patterns must be smooth, flowing from one pulse point to the next in an unbroken line. However, the strokes in patterns for *marcato* or *staccato* passages must be articulated with short, stopped movements.

Examples of both strokes in various meters have been provided.

CHAPTER TEN

MIXED-METERS

Prior to the twentieth century, most orchestral repertoire was written (metered) in consecutive groupings of two-, three-, or four-beat units per measure. Entire movements could be performed without a meter change.

During the twentieth century, composers began to explore new rhythmic possibilities with consecutive measures that did not always contain the same number of beats.

A sequence of measures might be:

5/8....5/8....9/8....5/8....7/8....3/8....4/8....7/4....3/4....7/4....3/8....4/8....7/4....6/8....5/8....9/8....5/8.

Or

3/16....2/16....3/16....3/16....2/8....2/16....3/16....3/16....2/8....3/16....3/16....5/16....2/8....3/16....2/8.

The first mixed-meter sequence above is from Stravinsky's *The Rite of Spring*, rehearsal Nos. 104 - 110. The second example is from the same work, rehearsal Nos. 167 - 170. Both are discussed in detail in the "Repertoire" section.

Delivering mixed-meter strokes correctly depends on the conductor's understanding of the **unequal height and speed of mixed-meter strokes.**

THE MIXED-METER EXTENDED STROKE

Problems arise when the conductor articulates two- and three-beat units with the **same** size stroke. **The equal height of the strokes** makes it difficult for players to distinguish which of the beats have the **greater** pulse value. If a player gets lost and looks for pulse identification from the conductor's beat, it will not be evident.

The Height and Speed of the EXTENDED Stroke

Height

The **largest unit of beats** in the measure must receive the **highest stroke, an extended stroke,** because the **highest stroke** is responsible for **more time** in the pattern.

Speed

If the baton **maintains a constant rate of speed** throughout a mixed-meter measure, the **larger unit of time will automatically receive a higher stroke. (The higher stroke becomes the extended stroke.)**

Examples:

5/8 measure: 3+2

The **first stroke** in the pattern (covering three pulses), **must be longer in time and higher than the second stroke** (which covers two pulses). The extra time needed for the first stroke is reflected in the height of the stroke. It is the extended stroke.

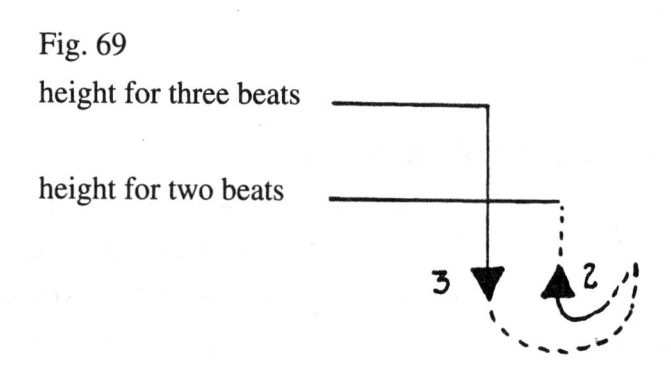

Fig. 69
height for three beats _____
height for two beats _____

5/8 measure: 2+3

The **second stroke** in the pattern (the extended stroke, three pulses) **must be longer in time and higher than the first stroke** (two pulses).

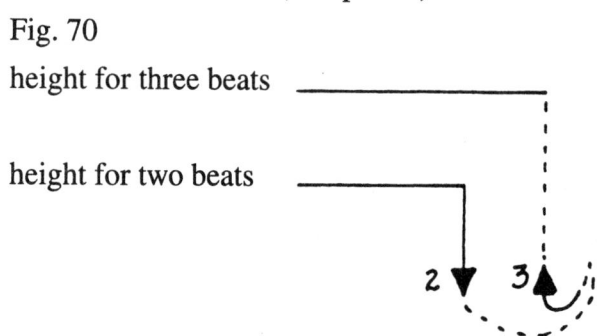

Fig. 70
height for three beats _____
height for two beats _____

7/8 measure: 2+3+2

The **second stroke** in the pattern (the extended stroke -- three pulses) **must be longer in time and higher than the other two strokes** (two pulses each).

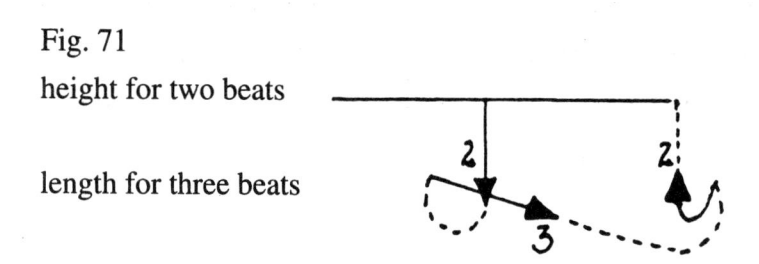

Fig. 71
height for two beats _____
length for three beats

7/8 measure: 2+2+3

The **third stroke** in the pattern (the extended stroke -- three pulses) **must be longer in time and higher than the other two** strokes (two pulses each).

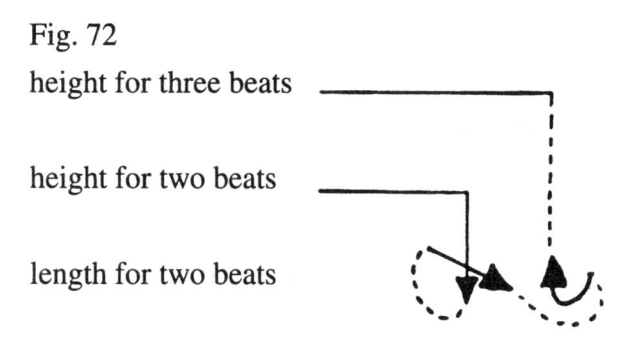

Fig. 72
height for three beats
height for two beats
length for two beats

THE BASIC MIXED-METER PROBLEMS

Let's reexamine the mixed-meter problem alluded to earlier. The 5/8 measures previously illustrated are conducted with two strokes, using the outline of a 2/4 beat pattern. However, when conductors physically beat 5/8 patterns, they generally conduct a **normal** 2/4 pattern, with **both strokes the same height. The extended** stroke is **eliminated,** and the **speed** of the baton stroke either **slows down or stops.**

Why is the speed of the baton effected? If the baton keeps moving, it **must slow down** to accommodate **three pulses** in a stroke that is designed to contain **two** pulses. On the other hand if the baton maintains its normal speed in both strokes, it fills the normal 2/4 pattern in **four** pulses and must **stop and wait** to account for the **fifth** pulse.

5/8 pattern

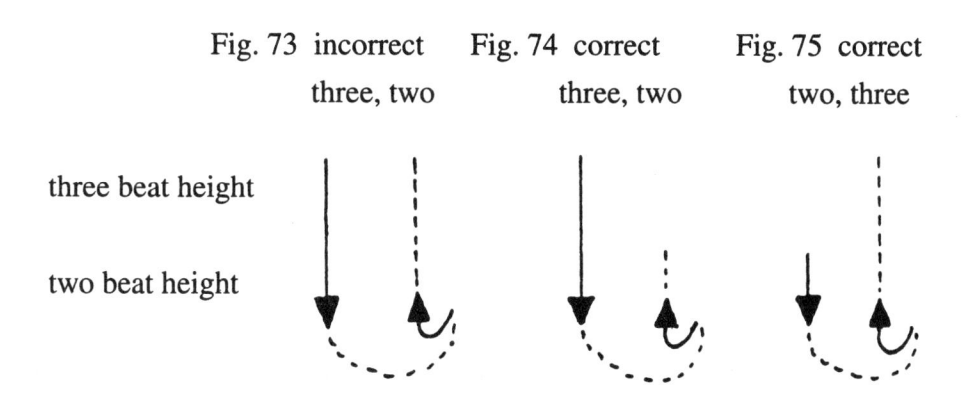

Fig. 73 incorrect   Fig. 74 correct   Fig. 75 correct
three, two   three, two   two, three

three beat height

two beat height

The problem illustrated above also exists for 7/8 measures. They are often conducted in a NORMAL 3/4 beat pattern, with **all three beats the same distance from one another.** The stroke responsible for the largest unit of beats, the **extended** stroke, is **eliminated. The speed** of the baton stroke is altered for the same reasons stated above.

7/8 pattern

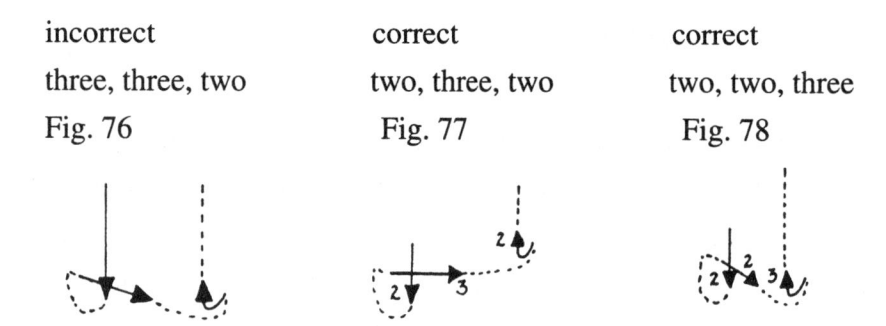

incorrect	correct	correct
three, three, two	two, three, two	two, two, three
Fig. 76	Fig. 77	Fig. 78

The Delivery: Tempo

The precise articulation of mixed-meter patterns is tied to the use of the wrist's **natural stroke,** the 'click,' which delivers the sharp, accurate pulses essential for mixed-meter conducting.

The method of delivery depends on the tempo. If the tempo is quick, the wrist is the **only** means of articulation worth considering. If the tempo is moderate, a combination of the forearm and the wrist may be a workable alternative. In either case the movement of the tip of the baton must be crystal clear to both the conductor and the players in the orchestra. I have insisted on the conductor's connection to the baton because **everyone on the stage depends on its clarity.**

The conductor's desire to have everyone in the orchestra see the changing patterns clearly sometimes causes problems. Conductors use the **upper arm's larger strokes, operating from the shoulder, believing it will clarify movement. It will not.**

The chances of completing quickly moving mixed-meter patterns from the upper arm are almost none. The tempo will **slow down.** The upper arm's natural stroke is geared to sustaining weighty sonorities in slow to moderate tempi. Conducting mixed-meter patterns with the arm is like rolling a large stone uphill. **When the meter is mixed, rely on the wrist and the 'click,' even in *fortissimo* passages.**

CHAPTER TEN SUMMARY

Success in conducting mixed-meter patterns depends on articulating the extended heights within the patterns and maintaining the speed of the stroke throughout the patterns.

In mixed-meter measures, the **largest unit of beats** receives the **highest stroke,** the extended stroke. If the baton maintains a **constant rate of speed,** it will make a higher, extended stroke to fill the larger unit of time. When a normal 2/4 pattern is used for a 5/8 measure, and both beats remain at an **equal height,** the speed of the baton either 1) **slows down** to allow the beat with the largest units (three beats) to accomodate the stroke meant for two beats, or 2) **stops** for a fifth pulse because both equal sized strokes have filled the normal four pulse pattern.

The wrist 'click' or 'flick' is the articulation of choice for mixed-meter measures, especially if the tempo is quick. If the tempo is moderate, a combination of the forearm and the wrist may be used. Rely on the wrist for mixed-meter conducting, even in *fortissimo* passages. The natural stroke of the arm is geared to slow tempi and weighty sonorities, and should not be used in quick tempi.

CHAPTER ELEVEN

THE UPBEAT

When we leave the realm of the time-beater and enter the world of conductor-generated performances, all baton strokes are equally important. However, one baton gesture earns a place of honor amongst equals. It is the very first stroke, the upbeat. It is special because it silently sets the musical table and creates the emotional agenda for what is to unfold. That silent signal must convey the following instructions to a waiting orchestra:

    1. The tempo

    2. The dynamic level of the first sonority

    3. The articulation of the first sonority

Moreover, it is the very first physical act the orchestra experiences! If the conductor is facing a new orchestra she/he ought to make certain the players will want to see and experience much more.

THE TEMPO

When a conductor prepares to start an orchestra, **the golden rule** should immediately spring to mind: **the upbeat must be one full beat in the exact tempo of the music that is to follow.**

One of the most common failures is the inability of the conductor to start a piece in the tempo she/he has chosen. Dynamic intent or an articulation may be visible in the upbeat stroke, but the tempo is often a mystery. Sometimes the preparation is twice as fast (half the tempo), or twice as slow (double the tempo). Sometimes the tempo jump-starts, causing rough bow scrapings from the strings and general rhythmic imprecision. But young conductors can take heart; even the most highly-respected professionals were not immune from the upbeat-sans-tempo virus.

Maestro Wilhelm Fürtwangler's upbeat was one of the most famous strokes in recent conducting history. Members of the Berlin Philharmonic are fond of relating that "we counted seven shakes, then we played."

Maestro Serge Koussevitsky's upbeat was also a cause of wonder "How does the orchestra know when to play?" was a question often asked by knowledgeable patrons in Boston's Symphony Hall. If you were on stage there were two choices and both worked. The first was to watch the concertmaster, Richard Burgin. When his bow came down everyone played. The second choice was a favorite of many players, which was to "attack after his baton passed the third vest button." Perhaps Maestro Burgin carefully timed his bow stroke to coincide with Koussevitsky's baton stroke as it passed the third vest button?

I was on stage when Maestro George Szell, a master conductor, tried, but could not begin, Beethoven's *Fifth Symphony* with the New York Philharmonic. His upbeat veiled his intent and the opening kept coming out solsol; solsol; solsol; mimi; instead of sol, sol, sol, mi. His wonderful orchestra in Cleveland had no trouble deciphering his upbeat: he had trained them to respond to his movements over a period of twenty-plus years. But in New York he was a one-week guest.

Upbeat solutions

If an upbeat fails to convey the expected tempo, try any or all of the following relatively simple and unobtrusive steps. <u>Before</u> the start of a movement rest the baton arm at the side of the body.

1. **Think** of the first three measures of music. If that is not enough to 'set' the tempo firmly in the baton, add a **physical sensation** to the thought by **pulsing** the tempo.
2. Set the **pulse** by squeezing the baton between the thumb and the forefinger. The pulsing will not be visible, because the baton is resting at the side. After thinking and pulsing the first three measures, raise the baton and make the upbeat in the **precise** tempo you have chosen.

The first two steps can be done within seconds, in the silence preceding the start of the music.

3. As a last resort, if the conductor still feels insecure, continue to pulse until the downbeat is delivered. After the first stroke <u>**do not** made and **move any part of the baton grip**</u>! The conductor is now properly launched on the musical journey.

If the podium occupant needs any further help to start the orchestra in a desired tempo, a career decision may be on the horizon.

Exercises:

Each of the seven exercises that follow consists of two strokes, an upbeat motion and a downbeat motion. It may be helpful to think of the two strokes as reflections of one another, **each stroke having the exact properties of the other.** Therefore, both strokes will begin and end in the same place in the Conductor's Space, the speed of the baton strokes in both directions will be the same, and the space used in creating the strokes will also be the same.

Use a metronome to indicate the changing quarter note pulses, and imagine that each upbeat starts a symphonic movement. Stand in front of a mirror and monitor every stroke. Add a 'click' to each pulse and repeat each set of strokes until the motions of the baton/arm are fluid and even. Then move on to the next metronome level.

Do the exercises beginning with fast baton strokes and conclude with slowly moving baton strokes. Use all components of the arm, i.e., wrist, forearm and shoulder. Remember that the upbeat **must** be made in the time of the downbeat, otherwise the musicians will not be able to gauge the speed of the tempo. Check the baton grip!

1. Quarter note = 156
2. Quarter note = 138
3. Quarter note = 112
4. Quarter note = 92
5. Quarter note = 76
6. Quarter note = 60
7. Quarter note = 46

After successfully moving through the seven-step exercise, **change the metronome markings** to quarter = 146, 120, 100, 84, 72, 62 and 52, and then vary the order. Begin with quarter = 100, then 52, then 84, etc. Repeat all exercises with the left arm.

The Dynamic Level

The intended sonority level of the upbeat is closely allied to the component of the arm which delivers the stroke. The upbeat stroke can be delivered to the orchestra from any part of the Conductor's Space.

If the *arm* **is at full extension** and the upbeat stroke is made from the shoulder, the dynamic level will be *forte* to *fortississimo*. The stroke will probably be large and delivered with vigor.

If the *forearm* is used to deliver the upbeat, the forearm will most likely be in the letter 'L' configuration. The stroke will be closer to the body and cover less space than a shoulder stroke. The dynamic range of the forearm stroke will generally be between *mezzo piano* and *forte*.

If the upbeat stroke is delivered from *the wrist*, it will cover the least amount of space and probably be in the *pianississimo* to *mezzo forte* range. The wrist stroke can be delivered with the elbow in a letter 'V' shape with the arm either close to the body or at full extension. Please recall that **the wrist can be used to articulate all dynamic levels up to and including the** *fortississimo* **level.**

Articulation

The upbeat stroke must contain the articulation of the sound or sounds it initiates. A straight- or curved line *legato* stroke can be used to start a singing musical text. A straight line short *staccato/marcato* stroke will produce a leaner, crisper sonority. *Legato* and *staccato sforzandi* can be achieved by adding a variety of 'clicks' to upbeat strokes. The forcefulness of the 'clicks' indicates to the players the degree of strength needed to attack the *sforzandi* articulations.

Placing the upbeat stroke within the Conductor's Space is covered in the chapters devoted to the technique of **Registration.**

The Sound

The color of the very first orchestral sound is the result of all the elements that combine to create the upbeat stroke. If the tempo, dynamics and articulation are clearly conveyed to the players, the attack on the first sound will be whole and in time. If any of the elements are **not** included in the stroke, the fabric of the first sound will suffer, and the players will compensate by adding the missing part or parts. The result will be **an unregulated sound created by committee** rather than a unified one guided by the conductor's intent.

While dealing with the character of the sound a conductor creates, it might be noted that all conductors carry a basic sonority within themselves. I heard Maestro Leopold Stokowski create the 'Stokowski-Philadelphia Orchestra Sound' with the Houston Symphony Orchestra, when he performed a work of mine while he was that orchestra's music director. The performance standards of each of the orchestras differed, but the sounds they produced were Maestro Stokowski's. The present-day Philadelphia Orchestra sound has no resemblance to the older Stokowski-induced sound. The sound they produce now belongs the their present music director. I have witnessed a variety of young conductors with the same level of expertise conduct the same group of musicians in the same repertoire. The overall orchestral sounds produced were wildly different.

I have also heard several excellent violinists eagerly play a very fine old instrument one after the other, and each produced a markedly different sound from the same violin.

We come in all sizes and shapes and look and feel differently, so it is not surprising that we also carry within ourselves our very own sound.

Beginning a work in different parts of the measure

To begin a work, a clear preparatory stroke must be made one full beat before the orchestra enters.

If the orchestra plays on the first beat, the preparatory stroke is the upbeat before the barline. (Note: While the stroke before the downbeat has been given a special name, the-upbeat, it is still a preparatory stroke.) **If the piece starts anywhere after the first beat in the measure, there must still be a preparatory stroke preceding the orchestral entrance.**

Assume the metric division in the measure under discussion is the quarter note and the tempo is *moderato*. The first orchestral sound within the first beat can be written:

1. On the actual downbeat, or beginning of the measure

Ex. 3

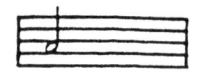

2. In the middle of the first beat

Ex. 4

3. On the last sixteenth of the first beat

Ex. 5

4. On the last part of a quintuplet in the first beat

Ex. 6

5. On the second part of a triplet in the first beat

Ex. 7

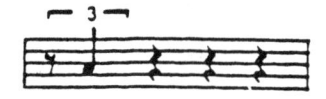

6. On the third part of a triplet in the first beat

Ex. 8

The placement of grace notes on or before the beat can also be included in this general grouping.

Since all the sounds are produced on or within the first beat in a measure, do all the first beat rhythmic variations receive the same or a different kind of preparatory stroke? If the tempo indication is sufficiently fast, the answer is 'yes' they **all** receive the **same kind** of upbeat. A clearly articulated, single in-tempo stroke, **without inner beats,** serves to initiate any of the indicated rhythms within the first beat of the measure. The answer would change only if the tempo slowed down substantially, causing a subdivision of the basic pulse. (In a subdivision the subdivided portion of the pulse generally acts as the upbeat.)

What is true for the first beat in a measure is also true for the second, third, fourth, fifth, sixth, seventh, or more beats. With one important change, the following sentence is repeated because it is vitally important in order to insure the clarity of orchestral entrances: a clearly articulated single in-tempo preparatory stroke, **without inner beats,** serves to initiate any rhythms anywhere **after** the first beat in the measure.

All the preparatory strokes described below are placed within the commonly recognized two-dimensional beat patterns.

Positions of the Preparatory Beats

1. Duple Meter

In the most commonly used time signatures in: 2/4—2/8—2/2—6/8 (in two)—6/16 (in two)—6/32 (in two).

If a piece begins on any part of **beat 1,** the preparatory stroke must be made on **beat 2,** the upbeat. The conductor's silent in-tempo preparatory beat is the signal to the orchestra that they are about to begin. (The placement of the stroke in the Conductor's Space is covered in the chapters dealing with **Registration.**)

Ex. 9

preparation

If the piece begins on any part of **beat 2,** the preparatory stroke in a duple meter must be made on **beat 1.**

Ex. 10

preparation

2. Triple Meter

Positions of the preparatory beats in the most commonly used time signatures in: 3/4—3/8—3/16—3/2—9/8 (in three)—9/16 (in three)—9/32 (in three).

If the piece begins on any part of **beat 1,** the preparatory stroke must be made on **beat 3,** the upbeat. As before, the upbeat is the silent preparatory beat. Note: **If there is silence in the measure after the preparatory stroke, add a clearly visible 'click' to the baton stroke immediately after the preparatory stroke.** Why? A 'click' defines the barline or pulse and helps the players accurately place the rhythm after the silence.

Ex. 11

preparation

If the piece begins on any part of **beat 2,** the preparatory stroke must be made on **beat 1.** ('Click' on one in rest after preparation.)

Ex. 12

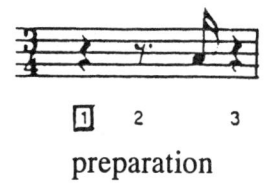

[1] 2 3
preparation

If the piece begins on any part of **beat 3** the preparatory stroke must be made on **beat 2.** ('Click' on one in rest after preparation.)

Ex. 13

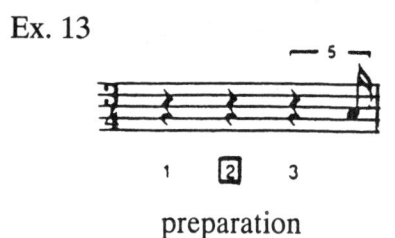

1 [2] 3
preparation

3. Meters in Four

Positions of the preparatory beats in the most commonly used time signatures in: 4/4—4/8—4/16—4/2—12/8 (in four)—12/16 (in four)—12/32 (in four).

If the piece begins on any part of **beat 1,** the preparatory stroke must be made on **beat 4,** the upbeat. As before, the upbeat is the silent preparatory beat. (Add a 'click' on the triplet rest.)

Ex. 14

[4] 1 2 3 4
preparation

If the piece begins on any part of **beat 2,** the preparatory stroke must be made on **beat 1.** (Continue to add 'clicks' on rests after preparations.)

Ex. 15

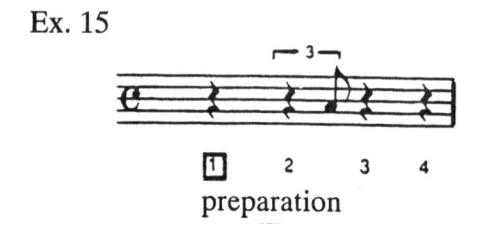

[1] 2 3 4
preparation

If the piece begins on any part of **beat 3,** the preparatory stroke must be made on **beat 2.**

Ex. 16

1 [2] 3 4
preparation

If the piece begins on any part of **beat 4,** the preparatory stroke must be made on **beat 3.**
Ex. 17

    1   2   3   4

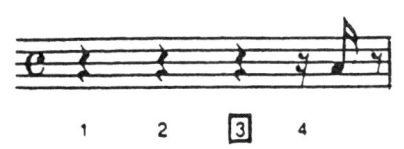

4. Meters in Five

Positions of the preparatory beats in the most commonly used time signatures in: 5/4—5/8—5/16—5/32—15/4 (in five)—15/16 (in five)—15/32 (in five).

If the piece begins on any part of **beat 1** and the measure is conducted in five, the preparatory stroke must be made on **beat 5,** the upbeat. It does not matter how the five beats are divided, 2+3 or 3+2, the upbeat remains the same.

Ex. 18

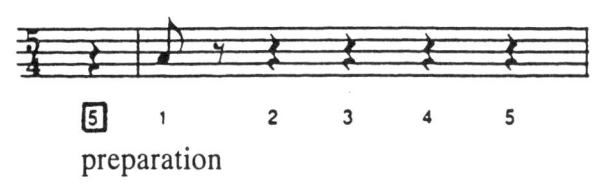

    5 1 2 3 4 5

preparation

If the piece begins on any part of **beat 2,** the preparatory stroke must be made on **beat 1.**
Ex. 19

  1 2 3 4 5

preparation

If the piece begins on any part of **beat 3,** the preparatory beat must be made on **beat 2 .** The placement of the preparation will depend on the pattern of the five. If the third beat is in a 2+3 pattern, the preparatory stroke begins in the middle of the body and moves to the left.

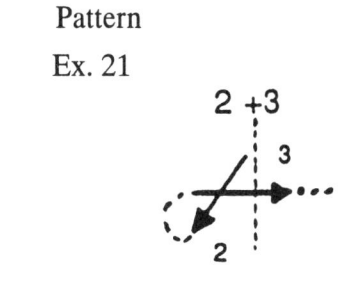

Ex. 20   Pattern

                                Ex. 21

 1 2 3 4 5

If the third beat is in a 3+2 pattern, the preparatory stroke can be made in several ways.

    A. To preserve the pattern, begin on the right side of the body and move to the left. This may prove awkward because of the continuing movement to the left to beat 3 in the pattern. This approach also negates the principle of approaching the next beat from the opposite direction.

    Ex. 22

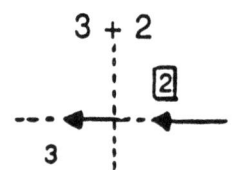

    B. Begin the stroke from the left side and move across the body to the right side. This approach breaks the pattern, but makes the continuing movement to the left easier and preserves the approach from the opposite direction principle.

    Ex. 23

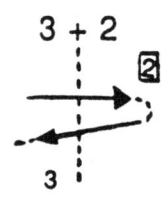

    C. Yet another option is to make a forward, **away** from the body preparatory stroke, and move the next stroke left, **toward** the body in the direction of the next beat in the pattern.

    Ex. 24

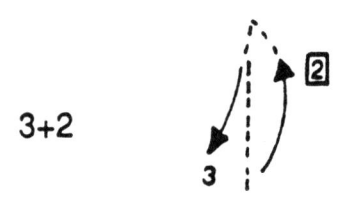

If the piece begins on any part of beat 4 the preparatory beat must be made on beat 3.

    Ex. 25

    preparation

    The placement of the preparation depends on the pattern of the five. If the fourth beat is in a 2+3 pattern, the preparation begins slightly to the left of the middle of the body and moves across and beyond the body to the right side.

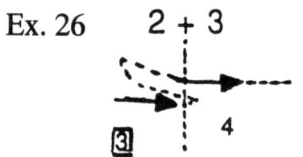

    Ex. 26

If the fourth beat is in a 3+2 pattern, the preparation begins from the middle of the body and moves to the left.

Ex. 27

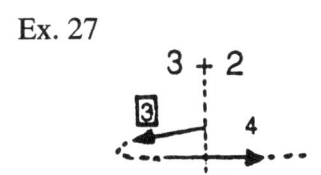

If the piece begins on any part of the **fifth beat,** the preparatory stroke must be made on **beat 4.** The division of the pattern does not affect the preparation.

Ex. 28

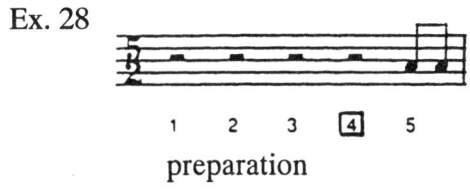

preparation

5. Meters in Six

Positions of the preparatory beats in the most commonly used time signatures in: **6/8—6/4—6/16—6/32.**

If the piece begins on any part of **beat 1,** the preparatory stroke must be made on **beat 6** the upbeat.

Ex. 29

preparation

If the piece begins on any part of **beat 2,** the preparatory stroke must be made on **beat 1.**

Ex. 30

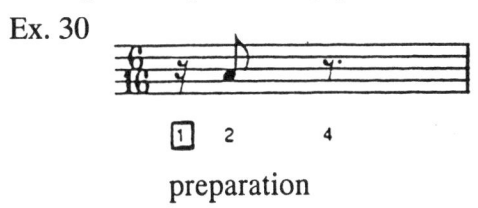

preparation

If the piece begins on any part of **beat 3,** the preparatory stroke must be made on **beat 2.** The division of the meter determines the position of the stroke. If the pattern of six is divided 3+3, the preparatory stroke begins on the right side of the body and moves to the left, and then back across the body to the right for the fourth beat. (If this proves awkward, refer to the 3+2 pattern described above (see Ex. 23) in the section dealing with meters in five and substitute the first part of that pattern for the beginning of this pattern.)

Ex. 31   Ex. 32

If the pattern is 2+2+2, the preparatory stroke begins in the middle of the body and moves to the left.

Ex. 33

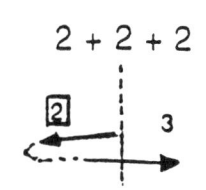

If the piece begins on any part of **beat 4** the preparatory stroke must be made on **beat 3.** The division of the meter determines the position of the stroke. If the pattern is divided 3+3 the preparatory stroke begins on the right side of the body, moves to the left side of the body and across the body to the right (the fourth beat).

Ex. 34

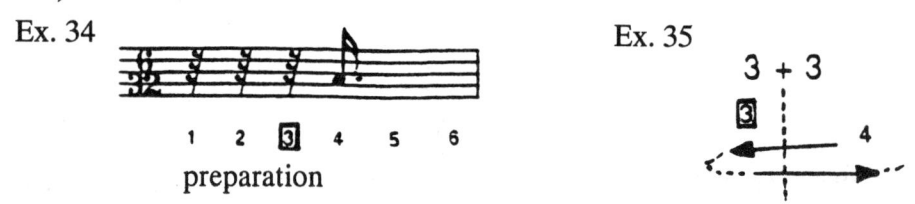

1 2 ③ 4 5 6
preparation

Ex. 35

3 + 3

If the pattern is 2+2+2, the preparatory stroke begins on the left side of the body and moves to the right. The fourth stroke continues to move to the right at a **higher level** than the third beat stroke. When meters expand beyond four beats to the measure, the "opposite direction" rule is a difficult one to keep intact, since measures in five, six, seven, etc., group themselves into movements of two's and three's, and the smaller units often move in the same direction. This is a case in point. The pattern works if the strokes are kept small and the second stroke, beat four in the pattern, is slightly higher than the preparation.

Ex. 36

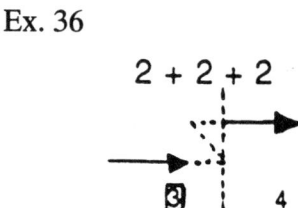

2 + 2 + 2

③   4

If the piece begins on any part of **beat 5,** the preparatory stroke must be made on **beat 4.** If the pattern is divided 3+3, the preparatory stroke moves across the body, left to right. The fifth beat is an upward and inward stroke to the left thus preserving the "opposite stroke" movement.

Ex. 37

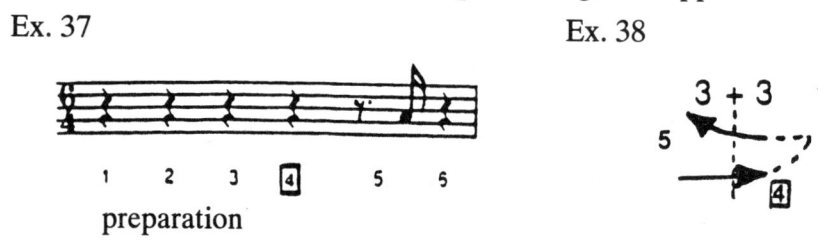

1 2 3 ④ 5 6
preparation

Ex. 38

3 + 3

5

④

If the pattern is 2+2+2, the preparatory stroke begins in the middle of the body and moves to the right outside part of the body.

Ex. 39

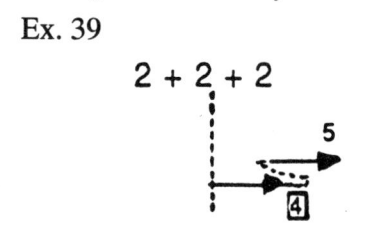

2 + 2 + 2

5

④

If the piece begins on any part of **beat 6,** the preparatory stroke must be made on **beat 5.**

Ex. 40

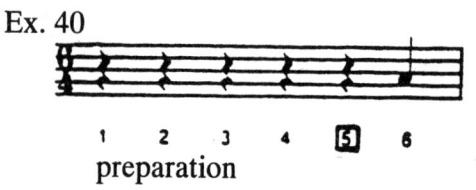

1 2 3 4 ⑤ 6
preparation

If the division of the meter is 3+3, the preparatory stroke starts in the middle of the body and moves well to the right of the body.

Ex. 41

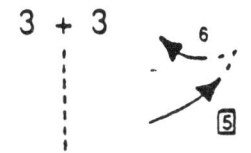

If the division is 2+2+2, the right to left upward stroke moves toward the middle of the body.

Ex. 42

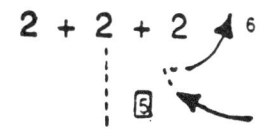

6. Other Meters

Meters in 7, 8, 9, and beyond follow the same general rules: the preparation must be made **one full beat before** the orchestral entrance, and whenever possible, the preparation comes **from the opposite direction.**

The most commonly used time signatures for **Meters in one:** 2/4 (in one)—2/8—2/16—2/32—3/4 (in one)—3/8—3/16—3/32—1/1—1/2—1/4—1/8—1/16—1/32.

A single in-tempo preparatory upstroke will start the orchestra, no matter where they begin within the measure.

Starting Mixed-Meters: The Unequal Stroke

Starting mixed-meter patterns means having to confront the extended stroke. There are two options:

1. **Honor the Beat Pattern**. If the beat pattern is honored, **the preparatory stroke may not contain the same number of beats as the upcoming unit of beats.**

Consider a 5/8 measure structured 3+2 and conducted in two. The first unit of beats in beat 1 in the measure contains three beats, the extended stroke, while the second unit in the measure, which forms the preparatory stroke, **contains only two beats.** If the mixed-meter pattern were honored, the preparatory upbeat would contain only **two** beats for the following **three-**beat unit.

Ex. 43

preparation contains two beats

If a 5/8 measure were structured 2+3 and conducted in two, starting the measure would still present a problem. This time the preparatory stroke, beat 2, contains **three** beats, the extended stroke, and the first unit of beats, beat 1, **contains only two beats.** If the mixed-meter pattern were honored, the preparatory upbeat would contain **three** beats for the following **two**-beat unit.

Ex. 44

preparation contains three beats

The extended stroke also exists in time signatures conducted as triple meters. In some basic 7/8 measures conducted in an overall three pattern, it is possible to honor the pattern and have equal preparatory beats. Starting a 7/8 measure conducted in three and structured 2+2+3, on **beat 2,** the third or fourth eighth notes in the measure work because the unequal stroke is not involved. In a meter which is conducted in three, **the preparatory stroke for beat two is made on beat one.** The preparatory stroke, beat 1, contains two beats, the same amount as the second beat. However if the piece were to begin on any part of the third beat -- notes 5, 6, 7 -- the conductor would again be facing the problem of the unequal stroke.

2. Option To Change the Beat Pattern. In the 5/8 2+3 measure change the **silent** preparatory **beat 2 from a three beat unit** to a **two beat unit in order to equal the two beat unit in the first part of the opening measure.**

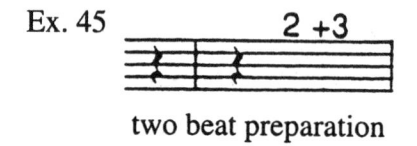

Ex. 45

two beat preparation

In the 3+2 measure the **silent** preparatory **beat 2 does not contain two beats,** but **three beats** to match the three beats in the first part of the opening measure.

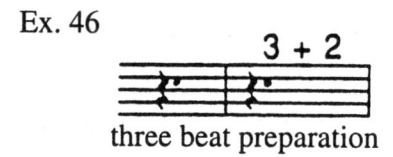

Ex. 46

three beat preparation

Despite the beat pattern, **the preparatory strokes are changed.** They are shortened or lengthened to conform to the amount of beats in the first unit of the mixed-meter measure. **Changing the time of a preparatory stroke** for a mixed-meter measure can be applied to all mixed-meters.

A note of caution: During a concert this change of pattern can **only** be done at the very outset of a piece, or after a *fermata* within a piece. In either case the preparatory beat begins from silence and has no effect on the flow of the music. In a **rehearsal** the conductor may choose to break the rhythmic structure whenever the orchestra begins again after a stop. However, the conductor must make it clear to the players that the changes are in place **for the rehearsal only -- not for the concert.**

I have noted the options because many conductors use a bit of both. If mixed-meters are conducted with a complete understanding of the extended stroke, including the differences in the height and speed of the strokes, the second option ceases to exist. The best way of realizing a composer's mixed-meter beat patterns is to conduct them as written. Do not change them unless the circumstances are very unusual.

CHAPTER ELEVEN SUMMARY

The **upbeat stroke** must convey the following instructions to a waiting orchestra:

1. The tempo
2. The dynamic level of the first sonority
3. The articulation of the sound of the first sonority

The golden rule is that the upbeat **must be one full beat in the exact tempo of music that is to follow.**

If the pulse is subdivided, the preparatory stroke is made on the subdivision.

A **single** in-tempo preparatory stroke is all that is necessary to cover the many different rhythmic possibilities within the upcoming beat.

Starting a work on different beats within a measure and in several different meters has been fully covered. The rule for using the preparatory stroke remains unchanged. Examples and discussions focused on meters in two, three, four, five, six, and seven as well as on preparatory strokes for each of the meters and for all beats in the patterns.

Beginning mixed-meter measures present a special problem because of the **extended stroke.** Various starting points within the measure were discussed for 5/8 and 7/8 meters. The question of whether to change and equalize the preparatory beat to match the opening segment of a mixed meter measure at the beginning of a work was addressed, with options offered.

As a general rule, the conductor should try to adhere to the mixed-meter patterns created by the composer.

CHAPTER TWELVE

THE ELEMENTS OF A NEW TECHNIQUE

Previous chapters articulated the fundamentals of conducting technique: control of the body, definition of the natural strokes of the arm, the baton, i.e. the tip of the baton, baton strokes including the upbeat preparatory stroke and basic beat patterns for various meters. It is important to learn how to use the conducting tools that are at the heart of our present technical system. The concept of the Conductor's Space has been introduced and within that space **a new set of guidelines for forming physical responses to music** will be offered and defined. It should be recalled that the rationale for physical motions generated by the conductor **must come from the composer's score.**

IS THERE A 'CORRECT' PHYSICAL RESPONSE TO A MUSICAL PROBLEM?

All that follows must be viewed in the context of this question. A single "correct" musical/physical solution to a musical problem **does not exist.** The very thought that any measure of music must be performed in a preordained "correct" manner robs music of one of its greatest attributes, **allowing the same succession of sounds to speak differently to different people.** It is a given that any two conductors confronted with the same musical problems will view them differently and devise distinct musical, thus physical, solutions. Even conductors who could agree fully on the musical meaning of a score would produce dissimilar results because of their individual motor and muscular skills and unique body structures. While all conductors have some technical limitations when compared to a mythic super-conductor, **every conductor is** capable of a wide variety of baton/arm strokes. The task of the conductor is to: 1) discover and profitably use the strokes that come naturally and work well for his or her body, and 2) add a variety of learned strokes to create a technical vocabulary that can cope with the needs of the composer. **Music may start in the composer's imagination, but it is delivered by the conductor via physical means.**

Conductors must think of stroke choices just as string players think of bowing possibilities; there are generally several solutions for most problems. **In theory, any baton stroke can be used for any solution, so ALL strokes may be 'correct.'** But in practice, the 'correctness' of the stroke depends on who chooses what stroke and when, and how and to what effect it is used.

THE SCORE

Those who yearn to conduct must never lose sight of the fact that it is the composer who makes the existence of the conductor possible. The composer's score is the conductor's holy book, the final word in most factual musical matters -- meters, metronome markings, pitch, pitch lengths, articulations, etc.

Even while accepting the constraints of the score, the conductor in charge of recreating the music must be wary. Reading a score is not an exercise in rigidity, and adherence to the factual elements of the text does not rule out insight or creativity. Music notation allows, in fact insists upon, personal involvement beyond the symbols. Automatons producing perfectly performed pitches do not generate music. The ingredients that make the recreation of music magical cannot be fully captured on the printed page.

Toscanini claimed that his only job was to adhere to the composer's musical text. Fortunately, he did not heed his own advice. He gave to each composer the gift of his musical vision. His recorded legacy makes it abundantly clear that a Toscanini performance carries an unmistakable personal quality which identifies and separates it from those of his colleagues. Even composers are not immune from deviating from their creations. Stravinsky asked that his music not be interpreted, maintaining that he had written everything into the music that he wished to be heard. Yet his own recordings, whether he was on the podium or in the control booth, belie his claims.

However, be warned that any fresh insights must arise from, and be seamlessly incorporated into, the flow of the score. Otherwise a conductor's flight of fancy, no matter how imaginative, cannot be musically justified.

Infusing the complete Conductor's Space with a probing mind and the united spirit of the performers on stage is the perfect way to pay homage to the composer and the score.

VISUAL SCORE STUDY - BATON PLACEMENT

Conducting music is a lifetime learning experience, geared to the three-step procedure mentioned on the opening page of this text:

1. Learning the score
2. **Installing a technical system to deliver the musical information in the score**
3. Delivering it

Step one and three are the basis for most conducted performances. Step number two has never been a high priority, if ever thought of at all.

Most conductors adhere to the time-tested methods of score study -- singing lines, considering pitch relationships, identifying harmonies, analyzing motives and phrase lengths, deciphering forms and playing through a score on the piano. All are important preparations directed to the substance of the score, the music itself.

It may seem strange to say that a conductor has only studied the music, but that is true. **Only the music has been studied and that is not enough.** A process that enables the conductor to **transfer newly acquired knowledge to the orchestra** has not been considered. Using predesigned, all-purpose formula patterns will not suffice. Because **music creates technique,** *a new technical language that is completely molded by the score is a necessity.*

Almost every measure in every score has some message that is relevant to the health of the music. Every composer has his or her own set of musical fingerprints and every score is or should be a reflection of individual thought. *Yet conductors continue to impose identical beat patterns on dissimilar music.* Why? One reason may be so simple it is overlooked.

When conductors study a score, they hear and analyze it, but few **see** the notated graphics on the page as **baton movement.** No attempt has been made to make a visual correlation between the changing shapes on the page with the placement of the baton. **If conductors paid closer attention to the visual structure of the composer's text, they would be forced to emulate those representations with comparable technical gestures.** Every composer and composition would benefit from a fresh, perhaps original, set of baton movements that is the mirror image of the music. **It would mark the beginning of the end of repetitive pattern beating.**

The topography of the score page is replete with clues for novel baton movement, yet it remains a veritable bonanza of untapped information. For example:

1. The length and character of the notes in the composer's musical text (dots, dashes, slurs, accents, holds, cut-offs, *accelerandi, rallentandi*, etc.) determine the **precise length of every stroke and the character of every baton articulation within the stroke.**

2. The registers and dynamic levels of the notes in the composer's score (*piano, forte, fortissimo, sforzando, pianissimo, crescendo, diminuendo*, etc.) indicate the **region in which the baton strokes are formed and how they are articulated.**

3. The orchestration in the composer's musical text indicates the **space in which the baton stroke functions.**

Practicing **Visual Score Study/Baton Placement (VSS/BP)** enables the conductor to assess the technical-physical demands of the score based on a *visual* impression of the printed page. The strength of Visual Score Study/Baton Placement is that the information it discloses can be used **prior** to the standard procedures for learning a score. **If properly used, the information has a direct impact on how the conductor will prepare and shape the music.**

Detailed explanations and examples of VSS/BP are presented in the next two chapters.

THE PATTERNCUBE

A NEW, TWO-PART, MULTI-DIMENSIONAL SYSTEM FOR CHARTING BATON MOVEMENT

A single, repetitive beat pattern cannot suffice if a conductor means to recreate a work that conforms to the composer's intent. The shape, direction, and placement of beat patterns have to change as the music changes. As decisions about baton placements are made, the movements derived from the score create their unique physical architecture and **the need to record and retain such technical decisions becomes necessary.**

Presently, the conductor's information about *baton movement* is restricted to a pattern drawing indicating beat contour, and nothing more. In contrast, the PatternCube **records _where_ the baton should be in the conductor's working space, _what_ strokes to use, and _how_ the strokes are delivered.** This new format also traces right hand/left hand movement.

PART ONE -- THE PATTERN

Part One of the PatternCube, **The Pattern,** outlines the contours of the beat patterns. (Part Two, **the Cube,** is covered in Chapter Fourteen.)

The shape of the pattern generally represents the melodic movement within one orchestral measure. The **new patterns, formed by the music, rarely conform** to the shapes or pulse locations of the older patterns.

REGISTRATION

When the composer's melodic structure embraces the entire range of the orchestra, the conductor should use his/her space in an equivalent manner. **Registration is the vehicle that frees the baton to explore all of the Conductor's Space,** guided by the composer's directions. It is a **multi-spatial VISUAL reflection of the composer's notation** and an essential element for creating the changing patterns that reflect the music's content. While Registration need *not be exact* it must be a close approximation and registration techniques should be a part of every stroke in **either** hand.

There are three Registration units:

Pitch Registration, Dynamic Registration and Spatial Registration. Pitch Registration forms the pattern in the PatternCube.

Pitch Registration

Pitch registration is the conductor's **spatial representation of the smallest components of the musical structure -- the composer's pitch contours.** The pitch contour may be a single melodic line, or the outline of a fully orchestrated harmonic segment. **Pitch Registration is most effective in slow to moderate tempi.** In fast tempi only the general direction of the contour of the pitch line need be indicated.

Exercise 1. For the following exercises, imagine a **vertical** keyboard in front of you. *A note is registered on the vertical keyboard when it is touched by the baton with a 'click' of the wrist.*

Begin with the metronome set at 60 and gradually increase the speed until the pulse rate reaches 120. Do not go faster. In Ex. 47 the right hand registers pitches covering a major ninth: middle C to fourth line D in the treble clef. Start the exercise at waist level, and gauge the hand movements so that the top D natural is at eye level. The space between the waist and the eyes is used to **Register** the pitches contained within the interval of the major ninth.

1. The first three notes (middle C) in the measure are registered on the imaginary keys with 'clicks' in the **same place** — at waist level.
2. The fourth pitch in the measure, **moves upward in a straight line** to the next note. 'Click' D natural.
3. In measure 2 the hand **moves down** to the C key at waist level and 'clicks' the first beat.
4. On beat 2, move upward in a straight line beyond D natural and 'click' E natural on the imaginary keyboard. For beat 3, the hand returns to the waist position and 'clicks' C again. The F key on beat four needs **a higher hand position** than the E, and the upward movement lengthens the space in order to reach the interval of a fourth.
5. Continue the **vertical** upward and downward movement until the scale is completed in both directions. Sing the pitches as they are registered.

Register all exercises in the same way. With practice, the hand quickly adjusts to pitch spaces and covers distances easily and accurately. **Remember that Pitch Registration is approximate, not exact.**

The diagram underneath the music is a representation of the hand movement for the exercise.

Ex. 47 Use straight line up and down strokes with either hand.

Vertical Hand Movement Diagram for Exercise One. (All up down hand movements are made within one vertical column, the bottom of the column being middle C, the top of the column the octave above middle C).

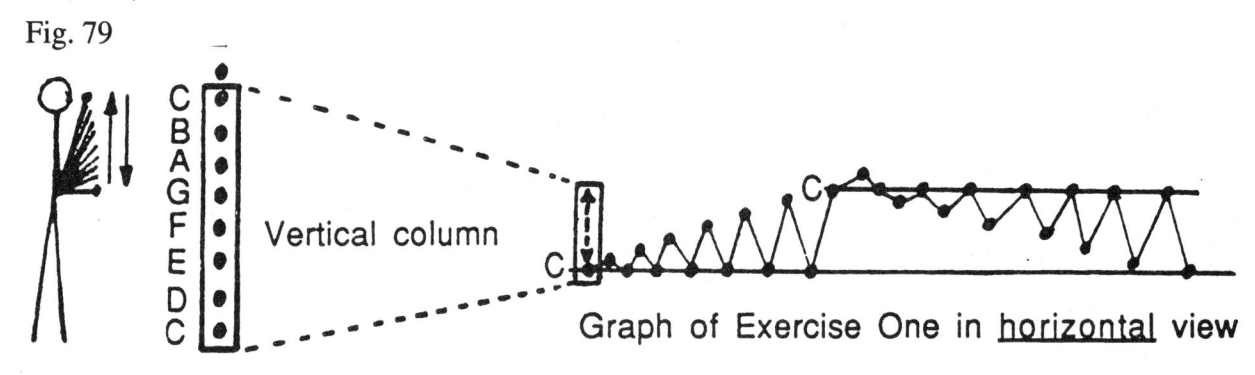

Fig. 79

Exercise 2. Begin with both arms resting at the sides, at full extension in front of and close to the body. The hands are at the **bottom** of the Conductor's Space. The right hand registers **ascending curved line strokes** to the right, **away** from the body, one stroke for every two notes until middle C is reached (a space above the waist). Return to the starting position with descending curved line strokes (one stroke for every two notes).

Repeat the exercise with the **left hand**, registering ascending curved line strokes to the left, away from the body, moving back to the starting position with descending curved line strokes (one curved line stroke for every two notes). The highest note in the exercise, middle C, occupies a space above the waist. **In this exercise an octave is registered from the lowest point of the Conductor's Space to an area above the waist.**

Note: **There are no fixed positions for pitches in the Conductor's Space.** Middle C is not in the same position in every musical situation. **Before** beginning, think of the amount of space to be covered in the registration. Do not put yourself in the position of trying to complete a registration beyond the limits of your Conductor's Space. The amount of space needed to cover the registered intervals can always be moderated since there are **no fixed pitches in the Conductor's Space.**

In Ex. 48 make one vertical stroke for each metronome pulse. (Each pulse will represent an eighth note.) Sing the pitches as they are registered.

Ex. 48

Vertical Hand Movement Diagram for Exercise 2. (All up down hand movements are made within one vertical column, from C in the bass clef to middle C.)

Fig. 80

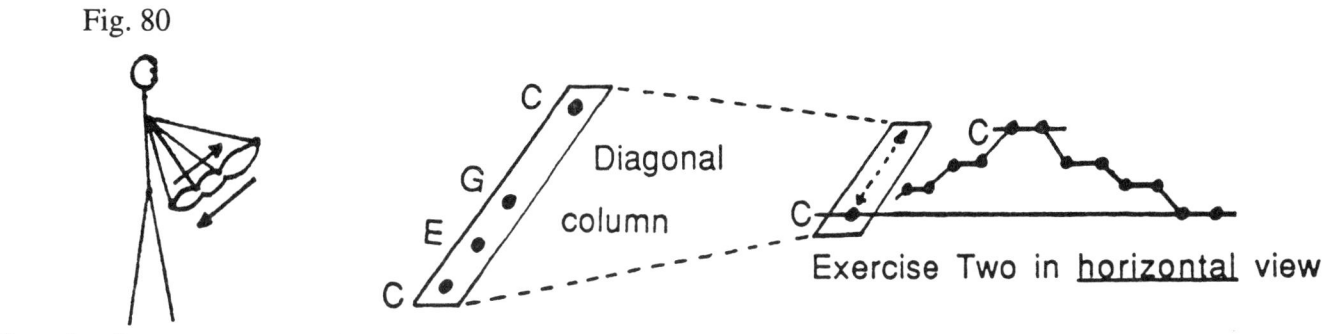

Exercise 3.

Begin and conclude the exercise **below the chest level.** The top note in the exercise ought to be registered slightly **higher than eye level.** Use **straight line** strokes moving upward and **curved line** strokes moving downward. Make one stroke for each metronome pulse in the exercise. (Each pulse represents an eighth note.) Complete the exercise with the right hand, and repeat with the left hand. Sing the pitches as they are registered.

Ex. 49

Vertical Hand Movement Diagram for Exercise 3. (All up-down movements are to be made within one vertical column, from middle C to the octave above.)

Fig. 81

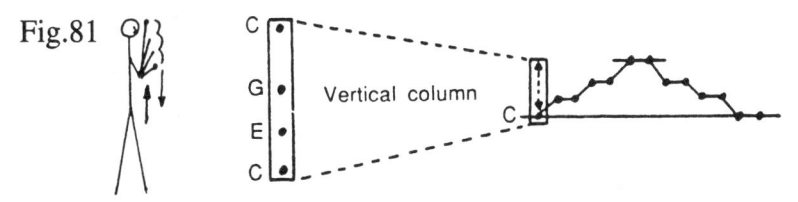

Exercise 3 - In Horizontal View

When **Pitch Registration** feels comfortable and the exercises are completed with ease, repeat and **begin each exercise in different areas in the Conductor's Space.** Think of the overall space to be registered before 'clicking' the first imaginary key. Finally, create your own exercises by singing slow or moderately paced familiar melodies and register the pitches on the imaginary keyboard. Employ a variety of strokes and use all areas of the Conductor's Space.

More often than not the composer's **pitch contours or phrase shapes** force a modification of the old pattern designs, and as the baton breaks **the old patterns it also creates new containers -- patterns -- for the music.**

Make it a habit to trace the shapes of singing *legato* lines with baton strokes whenever it is musically possible. Properly used, **Pitch Registration is a great technical tool.**

GLOSSARY OF SYMBOLS IN THE PATTERN

Add the following easily recognizable pattern symbols to those given in chapter nine.

Fig. 82

The **solid line** indicates the shape of the stroke (straight or curved).
The **arrow** shows the direction of the stroke.
The **tip of the arrow** marks the pulse point (or beat).
A **circle around a dot under the arrow** indicates a momentary stop of the stroke.
A **line under the arrow** indicates an uninterrupted stroke.
Numbers near the arrow identify the beat count.

↓ = straight line stroke, downward

↙ = straight line stroke, downward to the left at various angles

↘ = straight line stroke, downward to the right at various angles

↑ = straight line stroke, upward

↗ = straight line stroke, upward to the right at various angles

↖ = straight line stroke, upward to the left at various angles

→ = straight- line stroke, across to the right

← = straight line stroke, across to the left

⊙ = a short stroke

— = a long stroke

↧ = repeated stroke **in the same place.** No horizontal movement between strokes.

↧ = a **short** repeated stroke.

↧ = a **long** repeated stroke.

→ ·· = a **STOP** after the stroke (and before moving to the next beat).

Fig. 83

····· ▄ = the rebound.

The Rebound

A broken line **after** the tip of the arrow (pulse point) indicates a rebound and shows **the continuation and the direction of the stroke.** The rebound is also the preparation for the next stroke and serves to equalize the time between beats. The placement of the short *staccato* stroke **rebound** needs special attention.

The *staccato* stroke can be made with an **immediate rebound and stop** after the stroke. The rebound acts as the preparation for the next baton stroke which is made on the following pulse (if the *staccato* stroke were made on the first of a group of 4 sixteenth notes, the rebound would be made on the 2nd sixteenth note and the stop on the 3rd and 4th sixteenth notes).

The *staccato* stroke can also be made with a **stop and a delayed rebound** after the stroke. The missing rebound which is needed to prepare the baton for the next pulse is placed *just before* the next stroke. If we use the same 4 sixteenth note example, the *staccato* stroke would be on the first sixteenth, the stop on the 2nd and 3rd sixteenths, and the rebound on the 4th sixteenth.

Pitch Line for Pitch Registration

All patterns should have a pitch line, **a fixed center from which to register pitch.** It is an **imaginary** line that may be thought of as a movable "do" in *solfege*. Because it can be adjusted, or moved throughout the course of the music, the fixed center need not be harmonically anchored, although the pitch line is often the tonic in music of the classical period. The pitch line is usually fixed on a single, central pitch, or on a recurring sonority.

All baton movement should relate to the imaginary fixed center. For example, if the pitch line were F above middle C, all notes above F would be registered **above** the imaginary pitch line, and consequently all notes below F would be registered **below** the pitch line.

The pitch line also fixes a physical location. If F were the midchest area, all pitches above the F would be above the midchest, and all the notes below 'F' would be below the midchest area.

In Beethoven's *First Symphony* (Ex. 50), the pitch line is F above middle C, the harmonic center in the pattern. *Adding the pitch line to a pattern is a simple matter.* The imaginary fixed center is translated into a single, straight line (the pitch line), and given a pitch designation. The patterns are created on, above or below the pitch line, as shown in Ex.50. (If Ex. 50 were transposed to G major, the pitch line would be labeled with the note G.)

A PATTERN WITH SYMBOLS AND A PITCH LINE

What does a new pattern using **Pitch Registration** look like? The newly created pattern for the beginning of the second movement of Beethoven's *First Symphony* bears no resemblance to the universally recognized three beat pattern (see chapter eight). However, the new pattern not only preserves the three pulse meter but also outlines Beethoven's pitch movement articulations and indicates the shape of the phrase.

This example appears again in chapter thirteen (Ex. 54), with a full explanation of the pattern and the reasons for the strokes that form the pattern.

Beethoven, *First Symphony,* Second Movement

Ex. 50 *Andante Cantabile Con Moto*

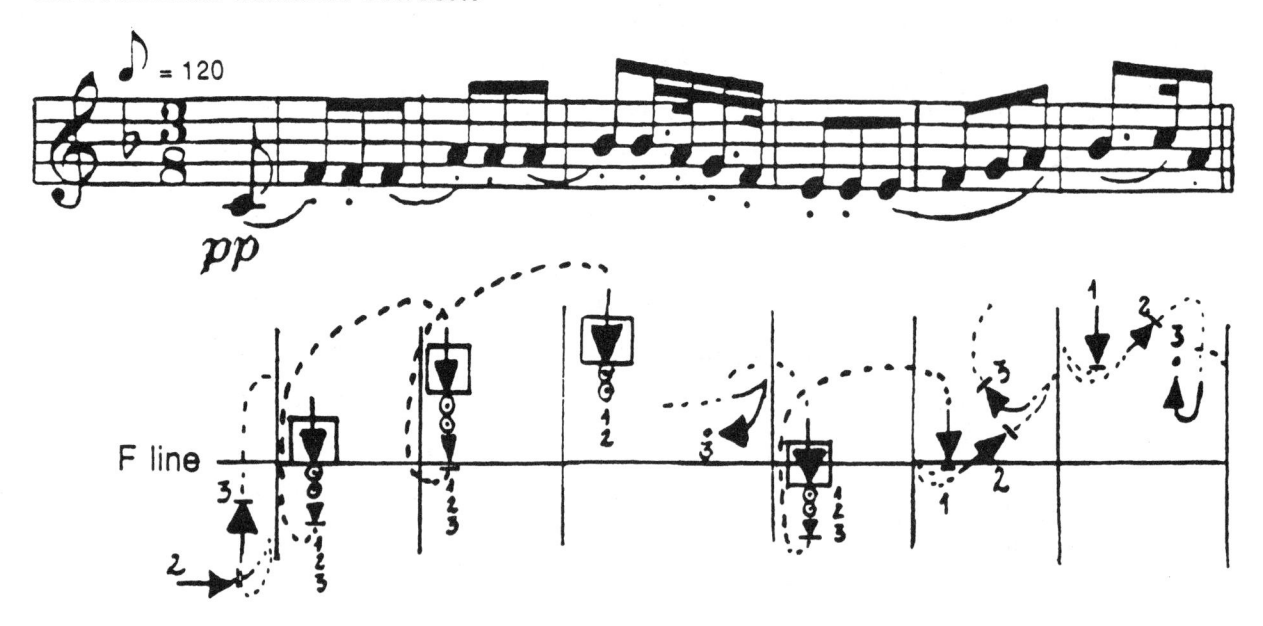

PITCH REGISTRATION LEVELS

How do we identify the areas we use in the Immediate Conductor's Space when we employ **Pitch Registration?**

The following diagrams identify **four Pitch Registration LEVELS.** Each **Level** corresponds to a general region in the **orchestra.**

W = **waist** area, the *lowest* region of the orchestra. From lowest note to circa middle C.

MC = **midchest** area, the *middle* region of the orchestra. From middle C to circa fifth line F in the treble staff.

UCN = **under chin** area, a *cross-over* area to the beginning of the *upper* region of the orchestra. From third line space C in the treble staff to circa first C above the staff.

E = **eye** area, any region, but considered first to be the *top* region of the orchestra.

Pitch Registration - Four Levels

Fig. 84

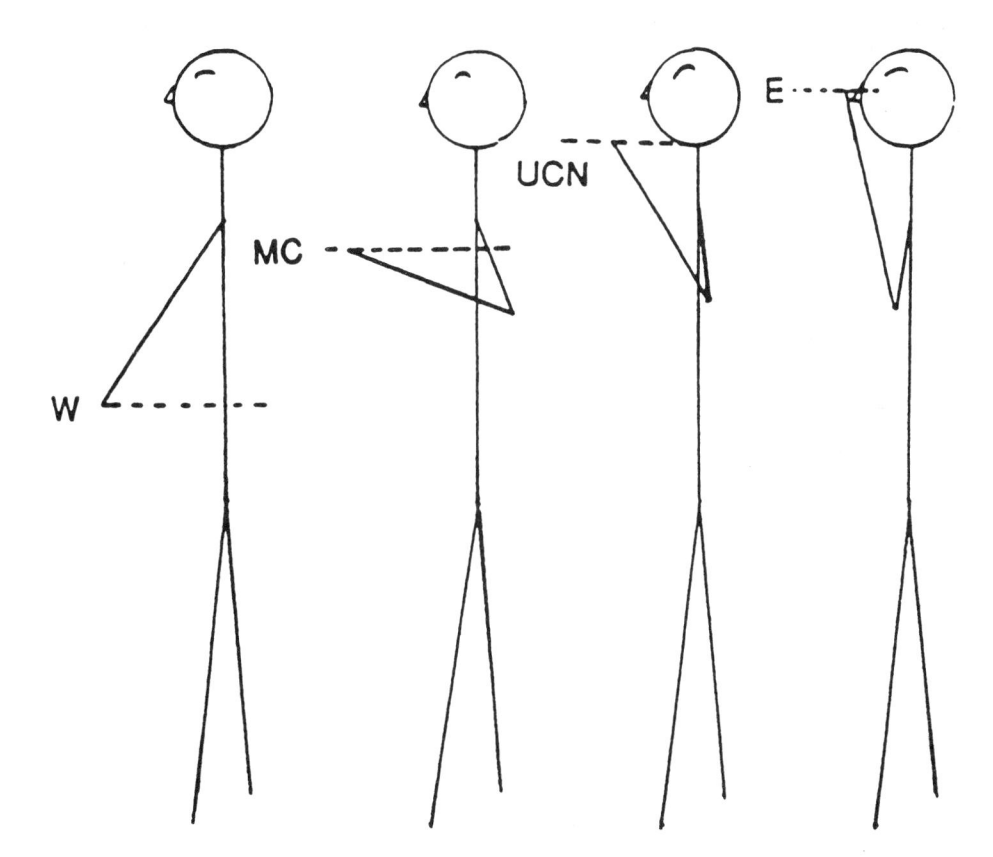

CHAPTER TWELVE SUMMARY

This chapter introduces some of the elements that create a new approach to conducting -- **a technical language completely molded by the score.**

Visual Score Study/Baton Placement, (VSS/BP), helps the conductor assess the technical/physical demands of the score based on a **visual** impression of the printed page. This technique is used in conjunction with the time-tested ways of studying and learning a score.

The PatternCube is a two-part system for tracking baton movement -- a measure-by-measure account of the conductor's baton/hand motions. The movement of the baton, for right and left hand, are codified in patterns signifying **where** the baton is, **what** stroke to use, and **how** to deliver it.

Part One of the PatternCube is **The Pattern.** (Part Two, the Cube, is introduced in chapter fourteen.) These new patterns rarely conform to the shapes of older patterns because they are formed by the music rather than a time-beating formula.

A **chart of symbols** for Pattern movement has been provided. Straight or curved strokes are represented by solid lines. The direction of the stroke is indicated by an arrow, the tip of the arrow showing the pulse point (the beat). Numbers above or below the arrow indicate the beat count within the measure. A broken line accounts for the rebound, the continuation of the stroke. All this information has been reduced to easily recognizable symbols. A chart has been provided with symbols.

The Pattern contains a **Pitch Line,** an imaginary fixed center from which to register pitch. It can be changed and adjusted as the music moves from section to section. The pitch line clarifies and outlines the range of the pitch materials and acts as an effective guide in detailing areas in which the baton operates.

Pitch Registration is the vehicle that frees the baton to explore all regions of the Conductor's Space, guided by the composer's directions. It is a multispatial visual representation of the smallest components of the musical structure, the composer's pitch contours. Pitch Registration need not be exact, but must be a close approximation and is most effective with moderately paced materials.

Pitch Registration and hand movement exercises have been provided.

A chart outlines the Four **Vertical** Pitch Registration Levels:

    E   =   eye level
    UCN =   under the chin
    MC =   the midchest area
    W   =   waist level

CHAPTER THIRTEEN

THE NEW BEAT PATTERNS

When **Pitch Registration** is used and new beat patterns are planned, a conductor's own perceptions of style, period and taste are helpful. It is equally helpful to resist the temptation to create patterns on a whim, following some unknown genetic urge -- patterns divorced from the music neither succeed, nor convince. It is accurate to conclude that **there is no single correct pattern** for any measure of music, but it is imperative that the conductor understand that his or her choice of **pattern must emanate from the music.**

New Beat Patterns: Examples

Legato Strokes-Straight and Curved

Ex. 51

Beethoven, *Violin Concerto,* First Movement

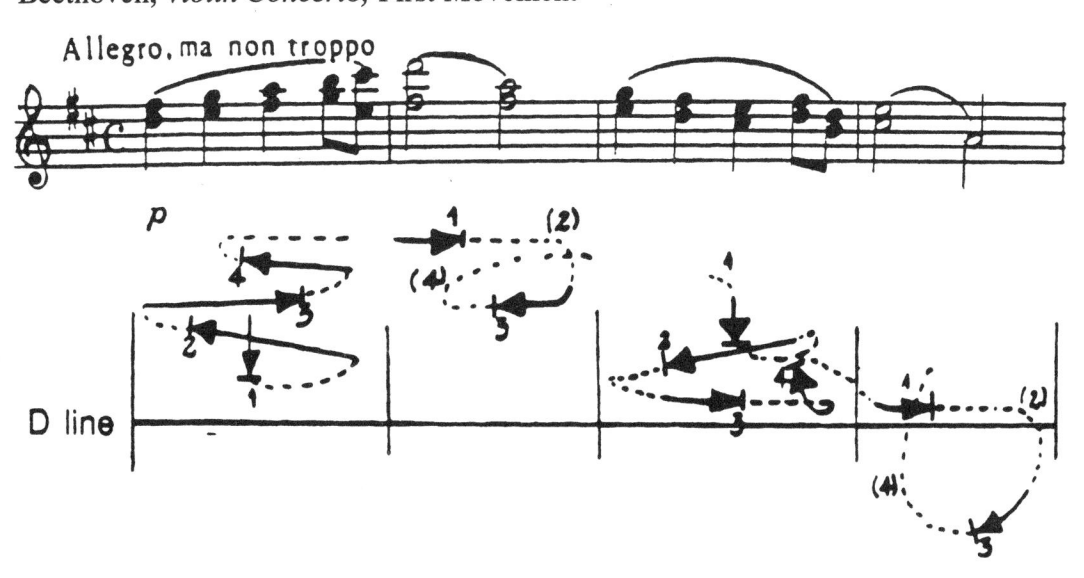

The D treble staff pitch line makes the shape of each of the patterns above, near and below the line, a fairly exact visual representation of Beethoven's pitch movement. The space covered in this example is an octave and a fourth.

Begin the example with the baton in the area under the chin. The top stroke in the pattern will be made at the eye level and the low A natural, the final note in measure 4, is registered in the area above the waist.

The four-pulse pattern is characteristic of measures 1 and 3. The second and fourth measures form a natural two-pulse pattern. This example uses both curved and straight line strokes.

Ex. 52
Brahms, *First Symphony*, Last Movement

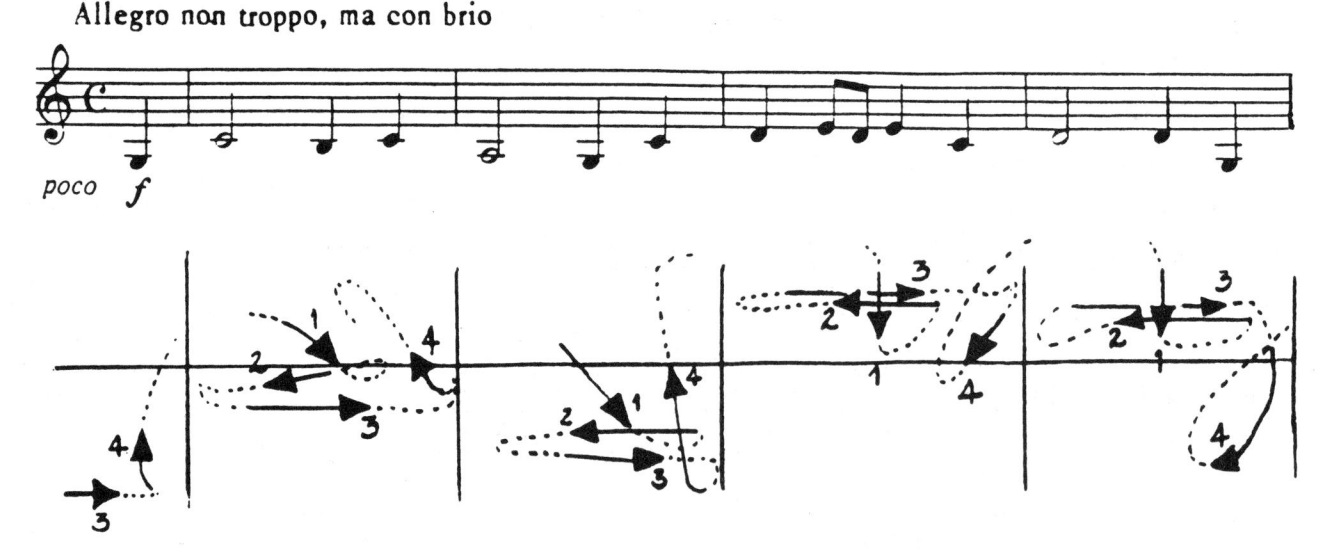

Allegro non troppo, ma con brio

poco f

The pitch line is middle C. The range of the conductor's movement in this example is spatially more confined than in the previous Beethoven example because the melodic material only covers a major sixth. The baton motions are straight line or curved line *legato* strokes.

Please note that the upbeat (G natural) to measure 1 comes from **below** the downbeat (C natural), rather than from above, as is the usual practice. If Brahms had written the first G an octave higher, an upbeat from above the C would be a physically *correct* movement.

The diagrammed pattern in four works perfectly and without difficulty. But let us suppose that a conductor decides that less pulse and more flow is necessary. An obvious alternative is two beats per measure. If that removes too much pulse, yet another alternative is available -- a combination measure which unites two pulses with one stroke and articulates the two remaining pulses. This combination preserves the flow and maintains the pulse. Beats 1 and 2 in measures 1, 2 and 4 are conducted with a single across-the-body stroke, as in the previous Beethoven example. (Beats 1 and 2 move to the right, beat 3 to the left and beat 4 is as written, except that the turn from beat 4 to beat 1 in the next measure comes from the opposite direction.) Measure 3 is articulated with four pulses.

Ex. 53
Copland, *Appalachian Spring*

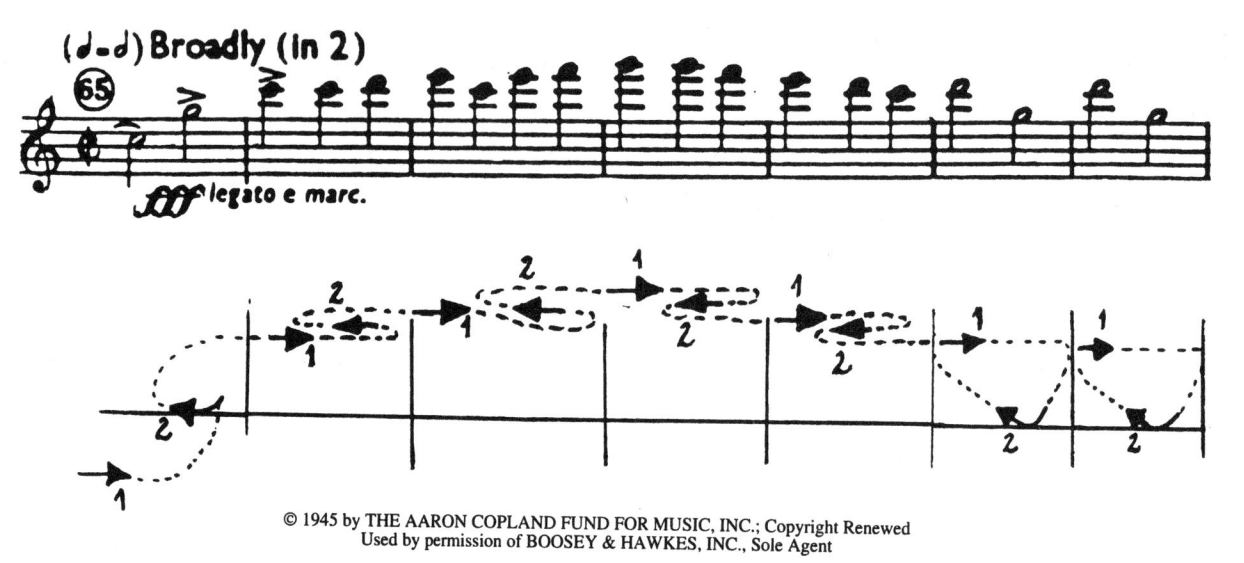

(♩=♩) Broadly (In 2)

㊻

fff legato e marc.

© 1945 by THE AARON COPLAND FUND FOR MUSIC, INC.; Copyright Renewed
Used by permission of BOOSEY & HAWKES, INC., Sole Agent

"The Shaker Tune" (No. 65 in the large orchestration) spanning an octave, lends itself to Pitch Registration (outlining the C major triad and the drop of the fifth), and robust across-the-body strokes in both directions. The pitch line is the G natural above the treble staff. The octave can be registered between the midchest and eye levels.

Legato and *Staccato* Strokes

Ex. 54

Beethoven, *First Symphony*, Second Movement

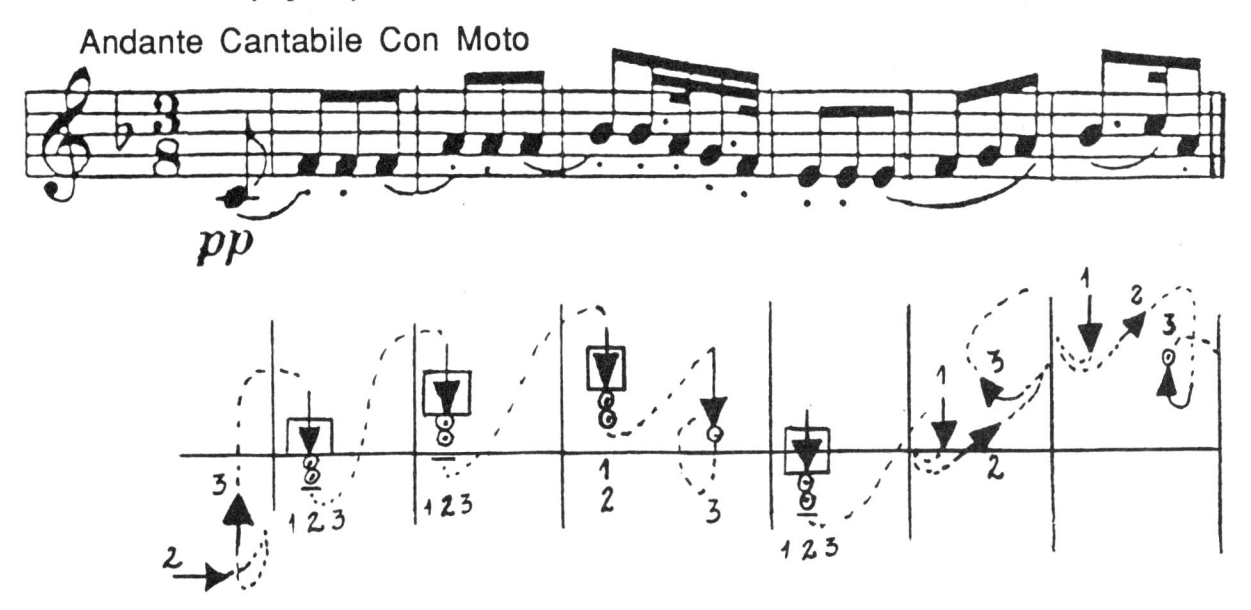

The beginning of the Second Movement (seen in Ex. 50) illustrates the proper use of long and short strokes, and contains compelling musical reasons for creating new patterns.

Measures 1, 2, and 4 resist any musical rationale for the usual three beat pattern. By design, Beethoven composed three measures of repeated pitches in eighth note values, with *staccato* markings under the first two beats. The repetitive music sits poised within the measures, awaiting direction. The conductor's physical translation of the composer's intent keeps the patterns static and within a single conducting space. Since there is no movement in the measures, the sideways motion between the first two beats of those measures should be eliminated. The third beat, a repetition of the two previous pitches, must also begin exactly where the first two beats began, the only difference is the substitution of a *legato* stroke for the *staccato* 'clicks.' The third beat is made within the same space by using a curved inward stroke. **The beat 'pattern' in each of the measures is three identical up-down strokes in the same space, with one articulation difference.**

Beethoven used the opening measures to carefully prepare the upcoming contrast -- the stepwise *legato* movement in measures 5 and 6. The baton can shape the stepwise music with a flowing pattern using *legato* strokes in new conducting spaces.

Fulfilling Beethoven's six-bar compositional scheme requires an almost stationary new pattern, breaking the usual 3/4 pattern and a combination of strokes, pitch and spatial registration. In contrast, a drawing of the traditional pattern reveals nothing about Beethoven's music other than that each measure contains 3 beats.

Ex. 55

Tchaikovsky, *Nutcracker Suite*, March

If the Tchaikovsky excerpt were conducted with four beats to every measure, twenty-nine of the thirty-two strokes needed to cover the eight measure excerpt would be short *staccati* with 'clicks.' This is definitely music to be conducted from the wrist.

In an alternative view, measures 5, 6, 7, could be conducted with two beats per measure, from the forearm, and measure 8 could be a combination measure of one stroke for the first two beats, plus single strokes for beats 3 and 4. The final note in measure 8 is articulated with the **left hand, which keeps the baton in the correct registration position to deliver the next stroke.**

One of the key elements in using registration is that it allows the conductor to plan precise music-derived baton movements with either hand which eliminates unnecessary body movement.

The pitch line is the treble D and the activity below the pitch line indicates that the basic hand position is higher than normal.

Begin this two-octave excerpt in the area under the chin. The first stroke in the second measure, F-sharp, is just below eye level. The lowest notes in measures 5, 6, and 7 are conducted in the area below the midchest level and above the waist. The left hand stroke in measure 8 is made above eye level.

CHAPTER THIRTEEN SUMMARY

The examples of new beat patterns included in this chapter make it clear that there is no single *correct pattern* for any measure of music.

Part One of The PatternCube allows the conductor complete freedom to form patterns with one proviso -- the conductor's choice of pattern must emanate from the music. **The composer justifies the presence of the conductor and the score creates conducting technique.**

The Beethoven, Brahms, Copland and Tchaikovsky new pattern excerpts contain pitch lines, stroke symbols and registration levels.

CHAPTER FOURTEEN

THE PATTERNCUBE - PART TWO
THE CUBE: COLUMNS ONE AND TWO

The **Cube** in the PatternCube is the information square under the beat pattern.
Fig. 85

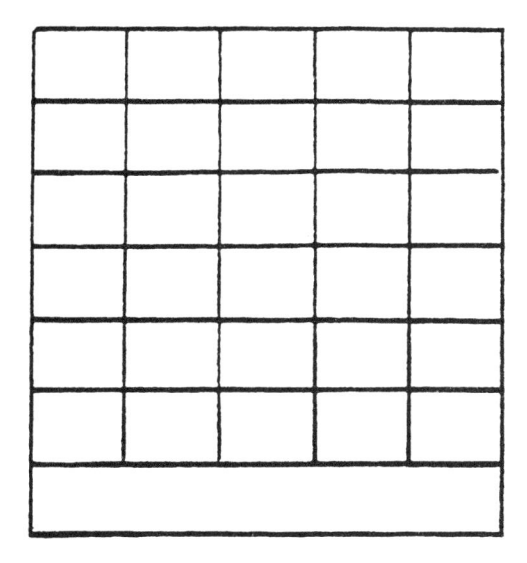

The five columns in the Cube **describe the physical movements that create the patterns.** The columns identify the strokes and the parts of the arm used to deliver the strokes. Registration **levels** and registration **zones** indicate the locations of the strokes. Placement of the left hand is addressed, assuming the baton is held in the right hand. Symbols are used throughout. A space at the bottom of the square is reserved for special comments.

The information in the Cube plus the Pattern completes the PatternCube.

The following series of short hand symbols will be used throughout the PatternCube.

GLOSSARY OF STROKE SYMBOLS IN THE CUBE

Fig. 86

FO ⌒ = Frontal **outward** curve, <u>top-down motion,</u> <u>away</u> from body. Zone 1 to Zones 2 or 3.

FO ⌣ = Frontal **outward** curve, <u>bottom-up motion,</u> <u>away</u> from body. Zone 1 to Zones 2 or 3.

FI ⌒ = Frontal **inward** curve, <u>top-down motion,</u> <u>toward</u> the body. From Zones 2 or 3 to Zone 1.

FI ⌣ = Frontal **inward** curve, <u>bottom-up motion,</u> <u>toward</u> the body. From Zones 2 or 3 to Zone 1.

SO ↻ = Sideways **outward** curve, <u>top-down or bottom-up motion</u>, <u>diagonally away</u> from body. Zone 1 to Zones 2 or 3.

SI ↺ = Sideways **inward** curve <u>top-down or bottom-up motion</u>, <u>diagonally toward</u> the body from Zones 2 or 3 to Zone 1.

LEFT HAND SYMBOLS

AR = At rest

FX = Full extension

OPD = Open palm facing the orchestra, wrist bent, *with fingers pointing to the floor.* OPD is used in all Zones and to indicate *crescendi*.

OPU = Open palm facing the orchestra, wrist straight up, with *fingers pointing to the ceiling*. OPU is used in all Zones and to indicate *diminuendi*.

OPS = Open palm facing the orchestra, UCN, with *fingers pointing to the right side*. OPS is used for *piano* to *pianissimo*.

ARM POSITION SYMBOLS

Fig. 87

FX = Full extension -- arm at full extension in all Zones

L̦ = Open L position -- midpoint between full extension and normal L

L = Normal L position -- elbow bent to L position

V = V position -- forearm close to body

THE CUBE -- <u>COLUMN ONE</u>

The **first vertical column** in the Cube indicates the meter (the number of beats in the measure.) That number may vary from a single beat to twelve or more beats. **Beat numbers start from the bottom of the column and move upward.**

If a meter is to be conducted with **one stroke per measure,** the first beat in the meter has **a diagonal line through the count.** (The bottom half of the box under the diagonal line will be shaded for easy recognition). If a meter has twelve beats but is to be conducted in four, **only the four beats with diagonal lines through them receive baton strokes.**

Figure 88, the 4/4 column one is conducted in four.

Figure 89, the 12/8 column one is conducted in four - diagonal lines through beats 1, 4, 7, and 10.

Figure 90, the 3/4 column one is conducted in one - diagonal line through first beat.

Figure 91, the 5/4 column one is conducted in five.

The examples illustrate charts for 4, 12, 3, and 5 beat meters.

Column One   Fig. 88   Column One   Fig. 89

Column One   Fig. 90   Column One   Fig. 91

THE CUBE: <u>COLUMN TWO</u> -- PITCH REGISTRATION LEVELS

Column Two in the Cube is used to identify the areas in the Immediate Conductor's Space where **Pitch Registration** creates new Patterns.

Pitch Registration deals with single pitches, harmonic blocks, or complete phrases. It works best in slow to moderate tempi and uses four **Vertical Levels** and both hands.

The following diagrams indicate the FOUR PITCH REGISTRATION **LEVELS and their symbols.** The levels outline areas which reflect **general orchestral registers.**

- W = **Waist** area, the *lowest* region of the orchestra. From lowest note to circa middle C.
- MC = **Midchest** area, the *middle* region of the orchestra. From middle C to circa fifth line F in the treble staff.
- UCN = **Under chin** area, a *cross-over* area to the beginning of the upper region of the orchestra. From third line space C in the treble staff to circa first C above the staff.
- E = **Eye** area, any region, but considered first to be the *top* region of the orchestra.

Pitch Registration - Four Levels

Fig. 84

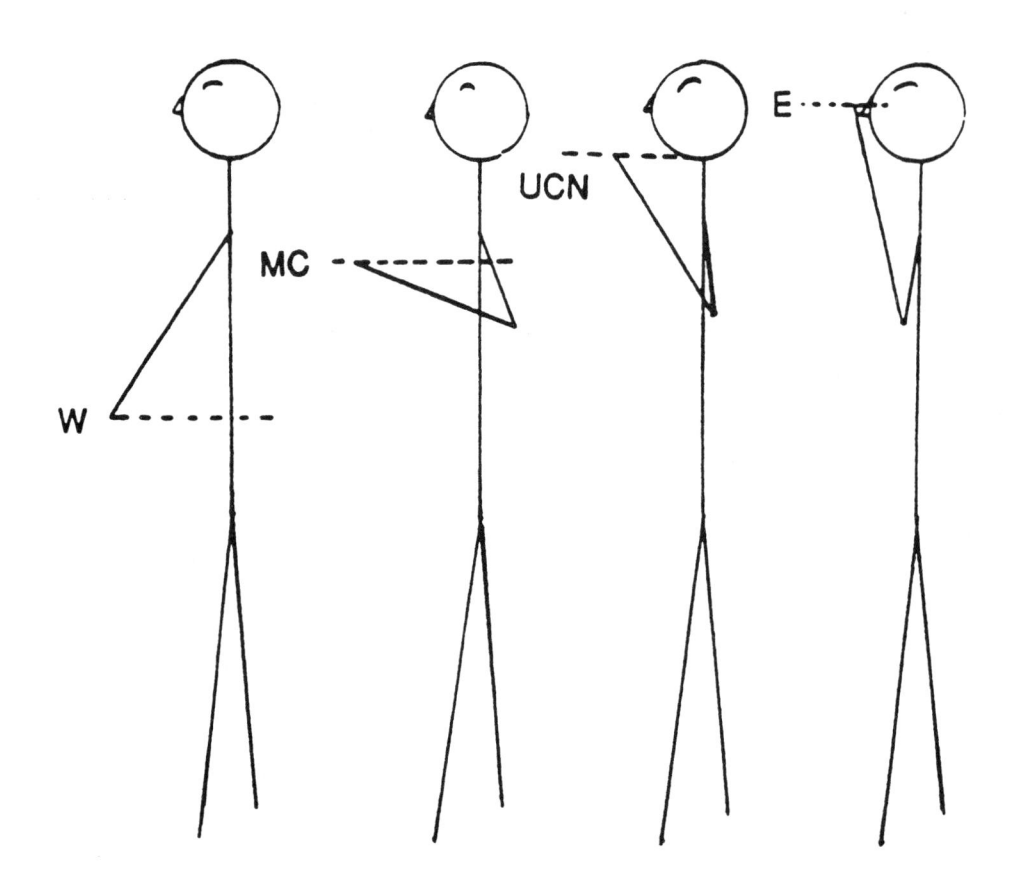

A blank space **above** a pitch registration level symbol means that there is **no change in the level.** For example, in Fig. 92, the nine-beat diagram, conducted in three, beats 2 and 3 remain at the W level. Beats 4, 5, and 6 are all at the C level. The only change in registration is within the third beat, after the UCN level for beat 7, an upward movement to the E Level for beats 8 and 9.

In Fig. 93, the four-beat diagram, the measure begins at the W level, and the second beat remains at the W level. A registration change comes on beat three.

In Fig. 94, the six-beat diagram, beat 2 remains at C level, and beat 5 remains at E level All other beats have registration changes.

In Fig. 95, the three-beat diagram, the third beat remains at the UCN level.

Fig. 92
Column Two

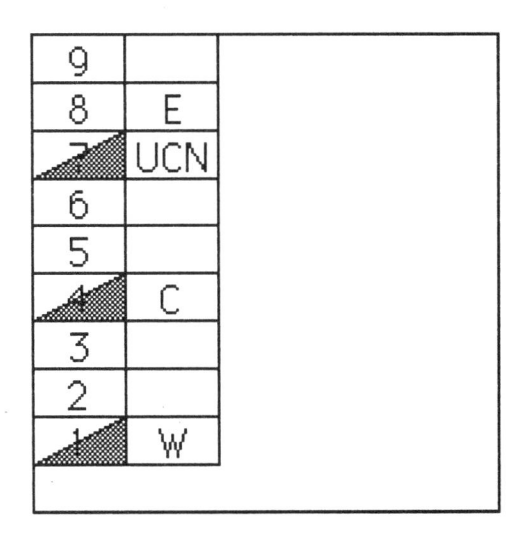

9	
8	E
7	UCN
6	
5	
4	C
3	
2	
1	W

Fig. 93
Column Two

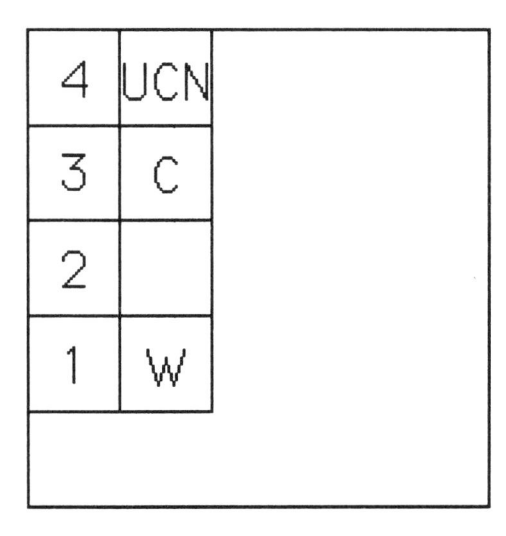

4	UCN
3	C
2	
1	W

Fig. 94
Column Two

6	W
5	
4	E
3	UCN
2	
1	C

Fig. 95
Column Two

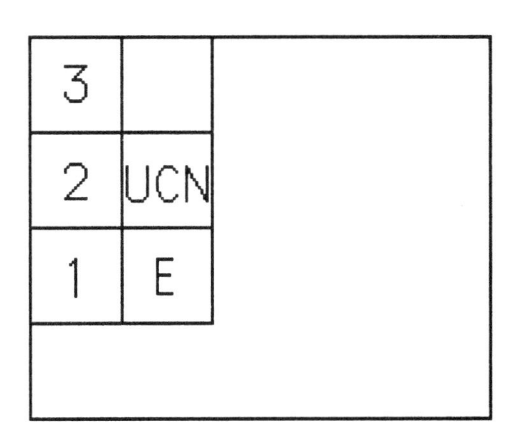

3	
2	UCN
1	E

Make Pitch Registration an everyday work habit. Its importance cannot be overestimated. It forces the conductor to examine and transform every note on the page from a **musical visual** experience to a **technical/spatial** one. **A conductor who believes in and employs Pitch Registration will know the external shape of every bit of ink on the page.**

CHAPTER FOURTEEN SUMMARY

Part Two of the PatternCube is **The Cube**, the information square immediately under **The Pattern**. The Cube consists of **five columns and an information box** containing a prescribed set of symbols for the physical movements that create the patterns. **Two** columns in The Cube, including a set of symbol definitions, have been introduced.

Column One indicates the **number of beats** in the measure (and the number of baton strokes needed to conduct the measure).

Column Two shows the **Pitch Registration levels.**

Pitch Registration deals with single pitches, harmonic blocks, or complete phrases. It uses four **vertical levels** and both hands.

The four Vertical-Pitch Registration Levels are:
- E = Eye level
- UCN = Under the chin
- MC = The midchest area
- W = Waist level

A pitch level symbol is added to a beat count and indicates the area in which the baton registers. A blank space in the column above a pitch registration level symbol (the next pulse in the measure) means that there is no change in that level.

CHAPTER FIFTEEN

THE PATTERNCUBE--PART TWO, CONTINUED
THE CUBE: COLUMN THREE

DYNAMIC REGISTRATION

Dynamic Registration is the conductor's **spatial** representation of the composer's dynamic scheme. Dynamics occur in varying contexts over periods of time and in infinite degrees. A composition may contain twenty *fortes*, all seemingly within the same context, yet each *could be* played differently and judged to be musically correct.

Dynamic Registration is the one device found in most conductors' performances. However, attempts to indicate dynamics with strong body movement instead of with arm/baton motion often disrupts the flow of the music. Guidelines for indicating dynamics, **Dynamic Registration** in the Conductor's Space, are provided for in three dynamic **zones.**

Dynamic Register Zones

The diagrams that follow divide the Conductor's Space into THREE DYNAMIC ZONES. The areas of the zones are **parallel to the body** and are defined by the lengths and positioning of the conductor's arms within the immediate Conductor's Space. Dynamic Registration is made horizontally, and within the three zones it is possible to meet the needs of the most sophisticated dynamic schemes. The zones are shown in column three of the Cube.

General Dynamic Range -- Arm Position

ZONE 1

Zone 1 is best for *piano* to *pianississimo*.

The baton is **close to the body. The forearm is bent at the elbow in the letter V position,** UCN (under the chin). The baton is pointed slightly to the left and tilted toward the ceiling. The hand is close to the face area, the eyes in line with, and looking over the baton. From this zone the conductor can 'paint' the most delicate nuances, with or without a baton. Be careful not to cover the eyes with the baton hand.

In special circumstances zone 1 accommodates dynamics in the *forte* to *fortississimo* range.

Fig. 96

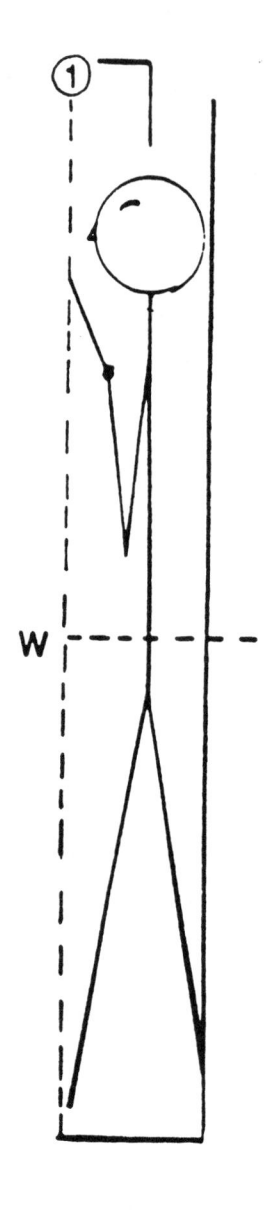

ZONE 2

Zone 2 is best for *mezzopiano* to *forte*.

Midpoint Zone. The elbow is at the side, the **forearm is in the letter L position,** between MC (midchest), and W (waist) levels.

This zone is also effective for *forte* to *fortississimo*, as demonstrated in the repertoire section.

Fig. 97

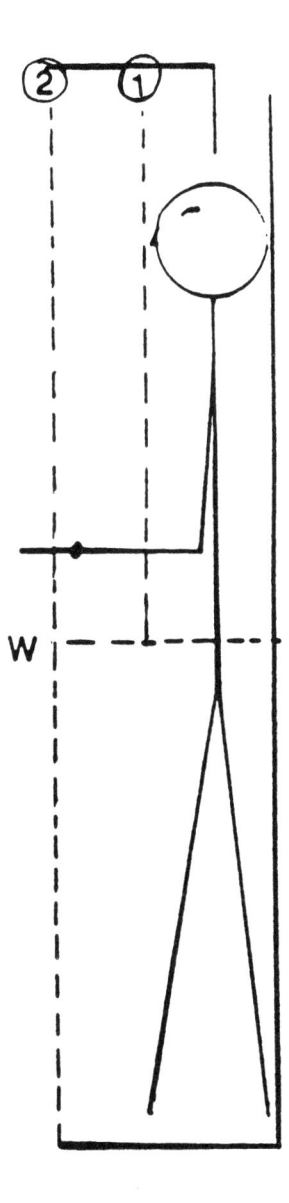

ZONE 3

Zone 3 is best for *forte* to *fortississimo*.

The baton is at the **furthest distance from the body.** The arm is at full extension (FX), and can be used in that position throughout the Conductor's Space. The arm at full extension can move through **all the zones.** Raise the arm upward, straight forward at full extension until it is parallel to the floor. The right arm has just passed through all the zones.

Zone 3 is also useful for the **opposite** dynamic range - *piano* to *pianississimo*. A conductor may choose to **paint with the wrist only** in *pianississimo*, while the arm is at full extension in zone 3. Zones 2 and 3 can contain a wide dynamic spectrum.

Fig. 98

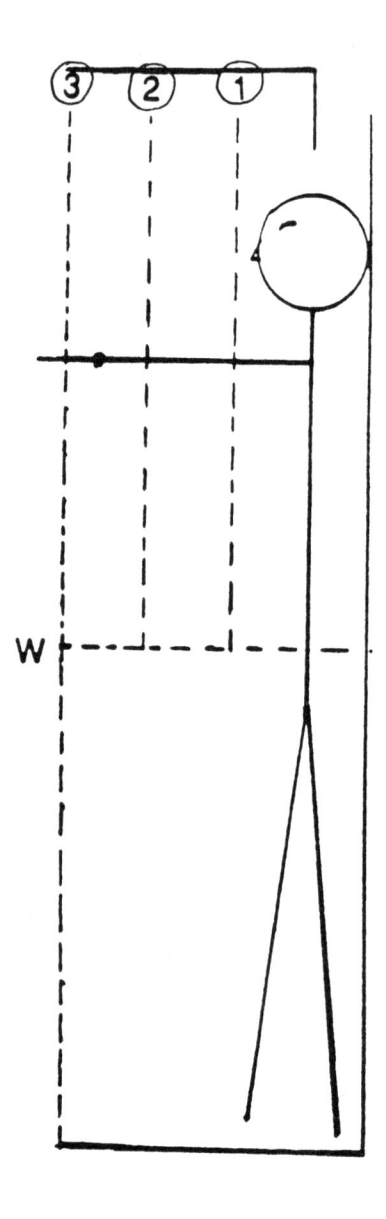

THE CUBE -- COLUMN THREE

The third vertical column indicates the **Dynamic Registration Zones** and includes **symbols for the positions of the arm.**

V = Arm in letter V position
L = Arm in letter L position
⌊ = Arm in open letter L position
FX = Arm at full extension

Fig. 99   Column Three

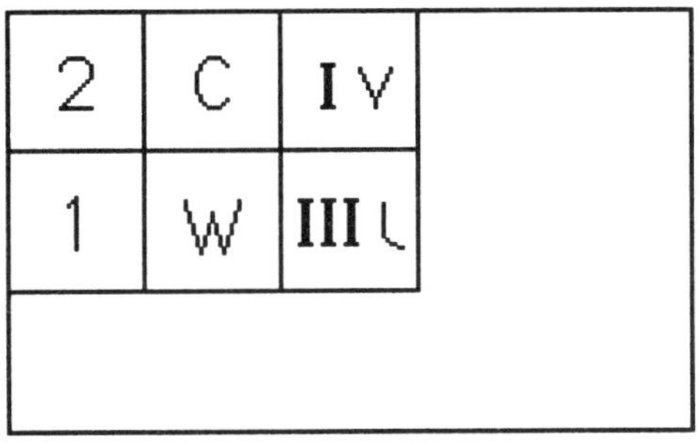

| 2 | C | I V |
| 1 | W | III ⌊ |

Beat 1 is at W level in zone 3, with the arm in the open letter L position, almost fully extended.
Beat 2 is at the C level in zone 1, with the forearm in the letter V position.

Fig. 100   Column Three

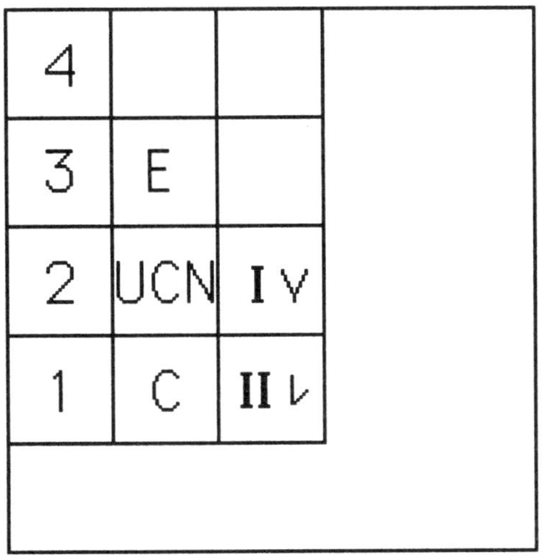

4		
3	E	
2	UCN	I V
1	C	II ⌵

Empty spaces above a registration indicate **a repetition of the position and the dynamic from the space below.** Beats 3 and 4 are a repetition of beat 2, in zone 1, UCN, with the arm

Fig. 101   Column Three

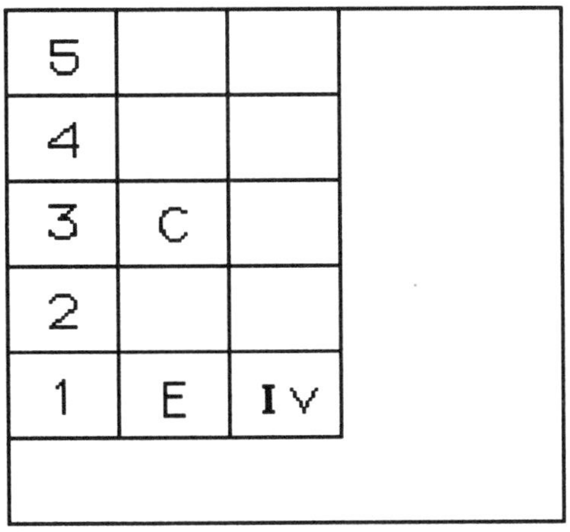

5		
4		
3	C	
2		
1	E	I V

In this example, beats 2, 3, 4, and 5 are the same as beat 1 -- at E level in zone 1, with the arm in the letter V position.

97

Fig. 102   Column Three

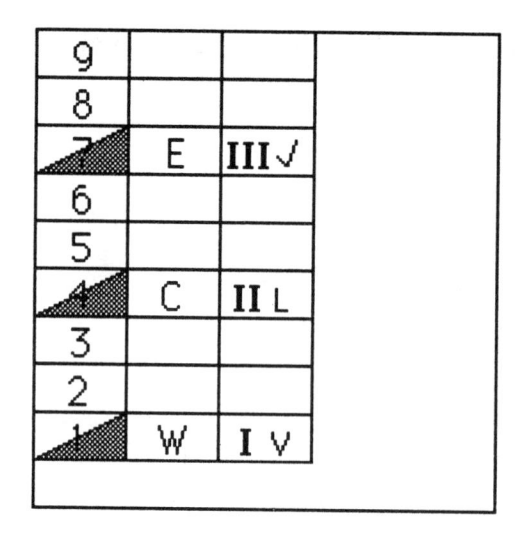

9		
8		
7	E	III √
6		
5		
4	C	II L
3		
2		
1	W	I V

Beat 1. Begin at W level, in zone 1 with the arm in the letter V position. There are no position changes for interior pulses 2 and 3.

Beat 2. Move up to C level into zone 2, and open the arm into the letter L position. There are no position changes for interior pulses 5 and 6.

Beat 3. Move higher to E level and into zone 3. The arm is now in an open letter L position. There are no position changes throughout beat 3.

CHAPTER FIFTEEN SUMMARY

This chapter has been devoted to **Dynamic Registration** which is shown in **Column Three in the Cube.** It contains the **three Dynamic Registration Zones** and the **symbols for the positions of the arms.**

Dynamic Registration addresses dynamics, uses both hands and involves movement in three **horizontal** zones:

Zone 1: The area closest to the body; the elbow in the letter V position at the side of the body, and the forearm UCN. Best for *p to ppp*.

Zone 2: The area midpoint in the Immediate Conductor's Space; the elbow in the letter L position at the side of the body, and the forearm in an area between the MC and W levels. Best for *mf to f*.

Zone 3: The arm is at full arm extension (FX); furthest distance from body. Best for *f to fff*, also *p to ppp*.

CHAPTER SIXTEEN

THE PATTERNCUBE -- PART TWO CONTINUED
COLUMNS FOUR, FIVE AND THE INFORMATION BOX

SPATIAL REGISTRATION

Pitch Registration involves **vertical** levels. **Dynamic** Registration uses **horizontal** zones. **Spatial Registration uses the entire Conductor's Space while directing** the movements of the horizontal and vertical baton strokes **toward specific players or specific sections of the orchestra.**

It is not unusual to witness an entire performance conducted from a single area in the Conductor's Space. Generally the baton is locked in the letter L position, in zone 2 at the MC (midchest) level. It is almost a certainty that the conductor who uses a constant baton position is one who is addicted to nonmusical repetitive time-beating. Much of the performance will be created by the players, not the conductor.

Spatial Registration involves both hands using the furthermost parts of the Conductor's Space, as well as the immediate podium area. Its use is mandatory when a chorus is added to the orchestra or when performers are off-stage or scattered throughout the auditorium. (**Cueing** is an integral part of Spatial Registration and will be covered in Chapter Nineteen.)

EXAMPLES
Covering the Entire Conductor's Space   Fig. 103

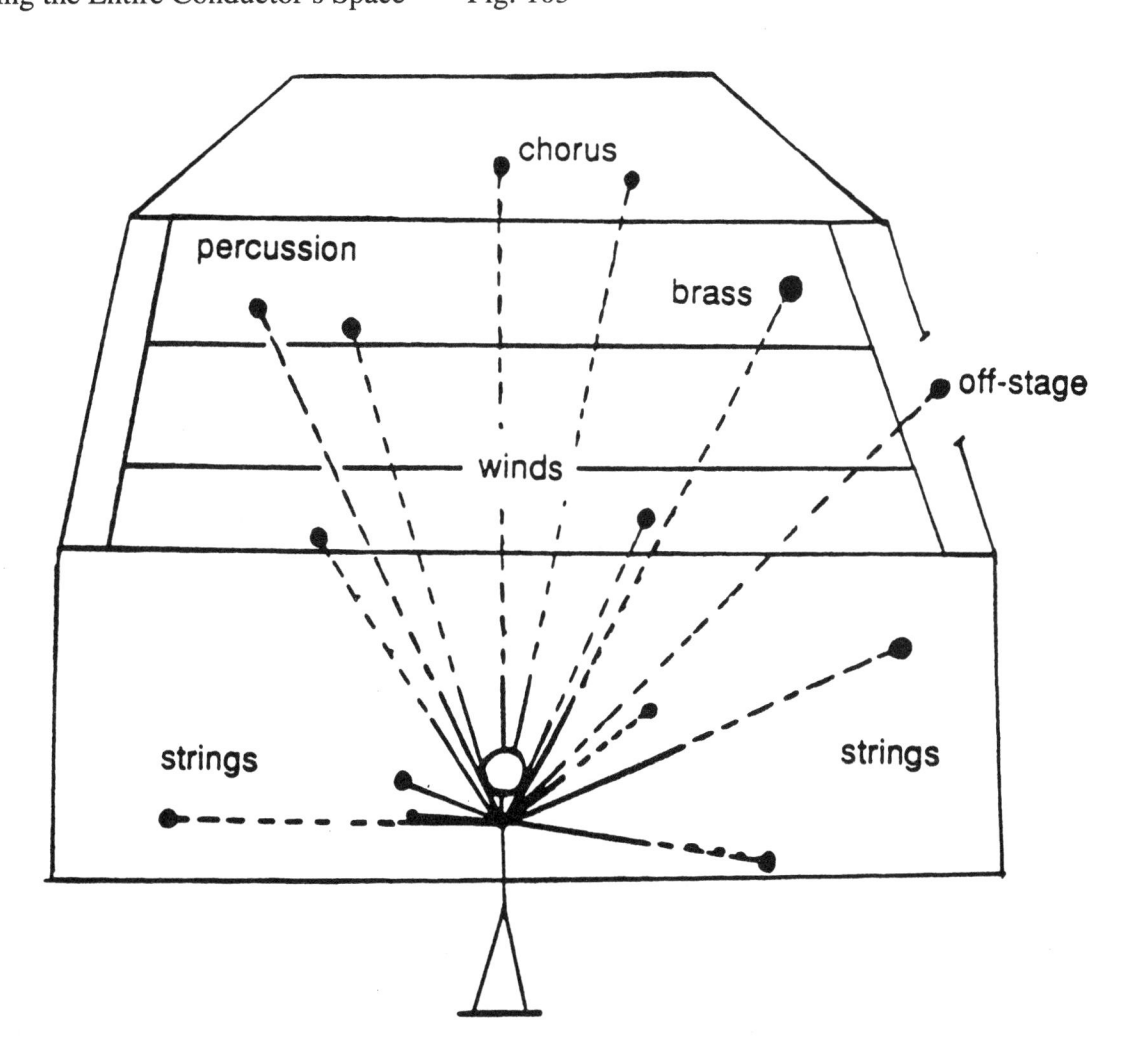

The Cube: COLUMN FOUR: SPATIAL REGISTRATION

Symbols for Column Four: Spatial Registration

Fr = In front of the body

SR = Right side of the body

LS = Left side of the body

Fig. 104   Column Four

6	W	III–	
5			Fr
4	E		
3	UCN	I v	SR
2			
1	C	II L	Fr

Beat 1 is in front of the body, as is beat 2. On beat 3 the baton moves to SR (right side of the body) and remains there for beat 4. On beat 5 the baton moves back to Fr (front of body) where it remains in place for beat 6.

Fig. 105   Column Four

3	C	III–	SR
2		II ∠	Fr
1	E	I v	SL

Beat 1 is SL (left side of the body). Beat 2 moves to Fr (front of body) and the third beat moves to SR (right side of the body).

With carefully *designed movements* of the baton, **Pitch, Dynamic and Spatial Registration** provide the players with pulse, linear shapes and articulations which are **the visible physical form of the musical text.**

Just as the composer carefully constructs an ongoing form, the conductor's Registration should conscientiously map a technical web of pattern designs to capture the composer's form.

Pitch, Dynamic and Spatial Registration, Columns Two, Three and Four in the Cube, are bound by a common tie -- **all flow from the composer's score.** Each is designed to induce conductors to observe music with fresh eyes to challenge them to study and learn the text from an entirely different perspective, to rethink baton technique and to provide the technical means to break the stranglehold of old formulas.

THE CUBE: <u>COLUMN FIVE</u> AND <u>THE INFORMATION BOX</u>

Column Five indicates the movements of the **left hand except** when the left hand assumes the responsibility for maintaining pulse. The switch in duties from right hand to left hand is shown in the space at the bottom of the Cube -- **The Information Box.** Column Five is then used for the **right hand while Columns One through Four will chart the motions of the left hand.** When the baton hand assumes time maintenance duties again, the Information Box notes the change and the activities of the left hand are once again indicated in Column Five. Important or unusual physical movements are also noted in the Information Box.

Fig. 106 Column Five

4				OPS I
3	C	I V	SR	OPU I
2				
1	W	II L	Fr	F X III
Left hand – moves from full extension III, toward body I				

Information Box: Left Hand Instruction

Column Five:

Beat 1: Left Hand FX (full extension), Zone 3.

Beat 2: Same as beat 1.

Beat 3: Left Hand OPU (open palm, facing orchestra, fingers pointing up), Zone 1.

Beat 4: Left Hand OPS (open palm, fingers pointing sideways to the right), Zone 1.

Fig. 107 Column Five

5		I V		
4		II ↙		
3	UCN			
2				
1	E	III –	SL	AR

Left hand – beats pattern
Right hand – at rest

Information Box: Right Hand AR (at rest). Left Hand beats pattern.

Column Five: AR (right hand)

Columns One, Two, Three and Four: Left Hand

Beat 1: E (eye level) zone 3, FX (arm at full extension), (SL) left side

Beat 2: Same as beat 1

Beat 3: Hand moves UCN (under the chin). No other changes.

Beat 4: Hand moves to zone 2 with arm in the closed letter L position. No other changes.

Beat 5: Hand moves into zone 1 with arm in V position. No other changes.

Conductors are encouraged to make their own PatternCubes and use maximum freedom in translating **musical decisions into physical movement.** After a short period of creating PatternCubes, the conductor will automatically 'see' baton strokes when learning a score. The use of VSS/BP (Visual Score Study/Baton Placement), covered in the next chapter, will make the creation of PatternCubes much easier.

CHAPTER SIXTEEN SUMMARY

The third component of registration is **Spatial Registration,** which gives **direction** to Pitch Registration and Dynamic Registration. **Column Four** in the Cube indicates **Spatial Registration,** the areas within the Conductor's Space where baton strokes are formed. Symbols have been provided to define spatial areas -- Fr (front of body), SR (side-right), SL (side-left). Spatial Registration uses both hands.

Every stroke in Part One, **The Pattern,** has been examined and described in Part Two, **The Cube. The result as shown in Columns Two, Three, and Four in the Cube, is a multi-dimensional symbol for every baton stroke.**

Column Five charts the movements of the left hand, unless that hand becomes the primary time indicator. The switch in duties is indicated in the **Information Box,** the space at the bottom of The Cube. The movements of the left hand are then shown in Columns One, Two, Three and Four and the right hand movement in Column Five. **Whenever the hands switch duties it is noted in the Information Box.**

The space at the bottom of The Cube is also used to note important or unusual events that involve physical movement.

Conductors who learn to create and use their own PatternCubes will have a thorough knowledge of the score and a musically informed baton.

CHAPTER SEVENTEEN
VISUAL SCORE STUDY/BATON PLACEMENT

The key to charting zones correctly lies in the **preparation of the space to be used.** The conductor's **eyes must be trained to see the score technically** just as the ears are trained to hear the score melodically and harmonically. **Visual Score Study/Baton Placement** (VSS/BP) is a quick-study visual guide for placing the baton in a space that corresponds to the composer's orchestration. **VSS/BP identifies the working space for registration.**

Ex. 56 Mahler, *Second Symphony,* First Movement

A **visual** reading of the Mahler example indicates a severe dynamic and tempo change for tutti strings at no. 15 (*Schnell*).

The preparation for the new tempo and dynamic character must be made on the fourth beat in the measure before no. 15. The key to the success of the fourth beat preparation is a very slight hold on the third beat, in effect, a preparation for the preparation. A slight hold on beat 3 allows the upbeat to be made in the **new** tempo on beat 4 and in the proper registration at the W level, due to the orchestration, and in zone 3 because of the dynamic character of the *Schnell*.

The composer has prepared a double jolt for the listener -- an unexpected musical surprise. To preserve the integrity of the surprise the conductor must make a powerful, but **discreet,** fourth beat 'click' preparation, clearly seen by the orchestra but **not by the audience.** Make a 'click' directly in *front of the body* at the waist level, in zone 1, as close to the body as possible and travel upward as short a distance as possible. The next two beats break the normal pattern; they are two strong downstrokes. The second stroke makes a short rebound to the left serving as the preparation for the third beat. The third beat is an outward and right across-the-body 'flick' toward the trombones and tam-tam, both arms moving into zone 3. On the fourth beat, the left hand engages the tam-tam (an extension of the musical surprise), while the baton hand fulfills its preparation for the other instruments.

Much of the drama in Mahler's music can be *seen* as well as read on the page, and the use of VSS/BP will reward the conductor with a preplanned and fully organized use of the Conductor's Space.

The analytical technique employed in **Visual Score Study/Baton Technique** is simplicity itself. Every conductor who can see a score page and has a cursory knowledge of orchestration will be able to participate in **VSS/BP.**

The following full score page examples demonstrate how looking at a page of music from a purely technical point of view **Visual Score Study** helps form technical solutions (**Baton Placement).**

Ex. 57 *Romeo and Juliet Overture*, Tchaikovsky

To the tutored eye the opening page of the Overture contains the following technical information:

Generally: There are only four players, clarinets in A (always check the key!). The *piano* sonority suggests small gestures, while mostly dark woodwind registers with no slurs indicate gentle 'clicks' for articulation. **Breathe** with the players, especially for the first entrance. Depending of the conductors choice of tempo, the opening chorale can be conducted with either 2 or 4 beats per measure.

Specifically: The first three *piano* bars are in zone 1 (Dynamic Registration). Begin at W or MC level because of the orchestration, and register throughout since the tempo moves at a moderate pace.

> **Measure 4.** The *crescendo* can be made by the left hand, or by moving the right hand to zone 2 from zone 1. (If the orchestra knows the piece, do not conduct a basic pattern for the first three beats; break the pattern and keep the baton in one place and mark the second and third beats.) Make the cut-off with the left hand on the fourth beat and prepare the entrance in measure 5 by moving the right hand into zone 2.
>
> **Measure 5.** Use small 'clicks' in the larger strokes for *poco piu forte* articulations. Sustain the *poco piu forte* in measure 6 -- there is no *diminuendo*!
>
> **Measure 7.** The silence means a small first beat ('mark' the beat) as hands move back to zone 1. Use a small second beat with a 'click' for the next entrance.

Even though the conductor has yet to pick up a baton, a swift *visual* perusal of the page yields a wealth of *technical* information.

Ex. 58 *Symphony No.93 in D Major,* Joseph Haydn - Third Movement, Menuetto

Before technical decisions are made, several interesting musical questions must be addressed. Is the piece to be beaten in three or in one, or with a combination beat -- in one, but with pulse points 'inside' the large one? The first phrase length is four measures overall, but is the first full measure the **first** part of the four measure phrase, or is it the **second** part of the four measure phrase? The technical solutions posed by the music are formed by the answers to these questions.

The first full measure is the **second** part of the four measure phrase -- the harmonic progression to measure four clarifies the phrase. Measure 4 is the beginning of the second phrase. It contains the pick-up note to measure 5, just as the note that begins the movement is the pick-up note to the second part of the four-measure phrase. However, the tempo is an open question and its resolution a matter of taste. Let us say 'in a moderate one' because Haydn's phrasing seems to emphasize beats 1 and 3.

Generally: Make it a habit to note and memorize the keys of the horns and trumpets. The opening is a strong *forte* statement, a single line scored throughout the orchestra until measure 4, a vigorous sound for that period. Use zone 2, perhaps zone 3 for the opening. Phrasing emphasizes *sf* downbeat slur to a short third beat with a *staccato* dot.

Specifically: The beginning needs a firm upbeat with a clear 'click' on the bottom of the stroke to insure a secure orchestral entrance to the first measure. (If the piece is conducted in three, a clear second beat with a 'flick' would achieve the same result.) Start at MC level and register down to W level in measure 3. The pitch registration moves to E level on the pick-up to measure 5, or on the cue to the horns, trumpets and timpani in measure 3.

> **Measures 1 and 2**: Begin in zone 2 or 3. The baton strokes are outward **legato** circles (first two beats) with a short, stopped, outward wrist 'click' for beat 3. Move beat 3 downward! **Break the pattern.**
>
> **Measure 3**: Make a short first downward stroke at W level, then cue the horns, trumpets and timpani at UCN level and move to E level for measure 5 registration for first violins and flutes.

The music of Haydn allows the conductor a great deal of latitude in shaping a performance, because the score invites inventiveness. If the tempo moved a few notches in either direction, other technical solutions would have to be devised. Or, if a newly discovered manuscript revealed different slurs and dots, the technical approach would have to undergo a radical change.

The opening of the last movement of the Dvorak *Symphony No. 9* is less problematical.
Ex. 59

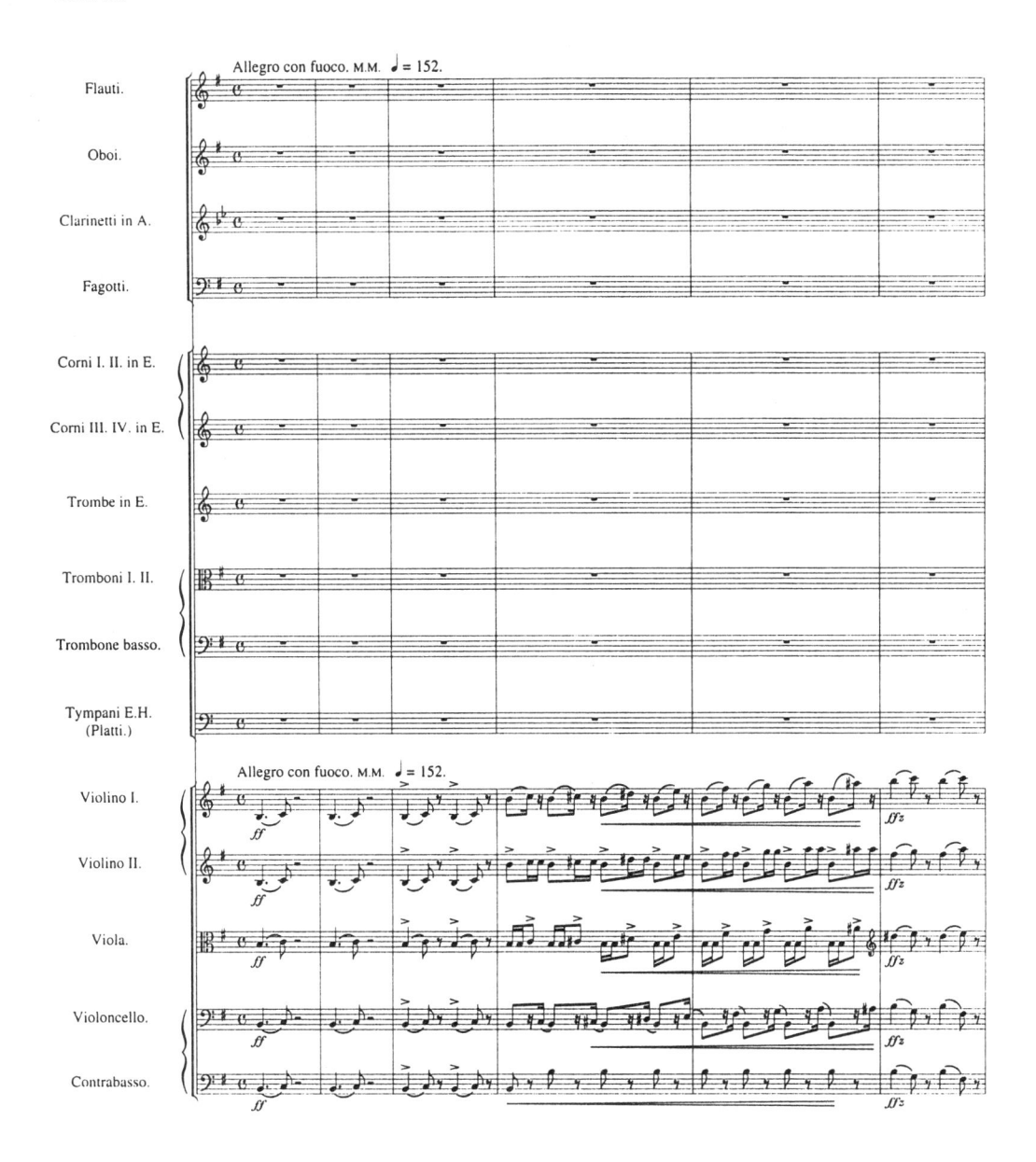

Generally: The beginning of this movement is conducted in four. Unlike the Haydn, there is a metronome marking -- quarter equals 152. Moving the arm four times per measure at 152 is a lot of baton movement. I suggest conducting the opening with two strokes in each measure for musical as well as physical reasons. (A switch to four strokes to the measure may be made at any of several places in the movement, but the momentum of the opening will benefit from a basic two pulses per measure.) The string opening has few problems once a decision on the beat pattern is made. Note the keys for horns and trumpets.

Specifically: Begin with a strong *fortissimo* upbeat at W level. Make a clear second beat with a 'click' as the preparation for a strong downbeat.

> **Measures 1 and 2:** Start in zone 1 and make a firm stroke across and away from the body. Then, 'click' a sharp second beat with the rebound toward the body.
>
> **Measure 3:** Make two similar long-short, down/up strokes and break the pattern! Note the accents; they are the first accents in this movement.
>
> **Measures 4 and 5:** Remain in two! Register upward (there is a three octave span within six measures), and make the *crescendo* by moving into zone 3. Note the accents and energy in the second violins and the differing viola accents.

Measure 6: The previous upward registration will take you to E level. Make two similar long-short, outward-inward wrist strokes at E level. Once again, break the pattern!

CHAPTER SEVENTEEN SUMMARY

<u>**Visual Score Study/Baton Placement**</u> (VSS/BP) identifies the working space for registration. It is the visual key to charting the zones correctly. **The eyes of the conductor must be trained to see a page as technical baton movement,** just as the ears are trained to hear melodic and harmonic progressions. **Learn to 'see' a page of music as baton movement.**

VSS/BP should be used as a quick-study guide for placing the baton in a space that corresponds to the composer's **orchestration.**

General VSS/BP rules:

- When the score indicates a *piano*, infer zone 1.
- When *fortississimo*, read zone 3.
- If the orchestration is in the bass clef, move to W level.
- If high winds are scored above the treble staff, think E level.

Make it a habit to carry a pocket score with you at all times. Visual Score Study/ Baton Placement (VSS/BP) can be practiced in spare moments in a variety of settings.

CHAPTER EIGHTEEN
THE LEFT HAND/ARM

Since the baton is the primary focus of orchestral attention and is usually held in the right hand, tradition has relegated the left hand to a secondary role. As a consequence, the left hand/arm is the least used musical weapon in the conductor's technical arsenal. More often than not the left arm duplicates the movements of the baton (mirroring) or hangs limply at the side of the body. In either scenario its existence is meaningless. Sometimes the left hand addresses a string section and vibrates quickly, the conductor's signal imploring the players to expend more emotional energy on behalf of the music. The vibrating motion looks suspiciously like the left hand version of the Shaker Stroke. The use of valuable left hand *crescendi* and *diminuendi* indications are often transmitted to the orchestra in an unclear manner. Even as the left hand maintains its traditional role, it confirms its lowly status.

The Palm

The palm of the left hand is used sparingly and is often overlooked. That is a mistake -- the palm is the perfect complement to the baton hand. Subtly or overtly it can influence dynamics, cut-offs and the shaping of phrases.

In previous chapters, I have alluded to the use of various positions of the palm facing the orchestra: OPD (open palm, wrist bent, *fingers down),* OPU (open palm, wrist straight, *fingers up*-stop sign), and OPS (open palm, *fingers pointing sideways).* When positioned correctly, the left-hand palm is a compact indicator of a wide range of specific dynamics.

Left Hand Dynamics

Basic Left Arm *forte* Indication

The palm is open and fully exposed to the orchestra; the wrist is bent in the direction of the floor, *fingers pointing to the floor.* In this OPD position, the arm is partially or fully extended at W level.

It is important that the extended fingers are close together, with no spaces between them. The sound should be collected in the hand rather than filtered through the spaces between the fingers.

Fig. 108   Fig. 109

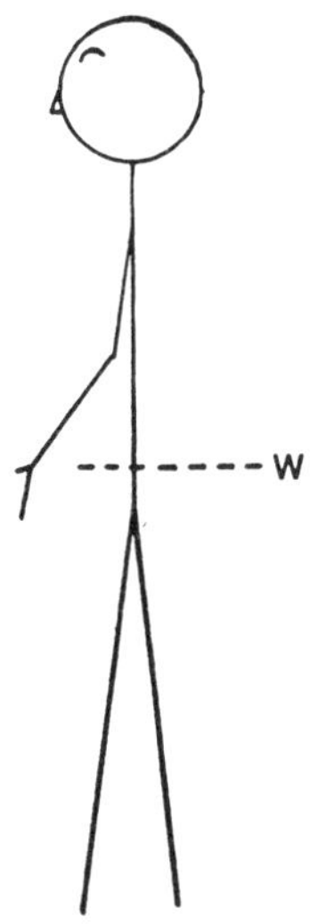

Partial Extension   Full Extension

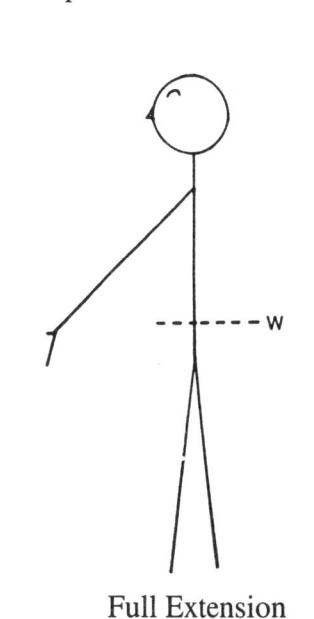

Left Hand *crescendo* Indication

The difference in the amount of sound requested by the conductor is the difference in the **position** of the arm. Keep all the elements of the *forte* position, except -- **raise the arm upward** from W level to MC level. This slight upward gesture will produce a **greater** volume of sound.

Left Hand *diminuendo* Indication

Making a *diminuendo* from a *forte* or *fortissimo* to a lesser dynamic level involves two physical moves. Assume the basic *forte* left arm position.

1. Make a complete right turnover of the left hand. As a result of the turnover the open palm will be *facing the floor.*

Fig. 110　　　　　　　　　　　　left hand　　　　　　Fig. 111
(1)　　　　　　　　　　　　　turn palm over　　　　　palm now facing floor
thumb

2. After completing the first move bring the arm toward the body, from zone 3 to zone 2 or into zone 1. The amount of *diminuendo* will determine the zone and the final hand position.

2A. Movement to zone 2. After the turnover, move the forearm straight up toward the body into zone 2. The forearm is now almost parallel to the body. **The palm is facing the orchestra,** *fingers pointing to the ceiling.* **This is the OPU position,** the classic police-officer-stop-sign. Remember to keep the fingers together.

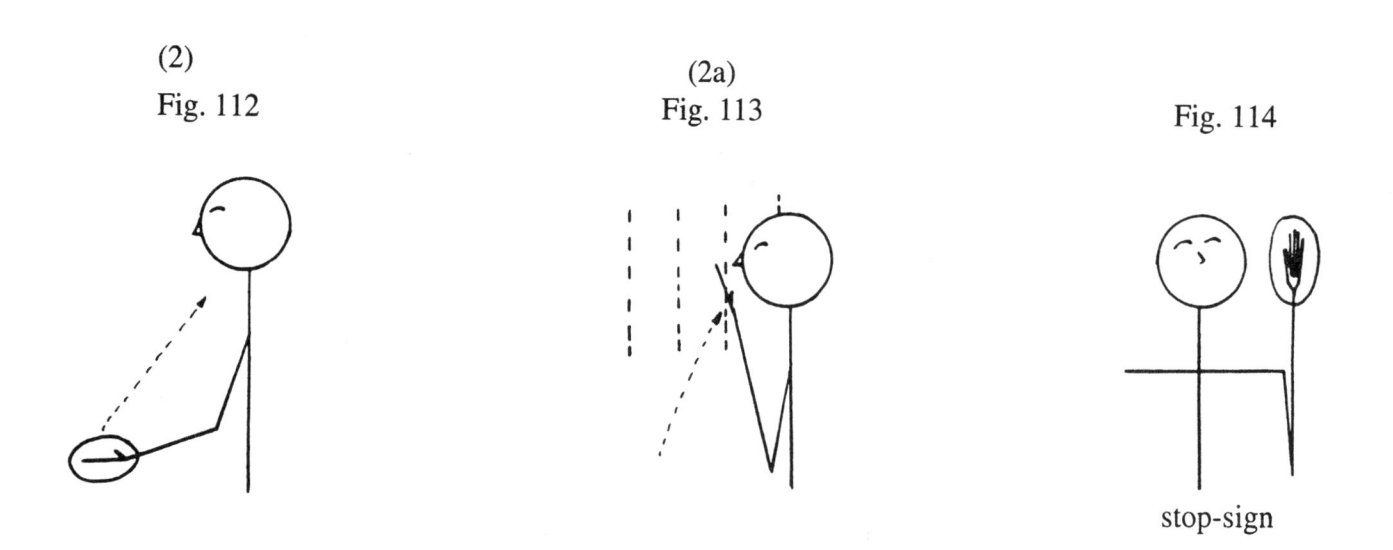

(2)　　　　　　　　　　　　(2a)
Fig. 112　　　　　　　　　　Fig. 113　　　　　　　　　　Fig. 114

stop-sign

2B. Movement to zone 1. With the open palm facing the orchestra, lower the forearm into zone 1, down to the right toward the face and right shoulder. The downward motion to the right will raise the elbow and move the forearm parallel to the floor.

The exposed palm is now under the eyes, in the middle or lower half of the face. ***The fingers of the open palm point to the right.*** **This is the OPS position**. This movement is excellent for *piano* to *pianissimo* and is especially useful for a *subito piano* indication.

Fig. 115 (2b)   Fig. 116

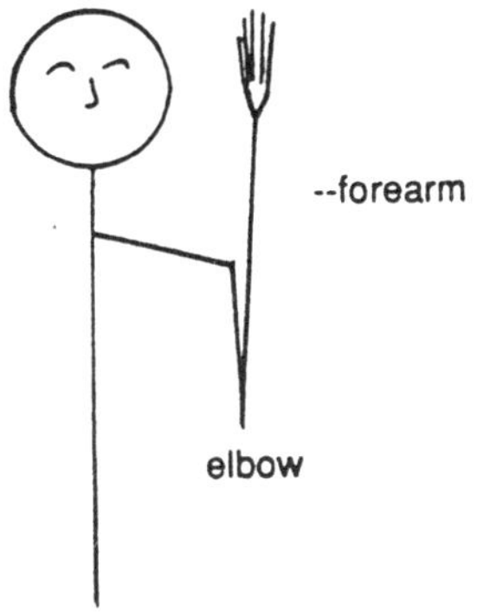

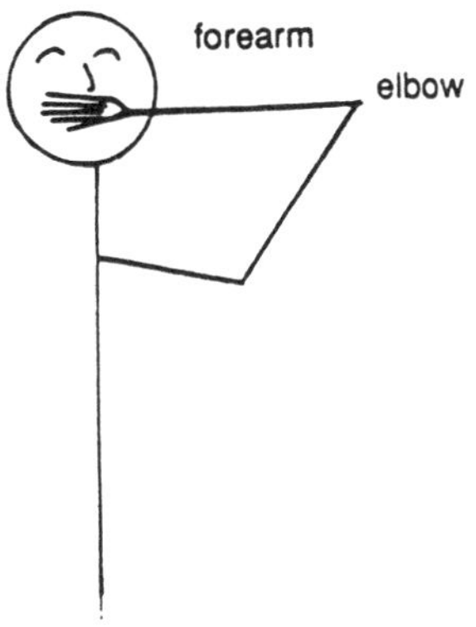

General Opportunities for the Use of the Left Hand/Arm

1. **When musical interest is focused on the string sections sitting on the left side of the stage,** the left hand can be used as the primary indicator of time. The first or second violins could be playing by themselves, playing different lines, or simply playing in unison. (In all cases the Information Box in the PatternCube would indicate the left hand as the primary indicator of pulse, and column five would show the right hand AR.)

The First Movement of the Sibelius *Second Symphony,* seventeen measures before letter B, is an example of a unison passage for the first and second violins. All other instruments are *tacit.* The use of the left hand, a fresh technical event, coincides with the composer's introduction of new material. The melody can be registered SL, from E to W level, and from zone 2 or 3 to zone 1 (twelve measures before letter B), and back to zone 2 or 3 two measures later. The right hand resumes time indication at the W level for violas and celli seven measures before letter B. (In the PatternCube, the Information Box would indicate that the right hand has resumed time keeping, and column five would revert to indicating left hand movement.)

If the percussion section is located to the left of center or on the left side of the stage, the left hand can supply effective and meaningful musical gestures.

The antique cymbal part in *The Afternoon of a Fawn* by Debussy is just such an instance. Three measures before the end of the work, the right hand continues to beat quiet pulses in zone 1, at MC level.

The left hand is at E level, FX in zone 3, and gives a small preparatory wrist cue to the antique cymbal player on the fourth pulse, four measures from the end. The percussionist plays the antique cymbal E natural downbeat, and the left hand maintains its position at E level. After the downbeat in the next measure, the left hand will move above E level on the second beat cue for the third beat B natural in the antique cymbal part. In that same measure the right hand, at W level, cues the celli and bassi for their fourth beat *pizzicato* entrance. In the final measure the right hand, still at the W level, accounts for the first beat *pizzicato as* the left hand concludes the work by cutting off the antique cymbal and the flutes. The difference in the range occupied by the right and left hands reflects the composer's orchestration, and in the quiet hush of the conclusion, unnecessary movement is eliminated by assigning the left hand to the antique cymbal player.

2. **When contrasting blocks of sound or different instrumental sections follow each other,** assigning the left hand to one of the groups of instruments can be musically meaningful.

In the "Finale" of the Tchaikovsky *Fourth Symphony,* measure nos. 26-29, the right hand (SR) assumes the responsibility for the woodwind entrances and the left hand (Fr or SL) for the string entrances. Alternating the hands makes it possible to register every section entrance in its own space. The right hand can begin **below** MC level in zone 2, and the first entrance of the left hand should begin **above** MC level also in zone 2. The registered movements of each hand get progressively higher as the pitch rises. Try to make E level coincide with the top of the phrase as both hands move into zone 3 in measure 28. In measure 29 the hands stay in zone 3 but register down from measure 28 to E level to account for the lower pitch levels.

The compositional scheme in the "Third Movement Trio" of the Beethoven *First Symphony,* a vastly different sound structure, also lends itself to the division of labor approach. The right hand covers the winds, making short wrist strokes in zone 3, Fr, below E level. The left hand is responsible for the strings, SL, and in contrast to the woodwind articulations, makes curved *legato* strokes in zone 1, working just above the W level. Keeping the hands in different levels and zones is deliberate and guarantees the clarity of the space each hand inhabits. The right hand left hand technical scheme mirrors the content of the composer's score until sixteen measures before the repeat sign. The conductor is free to change the technical scheme at the conclusion of any of the phrase endings in the ongoing structure.

3. **When solo or section woodwind lines are highlighted in the score,** using the left hand is usually a viable option. In the second movement of the Dvořák's *Ninth Symphony* the English horn solo beginning in measure 7 is excellent left hand material. Begin at the MC level, Fr, use zone 1 or zone 3, and make small gestures from the wrist or forearm. Register as much or as little as is necessary, based on the information in the following paragraph. The four measures written for the first and second French horns four measures before no. 2 is another example. Begin in zone 1, MC and Fr, and then move out to zone 2, UCN level in the second measure. Move back to zone 1 in the fourth measure finishing just under the E level. The seven measure flute and oboe lines beginning at no. 2 are musically rich for left hand movement. Since two performers are involved, the conductor ought to register the line throughout, beginning in zone 1, using zone 2 or 3 in the third measure, and moving into zone 3 for the *forte* conclusion. The range of an octave and a fourth is registered between the MC and the E levels. In each of the three examples cited, the accompaniments are uncomplicated and with the possible exception of the eighth measure after no. 2, no extra right hand attention is needed.

When the conductor works with woodwinds performing solo lines, the left hand may be reduced to minuscule motions, if used at all. Before making demands of the player, the conductor must **first listen** to what the player has to offer musically. If the conductor agrees with the player's interpretation, left hand motions should be discreet. After rehearsals the conductor may decide that the solo line needs no extra shaping and may forego the use of the left hand entirely. If the conductor feels the solo line requires attention, the left hand becomes an active participant in helping the player realize the conductor's intentions.

4. **When there is a quick dynamic alteration,** the left hand can be very useful. The last movement of Beethoven's *Eighth Symphony,* which carries a metronome marking of whole note equals 84, contains perfect examples of rapid and unexpected dynamic shifts that surprise the audience as well as interrupt the flow of the music. Within measure nos. 279-281, the dynamic level moves from *pianissimo* to *forte* with lightning speed. The baton hand is generally used throughout the indicated measures and negates the musical surprise because the downbeat is made with a *forte* gesture that telegraphs the event. If the conductor applies VSS/BP, a technical solution is available in which the left hand, as well as the baton hand, maintains the tempo and preserves the surprise.

The *pianissimo* in the first half of the measure is assigned to the left hand, E level, Fr, in zone 1. The *forte* in the second half of the measure, is conducted by the right hand with a short, quick wrist stroke, W level, Fr, in zone 1. Where exactly should the left hand take over the time keeping duties? The clear choices are measure no. 269 or 273. The right hand resumes the role of primary time keeper at measure no. 282.

5. **When a fresh color is added to a static or sustained orchestration**, it is usually a signal to use the left hand. In measure no. 28 of the Tchaikovsky *Romeo and Juliet Fantasy Overture,* the entrance of the harp is a natural left hand indication. Small circular upward wrist pulses begin below MC, Fr, zone 3, and conclude at E level in zone 3. The right hand, above the W level, does not pulsate, but moves from zone 2 to zone 1 for the *diminuendo* and 'holds' the F minor sonority.

6. **When an overtly dramatic moment is highlighted in the music**, the left hand is the likely candidate to articulate its arrival. The Third Movement of the Prokofieff *Fifth Symphony* six measures after no. 77 is just such a moment. The fifth measure is scored for low-pitched instruments including the tam-tam over a moving repeated bass figure. It is the musical preparation for the sixth measure downbeat which is meant to jolt the listener. It is scored for high trumpets and trombones, cymbals, and high-pitched shrill flutes and piccolo. It is a perfect place for the left hand to shoot straight up into the air at FX, high above the head. Keep the hand aloft for two full beats and quickly move to the left to the string tremolo. It is a dramatic gesture to fit the scoring and drama of the music.

7. **When a composer writes staggered entrances for various sections of the orchestra,** especially if the tempo is moving rapidly, the left hand can be very helpful.

STRING SEATING

Let us digress for a moment. Composers writing in the eighteenth and nineteenth centuries used the seating of strings in their orchestras to great advantage. They regularly moved the string sound from area to area in various sonic combinations: from the outside right side to the outside left side and back; the inside right side to the inside left side and back; the entire right side of the stage to the entire left side of the stage, etc.

The first and second violins faced each other, seated on opposite halves of the stage, separated by a standing conductor with a baton. (The separation would be less apparent if the 'conductor' were the concertmaster leading the ensemble from his chair with his violin bow, or if the 'conductor' were a harpsichordist seated amidst the ensemble and keeping the musicians together while playing his instrument.) The violas and celli were also placed opposite each other but inside of, and behind, the violins. The basses were usually placed behind the celli.

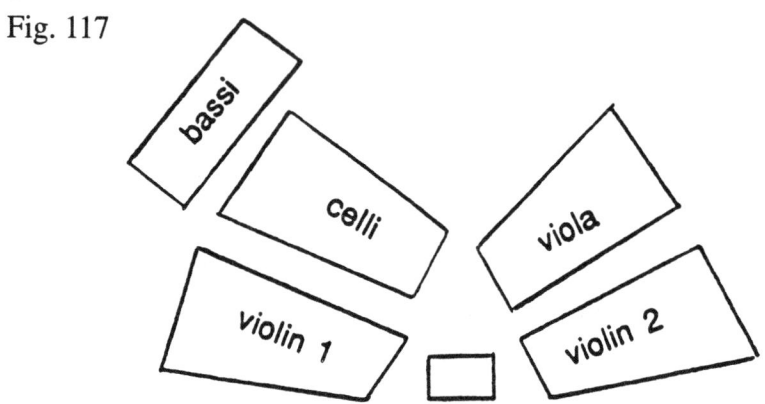

Fig. 117

The seating of the violas and celli was not as well defined as the seating of the first and second violins. Either section could be on either side of the stage.

The first movement of the Beethoven *Fifth Symphony* is a case study of quick moving units of sound emanating from various sections of the orchestra. The symphony will be discussed in detail in the Repertoire section, so let us concentrate on Beethoven's musical use of the *placement* of the string sections and assume the string seating to be the one outlined in the diagram. **The right hand** is assigned to the string instruments on the right side of the stage, the **second violins and the violas;** and the **left hand** to the string instruments on the left side of the stage, the **first violins, the celli and basses.** When the string passages are isolated in the first half of the movement it is clear that Beethoven was fully aware of the sources of his string sounds. Not only is there energy in the fast moving units of sound he created, but there is **additional** energy when the string sounds emerge in bursts from constantly shifting areas of the stage. In the measures below, the left hand directly addresses the left side of the stage, freeing the right hand for its side of the stage.

    Measures 6-7:   Violin 2, viola, right side = <u>right hand</u>
    Measures 8-9:   Violin 1, left side = <u>left hand</u>
    Measures 10-11:   Violin 2, viola, right side = <u>right hand</u>
    Measure 12-14:   Violin 1, left side = <u>left hand</u>
    Measure 15:   Violin 2, viola, right side = <u>right hand</u>
    Measure 16:   Violin 1, left side = <u>left hand</u>
    Measure 17-18:   Violin 2, viola, tutti, right side = <u>right hand</u>

Measure 25:   Violin 1, left side = <u>left hand</u>
Measure 26:   Violin 2, right side = <u>right hand</u>
Measure 27:   Viola, right side = <u>right hand</u>
Measure 28:   Celli, basses, left side = <u>left hand</u>
Measures 29-32: Repeat of measures 25-28

The above are examples of the string sound **moving from one side of the stage to the other side of the stage.**

Measure nos. 94 to 105 are examples of the string sound from the instruments which sit on either side of the conductor in **the very front of the orchestra** -- the first and second violins. Usually they play in unison or at the octave.

Measures 94-105: Violins 1 and 2 = **right hand**.

Note: In measure nos. 101-102 the **left hand** should be the primary time indicator. The right hand assumes time indication duties in measure no. 103.

In the development section Beethoven moves the string sound from the front of the orchestra the **outside string players** to the violas, celli and basses (the **inside string players**).

Measure 129:   Violin 2, <u>out</u>side right side = <u>right hand</u>
Measure 131:   Violin 1, <u>out</u>side left side = <u>left hand</u>
Measure 132:   Violas, celli, <u>in</u>side, both sides = <u>right hand</u>
Measure 133:   Violin 2, <u>out</u>side right side = <u>right hand</u>
Measure 135:   Violin 1, <u>out</u>side left side = <u>left hand</u>
Measure 136:   Violas, celli, <u>in</u>side, both sides = <u>right hand</u>
Measure 145:   Violas, celli, <u>in</u>side, both sides = <u>right hand</u>
Measure 146:   Violins 1 and 2, <u>out</u>side, both sides = <u>left hand</u>
Measure 147:   Violas, celli, <u>in</u>side, both sides = <u>right hand</u>
Measure 148:   Violins 1 and 2, <u>out</u>side, both sides = <u>left hand</u>
Measure 149:   Violas, celli, <u>in</u>side, both sides= <u>right hand</u>

Beethoven and other composers offer conductors many opportunities for left hand use. The left hand can participate as the primary time indicator, share time indication duties, or assist the right hand in clarifying dynamic content and phrase structures.

CHAPTER EIGHTEEN SUMMARY

This chapter explores the use of the left hand/arm. The traditional use of the left hand has placed it in a subordinate role, making it the least used weapon in the conductor's technical arsenal. Its role should be expanded.

The open left hand palm, OPU, OPD, and OPS can be used to shape a wide range of dynamics. Diagrams and symbols have been provided. The left hand shapes and influences sound and phrase structure and plays an essential role in the cut-off motion, explained in Chapter Nineteen. Whenever possible, the left hand should be used as an alternate to the right hand as the basic indicator of tempo. Some opportunities are:

1. When musical interest is focused on the left hand side of the stage.
2. When contrasting blocks of sound or different instrumental sections follow one another.
3. When solo or section woodwinds are highlighted.
4. When there are quick dynamic alterations.
5. When a fresh color is added to a static or sustained orchestration.
6. When an overtly dramatic moment occurs in the music.
7. When staggered entrances are written for various sections of the orchestra.

Works are discussed in each of the categories, and examples, including registration, have been provided.

CHAPTER NINETEEN

CUEING

A conductor's cue serves as a signal, a preparation for an upcoming musical event. It is a clear, physically precise motion in the direction of a player, players, or an entire section that indicates that performers are to play **momentarily.** The cue is most often a movement of the baton, but it can also be a movement of the left hand/arm. When a trusted player, or group of players, is about to perform, the cue may be no more than an arched eyebrow or a nod of the head.

The Cue, Two Separate Parts: Visual Preparation and Physical Execution

Part One - Visual Preparation

The conductor's visual contact with the performer creates expectation. **If possible, the conductor should make eye contact with the performer(s) a measure or two before the cue is given.** An experienced player is reassured when the conductor makes eye contact, and the inexperienced player needs the encouragement to prepare the entrance.

If the performers are seated in front of the conductor, eye contact can be achieved without moving the body. If the performers are seated to the right or left of the conductor, eye contact should be made by moving the head slightly in their direction. Do not move the body. (Consult the chapter on Body Technique.)

Part Two - Physical Motion: The Cue

The conductor's physical motion, the cue, initiates sounds and fulfills the expectation of the performer. **The cue must be made one full beat before an entrance, or if the performer plays after a rest (but within the beat), the cue may be given on the rest. A cue should never be made ON the entrance,** for the motion comes too late to influence the sound and character of the music. A well-delivered cue **prepares** and instructs the performer **how** to play: short, long, fast, slow, *forte* or *piano*. Wind and brass players need time to gather breath for the indicated attack. String players need time to lift and place their bows. Percussionists need time to raise their sticks to the appropriate height for proper articulation. *If the cue is made on the players entrance, the conductor has given the **player** the right to shape the performance.*

How to Make a Cue

A cue is a **stroke** and is subject to all the demands of the score. Direct a cue to a specific area in the Conductor's Space (Spatial Registration), adhere to the score's dynamic structure (Dynamic Registration), and to its pitch contours (Pitch Registration) whenever possible.

Spatial Registration

Either hand may be used to make a cue, but cues **must be made in the direction of the performer and registered spatially.**

If a cue is meant for the trumpet section, direct the arm toward the trumpets and deliver the cue with the wrist, forearm or from the shoulder. If a cue is meant for the snare drum, cue the snare drummer and not the timpanist or the bass drummer. **If spatial registration is not used, a well-conceived cue will fail.**

Generally, string section cues are directed toward the first stands. That is the rule unless the composer has written specific and differing music for stands beyond the first desk. In that case, the conductor should decide whether a special cue is necessary. On occasion players in the back of the section are cued **if they are not as responsive as the rest of the section.** If **all** the strings play an entrance together, make the cue in the direction of the first stand of the first violins.

Dynamic Registration

Once a player or section has been addressed, observe the dynamic character of the music. Cues may be made by both hands from all dynamic zones.

Zone 3: A *pianissimo* cue from zone 3 can be made by the wrist with a small, sharp 'click' directed toward a player or section. A *fortissimo* cue from zone 3 can be indicated by a large forearm stroke. Wrist 'clicks' in the preparation and conclusion of all cues help the pulse points in all zones.

Zone 2: The dynamics in this zone are best served with moderate forearm strokes.

Zone 1: The entire range of the *piano* dynamic can be delivered by wrist movement.

Pitch Registration

Unless the pitch is in the E level area, **pitch registration ought not be a primary consideration when delivering a cue.**

Keep all cues clearly visible, at MC level or above. It is possible to register pitch below the MC level for celli, basses and other instruments whose natural range lies in the bass clef, but the conductor's first consideration should be a clean signal, clearly seen.

The Performer

As the cue is delivered, the conductor should not turn away from the player or section until the sound has been safely produced. After the entrance, the conductor should try to maintain contact with the line or sonority as long as it is musically reasonable to do so before turning to other musical matters.

The Body

As noted earlier in the section on spatial registration the hands and eyes may give cues, but **the body is not to be used as a cueing instrument.** Maintain the clarity of the cue.

In the cueing exercises that follow, the imaginary orchestra conforms to the standard twentieth century seating arrangement: The first and second violins on the left side and center of the stage, the violas, celli, and basses seated in the center and on the right side of the stage. The first center row of winds left to right contains piccolo, flutes, oboes and English horn. The second center row of winds, left to right contains bass clarinet, clarinets, bassoons and contra-bassoon. A long third row of instruments stretching across the stage from left to right contains 4 horns, 3 trumpets, 3 trombones and tuba. The percussion section includes players in the back left hand corner of the stage behind the third row, and the timpanist in the back and center of the stage. A harp would be in the back right hand corner of the stage.

Fig. 118
Orchestral Seating Arrangement

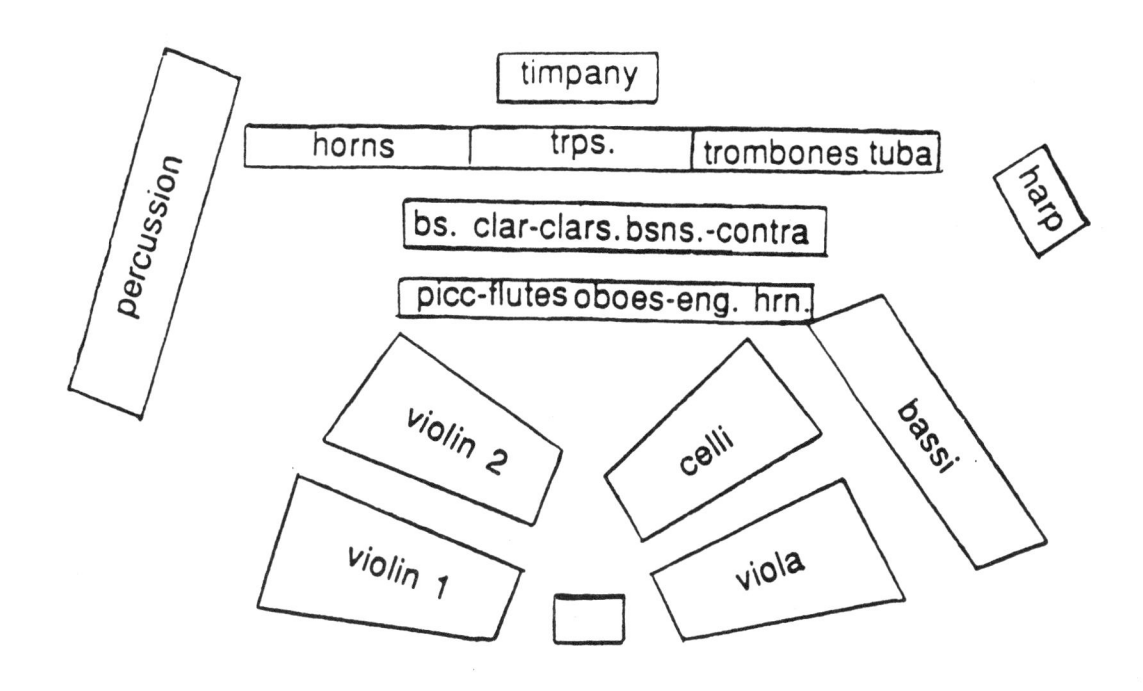

Cueing Exercises

Each of the exercises is based on the following five measures. Each exercise has its own set of instructions. Do all exercises with the **left hand** and then repeat the exercise with the **right hand.** Note the exercises where both hands are indicated.

Cue Points. The eight **encircled crosses** under the staff indicate the actual beats in the measure **where cues are to be made.**

Instrument **Entrances.** The eight **encircled arrows** over the staff indicate the **entrance points** of the cued instruments.

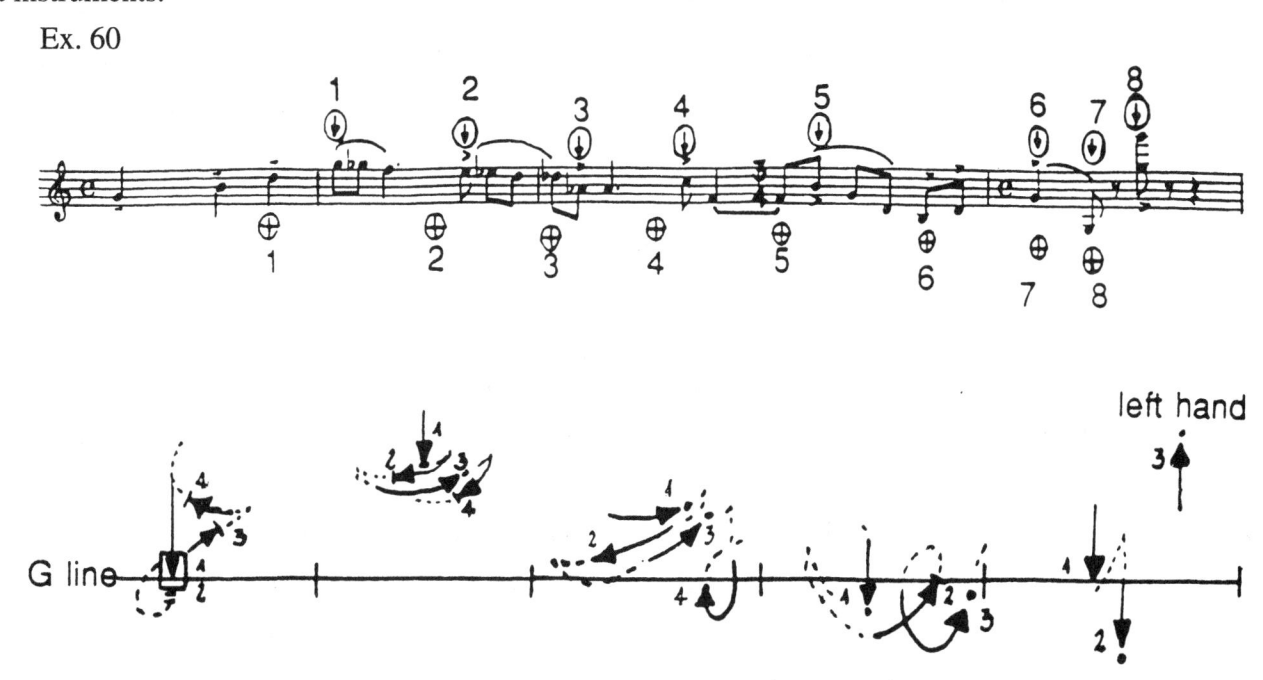

Ex. 60

119

This PatternCube is one technical solution for the five measures but there are many other solutions. Create your own PatternCubes as you move through the exercises.

Exercise 1: quarter equals 120

Trumpet 1	Horns	Strings	Winds
	cue 3	cue 5	cue 8

This exercise contains three cues. It begins with the first trumpet, *forte* throughout. Place the arm in zone 3, FX, Fr. Move from the trumpet to the horns (cue 3), then to the tutti strings (cue 5) and finally to the tutti winds (cue 8). A look at the closely seated group of first chair players in the middle of the woodwind section serves as a cue to the entire woodwind section when they play together.

Look at the horns on beat 4 in measure 2 at the first stand of the first violins on beat 4 in measure 3 and at the winds on the first or second beat of measure 5. The **movement** of the left arm is to the left of center for the horn cue, to the left side for the string cue, and to the right center for the woodwind cue. The right arm, the baton hand, maintains tempo.

Exercise 2: quarter equals 68

Flute 1	Oboe 1	Clarinet 1	Vln. 1
	cue 3	cue 5	cue 8

Exercise 2 contains three cues. The cue points remain the same, although the instruments change. The dynamic character is *mezzo forte* throughout. Use zone 2 and begin the exercise with the arm in front of the body (Fr). Register the strokes.

Visual contact before the cues are made remain the same as in exercise one, but directed toward different instruments. **Look** at the first oboe on beat 4 in measure 2, at the first clarinet on beat 4 in measure 3 and at the first stand of the first violins on beat 1 or 2 in measure 5. The three woodwind players sit next to and behind one another, and the woodwind cues can be made with small adjustments in a compact space in the Fr position. The third cue is a move to SL to address the first violin section.

Exercise 3: quarter equals 72

Violin 1	Vln. 2	Violas	Celli-Basses	Tutti Stgs.
	cue 2	cue 4	cue 5	cue 7

Exercise 3 contains four cues, each for a different section of the string orchestra. The beginning is *piano*, with the arm in a letter 'V' position in zone 1. The second violin entrance is *mezzo piano*, and the arm moves forward in zone 1. The viola entrance is *mezzo forte*, and the arm moves into zone 2. The celli/bass entrance is *forte*; the arm should move into the open letter 'L' position in zone 3. The *tutti* string entrance is *fortissimo*, the arm in the FX position in zone 3. **Look** at the first desk of the second violins on beat 3 in measure 2 and at the first stand of the violas on beat 3 of measure 3. **Look** at the first stand of the celli on beat 1 in measure 4. Notice the **difference** in the visual preparation of this cue (cue 5 under the music) as opposed to the visual preparation of the same cue point in the first two exercises. In this exercise the preparation comes **later** because the previous cue to the violas needs at least one full beat of visual contact with the section after the cue is made and before the next cue is given. **Look** at the first stand of the first violins on beat 1 in measure 5 before the final cue.

Exercise 4: quarter equals 138. All strings *pizzicato*.

Violin 1	Vln 2	Harp	Harp	Tutti Stgs.
cue 2	cue 4	cue 5		cue 7

The visual contact and cue points in this and the previous exercise are the same, but they have to be made almost twice as fast since the quarter now equals 138.

This exercise is *pianissimo* throughout. Stay in zone 3 and use small wrist strokes for the *pizzicati*. The left wrist begins the piece and makes the first cue to the second violins. The right hand gives the next two harp cues, and the left hand gives the final cue, this time to the first stand of the second violins. When the exercise is repeated the right hand begins, the left hand makes the two harp cues, and the right hand makes the final cue to the first stand of the basses. On the repeat, the hands will be forced to move across the body--left hand to the right side, and right hand to the left side into technical spaces better served by the other hand. Therefore, when the right hand begins the exercise, **suspend all registration** and remain at E level.

Exercise 5: quarter equals 86

Vibraphone	Chimes	Eng. Hrn.	Winds
cue 2		cue 5	cue 6

This exercise contains three cues and is *mezzo forte* throughout. Conduct in zone 2 and register throughout this exercise. Before beginning, know the exact placement of the vibraphone and the chimes! **Make the cues directly to the performers** rather than in the general direction of the percussion section on the left side of the stage.

Look at the performers or section at least one full beat before their entrances. Continue to create new PatternCubes.

Exercise 6: quarter equals 54

Xylophone	Picc	Tpt3	Trb Timp Picc
cue 1	cue 4		cues 6 7 8

This exercise contains five cues starting *fortissimo*, making a gradual *diminuendo* and concluding at *piano*. Begin the exercise in zone 3 at FX, and make the last cue from zone 1 with the arm in the letter 'V' position. Even though the quarter equals 54, do not subdivide.

Make visual contact with the **third** trumpet before the cue is delivered. The tempo is slow enough to make the visual preparation for the fourth cue to the timpanist **on the 'and' of beat 1 in measure 5** as well as the preparation for the final cue to the piccolo player **on the 'and' of beat 2 in measure 5.**

Exercise 7: quarter equals 32.

Subdivide each quarter (the eighth note equals 64), and transpose all pitches down one octave. The entire orchestra plays on the final note, but the cue is directed toward the cymbal player.

Basses-Tymp	celli	trombones	tuba	tymp	cymb
cue 1	cue 2	cue 4		cue 6	cue 8

This exercise contains five cues, starts *pianissimo*, makes a gradual *crescendo* and finishes *fortissimo*. Begin the exercise in zone 1 and conclude the exercise at FX in zone 3. Maintain registration throughout the exercise. **Because of the subdivision, the second full beat should occupy a space of its own, so move the stroke to the left after the first full beat in the pattern.**

There is plenty of time for visual contact with the players or sections in this slow tempo. **Experiment and alter the moment of visual contact from the pulse point of the beat to the 'and,' or middle of the beat.**

Remember to repeat all exercises, first with the left hand then with the right hand. Alter the shape of the patterns often, and change the tempi of the exercises after the technical problems in each have been solved.

When used, the left hand can encompass all areas of the Conductor's Space, and the left hand/arm is capable of forming a variety of strokes. Several exercises that add mobility to both hands were included in chapters six and seven. The following exercises for the **left hand only** should now be added to the conductor's practice schedule.

Left Hand

Exercise 1: A **straight line diagonal stroke** upward and outward, and a return stroke to the starting position. Begin at W level on the right side, in zone 1, elbow close to the body in an open letter 'L' position. Lock the wrist. Move the forearm upward, away from and across the body in a straight line diagonal stroke. Continue to move to the left until the arm is fully extended (FX) at the far left side of the body, in zone 3 at E level. Do not move the arm behind the back. After completing the stroke follow the path back to the original position. Repeat the stroke several times at various metronome markings in continuous uninterrupted movements. This left hand gesture is a dramatic energizer of volume, especially if the left hand palm is open and the fingers outstretched.

Exercise 2 : A **curved line outward, across-the-body stroke** and a return to the starting position. Begin with the left hand resting on the right shoulder. The forearm under the chin (UCN), and the elbow in a letter 'V' configuration in zone 1. Keep the arm parallel to the floor and move in an outward curved stroke, away from and toward the left side of the body, to FX, in zone 3. The position at the end of the stroke is the same as in Exercise 1, but at the UCN Level.

Repeat the stroke and use the instructions for Exercise 1. This is an excellent stroke for left hand cues to any area of the Conductor's Space.

CHAPTER NINETEEN SUMMARY

A left or right hand cue is a clear, precise motion in the direction of a player, players, or a section of instruments that alerts performers to play **momentarily.** A cue consists of two parts: the visual preparation and the cue itself, a physical motion.

Visual Preparation: The conductor should make **eye contact** with the performers a measure or two before the cue is given, a signal that they are expected to perform.

The Cue itself is a physical motion **in the direction of** the players and must be made **one full beat before the performer's entrance. If the performer plays after a rest, the cue may be given on the rest.**

A cue should never be made **on** a player's entrance. The moment for player preparation has passed and the cue has lost its musical validity. The conductor has failed to instruct the player on **how** to perform, letting the player assume the responsibility for the production and content of the sound.

Do not use the body as a cueing instrument. Make all cues with the hands/arms. On occasion, direct eye contact or a slight nod of the head are all that are needed to insure a player's entrance.

A cue delivered by the hand fulfills a specific technical role, but still functions as a stroke and is subject to all the demands of the score. The cue should be registered spatially, dynamically, and if possible, pitch-wise. Cueing exercises, including an orchestral seating plan, have been provided.

Chapters six and seven outlined several stroke exercises to be practiced by both hands. This chapter adds two new exercises for the left hand only. The first is designed to expand dynamic possibilities, the second to enlarge the cueing range.

CHAPTER TWENTY

THE FERMATA or HOLD, WITH CUT-OFF MOTION

All baton strokes are linked to the flow of the music and are bound by ongoing movement. *Fermati* are the composer's calculated effects to prolong a note or a rest, most often at the end of a phrase. Compositionally this is usually a cessation of rhythmic movement while sustaining or eliminating sound.

Two Parts of the Hold

The hold (*fermata*) may be thought of as a single musical gesture consisting of two parts:

1. **The Hold** is a relatively simple physical gesture. The **right hand** stops beating wherever a hold is indicated. It may be on the downbeat, in midmeasure, at the end of the measure, or at any rhythmic point within the measure. The dynamic level of the hold is determined by the zone in which the baton is held. Resist the temptation to shake the baton during a hold for reasons previously noted.

2. The **Cut-off** is a single left hand gesture if the music stops completely, or a two-handed technique if the music continues. The **cut-off motion,** the actual cessation of the sound, is the responsibility of **the left hand. Make it a habit to execute all cut-offs with the left hand.**

The preparatory motion for **the resumption of tempo** belongs to the **right hand. That right hand movement begins only when the left hand starts its cut-off motion.** The preparation may be in the old, or in an entirely new tempo.

Important General Cut-Off Rule

If a work continues after a hold, the right hand should **not** make the cut-off, because the right hand will require an extra motion, a preparation, to regenerate tempo. **The extra motion adds one full beat of silence within the measure.** But if the **left hand** makes the cut-off, the right hand preparation (to regenerate the tempo) can be made **simultaneously** with the left hand cut-off motion, **eliminating the silent beat within the measure.**

How To Make A Cut-Off

The Left Hand - Basic Movements

After the right hand has established the hold, the left hand cut-off movements are:

- made in **exactly one beat in the upcoming tempo,** and
- made in **one continuous motion,** and
- made from a stationary left side **starting** point A (OPD). Move to the right in a slightly curved upward motion to point B (begin to close OPD into a fist), return (left) to the original starting point A in a slightly curved downward motion (the hand is now in a closed fist position). Remember the move from starting point A, to point B, and back to point A, must be made in **one beat and in one continuous motion.**

Fig. 119

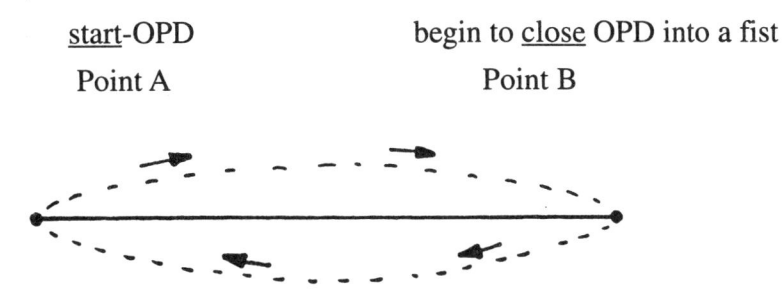

start-OPD   begin to <u>close</u> OPD into a fist
Point A   Point B

finish-hand is in a closed-fist position

The cut-off is made by the wrist and the palm in a combined movement. If it is initiated from the **forearm,** the wrist is locked until the cut-off is made. If the cut-off is initiated from the **wrist,** the forearm does not move.

Fig. 120

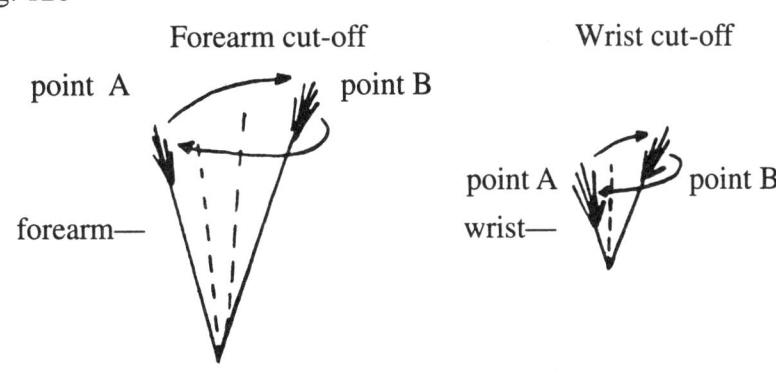

Forearm cut-off   Wrist cut-off

point A   point B   point A   point B

forearm—   wrist—

The Left FOREARM Movement In Cut-Offs: *Mezzo forte* **to** *Fortississimo*

The **left forearm** is most effective in cut-offs when the dynamic level is *mezzo-forte* and beyond. The left elbow may be in a letter 'L' position in zone 2, W level. The palm is open, facing the orchestra with <u>fingers pointing to the floor</u>, OPD.

From left side starting point A, move the forearm to the right, either in a straight or an upward curved line to point B. **Point B is not a fixed place.** It is the point where the hand stops moving to the right and begins the left return to point A. That point will always be affected by the tempo. (The location of point B moves further to the right as the tempo becomes slower.)

When point B is reached, the motion to the left to return to position A begins; the hand turns over; the **palm** faces the orchestra with the <u>fingers momentarily</u> pointing to the ceiling, OPU. The left movement is a straight across-the-body stroke and resembles a blackboard-erasing motion. During the return to the left motion the fingers begin to close into a fist.

When the hand reaches the original point A, the **hand is closed** into a fist. Within the leftward flow of the stroke, **'flick' the wrist strongly** to the left. This strong 'flick' movement stops the orchestral sound and moves the forearm well to the left of, and away from the body. This is an essential part of the cut-off, because **it clears the space in front of the body and allows the right hand ample room to complete its own preparatory procedure.**

The left hand movement between A-B-A can be considered the **preparation** for the cut-off. <u>The left hand closed fist wrist 'flick'</u> **is** <u>the cut-off</u>.

The Left WRIST/FOREARM Movement In Cut-Offs; *Pianississimo* to *Mezzo Piano*

The **left wrist** cut-off is most effective in *pianississimo* to *mezzo-piano* dynamic levels. Less space is used in this cut-off. The starting position, A, places the left hand under the eyes, the elbow raised in a "V" position parallel to the floor in zone 1, close to the body. The palm is open facing the orchestra, with the fingers pointing to the right, OPS. From this point, move the wrist downward **toward** the body in an inward circular motion to point B.

Point B is **below** the face and **closer** to the body.

From point B, which is below the original starting point A, move the forearm in a **diagonal line** across the body to the left to point C, and begin to close the fingers into a fist. (The starting angle is different, but movement to the left is the same motion employed in the *mezzo-forte, fortississimo* forearm cut-off to get back to point A.)

When point C is reached, close the open palm (hand) into a fist, and within the left flow of the stroke, 'flick' the wrist strongly to the left. This strong 'flick' movement stops the orchestral sound. Even in this dynamic range the 'flick' movement moves the forearm to the left. At the conclusion of its cut-off the left hand is on the outside part of the left side of the body.

The left hand movement between A, B, and C can be considered the **preparation** for the cut-off. The left hand closed fist wrist 'flick' **is** the cut-off.

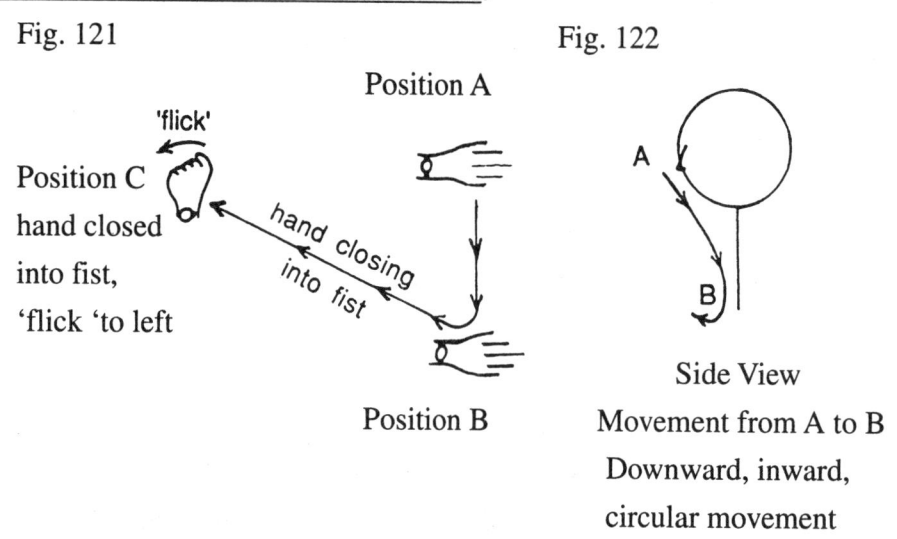

Fig. 121

Position C
hand closed
into fist,
'flick' to left

'flick'

hand closing into fist

Position A

Position B

Fig. 122

Side View
Movement from A to B
Downward, inward,
circular movement

The Right Hand - Basic Movements

The function of the right hand during holds is simple when compared to the work of the left hand. It has a two-part responsibility:
- to sustain the sound during the hold, and
- to prepare the next orchestral entrance **during** the cut-off if the piece continues. If there is any difficulty for the right hand, it is coordinating its movement with the cut-off of the left hand.

The right hand begins to move **only** when the left hand starts its preparation for the cut-off. That movement is a straight up-stroke, or a sideways up-stroke. The direction of the stroke depends on where the hold is placed within the measure.

A **half 'click'** is made near the top of the right hand stroke **at the precise moment the left hand makes its cut-off wrist 'flick.'**

The right hand is now in perfect position to deliver a clear downbeat that indicates the upcoming tempo. **When the hands are in sync the separate parts of the cut-off become a single, fluid, automatic movement.**

Fermati: Concluding Hold and Cut-off: Basic Movements

This is the simplest of holds, for the cut-off does not function as a preparation for a renewal of tempo.

1. **The right hand** stops beating to make the hold.
2. **The left hand** helps support the dynamic level, especially if *forte* to *fortissississimo*.
3. **The left hand** makes the cut-off in the appropriate zone.
4. **Both hands.** While the left hand executes the cut-off, the right hand returns to a neutral, elbow-at-the-side (in an L shape), midbody position.

Many conductors add a right hand cut-off to the left hand cut-off on the **final** hold, especially if the sonority is *forte* or *fortissimo*. A left hand cut-off is all that is necessary, but a two fisted vigorous cut-off in the spirit of the music often works well. If both hands are used they **must** be totally coordinated, or the result will be a work with two endings!

Fermati on Different Beats Within the Measure

Generating a tempo after a hold within a measure involves an important technical principle. During left hand cut-offs the right hand stroke **should repeat the held beat because the beat is the preparation** for the next beat in the measure. For example, if the hold is on beat 1, the preparation for beat 2 should be a **new beat 1 in** the old or a new tempo. If the hold is on beat 2, the preparation for beat 3 should be a **new beat 2** in the old or new tempo. And so on. The repetition of the held beat maintains the flow of the music and preserves the structural integrity of the measure.

Fermati with Four Beats in a Measure

Fermata on **beat 1**. As the left hand begins the cut-off, the wrist of the right hand moves in a small circular motion **underneath** (to the right or left) **the first-beat-hold baton position. The wrist 'clicks' 1 again** as the forearm moves **upward** through the first-beat-hold position in a **straight, diagonal line.**

Beat 1 has just been repeated. Move to beat 2 -- from the top of the stroke move down and to the left. Midway through the downward stroke, 'flick' strongly to the left. The strong left 'flick' will create the rebound that will fulfill beat 2 in the pattern.

Fig. 123

Fermata on **beat 2**. As the left hand begins the cut-off, the right forearm moves in a small circular motion to the right, **underneath the second-beat-hold baton position.** The right hand then moves **upward** and to the far left, strongly 'clicking' two again as it moves through the second-beat-hold position.

Beat 2 has just been repeated. Move to beat 3 -- from the far left position, move directly across the body in a straight line stroke, to beat 3.

Fig. 124

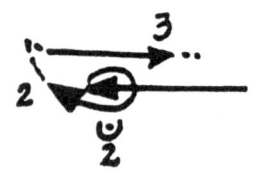

Fermata on **beat 3**. As the left hand begins the cut-off, the right hand moves in a small circular motion to the right, **underneath the third-beat-hold baton position.** The right forearm then moves **upward to the right diagonally,** strongly 'clicking' three again as it passes through the third-beat-hold position.

Beat 3 has just been repeated. Move to beat 4: The upward stroke will lead to the fourth beat.

Fig. 125

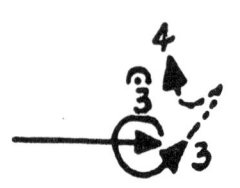

Fermata on **beat 4**. As the left hand begins the cut-off, the right hand moves in a small circular motion, **underneath** (to the right or left) **the fourth-beat-hold baton position.** The right hand then moves **straight upward,** strongly clicking four again as it passes through the fourth-beat-hold position.

Beat 4 has just been repeated. Move to beat 1 -- from the top of the stroke come straight down to the first beat in the next bar.

Fig. 126

Fermati with three beats in a measure

Fermata on **beat 1**. Move the right hand in a circular motion to the left underneath beat 1, then across the body to the right. (Note that the first beat in the 3/4 measure will be in front of the body, instead of to the left of the body.)

Fig. 127

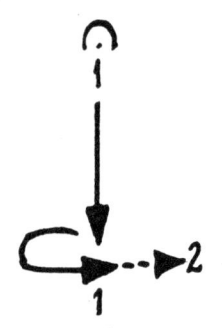

Fermata on **beat 2.** Move the right hand to the right and underneath the second beat, then upward to the left.

Fig. 128

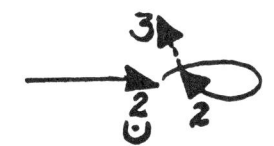

Fermata on **beat 3.** Move the right hand slightly to the right underneath the third beat, and then to the left and straight up.

Fig. 129

Fermati with two beats in a measure

Fermata on **beat 1.** Duplicate a **first beat hold in a 4 beat measure.** But the move to the second beat will be straight up rather than to the left.

Fig. 130

Fermata on **beat 2.** Duplicate a **fourth beat hold in a 4 beat measure.**

Fig. 131

Fermati with six beats in a measure

Fermata on **beat 1.** Duplicate a **first beat hold in a 4-beat measure.** The movement is generally a shorter, downward-slanted stroke.

Fig. 132

Fermata on **beat 2**. The right hand **moves to the right and back across to the left with a wrist 'flick'** which fulfills the third beat.

Fig. 133

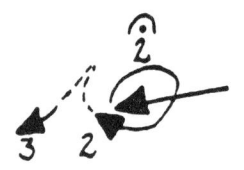

Fermata on **beat 3**. Duplicate a **second beat hold in a four beat measure.**

Fig. 134

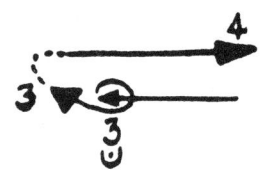

Fermata on **beat 4**. The right hand moves to the left with a wrist 'flick' and **back directly across to the right** for beat 5.

Fig. 135

Fermata on **beat 5**. Duplicate a **third-beat hold in a four-beat measure.**

Fig. 136

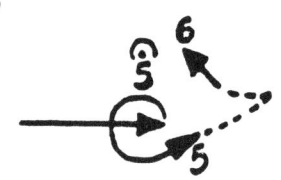

Fermata on **beat 6**. Duplicate a **fourth beat hold in a four-beat measure.**

Fig. 137

Measures with **7 or more beats** adhere to the same movement-between-beats principle. All structural beats within a measure must be approached from the **opposite** direction. All inner beats within a measure move in the **same** direction.

Fermati with *diminuendi* - Basic Movements

Fortississimo to *Pianississimo*: The role of the left hand in *diminuendi* was covered in chapter seventeen. The following is for both hands.

1. **The right hand** in zone 3 at *fortississimo* (or *fortissimo* or *forte*) stops beating and makes the hold.

2. **The left hand** is fully extended at the W level in zone 3, and the palm is open to the orchestra, fingers pointing to the floor (OPD). As the left hand begins the *diminuendo* moving **upward and inward** through zone 2 **toward the body** into zone 1, it will change to an elbow-up position, with the fingers positioned under the eyes and pointing to the right side (OPS). (The speed of the preparation for the cut-off is determined by the previous tempo.)

3. At the same time the left hand begins its movement, the right hand begins its *diminuendo*. It moves the forearm straight back **toward the** body through zone 3 into zone 1. (The speed of this movement is determined by the previous tempo.)

4. The left hand, now in position under the eyes in zone 1, makes a small wrist *pianississimo* cut-off. The right hand, now in zone 1, elbow tucked at the side, remains motionless during the cut-off.

Pianississimo to *Fortississimo* --Basic Movements

The role of the left hand in *crescendi* was covered in chapter seventeen. The description that follows is for both hands.

The **starting** position for this cut-off is the **final position** described in number 4, above. (The final position in this description is the starting position for the *fortississimo* to *pianississimo* hold described above.)

1. **The right hand** stops beating and makes the hold in zone 1, at *pianississimo* (or *pianissimo* or *piano*).

2. **The left hand** is in zone 1. The open palm is under the eyes, fingers pointing to the side (OPS). The palm turns over as the left hand begins the *crescendo* by moving **downward and away from the body** through zone 2, to a fully extended W level position in zone 3. The palm is open, facing the orchestra, with the fingers pointing to the floor (OPD). (The speed of this movement is determined by the previous tempo.)

3. At the same time the left hand begins its movement, the right hand remains in zone 1 and allows the left hand to make the *crescendo*, or it can begin an assisting gesture by moving straight out, away from the body through zone 2 into zone 3. (The speed of this movement is determined by the previous tempo.)

4. The left hand, now in zone 3, makes the *fortississimo* cut-off. The right hand, now in zone 3, remains motionless during the cut-off. (The conductor may add a right hand cut-off to the left hand cut-off, as previously described.)

There is another way to induce an orchestral *crescendo* during a hold. Once the *forte* or *fortissimo* is established, the decibel level of the sonority can be increased by holding the right arm at full extension and raising the baton ever so slightly, but only for a short period of time.

String players enjoy drawing extra bows, and percussionists delight in their *fortississimo* rolls. Wind players will survive by drawing discreet breaths, but brass players may feel challenged. Before taking a breath, first-rate brass players turn green, then red in the face if the cut-off is not made at the appropriate moment.

This particular *crescendo*-inducing device ought to be used carefully.

The Final Upward Gesture Cut-Off

A concert was held which contained three works with a combined total of thirteen movements. The odds of every movement in an eighteenth century work (four movements), an early twentieth century work (four movements), and a newly written work (five movements) concluding in the same **physical** manner are astronomical. Yet at the conclusion of every movement, whether slow, fast, loud, soft, major, minor or atonal, the conductor's right hand shot straight up, high above his head. At full extension, he added a larger than life right to left to right, swooping, looping, cut-off gesture that covered the entire upper area of his Conductor's Space. It was a show-biz spectacular but another form of mindless time-beating. The concluding hand-above-the-head gesture had nothing to do with the music.

If the final utterance of a composer leaves a work suspended and unresolved, a final **upward** gesture can work. It could be argued that the conclusions of the majority of works that make up our symphonic repertoire suggest a grounding and the use of some kind of **downward** stroke to supply a sense of closure, of mental resolution and physical finality.

Fermati without Cut-offs

Some holds do not need left hand cut-offs or cut-off strokes of any kind. In certain instances the composer's rhythmic construction in the measure **following the hold** eliminates the use of the cut-off technique.

The most famous *fermati* in the symphonic repertoire, the opening measures of Beethoven's *Fifth Symphony,* are the perfect example. By using eighth note rests between the holds and the resumption of sound in the following measures, Beethoven has supplied a **compositional** cut-off. **Despite the hold in measure 2, measure 3 needs only a right hand, in-tempo down beat with a strong click to activate the sound; no cut-off is necessary.** Please note: **If a cut-off is made, the preparation will add a full measure to Beethoven's structure.** Make the same right hand in-tempo downbeat for measure 6 even if it is a *piano* entrance after a *forte* hold, as well as for the oncoming *fermati*. The left hand remains inactive during the holds, unless it is used to reinforce the dynamic structure.

CHAPTER TWENTY SUMMARY

This chapter has been devoted to *the fermata* or hold, a calculated effect by the composer to halt the flow of the music and bring it to a momentary or a complete stop.

The *fermata* is a **single gesture with two parts:** the hold and the cut-off. The **hold** is generally accomplished with the right hand; the **cut-off** gesture employs both hands if the tempo resumes. While the left hand stops the sound (the cut-off), the right hand makes the preparation for the resumption of sound. **Both movements occur at the same time.**

If a right hand cut-off is made it adds an extra beat to the measure because it must make a new preparation to resume the tempo. The preparation is the **extra beat.** When the left hand makes the cut-off, the extra right hand stroke is eliminated.

All the technical movements necessary to make a successful cut-off have been analyzed. Examples have been supplied for forearm movement in *mezzo-forte* to *fortississimo* cut-offs and for the wrist and forearm movement in the *mezzo-piano* to *pianissimo* cut-offs.

Fermati with cut-offs at the **end of *crescendi*,** as well as cut-offs at the end of *diminuendi* were illustrated. Examples were provided for holds on different beats within the measure in the following meters: 2/4, 3/4, 4/4, 6 and 7 beat measures.

Also discussed were *fermati* without cut-offs and concluding holds. The application of the same final cut-off gesture for differing works, another form of time-beating, was covered as well.

CHAPTER TWENTY-ONE

RESTS

Written rests offer various technical opportunities for an array of baton strokes. Rests are perfect tools for registration because the silence created by rests allows unhindered and varied baton movement. The length of the silence determines how much baton movement is possible, an important factor in choosing and delivering the strokes before, during, and after the rest.

Rests in the Opening Measure

If a composition is new to the orchestra and:
1 - the opening measure begins with two or more rests, or
2 - the first orchestral entrance is made by some but not all the players,

conduct all the beats in the measure. The players who do not participate in the first sound will expect to see all the beats in the measure articulated by the conductor. While preparations for orchestral entrances should be made one beat before the entrance, the conductor is obliged to break that rule for musical reasons, just as patterns must be broken for musical reasons.

If a new work with four beats in a measure **begins** on the **fourth beat,** the first two strokes are used to 'mark' the tempo and be made in a recognizable pattern. When there is nothing written for the orchestra, **the motions of the conductor must reflect that lack of musical activity. Lightly indicated strokes** must be clear, small and without the physical impact or intensity that may stimulate a response from a player. The **third beat preparatory stroke** should begin with a firm wrist 'flick' and contain all the necessary information to start the orchestra on or after beat 4. If there is a **rest on the downbeat of beat 4** and the orchestral entrance is made in any other part of beat 4, indicate the first 3 beats lightly and make a firm preparatory 'click' **on the fourth beat.**

If a work in four begins on the **third beat,** the first small stroke 'marks' the tempo. Beat 2 is the preparatory stroke and begins with a firm wrist 'flick.'

If a work with five beats in a measure begins **on the fifth beat,** the first three small strokes are used to 'mark' the tempo. The fourth beat preparation must be a firm wrist 'flick' and contain all the necessary information to start the orchestra on or after beat five. Use this formula for as many rests as the composer has written before the orchestra's entrance. As the number of beats in a measure increases, the likelihood for an extended number of rests decreases.

There is an other option -- after a number of rehearsals the conductor may choose to dispense with the silent rests and begin the work with a **single** preparatory stroke. In that case the conductor, or the personnel manager of the orchestra, must be certain that every player including last minute substitutes, understands the new procedure!

Rests in Final Measures of a Movement

When a composition concludes on the downbeat of the final measure and is followed by one or more rests, the rests need not be conducted. They are a silent mechanical formula that complete the measure.

As long as music is being performed, rests shortly before the end of a work **do** have a value which transcends the printed page. Often the conclusion of a work is ruined by on-stage players who do **not** produce instrumental sounds. For example, let us assume that while the bulk of the orchestra has finished playing, a five measure post-script for four solo players remains to be heard. Those five measures cannot be used to fold music, dismantle woodwinds, blow spit out of brass instruments, pack up percussion instruments, or open instrument cases for their nightly deposits. The character and mood of the work must be sustained until the final sound has faded.

Moving Toward and Leaving a Rest

In the flow of a composition, moving toward and leaving a rest does not require extra attention from the conductor. The pattern of strokes derived from the music's shape serves the qualities of all rests, especially if they are within an easily felt rhythmic base.

Arriving at a *tutti* rest after a pulseless sonority has been held in place for several measures may require technical attention. To assure a clean cessation of sound before the rest, the left-hand cut-off is advisable. However, if the held sonority has a clear and repeated rhythm moving underneath or over it, the left hand may not be necessary; a sharp right hand 'click' or 'flick' within the beat pattern accomplishes a clean release before the rest.

Strokes After Rests Need Careful Consideration

In the following example a variety of different strokes must be employed for rests that look the same on the page. In this example consider each single pitch a fully scored orchestral *tutti*. Prep = preparation.

Ex. 61

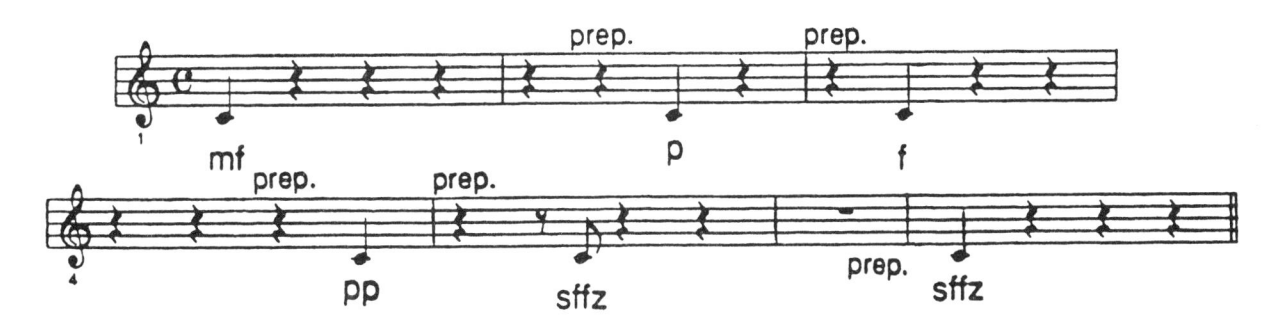

Measure 1. Rests are 'marked' because there is no other activity in the measure. The beats are small but clear.

Measure 2. The first beat is 'marked,' but beat 2 is the preparatory stroke to beat 3. The preparation must be a *piano* preparation from the wrist in zone 1, with the elbow in the letter 'V.' Beat 4 is 'marked.'

Measure 3. Beat 1 is the *forte* preparation from the forearm for beat 2. 'Mark' beats 3 and 4.

Measure 4. 'Mark' the first two beats. Beat 3 is a *pianissimo* wrist preparation for beat 4.

Measure 5. Make a sharp wrist 'click' downstroke preparation for the *sffz* second stroke. 'Mark' beats 3 and 4.

Measure 6. Do not conduct beats 1, 2, or 3. Make a strong upstroke preparation on beat 4 for the *sffz* stroke on the downbeat of measure 7.

A conductor confronted with a series of interjected notes in a field of rests must be able to choose from a variety of baton strokes. Under no circumstance should all the strokes in the example be the same, nor should they be delivered in the same manner. Measures of rests make the preparation of Pitch Level and Dynamic Registration relatively simple.

Beethoven's *Ninth Symphony*

Molto Vivace: (dotted half note equals 116, in one)

Ex. 62

Use the right hand throughout unless otherwise indicated. Make a strong, straight upward upbeat half-click in zone 1, starting at MC level and moving up to E level.

Measure 1. Begin at E level in zone 1. The *fortissimo* forearm stroke moves outward and away from the body into zone 3.

Measure 2. During the G.P. 'click' the forearm back toward the body into zone 1 at the MC level. The 'click' accounts for the measure and acts as the *sf* preparation for measure 3.

Measure 3. Make an outward stroke to zone 3 at the UC level.

Measure 4. 'Click' the right hand back to the body into zone 1 at E level. Once again the 'click' in a G.P. accounts for the measure of silence and serves as the preparation for the timpani *sf* in measure 5.

Measure 5. Direct the left hand (CF-closed fist) toward the timpanist seated in the left-center rear of the stage. The stroke moves downward, from the MC level to the W level. As the left hand articulates, the right hand moves upward into E level and 'clicks' a preparation for measure 6.

Measure 6. Repeat measure 1.

Measures 7 and 8. The right hand moves back and toward the right side of the body and 'marks' the G.P. measures with small beats in zone 1, under the E level. (The second violins are seated to the right of the conductor.)

Measure 9. The right hand is in place in zone 1 for the *pianissimo*. Make a small, curved *legato* wrist 'click' at the E level.

Attacks after Rests

Regenerating music after a rest is exactly like making the first stroke in the first measure. The stroke must contain all the elements of the sound it elicits. (Review chapter eleven.)

Pauses

There are other silences that belong to the rest family. They are not called rests but serve the same purpose. Each create momentary silences and break the flow of the pulse. They are pauses. Some are rhythmically defined, others are not. The "Scherzo" of Beethoven's *Ninth Symphony* contains the "grand pause," indicated by the initials G.P. Three other pauses are often grouped together and mistakenly interpreted in the same way. One of the three, the hold over the barline, should be separated from the other two -- the breath mark (') and the *luftpause* (/).

The confusion centers on the length of the pauses, which is not clearly defined.

Ex. 63

Beethoven, *Ninth Symphony*

Vivace: (dotted half note = 116)

In example 63, Beethoven adds a *fermata* over the barline to create a momentary silence before the music continues. Groves *Dictionary of Music and Musicians* defines the hold or *fermata* as "...indicating the prolongation of a note or rest beyond its usual value."[9] The length of the hold, or pause, is not discussed and is left to the discretion of the conductor.

An effect similar to the *fermata* over the barline might have been achieved with either the *luftpause* (/), or the breath mark (’), which are very like one another. The same music is used in examples 64 and 65, but with different pause signs.

Ex. 64

Ex. 65

What is the difference? The difference lies in the amount of **time** allotted to the two pauses. The *Harvard Dictionary of Music* does not mention the *luftpause* (/) but defines the breath mark (’) as "a **slight** break to allow for breath, or to mark the end of a phrase."[10] The implication is that the hold, including the one over the barline, should be allotted **more time** than the other two pause signs. In fact, the *fermata* is used to indicate varying periods of rest in a composition, including the long rest that marks a *cadenza*.

Conductors should be mindful that pause signs are not interchangeable because the musical effects each produces can differ. Composers make specific choices for specific pauses, and conductors are obliged to treat each pause mark with care and consideration.

The technique used for articulating a hold on the barline, a *luftpause,* or a breath mark, is to **make a slight stop in the stroke before moving onto the next unit of time.** Orchestral musicians often overlook the sometimes small markings that indicate the pause, so the conductor might consider the added precaution of a left hand cut-off as part of this technique.

---

[9] Heinrich Schenker, "Konzertdirigenten" in *Die Zukunft* Vol. 7 (Berlin 1894) reprinted in Hellmut Federhofer, editor, *Heinrich Schenker als Essayist und Kritiker* (Olms Hildesheim 1990) pp. 81-82.

[10] Harvard Dictionary of Music

CHAPTER TWENTY-ONE SUMMARY

If there are two or more rests **before** the first entrance of the orchestra in a newly composed work, articulate the rests in the opening measures. The orchestra players who do not perform in the first measure will expect the conductor to account for all the rests in their parts. Once a piece has been rehearsed and the orchestra knows it well, the conductor may choose to eliminate the silent preentrance beats.

Rests that are added to the last measure, **after** the final orchestral sound, should not be conducted. They are added to fill out the required number of beats in the measure and to balance the end of the work.

Approaching and departing rests need special care. Rests are a natural preparation point for generating oncoming orchestral attacks of every variety. Examples have been provided for different kinds of articulations that must be made during a series of rests that look alike on the page. Techniques have been discussed.

Pauses, like rests, create silence. Some silences, like the G.P. (the Grand Pause), are measured; others like the *fermata* over the barline, the *luftpause*, and the breath mark are not.

The length of the pause generated by the *fermata* **over the barline** is generally longer than the length of the pause created by the *luftpause* or the breath mark. The length of these pauses has not been clearly defined and as a result the timing of the pause is left to the conductor.

Definitions of lengths of rests are discussed, and a technique for dealing with pauses has been provided.

CHAPTER TWENTY-TWO

ACCENTS — SYNCOPATION

Without defining the process, the preparation and delivery of accents were covered in chapter nineteen. An accent, like a cue, **must be prepared one beat <u>before</u> it occurs and the preparation must indicate the exact dynamic and rhythmic properties of the accent.** Preparations for accents are often overlooked or taken for granted. The conductor shows the accent as it occurs, with a heavier than normal stroke. An unprepared, simultaneous conductor-orchestra arrival at an accent suggests that the conductor is in danger of following the orchestra. The conductor must always be a musical step ahead of the orchestra!

The wrist is the important ingredient for the production of an accented note. We already know that a preparatory 'click' or 'flick' indicates the point of attack to an orchestra with precision and clarity. It may also be noted that a *pianissimo* preparatory 'click,' as well as a *fortissimo* 'click,' can **both** be delivered to the orchestra from the same general area in the Conductor's Space. **The shorter the distance the preparatory stroke travels, the better the chance is for a precise, unified attack on the accented note.**

Within a small conducting space the wrist can produce any kind of preparatory stroke: *legato, staccato,* or *tenuto*. It can also produce any dynamic: a *piano tenuto* or a biting, quick snap-of-the-wrist *ffz*. If the wrist 'click' or 'flick' is used, the preparatory principles demonstrated in example 61 can be applied to the similar rhythmic music in the *Romeo and Juliet Overture* by Tchaikovsky. (The strings are omitted in this example.) In performance, particular attention should be paid to the cymbal player. The cymbal sound should be short, with a high-pitched quality.

The right hand can manage the passage without difficulty, but the left hand can also effectively indicate accents, especially if the accents are scored for instruments on the left side of the stage. When the wrist is used the preparations must be clear and, if it is convenient, the accented beats directed toward the instruments responsible for performing them. The pattern determines the movement of the forearm or wrist. **Occasionally the left hand might be used to arrive simultaneously on a rhythmic accent,** usually *forte* or *fortissimo,* with the orchestra, but **only** if the right hand is initiating the preparation for the accents while it maintains tempo.

Ex. 66
Tchaikovsky, *Romeo and Juliet Overture*

Measure 1. Prepare the fourth beat entrance on the third beat with a clear wrist 'flick' in zone 3, Fr, at E level.

Measure 2. Make a sharp 'click' on the downbeat for the entrance **after** the first beat. The stroke on beat 2 should not be as strong as the third beat stroke, which will have a sharp wrist 'click' to prepare the fourth beat entrance.

Measure 3. Make a sharp 'click' on the first beat to prepare for the second beat entrance and another sharp 'flick' on beat 3 for the entrance after the third beat. Remain in zone 3, Fr, at E level throughout unless all the strokes are directed at the cymbal player. In that case either hand may address the cymbals.

In the *Romeo and Juliet Overture* excerpt use the left hand for the four accents that occur on the beat. When that can be done easily, make left handed strokes on the accents that are written **after** the beat (there are two in measures 2 and 3) by preparing for the stroke **on** the beat.

Preparing a *Fortissimo* Accent during a *Pianissimo* Sonority

A conductor may find that the composer has not allotted enough time to address a specific situation, such as a fully scored *fortissimo* immediately upon the heels of a thinly scored *piano* or *pianissimo*. If a *fortissimo* preparation is imposed on the final *pianissimo*, the *pianissimo* is sacrificed. If no preparation is given for the *fortissimo* accent the conductor is in danger of losing control of the sonority. **The ingenuity of the conductor is tested to find a compromise.**

If the accented *fortissimo* is a textural and musical surprise, the conductor is obligated to hide the preparation from the audience, as explained before (see Mahler ex. 56). Therefore, the preparation is short and **directly in front of the body, out of sight of the audience.** The wrist is responsible for the instigation of the preparation and for the delivery of the accent.

If the accented sonority has been heard before, the surprise factor is no longer a concern, but the preparation must not be obvious and can be made by using both hands as follows:

Begin with the left hand in front of the body in zone 2, palm up (OPU), MC level to establish the *piano* or *pianissimo* character of the music for at least one full measure before the *fortissimo* entrance. The right hand is behind *and above* the left hand in zone 1 'and' initiates a wrist *fortissimo* 'click.' In this physical frame the orchestra sees the left hand *pianissimo* indication in front of the right hand *fortissimo* signal. If properly executed the right hand will be mostly hidden from the audience's view.

If the conductor wishes to **fully conceal the preparation from the audience** there is yet another way to deliver the *fortissimo* stroke preparation. Position the right hand beat in front of the middle of the body at W level in zone 3 **before** the preparation. If it is necessary, break the pattern. The *fortissimo* preparation will come **back** toward the body and **out** again to zone 3 for the accented *fortissimo*. The left hand ought to be in the same position described in the previous paragraph, except that it will be at E or UC level, **above and away from the movement of the right hand.**

Preparing a *Piano* Accent during a *Fortissimo* Sonority

During a *fortissimo* passage a warning sign that a *piano* or *pianissimo* is coming **should not be shown prematurely.** It is disconcerting to see a conductor raise a left arm and display a clearly visible *piano* signal in the midst of a huge orchestral sonority. If the dynamic does not immediately change, the audience cannot be faulted for thinking the players are not watching the conductor. Actually, the players **are** watching and helping the conductor by disregarding a signal that is clearly incorrect.

The *piano* signal ought to be delayed and displayed as late as possible. If the quarter note is the time unit, a quick upward motion of the left palm, OPU, on the last sixteenth of the quarter note before the change will be time enough for the *piano* indication. The orchestral response will be immediate and controlled.

Because the sonority level drops rather than rises, another technique is available that ordinarily should not be used. **It is understood that dynamic changes should be prepared and not arrived at simultaneously by orchestra and conductor.** It is a basic rule and should always be observed with the one following **exception.**

If the conductor carries the written *forte* or *fortissimo* as far as indicated and then **freezes the motion** of the baton on the very next beat, **the inert baton will secure an immediate *piano* or *pianissimo*, with or without an accent, on that beat.** After the single stopped beat, the conductor must resume the pattern. In this special instance the conductor's lack of motion, and the orchestra's *piano* or *pianissimo*, will be simultaneous and achieved **without** preparation. It must be noted that there is a huge difference between this kind of conductor-orchestra simultaneous arrival and the kind which occurs because of lack of conductor preparation. The body language confirms that the conductor is in full control of the event. **The means to achieve the dynamic change is a willful, carefully conceived and fully prepared technical maneuver imposed upon the orchestra.**

Syncopation, Accents within Syncopation

The treatment of an accent or accents within syncopated figures brings us to the larger subject of syncopation, "an alteration of the normal time accents of the bar brought about by the setting up of contrary accents," *Groves Dictionary*.[11]

Early in their studies conductors may encounter difficulties with heavily syncopated music, finding themselves pulled away from the basic pulses (beats) within the measure and stroking on the syncopation. If the conductor wavers and moves away from the bedrock of the basic pulse, **there is no syncopation,** because syncopated rhythms **depend** upon a **firm basic pulse.** The consequences are likely to be dramatic and destructive.

If the tendency to stroke on the syncopation persists, the conductor can confirm the basic pulse by:

1. **Shortening the stroke.** When the baton stroke uses less space it cuts down the possibility of being pulled onto the syncopation, especially in quick tempi.

2. **Adding a 'wrist click' or 'flick' to the stroke.** The addition of a wrist 'click' or 'flick' emphasizes the pulse, helps define the basic beat, and 'springs' the actual syncopation.

3. Work on the syncopation problems in Exercises 70, 71, 72.

The very nature of a syncopated rhythm presupposes some sort of accent, whether or not it is indicated in the music. When a composer <u>adds</u> accents to a syncopated figure, the realization of the composer's intention requires specific technical expertise.

An example from Stravinsky's *Firebird Suite,* here notated both with and without accents, should produce different physical reactions from instrumentalists and/or conductors.

---

[11] H.C.C., "Syncopation," Eric Blom, ed., Grove's Dictionary of Music and Musicians (St. Martin's Press Inc., New York 1954) Fifth Edition, Volume Eight

The stroke the conductor chooses will make a difference in the weight and delivery of the syncopation. Strokes for accented syncopated passages can be made in any dynamic, placed in any register, and delivered to any level.

Stravinsky, *Firebird Suite*

Ex. 67

Ex. 68

The unaccented version (ex. 67) should be conducted with normally registered baton strokes, above W level, Fr, with the elbow in the letter 'L,' addressing the horns, bassoons and the tuba, with well-articulated pulse points to 'spring' the syncopations. The difference in the dynamics, *mezzo-forte* to *forte* (preparing the last beat in measures 2 and 4 for the *forte*), requires a quick movement from zone 2 to zone 3 on the second beat in measures 2 and 4.

The accented version (ex. 68) requires a different technical approach. After accounting for dynamics and registration, each of the accents receives short, stopped strokes. The **rebounds are eliminated,** highlighting the basic pulse in the measures. Every stroke is delivered with more weight and with more forward push than was used for the first version (ex. 67). <u>The pattern the player sees is compact, focused and powerful</u>. The heightened energy level ignites each of the accents on the syncopations.

Brahms, *Second Symphony,* Fourth Movement

Ex. 69

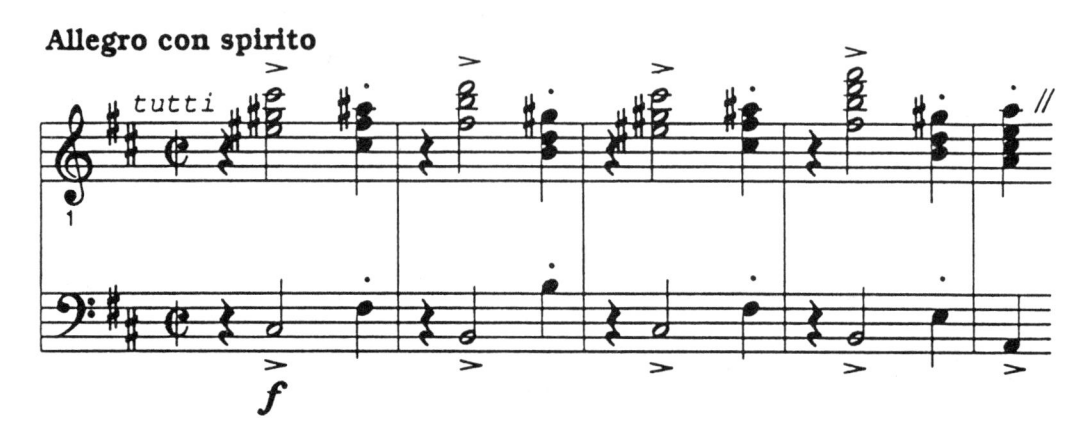

The Brahms example benefits from two kinds of strokes in each of the four measures; an outward accented *legato* stroke and a returning *staccato* stroke. The initial stroke for the silent first quarter note in the measure must have the push and energy of the stroke in Stravinsky example 68. Unlike the Stravinsky, the stroke must also have **length** because of the duration of the first note in the measure, the accented half note. On the first beat in the measure, a sharp right wrist 'flick' begins a *legato* **horizontal stroke,** from zone 1, at the UC level, Fr, which **quickly** moves outward and away from the body into zone 3. **The space used in the movement from zone 1 to zone 3 is essential.** The quickness of the stroke generates the necessary attack, but the length of the stroke compels the orchestra to sustain the attack. The second stroke quickly moves back toward the body and into zone 1, but comes to a **full stop** because of the dot above the fourth beat quarter note. The same beat pattern is repeated in each of the measures with the addition of pitch registration. (A workable substitute for the horizontal stroke motion is an outward and downward curved stroke motion.)

Syncopation Exercises

The following exercises help the baton stroke prepare and articulate syncopated passages. Rhythm and accents are the major considerations. Pitch classifications are a secondary concern. Dynamics, zones and levels remain constant throughout each exercise. Sing the rhythms, and pay particular attention to the accents and lengths of the notes as the metronome markings change.

Exercise 1.

Ex. 70

Establish the pulse in measures 1 and 2. Add wrist 'clicks' to beats 3 and 4 in measure 3 for the off-beat accents.

- **First time.** Use the right hand. Set the metronome at a quarter equals 62. The dynamic is *piano*, and the arm is at FX, in zone 3, Fr, at the MC level.
- **Second time.** Use the left hand. Set the metronome at a quarter equals 84. The dynamic is *mezzo-forte*, and the elbow is in the letter 'L,' in zone 2, SL, at the W level.
- **Third time.** Use the right hand. Set the metronome at a quarter equals 146. The dynamic is *fortissimo*, and the elbow is in an open letter 'V,' in zone 1, Fr, at E level.

Exercise 2.

Ex. 71

The key preparatory strokes in this exercise are to be short, with forearm push, and wrist 'clicks.' They will be found in:

measure 2, fourth beat
measure 3, third beat
measure 4, second beat
measure 5, all beats
measure 6, fourth beat

- **First time.** Use the left hand. Address the brass section. Set the metronome at a quarter equals 160. The dynamic is *fortissimo* throughout, and the arm is at FX in zone 3, Fr, at E level.
- **Second time.** Use the right hand. Address the woodwind section. Set the metronome at a quarter equals 100. The dynamic is *mezzo forte* throughout, and the elbow is in a letter 'L' position in zone 2, Fr, at the UC level.
- **Third time.** Use the left hand. Address the bass and cello sections. Set the metronome at a quarter equals 56. The dynamic is *pianississimo* throughout, and the elbow is in a letter 'V' in zone 1, Fr, at the MC level.

Exercise 3.

Ex. 72

The first stroke in measure 1 should not be forceful, in contrast to the stroke for the second beat which has all the properties described for the key preparatory strokes in example 71. All preparatory rests before the accented notes must be well articulated. The final stroke must be short and sharp. The entire percussion section, timpani plus three percussionists, is addressed in measures 1, 2, and 3, and the entire orchestra plays the final three measures.

- **First time.** Use the left hand. Set the metronome at a quarter equals 76. The dynamic is *forte* throughout, and the arm is in zone 3, SL, at the UC level.
- **Second time.** Use the right hand. Set the metronome at a quarter equals 128. The dynamic is *pianissimo* throughout, and the elbow is in a letter 'V' in zone 1, Fr, at the MC level.
- **Third time.** Use the right hand. Set the metronome at a quarter equals 172. The dynamic is *mezzo forte* throughout. The elbow is in an open letter 'L' in zone 2, Fr, at the E level.

CHAPTER TWENTY-TWO SUMMARY

An accent, like a cue, must be prepared one beat before it occurs, and the preparation must indicate the exact dynamic and rhythmic properties of the accent. The shorter the distance the preparatory stroke travels, the better are the chances for a unified attack on the accented note. To insure the points of attack with clarity and precision use wrist 'clicks' and 'flicks.'

Both hands are used in preparing and indicating accents.

The techniques involved in preparing a *fortissimo* accent after a *piano* sonority, and a *piano* accent after a *fortissimo* sonority are discussed in detail. Dynamic changes are always prepared to avoid simultaneous conductor-orchestra arrival points, but one **unprepared** dynamic change, freezing the motion of the baton, can be used to good effect.

Syncopation, with and without accents, creates problems for beginning conductors who stroke on the syncopation rather than on the basic pulse. If syncopation causes problems, concentrate on the basic beats, shorten the strokes that outline the basic beats, and add wrist 'clicks' to all the pulses that precede the syncopations.

Syncopation exercises have been provided for both hands, in all dynamics, levels, and zones. Examples of accented syncopation with differing properties have been supplied using the music of Stravinsky (short, powerful) accent and Brahms (*legato* accents).

CHAPTER TWENTY-THREE

TEMPO

What is tempo? The speed of the baton as it moves from pulse point to pulse point in a pattern creates pace. **Pace is tempo,** and tempo is a reflection of how the conductor perceives the music unfolding over a period of time. A work may be conducted in a single, unwavering tempo from the first note to the last; for instance, a march with an unchanging metronome mark of 120 per beat. A performance might also be made up of a combination of tempi which bear no metronome markings: an Introduction marked *Lento* may lead to a section marked *Allegro*, which concludes with a Coda marked *Presto*. *Lento, Allegro* and *Presto* are generic terms and all such descriptive terms have a common factor -- they are devoid of fixed tempi.

Choosing a Tempo

Choosing the tempo (pace) for music that does not have clearly defined instructions is a challenge conductors face constantly. The determination of tempo for the bulk of pre-twentieth century repertoire relies on the taste and education of the conductor. Traditions and performance practices of the period have to be considered, as well as the position of the composer in his or her musical era. Reality may alter carefully considered decisions: 'boomy' or 'dry' acoustics in the performing space, the ability of the orchestra to articulate fast tempi or the lack of quality in the orchestral sound in slow tempi.

Please notice that I have not referred to the 'right' tempo. Even when metronome marks exist, as in Beethoven symphonies, there is unending controversy. Over the past twenty or more years, I have known many composers who have disavowed, and changed their original tempo indications. The tempi they felt and put on paper in their workrooms were not what they experienced nor expected in the workplace, the concert hall.

Well then, is there a 'right' tempo? **Not one, but many.**

The tempi of Beethoven's *Fifth Symphony* are 'right' when Maestro A can convince an audience that the reading is precisely as Beethoven imagined.

The tempi of Beethoven's *Fifth Symphony* are 'right' when Maestro B's vastly different pacing convinces an audience that the reading is precisely as Beethoven imagined.

If one eliminates the obvious attempt to shock, almost all rationally conceived tempi can be the 'right' tempi. If musically astute listeners agree, the conductor has served the composer well and the tempi must be judged to be 'right.'

CHANGING THE TEMPO

A tempo change occurs when the composer signals that the **pace** of the music be redirected. The signal, conveyed in a variety of ways, must contain instructions on how and where to shift the tempo. Some signals are exact (metronome markings) and require the conductor to be alert to the formula for making the change. Other signals (written instructions) are imprecise and allow a great deal of artistic freedom. In the latter category, the opening movement of Mahler's *Fourth Symphony* carries no metronome marking; the only tempo indication is an ambiguous *Bedächtig*, or *Moderato*. Yet within the first sixty-seven measures (to no. 5) there are fifteen separate instructions that directly affect the formulation of the tempo. The burden of the initial choice of tempo and its later nuances are the responsibility of the conductor. When one remembers that the music was written by a composer who was also an immensely gifted conductor, the multiple directions are not surprising.

The Effect on Tempo when the Rhythmic Unit of Propulsion <u>Does Not Change</u>.

Many conductors believe that **moving a barline** creates a tempo change. **It does not.** Tempo is established and maintained by an unchanging **rhythmic unit of propulsion:** the quarter, the half, the sixteenth, etc. The barline simply **divides** the tempo.

In consecutive bars of 4/4, 5/4, 3/4, 2/4, 6/4, 4/4, 3/4, **with no specific instructions for altering the tempo,** the **quarter note is the basic unit** of rhythmic propulsion and is **constant.** So, while the **barline** changes, the movement of the time, the **tempo,** remains the same. In a sequence of 3/8, 5/8, 2/8, 6/8, 3/8, 7/8, the **eighth note is the basic unit** of propulsion, and is constant. Again, the **barline** changes, but the *tempo* remains intact. If different meters are combined, 4/4, 3/8, 5/4, 5/8, 3/4, 6/8, etc., the common rhythmic denominator, the **eighth note, becomes the basic unit** of propulsion. Even though the **barline** divides the measures irregularly due to changing **time signatures, the tempo (basic pulse) remains the same** since the basic unit of propulsion, the eighth note, has neither gotten slower nor faster; it remains unchanged.

Bernstein *Serenade*, Third Movement, Violin Solo, letter E.

In this example the eighth note is the basic unit of propulsion, and remains constant. Moving the barline does **not** change the tempo.

Ex. 73

Presto ($\quarter$=138)

© 1956 by THE ESTATE OF LEONARD BERNSTEIN; Copyright Renewed
LEONARD BERNSTEIN MUSIC PUBLISHING COMPANY LLC, publisher,
BOOSEY & HAWKES, INC., Sole Agent
Used by permission

The strokes that account for **three** eighth notes in measure 3 and the beginning of measure 5, must be **higher** than the strokes that account for **two** eighth notes. (See chapter ten)

Bernstein *Serenade*, Fifth Movement: orchestra, after number 34

This example contains **two concurrent** duple meters, 6/8 for the bottom strings, and 2/4 for the violins. The basic unit of propulsion is the mix of three eighth notes against two eighth notes. Despite the change of time signatures, 2/4-6/8 to 3/4-9/8, and the reverse, the tempo remains unaffected because of the **equal** time values of the quarter and the dotted quarter.

Ex. 74

[musical example]

© 1956 by THE ESTATE OF LEONARD BERNSTEIN; Copyright Renewed
LEONARD BERNSTEIN MUSIC PUBLISHING COMPANY LLC, publisher,
BOOSEY & HAWKES, INC., Sole Agent
Used by permission

The first two measures, 2/4-6/8, are conducted in a two pattern, and measures 3 and 4, 3/4-9/8, in a three pattern.

Beethoven, *Third Symphony,* Scherzo

This example involves not only a meter change, but a mathematical equation as well. To what purpose? The composer wants to be certain that the tempo is preserved and **not** changed! The tempo marking for the 3/4, the dotted half note equals 116, and for the Alla Breve, the whole note equals 116, means that **both measures are equal in time to one another.** Despite the physical appearance of the music, a single stroke is made for both the Alla Breve and the 3/4. The change in meter has **no** effect on the tempo.

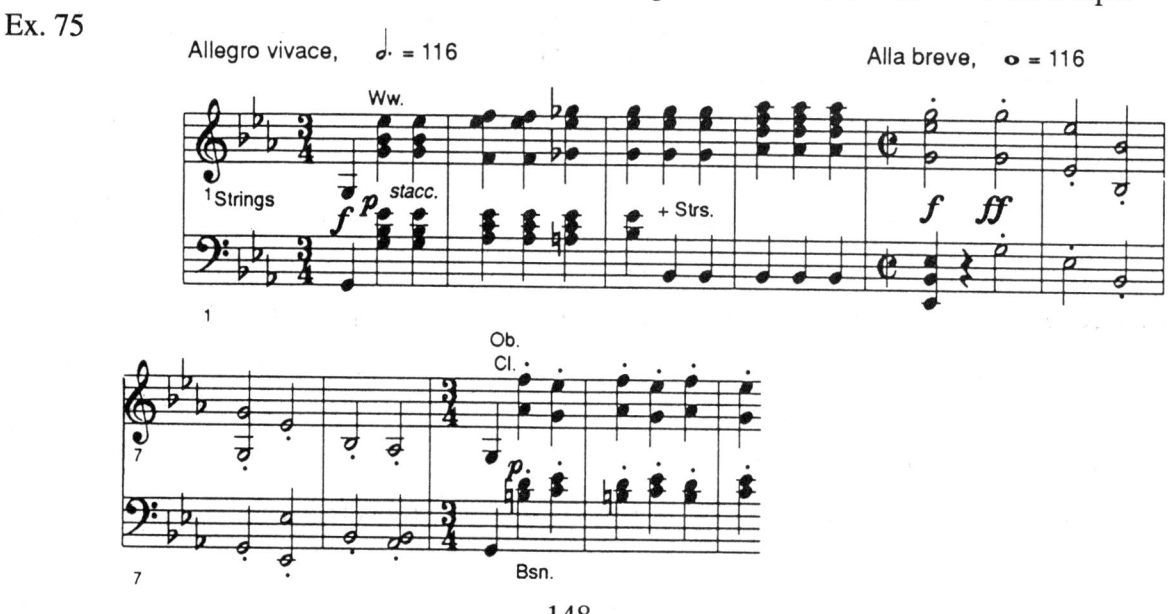

Ex. 75

(The strokes in measures 5 - 8 should be short, pushed, forearm strokes with wrist 'flicks,' in zone 1, Fr, from E level down to W level.)

Why did Beethoven choose to organize his rhythmic materials as he did? Had he wanted to, he certainly could have avoided a change of time signature by writing measures 5 - 8 in the following manner:

Ex. 76

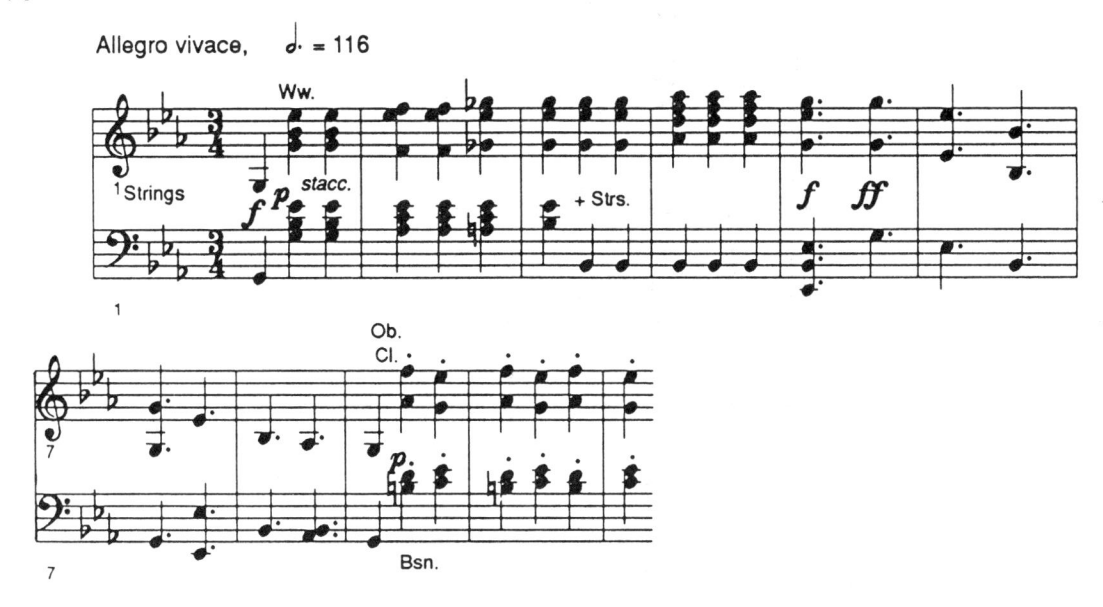

The answer probably lies in yet another question, would the musical effect be the same? The physical energy the players generate during the Alla Breve gives it a visceral quality, a sound quite different from that generated in the ongoing 3/4 signature.

The Effect on Tempo When the Rhythmic Unit of Propulsion Changes

As noted, a change of tempo occurs when a composer alters the **pace, or speed,** of the **basic rhythmic unit of propulsion.**

In ex. 77 the longer note value has been transferred to a shorter note, **slowing** the tempo.

Ex. 77

The **eighth note** in measure 4 has been changed to equal the **quarter note** in measure 3. The tempo in measure 4 has been cut in half, and the result is a **new tempo** that is **twice as slow. (The baton stroke in measure 4 is twice as slow as in the previous measure.)** The metronome reads as follows: the 120 metronome marking per **quarter** note of measure 3 has been transferred to the **eighth** note of measure 4. The eighth note now equals 120, which **reduces** the quarter note to 60. Because the basic unit of propulsion has been altered, **the tempo has changed.**

If a composer wants to make a tempo **twice as fast,** he reverses the signal.

Ex. 78

[Musical notation: 3/8, 5/8, 2/8, 6/8 measures with eighth/sixteenth notes; tempo markings ♪ = 50 and ♪ = ♬ = 100]

The **eighth note** in measure 4 has been changed to equal the **sixteenth note** in measure 3. The result is that the tempo in measure 4 has doubled and is now **twice as fast. (The baton stroke in measure 4 is twice as fast as in the previous measure.)** The metronome would read: the 100 metronome marking per sixteenth note in measure 3 has been transferred to the eighth note of measure 4. The eighth note now equals 100, which doubles its previous value (which was eighth note equals 50).

Brahms, *Second Symphony,* Third Movement, Measure No. 31

The change from the character of the *Allegretto grazioso* to the *Presto ma non assai*, to half note equals quarter note, is another example of a composer faced with options and making what seems like the inevitable choice. In the context of this chapter let us suppose that Brahms eliminated the *Presto*, the change of tempo indication, and wrote:

Ex. 79

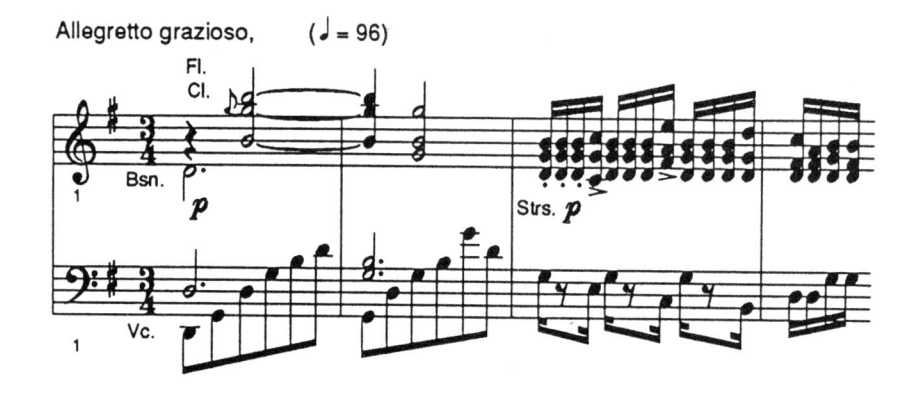

[Musical excerpt: Allegretto grazioso, (♩ = 96), 3/4 time, with Fl., Cl., Bsn., Strs., Vc. parts]

instead of the version we all know:

Ex. 80

[Musical excerpt: Allegretto grazioso, (♩ = 96), 3/4 time changing to Presto ma non assai, ♩ = ♩, 2/4 time]

The entire character of the music divides itself into a before and after status; the dividing line is the alteration of the tempo. Brahms had two musics in mind and his solution to change the tempo is essential for the preservation of the differing nature of the materials.

In technical terms, the continuation of a three pattern in ex. 79 robs the baton of the energy produced in the recurring downbeat strokes in the tempo change in ex. 80. The small working area needed to produce the sharp wrist 'click' strokes, MC level, zone 3, Fr, helps to keep the sound tight and focused from 2/4 measure to 2/4 measure.

Copland, *Appalachian Spring*, five measures after no. 16

In the fourth measure, the eighth note takes on the value of the quarter note in measure 3, **cutting the tempo in half.** In measure 7, the quarter note takes on the value of the eighth note in measure 6, **doubling the tempo.**

Ex. 81

© 1945 by THE AARON COPLAND FUND FOR MUSIC, INC.; Copyright Renewed
Used by permission of BOOSEY & HAWKES, INC., Sole Agent

The **speed of the baton stroke is cut in half** in the fourth measure, and **resumes its original speed** at the Tempo Primo in measure 7.

Strauss, *Till Eulenspiegels lustige Streiche*, nine measures after no. 12

The dotted quarter of the 6/8 becomes the eighth note in the 2/4. In effect, two measures of 6/8 become one measure of 2/4.

Ex. 82

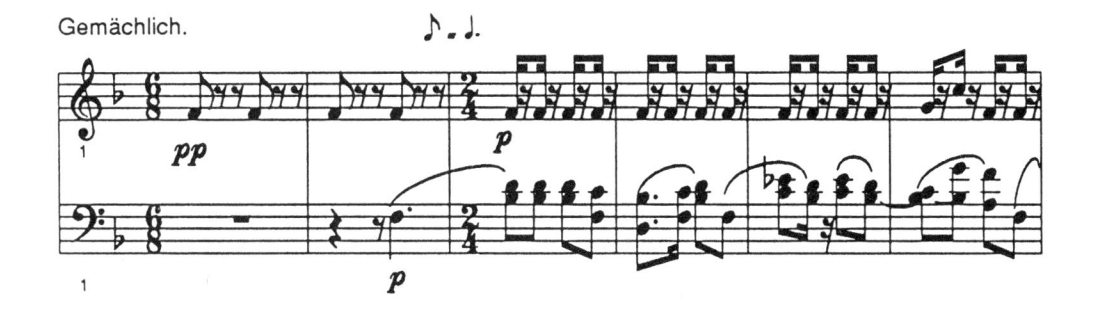

While the speed of the strokes remain constant, the conductor must make a distinct four beat pattern in the third measure of this example. As always, registration helps clarify orchestration. Make *staccato* left hand wrist strokes in zone 3, Fr, UC level for the horns in the first two measures. In the second measure address the viola, bassoon, and clarinet entrance with a right hand curved *legato* stroke in zone 1. Begin the stroke at the W level on SR, in zone 1 and move up to C level in measure 3, in a clear four beat pattern. In measure 3 the left hand moves to the first violins, SL, MC level, zone 3, and 'clicks' a small four beat pattern from the wrist for one measure only.

CHAPTER TWENTY-THREE SUMMARY

Tempo is pace.

A change of tempo occurs when the pace of the music is altered. Changing the barline does not affect the tempo. When a composer writes consecutive measures of 4/4, 5/4, 3/8, 9/8, 2/4, 5/8, the **meter** has been changed but the **tempo remains the same** because the unit of propulsion, in this instance the eighth note, remains unaffected. When the **unit of propulsion,** which governs the speed, or pace of the music **is changed, the tempo changes.**

The composer achieves an unspecified alteration of tempo by written direction: *piu mosso, rallantando*, etc., or a precise modification of tempo by changing the metronome marking.

The use of the metronome assigns specific speeds to units of propulsion, and the speed of the pulse/tempo can be altered by assigning different note values to the same metronome marking.

For example, a tempo based on a **quarter note** marking which equals 120 can be **cut in half** by transferring the same 120 pulse marking to an **eighth note,** or made **twice as fast** by transferring the same 120 pulse marking to a **half note.**

CHAPTER TWENTY-FOUR

TEMPO, PART TWO

Tempo Modification—*Accelerando—Rallantando*

Modifications in tempo are made away from and back to the same tempo, or toward an entirely new tempo. The key to successfully moving a tempo ahead, an *accelerando*, or successfully slowing tempo down, a *rallentando*, is deciding **beforehand** what the new tempo will be. If the new tempo is not carefully gauged there may be an abrupt backward or forward lurch; a corruption of the composer's intention.

A tempo change must be perfectly launched. A clear pacing of a *rallentando* in the first three or four strokes of the baton allows the orchestra to continue an ongoing *rallentando*, **without conductorial guidance** for possibly 9 to 12 beats. A clear pacing of the first three or four strokes in starting an *accelerando* yields the same results.

The technical requirements are not difficult. As the tempo decreases the **size of the baton stroke becomes larger** to fill the longer periods of time between pulses. If the conductor wishes to keep the size of the stroke the same, the **speed** of the baton stroke has to slow down in order to compensate for the lengthening of the time between pulses. Conversely, as the tempo increases **the stroke becomes smaller.** No workable alternative exists for the *accelerando*, because increasing the speed of the strokes within the same sized beat is not practical. Whatever method the conductor employs, **the strokes from pulse point to pulse point must be perfectly executed to create a seamless modification of time.**

The following examples need a carefully conceived plan to meet the composer's intent.

Ex. 83

Tchaikovsky, *Serenade for Strings*

Moderato, Tempo di Valse, dotted half note = 69

Tchaikovsky's metronome mark dictates that the measures be beaten in one. Measure 4 contains a *ritenuto* and is beaten in three. Depending on how much of a *ritenuto* is made in measure 4, the conductor has the option of beating 3 pulses within <u>one vertical movement</u>, thus preserving the single stroke per measure, or <u>creating a 3 beat pattern</u> with a very slight right movement for beat 2. The *a tempo* return in measure 5 is immediate. From measure 5 through the *a tempo* marking in measure 19, **the conductor must have a precise plan for pacing the *stringendo* (accelerando), moving away from the *a tempo*, and the** *ritenuto (rallentando)*, moving back to the *a tempo*.

The tempo remains constant in measures 5 - 10 which can be read as three two-measure phrases. Thus every two measures could be combined and conducted with a two-beat pattern, rather than beating 6 single stroke downbeats for each of the six measures. (Measure 6 must have a strong *staccato* 'click' on the downbeat for the *subito fortissimo*, the eighth note run.) The midpoint of measure 10 can be used as a springboard to the *stringendo* and the hemiola in measures 11 -14. The two, two-measure phrases **must move briskly ahead** to measure 15! (Measures 11-14 can also be conducted in two-beat patterns, but the conductor must make certain that the second stroke in the patterns, measures 12 and 14, are very clear, allowing the players to place the second beats precisely.) **Measure 15 is the key measure; it is both the culmination and the release of the tempo modification.** Measures 15, 16, and 17 gradually slow down and continue in one. With measure 18, the tempo has slowed sufficiently to beat a comfortable 3, and make the *fermata*, with a *diminuendo*, on beat 2. The upbeat stroke on beat 3 in measure 18 acts as the *a tempo* preparation for measure 19. Note that the eighth note after the *fermata* is played as an upbeat in the new tempo.

The right hand can accomplish what has been described above, mostly at E level, moving between zones 2 and 3 until the *fermata*. As always, the wrist is useful, and the largest movement should be restricted to small forearm strokes. Despite the *fortissimo* marking, do not use the upper arm in this example!

Ex. 84

Debussy, *La Mer*, Third Movement, twelve measures before no. 55

The third movement of *La Mer*, "*Dialogue du vent et la mer*," provides an excellent example of tempo modification. While there is little in common between the brilliant scoring of the Tchaikovsky, ex. 83, and the lovely oboe solo in the Debussy, ex. after no. 54, the successful realization of either depends upon the conductor's sensitivity to tempo movement. If it is true that Debussy's detailed instructions for the flow of the line places certain restrictions on the conductor, it is equally true that the same instructions allow a conductor with imagination and taste the fullest measure of freedom in realizing this glorious music.

The tempo indication at the opening of the movement is half note equals 84, but well into the movement, five measures after no. 54 at the D-flat major, a marking of *Plus Calme et tres expressif* precedes the entrance of the two solo woodwinds. The illustrated solo oboe line shows a four measure *ritard*, a six measure *accelerando*, and a final two bar *ritard* to no. 55, and a return to the opening material.

Every measure is beaten in 2, with the possible exception of the *ritard* in measure 12. The first four measure phrase is structured two plus two. The conductor has the option of slowing down every second stroke in <u>each</u> measure, which helps to create the ongoing *rallentando*, or slowing down the <u>second stroke</u> in every second measure, which moderates the *ritard* and highlights the articulation of the triplets, the *crescendo,* and the dynamic levels in the measures that follow. Whatever method the conductor decides to use, the time consumed in either presentation must be the **same!** In contrast, the next six measures must move ahead constantly; three phrases of two measures each. Each two-measure phrase is an exercise in dynamic structure and must be fully realized; two measures of *crescendi*, two measures of *crescendo-diminuendo*, *piu piano*, and finally *pianissimo*. The conductor must have a clear idea of the outer limits of each *crescendo* within the context of the twelve measure structure. The composer does not supply that information. The final two measures before no. 55 act as the pivot for the *ritard* back to the fixed tempo and the high double B-flat which began the section.

Registration is essential and helps shape the material. Pitch Registration covers one and one half octaves, E level (the beginning) to above W level (measure 11). Dynamics move between zones 1 and 2, with the palm of the left hand (OPD) playing a very important role in implementing the many dynamic changes. (Measures 2, 4 and 6 move into zone 2 from zone 1. The middle of measures 7 and 8 also move into zone 2 from zone 1.) All strokes (wrist, forearm), a combination of straight line and curved, are delivered in a fairly confined Conductor's Space. (The dynamic structure, a study in shades of *piano*, restricts the movement of the baton to zones 1 and 2.) The entire section could be conducted with the right hand, but looking ahead, the first four measures might be given to the left hand. If the left hand is used **it eliminates the Pitch Registration leap for the right hand in measure 13** and outlines the return of the opening material. (The left hand would begin in zone 1, E level, Fr, and move into zone 2 in measure 2, OPD. After making a slight *rallentando* in the second half of the measure, the left hand would move back into zone 1 in measure 3.)

Moving to a New Tempo

Ex. 85

Beethoven, *Fifth Symphony,* Last Movement, twelve measures before *Presto.*

Unlike the freedom Debussy gives the conductor in making tempo modifications in *La Mer*, Beethoven's metronome markings in the last movement of the *Fifth Symphony* take the guesswork out of the arrival point of the *accelerando*. The thirteenth measure in this example, the *Presto*, is beaten in one, the whole note equals 112 per measure. The point of departure is the half note, which equals 84, with two beats per measure. **The forward motion to the new tempo is made over nine measures, beginning in measure 4.**

This transition works best if the conductor is already beating one to a measure **before** the arrival at the Presto. The first three measures will be steady, with two beats per measure. Measures 4, 5, and 6, the beginning of the *accelerando*, move ahead but remain in a distinct two beats per measure. Measures 7 and 8 continue to move ahead, but are beaten **with one vertical down/up stroke per measure.** The second beat in the pattern is made **within** the upward vertical movement. As the tempo gets faster the speed of the baton stroke, approaching a half note equals 224, is difficult to read in the basic two beat, second beat side right configuration. However, retaining the beat but changing the pattern facilitates the forward motion. In addition, the movement to a **divided one** acts as the pivot for moving into a non-divided, one beat per measure pattern. The four measures before the *Presto* continue to move smoothly ahead, now unmistakably in one, arriving at the *Presto* in the new tempo -- whole note equals 112.

Conduct the *accelerando* with the right hand, wrist and forearm, E level, beginning in zone 2 and moving into zone 3 on the downbeat of the *Presto*, where the registration will change to W level.

Listen for Momentum

The most important factor for moving an orchestra from one tempo to another is creating and **listening** to the progress of **the momentum of the music.** Once the momentum, **the beginning of the**

movement toward a new tempo has been clearly established, the orchestra will sense the shifting of the pulse and 'carry' the conductor to the arrival point of the new tempo. In a real sense the conductor 'rides' the momentum of the orchestra into the new tempo, especially in an *accelerando*.

Often the conductor is so concentrated on getting to the new tempo, she/he does not listen to the orchestra, and moves the tempo before momentum is clearly established. The inevitable scrambled result is the conductor's fault because the orchestra is left without any transitional pulse and is forced to catch up to the speeding conductor. With experience the conductor learns that a forward or retarded motion has to be established **before a tempo transition can be accomplished.**

Metric Modulation

Written instructions and explicit transference of metronome markings to change tempi are two forms of tempo alteration. Neither allows for **instantaneous changes of tempi without preparation.**

Metric Modulation answers that need and provides a method of binding totally **unrelated tempi with precision. Metric Modulation uses a part of a unit of pulse from a previous tempo to create a new tempo.** The conductor must be able to mentally extract a part of an established pulse and physically beat the extraction as the **new** unit of propulsion.

Metric Modulation Exercises

The boxed areas indicate the value of the old tempo to the new. In ex. 86, three sixteenths equal the new quarter. In ex. 87, two parts of a triplet equal the new quarter. In ex. 88, two sixteenths of a quintuplet equal the new quarter, and in ex. 89, three eighths equal the new half note. In the first three examples the tempo **increases,** in the final example the tempo **decreases.** Practice each of the following examples in varying tempi, starting with the quarter note at 60 and increasing the speed to a maximum of quarter note equals circa 148.

Ex. 86

Ex. 87

Ex. 88

Ex. 89

Elliott Carter, *A Symphony for Three Orchestras*

Elliott Carter is a leading exponent of metric modulation. The short two-measure example, moving to the *piu mosso* triplets based on the preceding quintuplets, is typical of the rhythmic complexity of his writing. This score is well worth investigating because of the clear-headed musical application of metric modulation.

Measures 132-133, third orchestra, violins 1, 4, 7.

Ex. 90

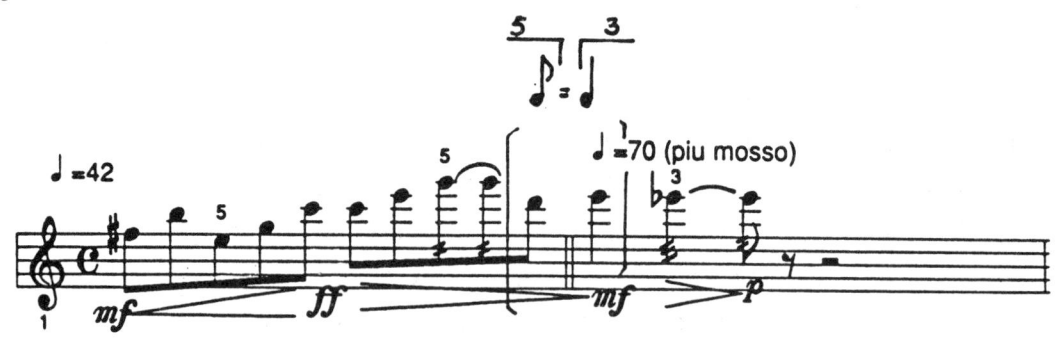

"Reprinted by Permission of ASSOCIATED MUSIC PUBLISHERS, INC. (BMI)"

Charles Wuorinen, *A Reliquary for Igor Stravinsky*

The example below is a beautifully prepared metric modulation. The lengthening *piano* sonorities, after a series of *forte* quarter note chords, almost brings the tempo to a halt, making the next event, the solo flute entrance in a metrically modulated unrelated quicker tempo, fresh and invigorating.

Mid-measure No. 180

Ex. 91

© 1978 Used by permission of C.F. PETERS CORPORATION

Beethoven, *Leonore Overture No. 3,* four measures before the *Presto*

Abrupt, unrelated tempo changes were written well before Metric Modulation became a reality in the twentieth century. Imagine Beethoven bringing a newly composed work containing an unprepared tempo change (like ex. 92) to the first orchestral rehearsal. The results must have been chaotic! In Beethoven's time, the solution to unrelated tempo changes was undoubtedly to rehearse and rehearse until the orchestra became familiar with the music.

Ex. 92

[musical example: allegro, ♩=126 ... presto, ♩=168, strings pp, cresc. poco a poco]

Technical solutions are available.

When a tempo has been established, as is the case of *Leonore Overture No. 3*, the following is possible: in the measure before the *Presto* the conductor's second stroke can be *delayed* while the orchestra continues to play in the **old** tempo for one beat. The slight delay allows the conductor to make a clear upward 'click' preparation **in the *Presto* tempo** without disturbing the old tempo. **The arrival of the conductor's downbeat after the delayed second stroke is precisely where it would ordinarily be both if strokes in the measure were equal in time.**

This excerpt is an excellent exercise for hand and ear coordination. Start three measures before the *Presto*, slowly at first, half note circa 72, and gradually increase the tempo to 120 per half note. (Sing the string line or play it on the piano with the left hand and beat the tempo with the right hand.) Do not move the wrist for the second stroke in the measure before the *Presto* until the E-natural. The wrist moves *after* the E and the delayed upward movement is the preparation for the new tempo.

Beethoven, *Fifth Symphony*, Second Movement, six measures before the *Piu moto*

The same principle applies to the following excerpt. In the measure before the *Piu moto*, initiate the third beat with a clear second beat 'click' in the rest. Delay the third beat until it has the value of the preparation for the *Piu Moto*. In this instance the baton makes the upstroke in the middle or latter part of the third beat triplet.

Ex. 93

[musical example: ♪=92 ... Più moto ♪=116, pp, stacc.]

Moving from an established tempo back to a **previous** tempo is far less difficult than moving to a completely new tempo. The orchestra's memory of the old tempo simplifies the transition. Ex. 94 is easily accomplished without preparation if measure 5 has a decisively 'clicked' downbeat stroke. The orchestra will know the tempo beforehand and will be waiting for a secure downbeat stroke to make the change.

Ex. 94 Beethoven, *Fourth Symphony*, Scherzo

CHAPTER TWENTY-FOUR SUMMARY

Composers make tempo modifications by moving toward and away from an established tempo or to an entirely new tempo. The conductor's use of *accelerandi* and *ritardandi* must be natural and unforced.

An important element in moving from one tempo to another is creating and listening to the progress of the **momentum** of the music. The shift in tempo cannot be accomplished if the beginning of the tempo transition, the momentum toward the new tempo is not clearly established.

If the conductor moves toward a new tempo with momentum clearly established, the orchestra will 'carry' the conductor to the arrival point of the new tempo in a smooth and musical transition. If the conductor does not establish momentum and moves ahead of the orchestra, the result will be a scramble as the orchestra tries to catch up to the conductor's abrupt and unprepared leap toward the new tempo.

Metric Modulation, in use since the mid-twentieth century, provides the composer with a mathematical tool to make abrupt, unrelated tempo changes smoothly and musically. Metric Modulation uses a **part of a unit of pulse from a previous tempo to create a new tempo.** The conductor must be rhythmically precise in moving from unit to unit, or the tempo change will not work. Exercises and examples have been given.

Well before Metric Modulation was a reality, composers wrote unprepared tempo shifts. Beethoven provides three excellent examples. Other than constant repetition to acclimate the orchestra to the unexpected tempi, the conductor can employ technical solutions for unexpected tempo changes.

Examples and technical solutions are offered.

CHAPTER TWENTY-FIVE

ACCOMPANIMENTS--INSTRUMENTAL

Accompanying a Soloist

An additional set of working principles is required when the conductor becomes an accompanist. The podium occupant still listens and reacts, but the technical process can be, and often is, different.

The Soloist

Arrange a private meeting with the soloist prior to the first rehearsal and play or sing through the orchestral accompaniment. Note the soloist's needs: time for an extra breath, a difficult string shift, a cascade of notes or *rubati*. Whether the conductor agrees with the soloist's interpretation or not, every effort must be made to support the soloist's musical vision; it is a collaboration geared to achieve the loftiest musical level possible. Know every note of the instrumental soloist's part and all the vocal soloist's words. That knowledge is the conductor's only protection when the unforeseen happens, and rest assured, at some time, somewhere, the unforeseen will happen.

Orchestral Balance

On stage an immediate consideration is orchestral balance; the soloist must be heard. Often the score is simply a dynamic guide and can be adjusted to the qualities the soloist brings to the music. A thorough understanding of orchestration will help the conductor make knowledgeable decisions. The conductor must listen and decide upon the best level of orchestral support since instruments and voices vary in different performing spaces. An Assistant Conductor, sitting in the hall and listening carefully can be a valuable asset and should be utilized.

Rests

The chapter on rests should be reread since much of the technique for successful accompanying lies in the conductor's ability to start an orchestra after a rest or a series of rests. As previously noted, rests before the actual preparation are 'marked' and the preparatory stroke must be clear and well articulated. If the total number of rests is spread over three to six measures it is best to 'mark' the downbeat of every measure. If the orchestra rests for six or more measures they should be told that the measures will not be beaten, and the conductor must indicate precisely where the beating will resume; "two bars before letter H," or "one full bar on the trill at the end of the cadenza." It is always wise to use the left hand to alert the orchestra for the resumption of tempo.

Soloist/Conductor Partnership

The partnership of soloist and conductor is one of trust. Soloists depend on conductors to follow their particular needs and the conductor relies on soloists to perform (more or less) as rehearsed. However, soloists are not machines and on occasion the conductor's job becomes, shall we say, exciting? Soloists have been known to jump or miss a series of measures leaving the conductor in musical limbo. It is easy for the conductor to jump with the soloist, but can an entire orchestra make the leap as well? Probably not, unless the orchestra is experienced, the repertoire very well known and often performed. There are three options available to the conductor, none of them less than chaotic:

1. **Continue to beat patterns in tempo** with the right hand and signal the soloist with the left hand. You may be certain that the soloist is fully aware that all is not well. Once contact is established wait for the soloist to adjust. Of the solutions available, this is clearly the best. Classical improvisation in the concert hall is not a dead art as some claim; when needed, soloists can improvise.

2. If the soloist does not respond, hold the left hand up while **the right hands maintains pulse, *but not pattern*.** The orchestra knows there is a problem and looks to the podium for help. The conductor should discreetly call a number/letter, or an obvious musical event and make a decisive downstroke. If necessary, this downstroke may be made with both hands, mirroring, so that both orchestra and soloist are aware of the need for an arrival point. In a musical emergency use all necessary techniques, even the bad ones!

3. The least desirable solution and the one to be avoided if at all possible is to stop the orchestra and begin again. A few seconds of unorganized chaos, option 1 or 2, is preferable to a complete stop.

Instrumental Soloists

Technical realities often intrude on musical aims. The Chopin *Piano Concertos* abound in measures that challenge the dexterity of the soloist. The following examples can be, and often are, played within an ongoing pulse; the soloist making the necessary rhythmic adjustments in the right hand. If, however, the soloist decides to treat the measures as quasi-cadenzas, as sometimes happens, the result is a suspension of predictable pulse. What should the conductor do? **Listen and look!** Here are two choices:

1. Listen to and follow the **treble clef** series of notes and catch the key pitch in the right place, F double sharp on the third beat in ex. 95, or the downbeat in the second measure of ex. 96.

2. Listen to the **bass line. Watch** the performers left hand through the measure. In the majority of cases the performer's right and left hand will arrive simultaneously at harmonic changes. **The eye helps the ear,** so the conductor should **arrange the placement of the podium** with a clear view of the movement of the soloist's left hand. As a supplement to knowing the soloist's music, the conductor should have visual contact with the performer.

The conductor should also be in a position to clearly view the bow arm of string soloists and watch singers and wind soloists for breaths at beginnings and endings of phrases.

Chopin, *Piano Concerto in E Minor*, Romance, measure No. 94

In ex. 95 the harmonic movement from the G-sharp major chord to the D-sharp seventh is clearly outlined in the left hand, as is the movement from the D-sharp seventh to the second measure barline G-sharp major chord in ex. 96.

Ex. 95

Larghetto, quarter equals 80

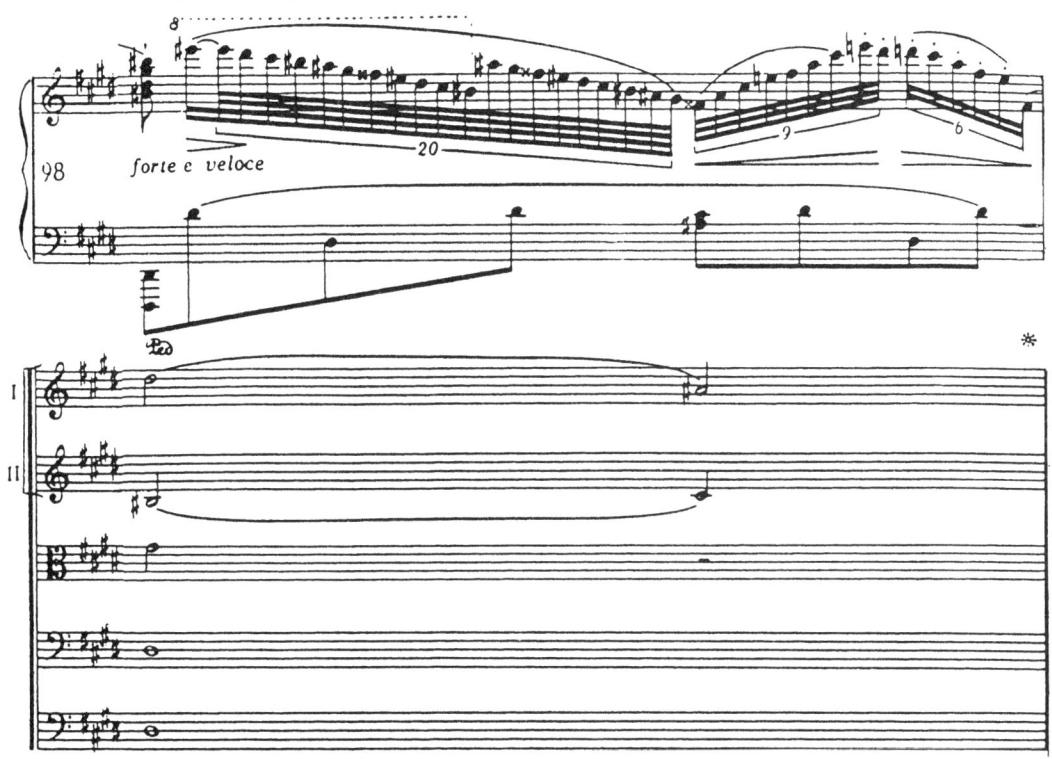

Ex. 96, (Romance), measures 98, 99

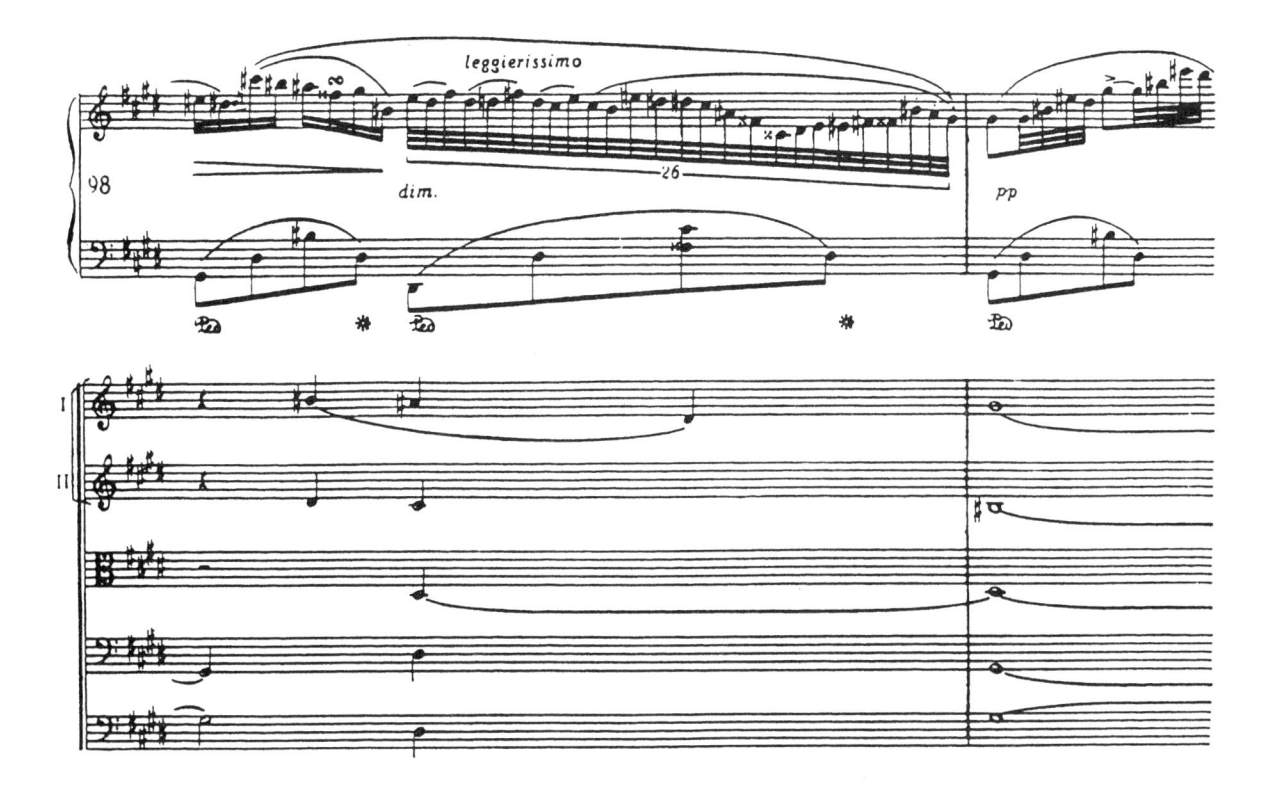

Conclusions of Cadenzas

A key point in any accompaniment is the resumption of tempo after a cadenza. **Does the conductor *follow* the soloist or does the conductor *lead* the soloist?** Both solutions are necessary. In most cases the score makes it clear who follows whom, but if there is any confusion, the soloist and conductor must decide their strategies **before** the performance.

Mendelssohn, *Violin Concerto*, First Movement, end of cadenza and orchestral reentry

In the Mendelssohn *Violin Concerto* (ex. 97), the score is very clear. The composer provides the soloist with written material for an exact in-tempo reentry of the orchestra after the cadenza, so the conductor follows the soloist. With a prearranged signal, usually by the left hand, the conductor alerts the orchestra two or three full measures **before** the orchestra plays. The right hand 'marks' these measures and then makes a larger active wrist 'click' on the downbeat of the measure with the *pianissimo* woodwind and first violin entrance. The right hand should be at E level, in zone 1, Fr.

Allegro Molto Appasionato
Ex. 97-end of cadenza

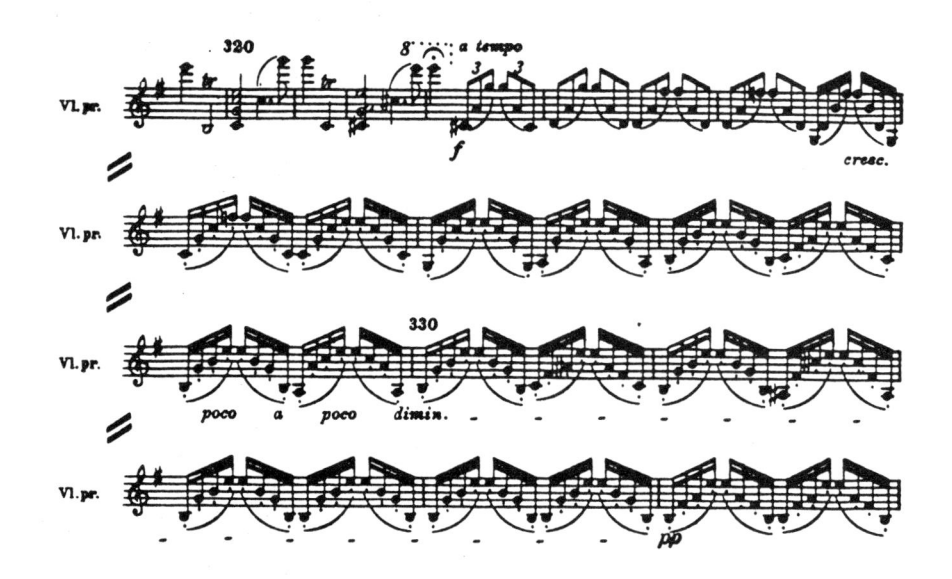

Ex. 97 continued, orchestral reentry

Beethoven, *First Piano Concerto,* end of last movement cadenza and orchestral reentry

The hold at the end of the cadenza in the last movement of Beethoven's *First Piano Concerto* allows the conductor to start the orchestra from silence. In this instance the soloist **follows** the conductor as the tempo resumes. (In performance the length of the hold preceding the tempo is mutually felt if the shaping of the sixteenth note figures immediately before the hold are well articulated by the soloist.)

Allegro Con Brio (Orchestra holds a C major chord)
Ex. 98-end of cadenza

Ex. 98, continued, orchestral reentry

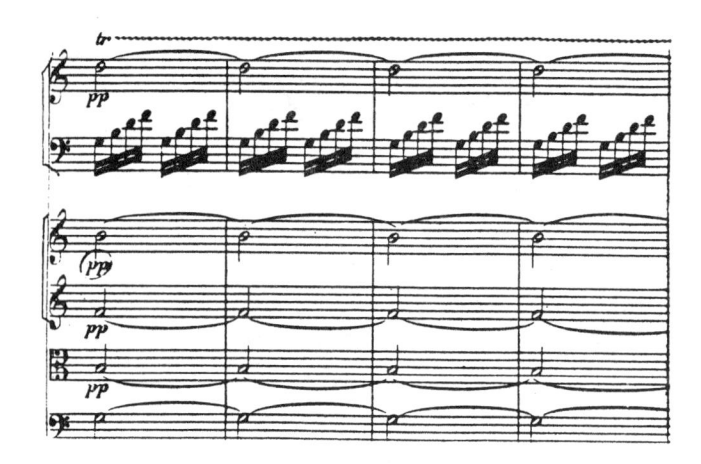

Beethoven *Third Piano Concerto*, end of last movement cadenza and orchestral reentry

Ex. 99 is another instance when the soloist **follows** the conductor at a crucial point in the music, the *Presto*. After the hold has been fulfilled on the G-natural, **the conductor must give an in-tempo (*Presto*) upbeat to the soloist for the cut-off of the *fermata* and a strong downbeat for the resumption of tempo.**

Even though the soloist is the only one playing in the first measure of the *Presto*, the conductor cannot follow the soloist because there is little or no chance to **prepare** the strings for the new tempo. A passive beat 1 of the *Presto*, waiting for the soloist to set the tempo, means the orchestra entrance will suffer due to lack of preparation. The conductor must lead the soloist.

Ex. 99

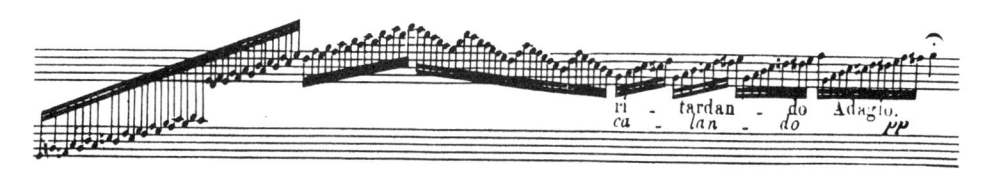

Beethoven, *Fourth Piano Concerto,* end of last movement cadenza and orchestral reentry

The *Presto* in Ex. 100 is a new tempo, and the conductor is responsible for its initiation. After the held D-natural trill, once again the conductor must **lead** the soloist into the *Presto*. The orchestra has the major material and the conductor's attention will be focused on the string entrances. The pianist will have no difficulty following the conductor's lead. The *Presto* is conducted with one beat per measure. The preparatory stroke must be small for the *pianissimo*, and made with an upward wrist 'click,' in zone 2, at the E level.

Ex. 100

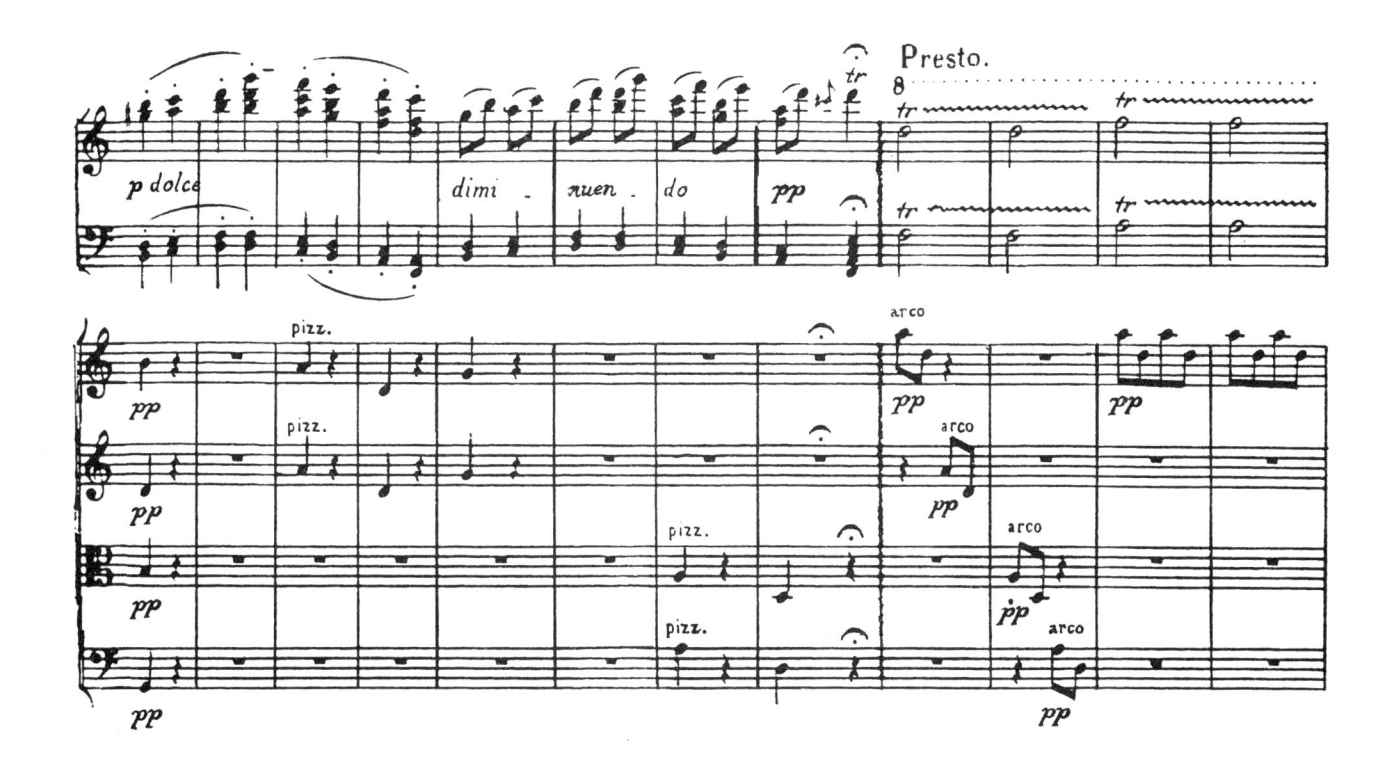

CHAPTER TWENTY-FIVE SUMMARY

The collaboration between soloist and conductor is geared to achieve the highest musical level. Working with a soloist or soloists requires an additional set of tools for the conductor. Listening habits have to be expanded and technical resources may have to be stretched.

The conductor must know every note in an instrumental soloist's part and every word of the singer's text. It is advisable to have a private meeting with solo performers prior to rehearsals so that musical differences, if they exist, can be discussed and resolved. The conductor must assist the soloist when special needs are required for technical or personal reasons. The balance between soloist and orchestra is the conductor's responsibility -- the soloist must be heard. Conductors should **use their eyes as well as their ears.** It is important for the conductor to be able to see vocal and wind soloists for breaths at beginnings and ends of phrases, and the bottom registers of the keyboard in piano concerti.

Specific accompanying techniques have been discussed for: soloists who jump or miss measures of music, and soloists who need extra time to complete technically demanding music.

Examples of conclusions of instrumental cadenzas and the resumption of tempi have been examined.

CHAPTER TWENTY-SIX

ACCOMPANIMENTS--VOCAL

RECITATIVE

A *recitative* is usually written for one voice at a time. The vocal line closely follows the natural rhythmic pattern of speech and is not bound by a regular pulse. Two basic forms of *recitative* are accompanied or *secco*.

Accompanied *recitative* (*recitativo accompagnato*, also *stromentato*) uses instrumental forces to support the vocal line. *Secco* (dry) *recitative,* originally known as *recitativo semplice*, uses a continuo as accompaniment, usually a harpsichord or organ. In accompanied *recitative* the conductor must know the musical line and every **syllable** of the text. More importantly, conductors need to identify the syllables that generate orchestral attacks or initiate harmonic changes.

A common problem in conducting vocal *recitative* arises because of **the suspension of the regularity of the pulse** due to the musical freedom required by the soloist.

During a *recitative* the **time between pulses/beats must be elongated.** The result is a suspension of predictable baton movement. If the conductor's baton stroke maintains its previous speed during an **elongated** pulse, it will have to **stop moving** before the soloist has completed the text in the *recitative.* The baton will be frozen; motionless and useless. A high placement of the inert baton leaves the conductor at a technical disadvantage because an even higher **extra preparatory stroke** must be made for the orchestra's next entrance.

Solutions

- If a *recitative* is not very long:

  Keep the baton in motion throughout the *recitative* by **slowing the speed of the** baton stroke in the elongated pulse/beat. **Near or at the conclusion of the** *recitative,* **'click' or 'flick' the wrist on the appropriate word or syllable and move the baton quickly into the next stroke.** The wrist movement within the moving stroke serves as the preparation for the orchestra's entrance. With this technique the conductor fills the beat, allows the soloist to interpret the text, and includes the necessary preparation for the next beat.

- If a *recitative* is very long:

  When a soloist decides to showcase his/her extraordinary gift with musical ornaments and dazzling vocal displays, **disregard the advice that has just been offered.** The conductor is no longer directing a short recitative and can treat the soloist's efforts as a *quasi-cadenza*. Use a pencil and simply add a *fermata* over the text, wait, and 'click' or 'flick' at the appropriate moment and resume tempo.

- If a *recitative* is neither long nor short:

  The baton should be held motionless at or near the W (waist) level, waiting to move into the next beat on the appropriate word/syllable.

Handel, *Messiah*

Every orchestral entrance must be preceded by a firm preparatory stroke from the conductor, on or before key words in the text. **The beats on which these key words occur should be memorized by the conductor or clearly marked in the score.** The two examples of accompanied *recitative* that follow are typical of Handel's style.

Sing and conduct each of the *recitatives* and vary the pace and delivery of the text. If possible, solicit the help of a singer or an instrumentalist to play through the solo vocal lines of the *recitatives*. They should be performed with the utmost freedom.

Conduct each of the examples in zone 2 or 3, at MC or UC level. It is essential that the orchestra see the baton at all times, so keep it in front of the center of the body unless a specific cue has to be directed toward a player or section. Use sharp 'clicks' for all preparatory strokes. The text will dictate which part of the conducting arm, the wrist or the forearm, is used when the 'clicks' are made.

Handel, *Messiah,* from no. 5, "Thus Saith The Lord"

Ex. 101

All beats are to be conducted in measure 2, but the first 3 beats are 'marked.' The fourth beat, the word *"come"* receives an active upward preparatory 'click' for the downbeat in measure 3. The downbeat, on the syllable *"tem*-(ple)" receives a downward 'click' that generates the orchestral punctuation after the first beat. In measure 4, make a preparatory 'click' on beat 2, on the word *"of,"* for the chord on beat 3. Make an upward 'click' on beat 4 for the downbeat in measure 5. In the fifth measure, 'click' on the syllable *"de*-(light)" on the third beat for the orchestral entrance after the third beat. In measure 6 'mark' the second and third beats and be prepared to **elongate** beat 4. **Remember to keep the baton in motion!** Make the downbeat in measure 7 on the word *"come."* In measure 8 place a *fermata* on beat 1, and wait for all the words. After the word *"Hosts,"* move on to beat 2 and prepare the final chords on beats 3 and 4.

Ex. 102

Handel, *Messiah,* no. 47, "Behold, I tell you a mystery"

'Mark' the first measure. Conduct a four beat pattern in measure 2, and add a 'click' on beat 2, the word *"you,"* for the change of harmony on beat 3. 'Mark' measure 3, and 'click' a preparation for the harmonic change in measure 4 on the word *"all."* **Keep the baton in motion** and allow the soloist complete freedom in the first four measures. In measures 5 and 6, the conductor might suggest to the soloist that the tempo remain steady for the sake of the effect of the sixteenth note exchange between soloist and ensemble. (If the soloist is not amenable, the conductor does have control of the ensemble and can articulate the sixteenth note figures as cohesive rhythmic units.) In measure 5 'click' on the syllable *"mo-*(ment)," and in measure 6 'click' on the word *"eye."* In measure 7 the conductor should be prepared for an **elongated second beat.** On the syllable *"trum-*(pet)" the forearm should move strongly into beat 3 to complete the *recitative.*

A conductor is expected to bring ideas and concepts about the meaning and pacing of the libretto, but at the same time she/he must be willing to partner contradictory views. The pacing of the words, thus the basic tempi, will vary considerably from interpretation to interpretation, as will the techniques employed by the baton.

Mozart, *Cosi Fan Tutti*, Scene 9, Recitative, Dorabella

Mozart's music and Lorenzo da Ponte's libretto provide the clues to the emotional state of Dorabella. Because her heightened feelings are open to an infinite number of interpretations, the conductor should be prepared to wield a flexible and quick baton.

Ex. 103

Measures 24 and 25 are conducted in four. Make a *forte* preparation in zone 3, E level for the first beat of measure 24, on the syllable *sco* - (sta-ti). Make a *piano* wrist 'click' preparation in zone 1, UC level on the first beat of measure 25, on the syllable *"fet-*(to)."

Measures 26, 28 and 32 is the *Allegro assai* for the orchestra, usually beaten in a moderate two. It can be conducted by the left hand with an upward, MC to E level, outward, zone 2 to 3 and a return, curved stroke on SL.

Measures 27, 29 and 31. Three measures remain in a modified, slower two, or can be beaten in a moving four, depending on Dorabella's delivery of the text.

Measure 27. The third beat must be clearly articulated by the conductor. A wrist 'click' in zone 3, E level, on the syllable *"lu-*(ce)" will generate the orchestra entrance.

Measure 28 is the same as above. The third beat must be clearly articulated, on the syllable *"spi-*(ro)."

Measure 30. After the downbeat, treat the rest of the measure as preparation for the quicker orchestral tempo. Let Dorabella complete her text and make an upward 'click' preparation for the tempo in measure 31.

Measure 35 is traditionally conducted in a slower four, while the pick-up to measure 34 is used to make the tempo transition. The pick-up to measure 34 is *piano* and should begin in zone 1. Register downward from UC to above W level. The *Maestoso* in Measure 41 is conducted in a broader four, with a sharp 'click' on the first beat and *legato* strokes for the second and third beats.

Measure 36 needs a decisive *piano* stroke in zone 3, MC level on the first beat to generate an accurate orchestral response.

Measures 41 and 42 require an **elongated** fourth beat in both measures. 'Click' on the downbeat in both measures, as well as on the downbeat in measure 43.

Measures 43 and 44 allow the singer a chance to display a high note. There are two ways to treat these measures:

1. On the high note, **move the baton through the measure to the beat before the concluding note of the singer's phrase.** In this instance Dorabella's high note is on beat 4 in measure 43, and the phrase finishes on beat 3 in measure 44. The conductor quickly moves the baton, **out of tempo,** from beat 4 in measure 43 (on the high G-natural) to beat 2 in measure 44, treating beat 2 as though it had a hold. The second beat is held to allow Dorabella to sustain the G and deliver the remainder of the text. On the syllable *"pie,"* the second half of beat 2, move the baton to beat 3,*"-ta,"* and on to beat 4 to the end.

2. Place a hold on the G-natural, the syllable *"fug,"* on beat 4 of measure 43. Follow the text as it unfolds, perhaps with a small subdivision on the syllables *"gi," "per," "pie,"* if the tempo slows down **considerably,** to beat 3 in measure 44.

Measure 45. Follow the vocal line and 'mark' the first two beats in the measure. 'Click' a full quarter note fourth beat preparation on beat three and hold the downbeat of measure 46 for a **full** half note!

CHAPTER TWENTY-SIX SUMMARY

There are two basic groups of *recitative:* the accompanied *recitative* with instruments, and the *secco* or 'dry' *recitative* with continuo. *Recitatives* allow singers interpretive freedom which may create problems in singer-orchestra interaction. During a *recitative,* a word, a phrase or a high note can be stretched and the conductor must manage with a lengthened, or ***elongated pulse/beat.*** Often the conductor makes a normal in-tempo stroke and then has to stop the motion of the baton and wait for the soloist to fulfill the text. The solution for the elongated beat is to **keep the stroke in motion by slowing down the speed of the baton.** Slowing the motion of the baton gives the soloist time to interpret the text, fills the beat, and allows the conductor to provide a preparation for the next beat.

The importance of knowing all the syllables of all the words when accompanying a vocal soloist cannot be overstated. Two examples of *recitative* from Handel's *Messiah* have been provided, as well as one of Dorabella's *recitatives* from Mozart's *Cosi Fan Tutti*. Techniques have been discussed for initiating orchestral entrances on specific words or syllables in each *recitative* as well as for the held high note toward the end of Dorabella's *recitative*. If the *recitative* is of moderate length, hold the baton at waist level and move to the next beat on the appropriate word or syllable. If the *recitative* is long, treat it as a normal hold.

CHAPTER TWENTY-SEVEN

SPEAKING TO AN ORCHESTRA

The conductor knows what she/he wants to hear from an orchestra, but what should an orchestra hear from a conductor? Very little! Note the following six points:

1. **Lack of preparation**. Unprepared conductors are a disgrace. They talk a lot. They are forced to waste everyone's time to cover their unpreparedness. When a conductor faces an orchestra, she/he must know the score!

2. **Technique**. Assuming the conductor knows the score and the conducting technique is exemplary there is little need for speech-making. If the technique is poor there will generally be huge amounts of conductorial verbiage.

3. **Prolonged Lecturing**. Many conductors teach and preach endlessly. A bit of both may be essential but a time line has to be drawn in rehearsals. See no. 6.

4. **Rehearsal time is precious.** All necessary musical information can be delivered by the baton. If special musical refinements are addressed verbally, instructions should be delivered in concise **musical** terms. Corrections should be made quickly and effectively. Do not pontificate.

5. **Important words. Most corrections can be made with six words:** faster, slower, louder, softer, shorter, longer. Omit abstract references -- "A Homeric colored dawn" (for a string sonority) "the inner rhythm of a Cubist painting" (for cross rhythms in winds, brass, percussion), or bland personal assertions -- "play like you are on a Sunday picnic with your family" (for a lively string and woodwind tune). None of the above time-wasting comments has absolute meaning for a diverse group of musicians.

6. **Be specific!** If a *string* sonority is not correct, try dynamics (less or more), bow placement (middle, tip or sul tasto), different fingerings (consult concertmaster), or change the character of the vibrato (less, more or non-vibrato). If you cannot achieve what you imagine, ask for help from the concertmaster. She/he will be more than willing to suggest a solution. If a solution is offered, try it, it will probably work. **The conductor must never forget that there are hundreds of cumulative years of experience on the stage.**

If **woodwind and brass** cross-rhythms are not clear, try section balances (more or less of each), lengths of notes (shorter or longer), and points of phrase completions, especially if they differ from section to section. Before beginning to work on the subtleties of balance and phrasing, be aware that musicians read baton strokes from different vantage points on the stage. When a variety of sounds emanate from different parts of the stage, the disparity in rhythmic articulation generally involves the point of attack. Players may be reading the baton correctly, but the sound may be speaking late in the low-register instruments, or perhaps a bit ahead in the high-register instruments. **Without rhythmic cohesion, balance and phrasing should not be attempted.** The conductor should address each of the section attacks separately. When the rhythmic foundation is sound and the performers have had a chance to hear what the other sections are playing, the conductor will discover that balances and phrases will emerge.

If the **percussion** sound is not correct ask for various sticks which can soften or sharpen the timbre, as well as the rhythm. Ask for a change of instrument if it is small enough to be carried on stage by hand like a snare drum, triangle, cymbals, wood blocks, maracas, tambourines, etc. Many instruments come in various sizes, generally from large to small, and each has a different color. Do not be afraid to ask percussion players for their suggestions. Unless the conductor is a specialist in percussion, the players will know more than the conductor about the sound and quality of their individual instruments.

General Advice

If the line or shape of the melody is incorrect, **explain what is lacking and offer precise solutions** (e.g. "play toward the top of the phrase in measure 6, sustain the B-natural, *diminuendo* on the G-sharp. Winds, breathe through the line, articulate with the strings in measure no. 42." If you cannot make yourself understood, **sing the line.** Do not worry about imperfect intonation. Toscanini sang out of tune but everyone on the stage understood the shape and movement he desired.

Address all points fully. If the orchestra is stopped for an intonation, pitch or rhythmic fault, correct the problem. **Do not proceed until it is done!** The orchestra expects the conductor to address the problem and correct it. A conductor who isolates a fault and then fails to provide a solution jeopardizes his or her authority with the orchestra. If a player is having severe difficulty with a part or intonation, address it off-stage and personally.

If an orchestral work is in the category of descriptive music, resist the temptation to explain the rationale of the work. Instead, secure copies of the program notes and put them on the players' stands. Don't waste time with an unnecessary lecture.

Rehearsal Order

Post a <u>rehearsal order before the first rehearsal</u>, and if at all possible stick to it. The options are clear. Either start with the largest number of players and let them go early, or start with the fewest number of players and call the rest of the orchestra at a specific time.

If sectionals are called, consider the time needed for the particular rehearsal. Make sure there is enough time allotted to clear up the problems that prompted a sectional.

Before the rehearsal begins

Know the music!

When the rehearsal begins

Greet the orchestra, get to work, be positive, control the verbiage. Let the baton do the talking!

Bowings—Supplying the Music—Building a Library

Complete sets of parts for most of the basic repertoire can be purchased without difficulty, and many conductors carry their own parts. Everything can be carefully marked before the first rehearsal: extra rehearsal numbers, additional dynamics for all sections of the orchestra, bowings for strings, breath marks for woodwinds, mallet indications for the percussion, etc.

Building a personal library of clearly marked parts **saves precious rehearsal time.** There is one drawback. Almost every string section has strengths and weaknesses as well as a tradition. The concertmaster, or leader, bows accordingly and in some circumstances the visiting conductor's bowings may not fit the character or style of the orchestra. If such a situation arises, do not argue and do not hesitate. **Change the bowings to conform to the best qualities of the orchestra's string section.** If the conductor insists on using a bowing which the strings resist, she/he risks losing the good will of the players.

If the Conductor is not a String Player

When a bowing doesn't work, ask for help. Listen to the leaders of each string section, they are more than willing to offer solutions. Remember, bowings that work for a string section in one orchestra may not work for a string section in a different orchestra.

When **more than one bowing is offered,** listen carefully and choose. If there is a subtlety that is not clear, ask to hear the bowing again. After a second hearing, make a decision quickly. **Section leaders may differ** on the merits of a bowing. If there is a real debate ask the concertmaster to make the decision. His or her word in such matters is final.

Know and understand the mechanics of producing sound on a string instrument before standing in front of a string body. Befriend a string player and ask about the placement and parts of the bow, kinds of bow strokes, bow pressure, how much hair to use, etc. Ask about the left hand, kinds of vibrato, and color production in combination with the bow. There is a real connection between the bow and the baton. **Very often baton strokes resemble bow strokes and can elicit the same sounds from a string ensemble.**

If at all possible learn how to play a string instrument. Learn the positions and fingerings for scales. It is not necessary to become a virtuoso, but the experience of holding a bow and successfully moving it across the strings helps produce coherent musical sounds.

The Negative Face

It is easy for some and difficult for others, **but conductors must learn to control negative emotions when they are conducting.**

We know that musicians help conductors in many ways. Rarely does an orchestra fail to live up to the demands of the music and its own personal, professional standards. However, orchestral musicians working in a stressful profession make mistakes. Conductors who think otherwise are unrealistic. Players do not play wrong pitches on purpose, crack notes to irritate the conductor or willfully miss entrances to destroy a performance. When a glaring mistake occurs the player is fully aware of what has happened. No one feels worse.

What is **not** needed is a look of disbelief, horror, or contempt from the podium. Screwing one's face into a mask of pain and scowling at the culprit will prolong an unhappy moment and almost certainly risk losing the respect of the orchestra.

The conductor is responsible for maintaining the musical integrity of the orchestra and cannot overlook consistently poor, or faulty playing. The proper place to address such a problem is either **in a rehearsal, or off the stage, but not during a performance.** Remember that all conductors, the greatest and the least gifted pretenders, make mistakes. How could we not? We are human and subject to the same performing pressures as the musicians sitting in front of us.

Every performance is a struggle for the unattainable and the journey cannot be made alone. The extent of the help conductors receive will depend on their sense of humanity and the recognition that few musical journeys are error-free. The wise conductor learns to come to terms with reality.

CHAPTER TWENTY-SEVEN SUMMARY

The social and day-to-day skills needed when a score is ready to be rehearsed and performed are many. This is an important chapter. Please re-read it carefully.

CHAPTER TWENTY-EIGHT

REPERTOIRE

Two paragraphs that appeared in chapter twelve should be reviewed before moving into the repertoire section.

Is there a Correct Physical Response to a Musical Problem?

All that follows must be viewed in the context of this question. A single "correct" musical/ physical solution to a musical problem **does not exist.** The very thought that any measure of music must be performed in a preordained "correct" manner robs music of one of its great attributes -- **allowing the same succession of sounds to speak differently to different people.** It is a given that any two conductors confronted with the same musical problems will view them differently and devise distinct musical, thus physical solutions. Even conductors who could agree fully on the musical meaning of a score would produce dissimilar results because of their individual motor and muscular skills and unique body structures. While all conductors have some technical limitations when compared to a mythic super-conductor, **every** conductor **is** capable of a wide variety of baton/arm strokes. The task of the conductor is to: 1) discover and profitably use the strokes that come naturally and work well for his or her body, and 2) add a variety of learned strokes to create a technical vocabulary that can cope with the needs of the composer. **Music may start in the composer's imagination, but it is delivered by the conductor via physical means.**

Conductors must think of stroke choices just as string players think of bowing possibilities, there are generally several solutions for most problems. **In theory any baton stroke can be used for any solution, so ALL strokes may be 'correct.'** But in practice, the 'correctness' of the stroke depends on who chooses what stroke and when, and how and to what effect it is used.

The PatternCubes

The PatternCubes attached to the repertoire section are workable solutions for musical problems in the score. **It must be stressed that the choices presented in the PatternCubes are single solutions from among many possibilities.** The PatternCubes are to be used as <u>guides</u>. Conductors should retain and refine the solutions which fulfill their musical concepts and match their physical means. However if a particular PatternCube seems physically and musically counterproductive, **do not hesitate to replace the PatternCube with a newly created original pattern design drawn from the music.**

Please review the contents of the PatternCube and the symbols outlined in chapters twelve through fifteen.

The Repertoire:

Magic Flute Overture - Mozart
Symphony No. 5 - Beethoven
Rite of Spring - Stravinsky

Excerpts from each of the works include complete **PatternCubes** as well as **Visual Score Study/Baton Placement** descriptions.

Ex. 104 Mozart, *Overture to the Magic Flute*—Introduction

This excerpt appears regularly in conducting auditions.

The Introduction is often subdivided and conducted in eight. The rationale for subdividing the pulse is the *Adagio* marking, and the belief that subdivision makes it easier to play the sixteenth note pick-ups into measures two and three. The opening measures have inspired some esoteric solutions. Some conductors move the last sixteenth note in the measure to the beginning of the next measure, forming two sixteenths on the downbeat. Others dictate each sixteenth note, slowly, without regard for the tempo they have chosen for the Introduction.

Mozart's *Adagio* is a cut-time signature, and *if* the conductor's stroke is firm and uncluttered, orchestral musicians are capable of placing a sixteenth note anywhere within a pulse, confirmed in exercises 3-20. Mozart's musical materials do not support the use of subdivided baton motions. The orchestration is clear, straightforward, and the movement of the color changes are immediate and evident. The rhythmic, harmonic, and melodic gestures are sparse eliminating the need for a pace that moves slowly.

In the PatternCube the Introduction to the *Magic Flute* Overture is presented in a moderately paced four beats per measure.

Seating—The violins are seated opposite one another, the violas seated next to and inside the first violins to the left of the conductor, and the celli next to and inside the second violins to the right of the conductor. (Viola and celli placements often differed.) Bassi are behind the celli, and the winds are generally behind the strings and in front of the conductor. The brass instruments are behind the winds and the timpani, and percussion, as needed, near the trumpets.

Visual Score Study/Baton Placement

The tempo has been discussed above. Note the keys for the clarinets, horns, trumpets, and the addition of three trombones to the orchestra. (In the PatternCubes the trombones are seated in the rear of the orchestra, on the right side of the stage.)

Measures 1-3 -- The E-flat major chord is scored for the entire orchestra, a commanding sonority—use zone 3, FX, C level. To insure exact ensemble use a left hand cut-off before the hold. The *fermata* on the silent third beat indicates that beat four needs a sharp *fortissimo* 'click' in measures 1 and 2, and a *piano* 'click' in measure 3. (Performance Note -- Many conductors treat the half note chords on the down-beats in the first three measures as **holds,** eliminating the pulses. However, beating the first two pulses at the **beginning** of the measure to beat 3 removes tempo ambiguity where it is most needed, at the **end** of the measure.)

Conclude the sonority of the first two beats in the measure on beat 3. Do not try to make the cut-off just before the third beat and avoid orchestral accents on the cut-offs. Make the *fermata* after the cut-off on beat 3. Beat 4 begins from silence, so treat it exactly like an upbeat. The orchestra will have no trouble placing the sixteenth in the upbeat if the tempo from beat 4 to beat 1 is the same as the tempo established in beats 1 and 2.

Measures 4-7 --The four measures make two 2-bar phrases. The celli, bassi, and bassoon lines are *piano*, and conducted at the W level, SR, in zones 1 or 2. Note that the *sfp* marking for the chords is still within an overall *piano* dynamic. Use the left hand (OPU) for dynamic control if necessary.

Measures 8-11 -- Again two 2-measure phrases. Note the second violin E-flats. They fill the silences in measures 8 and 9 with an added *crescendo* in measure 9. The trombone chords in measures 9 and 11 must be carefully prepared on the downbeat with a *piano legato* wrist 'click'- zone 2 or 3, E level, SR.

Measures 12-15 -- In measures 13 and 14, check the balance between the horns, *sfp*, and the trombones, *mfp*. Fill measure 15 with full sounding quarter notes -- use *legato* strokes and add a 'click' on beat 4 to initiate the new tempo.

Measure 16 -- Moving to the *Allegro*, 4 eighth notes in the new tempo may equal the previous (*Introduction*) quarter note. The first beat is *piano* -- use a short *staccato* stroke from the wrist with no rebound - zone 2, W, SR. On the second beat make a short round stroke with a sharp rebound for the *forte* and the slur.

(Performance Note -- If the conductor prefers *not* to maintain the tempo relationship indicated above -- place a very slight hold on beat 4, and then add an additional preparatory 4th beat which will act as the upbeat to the new tempo of the *Allegro*.)

Fig. 138. **PatternCubes**

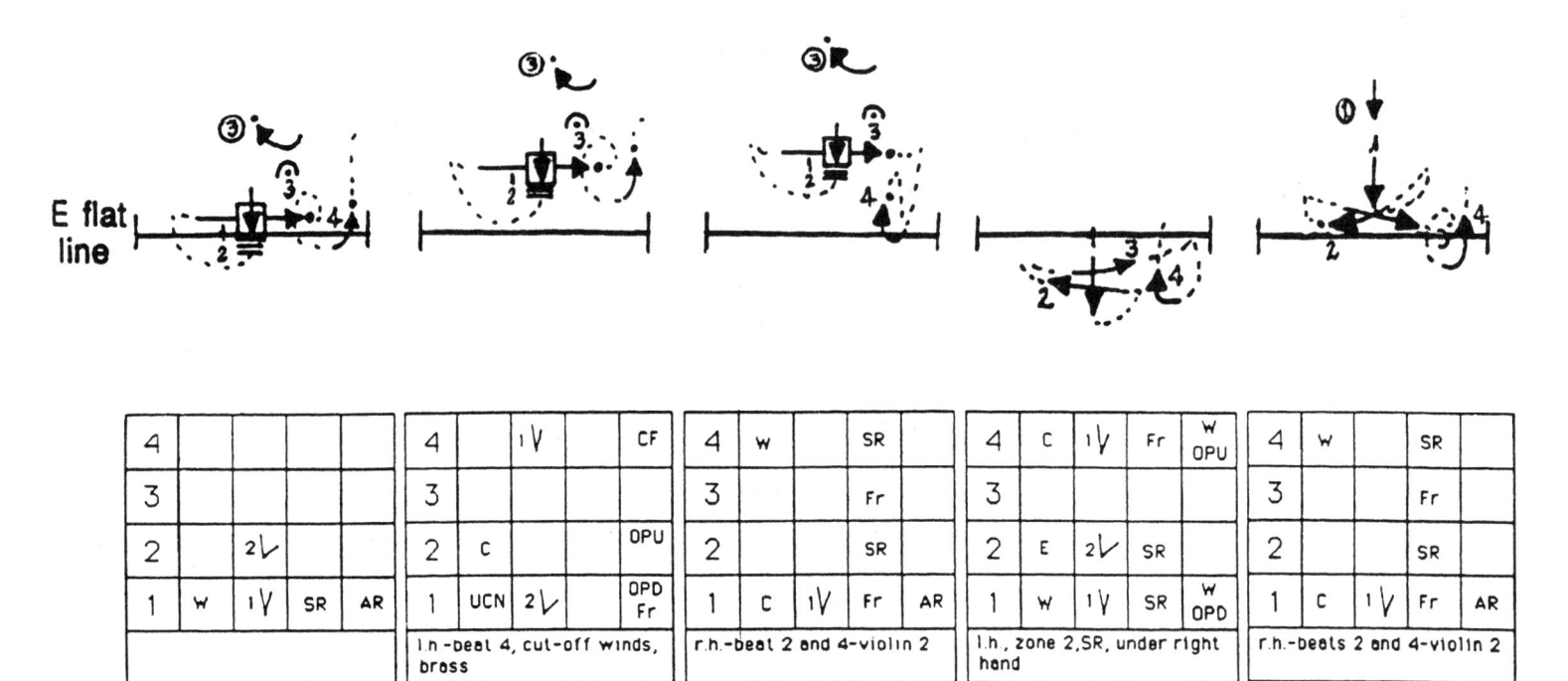

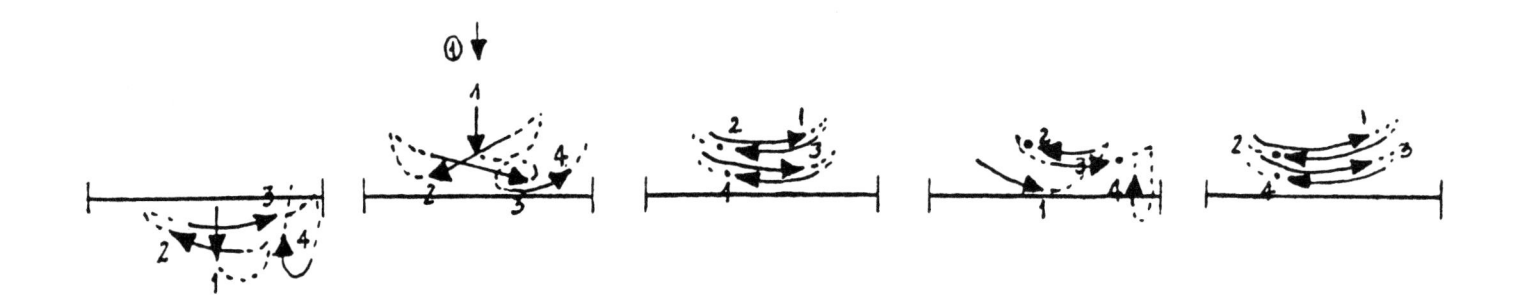

4	C	1V	Fr	W OPU
3				
2	E	2V	SR	
1	W	1V	SR	W OPD

l.h.-beats 1-4, zone 2, SR under right hand

4				
3			Fr	
2			SR	
1	C	1V	Fr	AR

r.h.-beats 2 and 4, violin 2

4	UCN	2V		E SR
3		1V		
2	C	2V		OPU Fr
1	UCN	1V	Fr	

l.h.- on and of beat 2, zone 1 beat 4, zone 2

4				
3	E	1V		OPU Fr
2	C	3FX		
1	UCN	2V	Fr	OPD SR

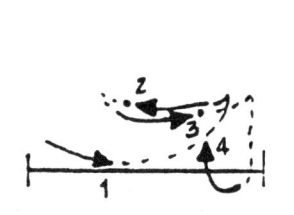

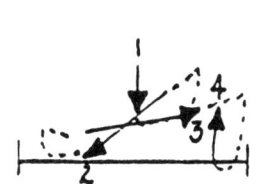

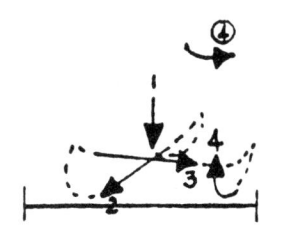

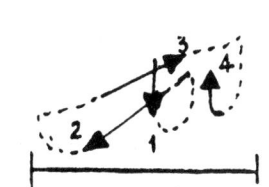

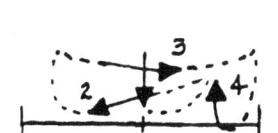

l.h.-beats 1,2-zone 2, beat 3-zone 1

4	C	2V	SR	
3	UCN	1V	Fr	
2	W	2V	SR	
1	C	1V	Fr	AR

r.h.-legato strokes

4			
3		2V	
2			
1	W	1V	SR

r.h.-short strokes, beat 2 sharp 'click', legato rebound

Ex. 105 Beethoven's *Fifth Symphony,* First Movement, measures 1-29

Fl.
p cresc. f
ff
Ob.
p cresc. f
ff
Cl.
p cresc. f
ff
Fag.
cresc. f
ff
Cor.
p cresc. f
ff
Tr.
p cresc. f
Tp.
p cresc. f
cresc.
f
ff
p
cresc.
f
ff
p
cresc.
f
ff
p
Basso p cresc. f
ff
p

The opening measures of this symphony have become an audition favorite.

In order to insure a clear orchestral attack, **THE UPBEAT** (in this case a complete measure) **MUST BE IN THE EXACT TEMPO OF THE OPENING MEASURE**

The treatment of the *fermati* poses a question the conductor must confront--whether or not to make a cut-off gesture after each *fermata*. If a cut-off is used the conductor must make a preparatory stroke to reengage the orchestra. The cut-off and preparatory stroke add a measure to Beethoven's structure. Proceeding immediately from the hold into the next measure without a cut-off gesture creates a natural cessation of orchestral sound and preserves the numerical structure of the music.

While the musical choice seems clear-cut, acoustics have to be considered. If the concert hall is overly resonant, the second violin *piano* entrance in measure six may not be heard after the *fortissimo* hold in measure five unless a cut-off gesture is employed to help clear the sound. The conductor must choose between the demands of the composer and the reality of the performing situation.

Seating. The PatternCube will be based on the seating Beethoven used in the Dec. 22, 1808 Vienna premiere. Seated to the left of the conductor will be the first violins, on the outside, the celli to the left of the first violins, and the bassi behind the celli. The second violins, on the outside and facing the first violins, and the violas to the right of the second violins, will sit to the right of the conductor. The winds in pairs will be in front of the conductor with the horns, trumpets and timpani behind the winds.

Visual Score Study/Baton Placement

Alongside *Allegro Con Brio* Beethoven provides a metronome marking (the half note equals 108) which is a clear indication that the movement should be conducted with one stroke per measure. Wrist 'clicks' on downbeats are the conductor's most important technical ally since the three eighth note motive units are preceded by an eighth note rest. Note the keys for the clarinets, horns and trumpets. The PatternCube contains one stroke per measure, presents two physical solutions for the opening measures, and does **not** employ cut-offs after the holds.

Preparatory Stroke, Measures 1-2

Note the scoring -- the entire string section plus the two clarinets. Remember the **GOLDEN RULE!** 'Click' a clear in-tempo preparatory stroke, and deliver the downbeat with a forceful 'click' at the conclusion of the stroke. *Do not alter the speed of the baton* between the preparatory stroke and the downstroke. Avoid the temptation of stopping the stroke at the high point and increasing the speed of the downstroke. Keep the stroke short and compact. If a vertical stroke is used, begin the stroke at C level, and move the forearm no higher than UCN level or just under E level. Connect to the tip of the baton!

Option: The PatternCube uses vertical strokes, beginning at C level, in zone 2, Fr, and includes registration. A very effective alternate stroke for the beginning of this movement is indicated below the PatternCube. It is also a stroke that begins at C level, in Zone 2, Fr, but it is a **horizontal** stroke instead of a vertical one. The stroke moves backwards and forwards rather than up and down. From the starting position 'flick' the baton backwards in a straight line towards the left shoulder. At the top of the stroke the elbow is in a V position. This movement to the V position serves as the preparation for the downbeat. From the V position thrust the arm straight out and forward towards the original starting position, adding a 'flick' at the end of the stroke. The return motion creates a very powerful downbeat. Do not alter the speed of the backward and forward motions. Either set of strokes will produce a rhythmically unified orchestral attack.

In the second measure maintain the hold for at least double the value of the half note.

Leaving the Hold in Measure 2

Repeat the vertical or horizontal preparatory stroke that was used to begin the movement. **Because there will be no cut-off gesture, the E-flat sonority will continue to sound throughout the preparatory stroke for the third measure.** The E-flats will cease only when the string players lift their bows and the clarinetists stop blowing air to account for the eighth note rest at the beginning of measure three.
If problems arise leaving a hold, the conductor must pay special attention to the 'click' in the preparatory stroke while the orchestra is producing sound. A very strongly articulated preparatory 'click' can sometimes inadvertently stop the sound *before* the arrival of the barline because the players 'read' the 'click' as a cut-off. The same kind of preparatory 'click' induces players to *jump ahead* to the next measure because they 'read' the 'click' as the next downbeat. If either event occurs, the conductor should *modify the strength and the size of the preparatory 'click.'*

The rest on the downbeat following the *fermata* in measure 3 makes a different kind of preparatory stroke possible.

During the *fermata* the baton hand resumes its preparatory motion by lifting the stroke upward, or moving it backwards, *without the benefit of the bottom 'click.'* This initial movement does not indicate the tempo! The following vertical downstroke 'click,' or horizontal forward 'click,' to the rest in measure three must show the tempo and be absolutely clear.

Measures 3-4-5-6

Many conductors place the hold on the fourth measure and eliminate the fifth measure. Move beyond the in-tempo fourth measure, and mark the fifth measure clearly while observing the *fermata*. The upward preparatory stroke, with a *piano* 'click' for the second violin entrance in measure six, should move to the right (SR) so the downstroke 'click' for measure six can be seen by the entire second violin section.
(Note: Measure 6 is not the beginning of a four-measure phrase. Measure 7 is the beginning of the first of three four-measure phrases. The bassoon and celli bass line confirms Beethoven's phrasing.)

Measures 7-8-9-10

Measures seven through ten are generally conducted with downward vertical strokes for each measure, a workable solution. However, Beethoven's four-bar phrase is better served if a normal four-beat pattern were employed for this grouping. *The across-the-body stroke, beat three in the pattern and measure 9 in the phrase, fits Beethoven's musical contour perfectly.* Measure 9 is the only measure *without* the three eighth note rhythmic unit, and should be conducted differently from the other three measures in the four-bar phrase. Wrist 'click' measures seven, eight, and ten. Do not 'click' the across-the-body stroke in measure nine. All baton motions should be small, *(piano)* rhythmically precise, and in Zone 1, possibly in Zone 2. Register as shown in the PatternCube.

Measures 11-12-13-14

Employ a four-beat pattern. Register as shown in the PatternCube and maintain rhythmic momentum.

Measures 15-16-17-18

Use 2 two-beat patterns for these four measures. Move the baton to the right for the second violins and violas in measures 16 through 18, and use the left hand (SL) in zone 2, for short 'click' cues in measures 16 and 18 for the first violins.

In measure 18 the right hand stroke moves to the left with a 'click,' out to zone 2, Fr, for the *crescendo* and the cue for the woodwinds, brass and timpani entrance. Continue to 'click' every barline that contains the three eighth note unit within the measure.

Measures 19-20-21

The three *forte* horizontal strokes shown in the PatternCube are made by the right hand moving from left to right in each of the measures. Please note that they are *forte*, not *fortissimo*. (In measure18 the right hand moved to the left, therefore positioning itself for the first left to right stroke to indicate the barline in measure 19.) These strokes are not short and do not have dots at the ends of the arrowheads in the PatternCube. Beethoven asks for full quarter note lengths on each of the barlines. In measure 21 maintain the held G-natural for at least double the value of the half note. Note the dotted rebound indications for the correct registration. In measure19 the rebound is backward and under the original stroke, in measure 20 backward and over the original stroke, and in measure 21 will move upwards after the hold.

Measure 22

Make a *fortissimo* 'click' for the upwards preparatory stroke and do not forget the GOLDEN RULE. This *fortissimo* preparation differs from the others because it is meant for every player on the stage with one exception -- the timpanist. (The hand tuned drums of the period are in the wrong key for this entrance.) The weight of this *fortissimo* sonority moves beyond the sonority level of the *fortes* in the previous measures. The upward preparatory stroke will move into zone 3, E level for the arrival of measure 22.

Measures 22-23-24

'Click' strong *fortissimo* downbeat strokes for measures 22 and 23. Use vertical downstrokes for each of these three measures. Make the hold <u>on measure 24</u>, not measure 23, and account for all the measures.

Measures 25-26-27-28

The right hand could conduct these four measures by remaining in Zone 3 and using *piano* wrist 'clicks' for all entrances. For the sake of diversity, the PatternCube indicates a two handed approach to these four measures, *dictated by the seating of the orchestra.*

Measure 25

Both hands 'click' a *piano* upbeat preparatory stroke, the right hand in zone 3, SR, the left hand in zone 2, SL for the first violin entrance. The <u>right hand</u> conducts measures 26 and 27 with two downward vertical strokes for the second violins and violas. The left hand is AR. The <u>left hand</u> assumes the primary time duties in measure 28 and conducts the celli and bassi with an upward stroke in zone 2, SL, and begins the next four bar phrase with a downward stroke for the first violins in measure 29. The right hand is AR for these two measures.

(Note that Beethoven changes the phrase structure after this hold. Unlike the second violin entrance in measure 6 which was *not* the beginning of a phrase, the first violin entrance in measure 25 *is* the beginning of a four-bar phrase which resolves to C minor in measure 29, and then immediately repeats itself. In this construction, every measure contains the three eighth note unit, unlike measures 7 through 10.)

Figure 139. **PatternCubes**

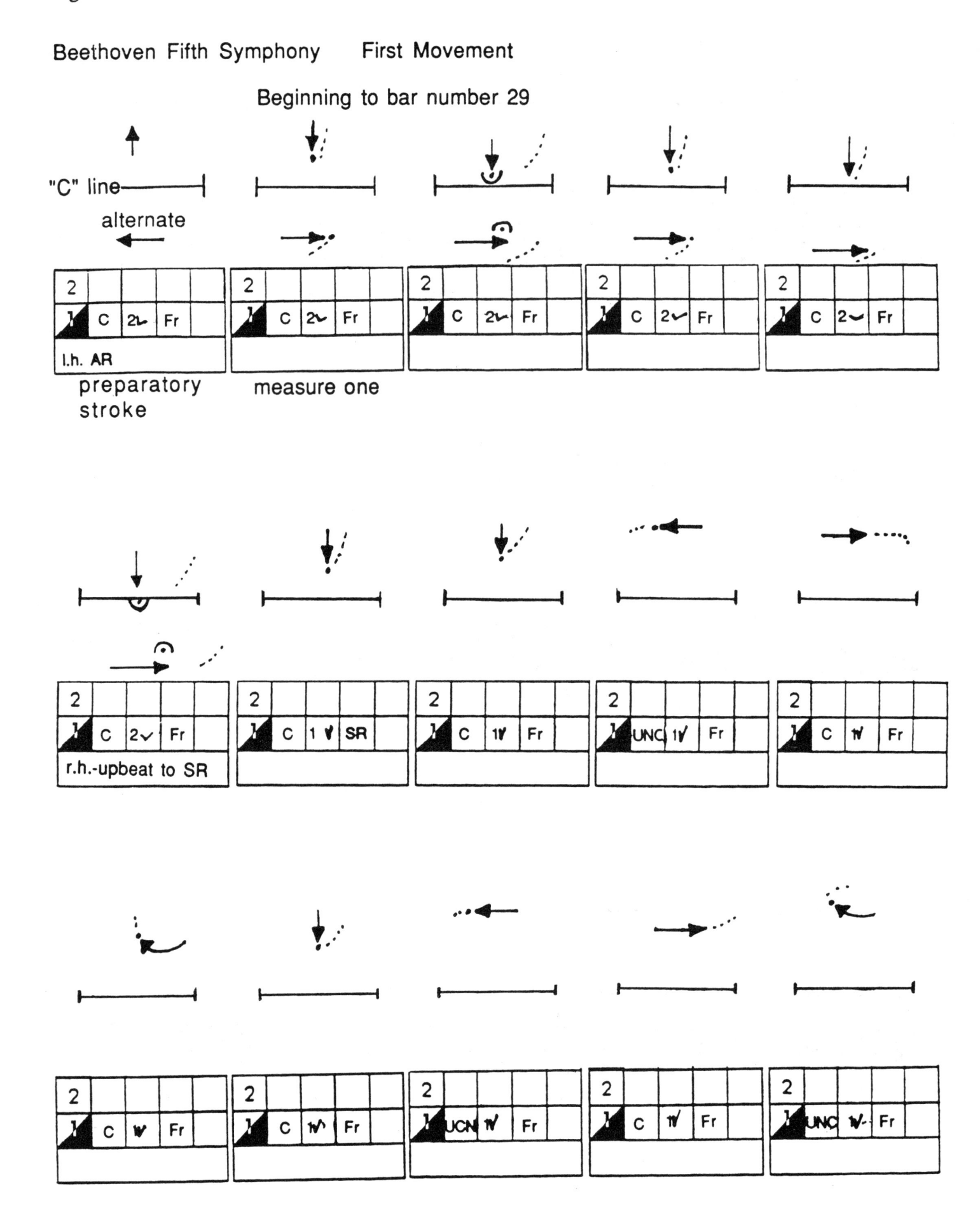

Beethoven Fifth Symphony   First Movement

Beginning to bar number 29

191

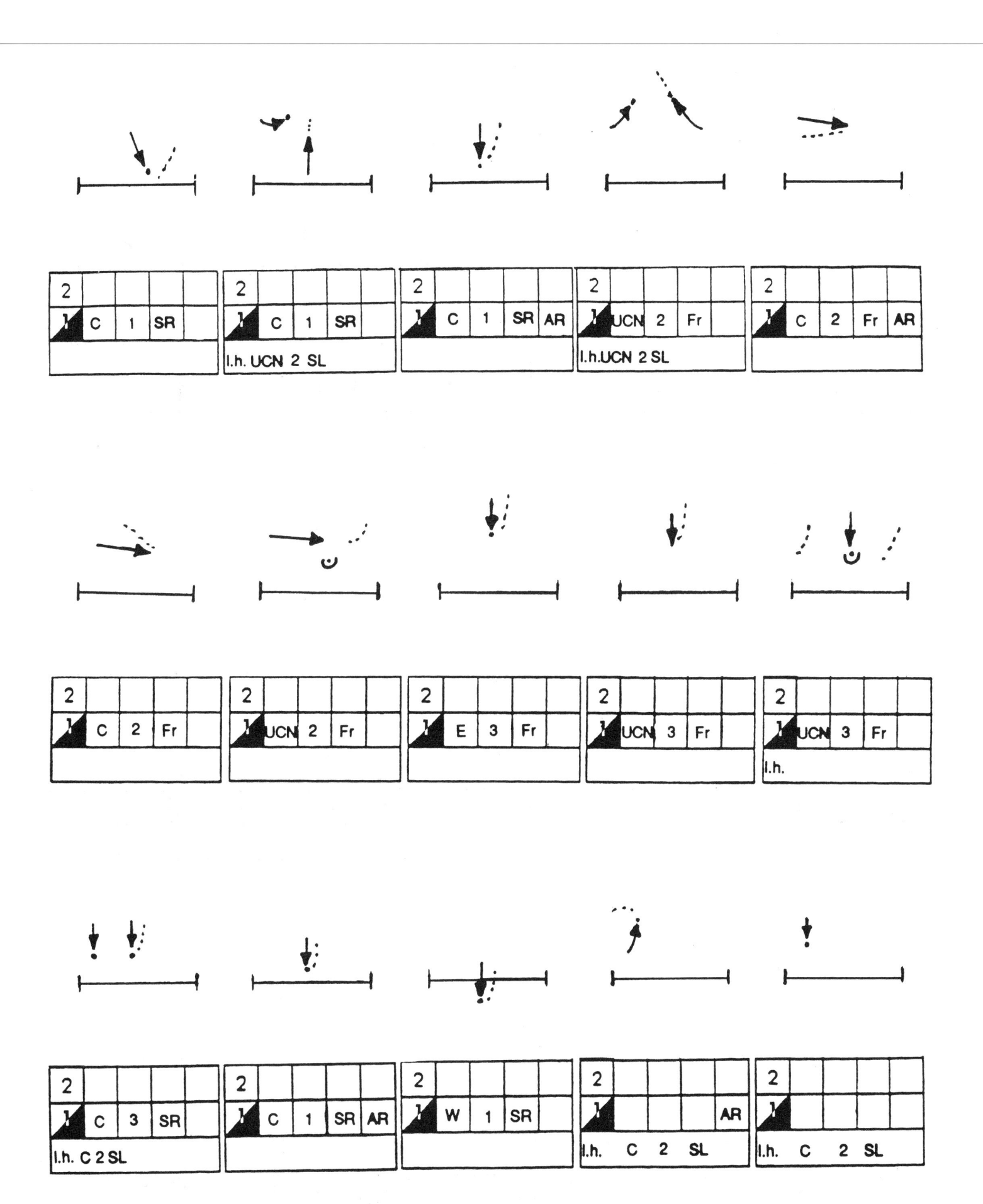

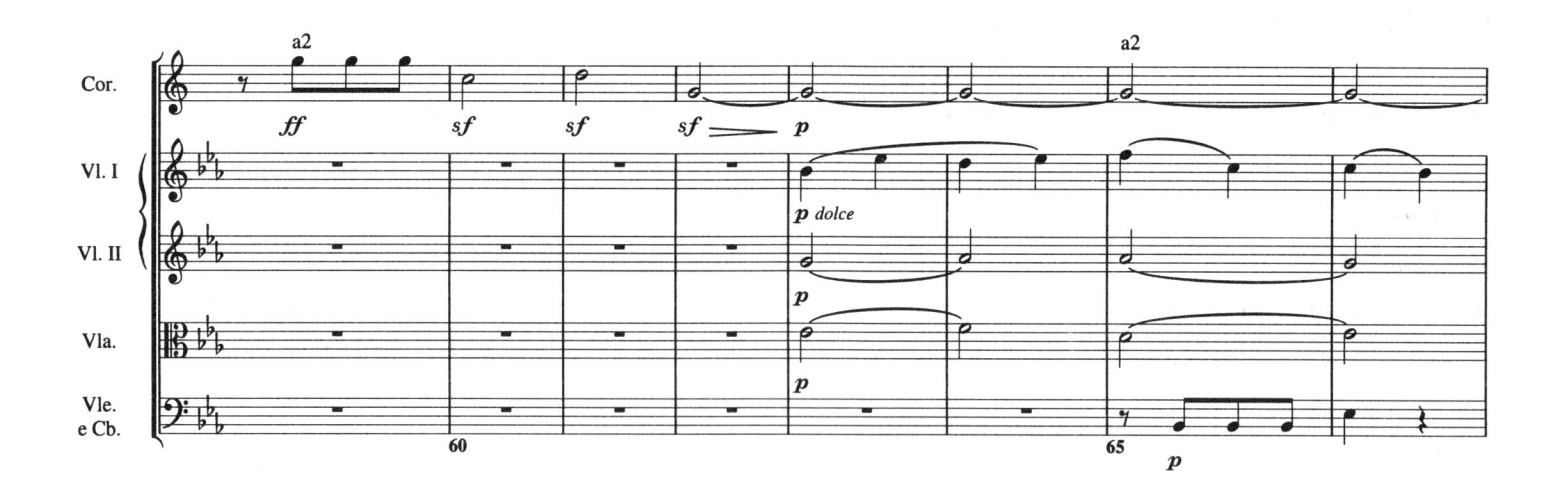

Ex. 106 Beethoven's *Fifth Symphony,* First Movement, measures 59 to 66

It is not unusual to hear performances which stress measure 63 as the *first* measure of a four-bar phrase, moving from measure 63 to measure 66.

The four-bar phrase actually begins on measure 62, with the horn B-flat pedal. The first violin entrance on measure 63 is the *second* measure of the four-bar phrase, which encompasses measures 62 to 65. The harmonic resolution to E-flat in measure 66 is the beginning of the next four-bar phrase.

The PatternCube uses a traditional four-beat pattern, rather than repeated vertical strokes, for two reasons. The first is to outline where the first measure of the phrase begins by relying on <u>only one</u> downstroke in a series of four strokes. The other is to employ the horizontal strokes contained in a four-beat pattern because of the lyrical quality of the material.

Visual Score Study/Baton Placement

Measures 59-60-61

The arm is fully extended into zone 3, E level, toward the horns. The *sf* indications in measures 60 and 61 are made with a downbeat 'click,' and a forward push as well as a quick backward motion of the hand, while remaining in zone 3. The *sf* in measure 62 will be treated the same way except that the quick backward motion moves back to Zone 1 because of the *diminuendo* to *piano*. If the horn line is registered, the movement from measure 61 to 62 will form a natural downstroke and indicate the first measure in the PatternCube four-beat pattern.

Measures 62-63-64-65

These four measures form a four-bar phrase and use a four-beat pattern. Make the *diminuendo* in measure 62 to the *piano* dynamic. The second, third, and fourth measures in the four-beat pattern are conducted by the left hand as indicated in the PatternCube, including the delivery of an essential cue to the celli and bassi in measure 65. (The first violins, celli and bassi are all seated to the left of the conductor.)

Measure 66

This measure marks the beginning of the next four-measure phrase, but is still conducted by the left hand. (In the following measures the right hand will complete the phrase, beginning with the clarinet entrance on the second beat in the pattern, just as the first violin entrance in the previous phrase was the second beat in the four-beat pattern.)

Fig. 140 **PatternCubes**

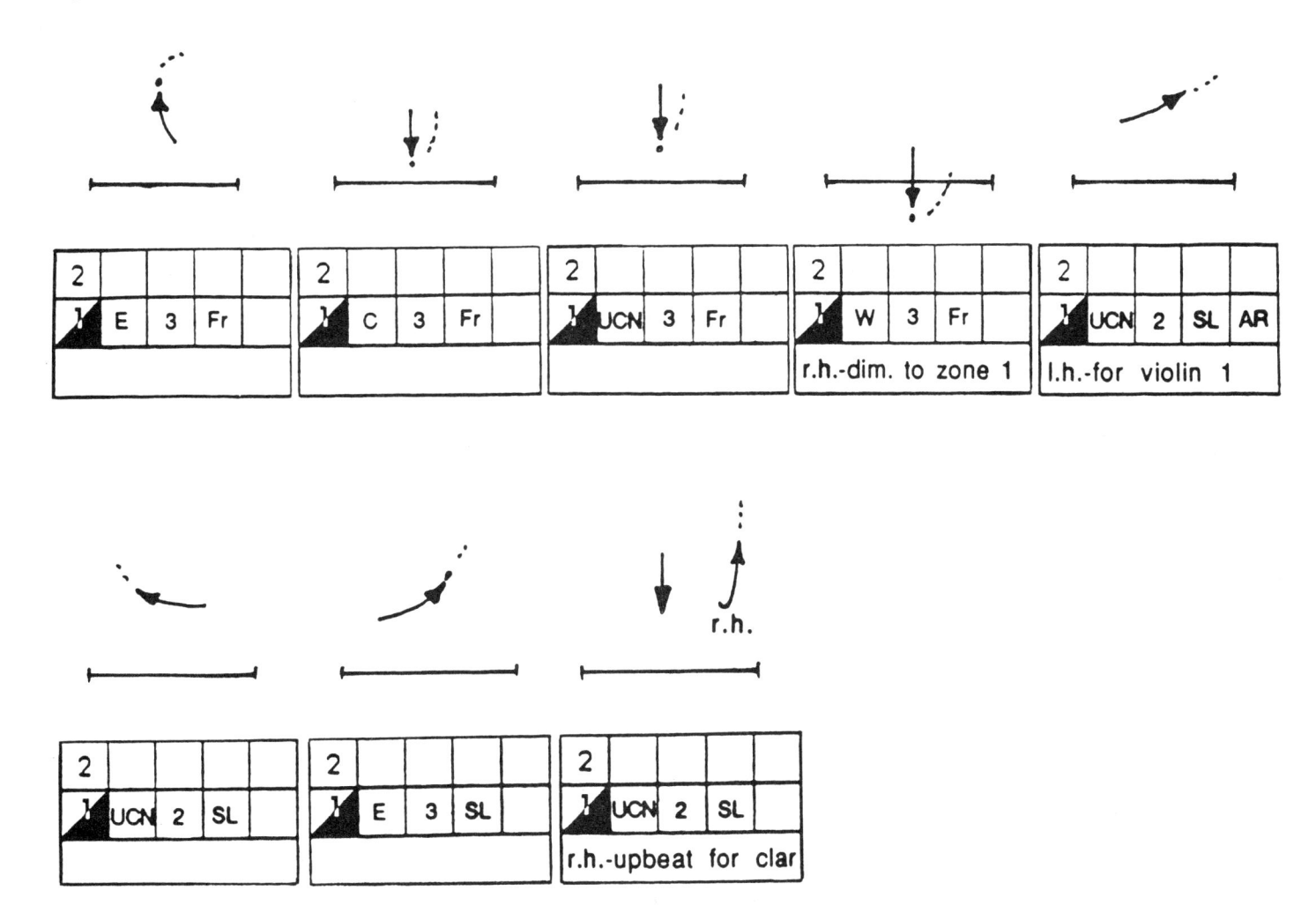

Ex. 107 Beethoven's *Fifth Symphony,* First Movement, measures 121 to 138

Measures 121 to 138

Apply previous technical solutions to this excerpt. The E-flat sonority in measure 122 is a full quarter note, not an eighth note. The *piano* preparation leaving the *fortissimo* hold in measure 128 for the second violin entrance in measure 129 is a repeat of the measure 5 to measure 6 articulation. Measure 129, like measure 6, is a pick-up to a four-bar phrase and not the beginning of the phrase. The measures from 130 to the end of the excerpt are usually conducted with the right hand, but the PatternCube emphasizes a two-handed approach for the sake of variety and, as before, utilizes 2 four-beat patterns.

Visual Score Study/Baton Placement

Measures 121-122-123-124-125

Everyone on stage is playing in measure 121 except the timpanist. Make a strong upward 'click' for rhythmic clarity and the *fortissimo* sonority in measure 121 -- zone 3, E level, Fr. Measure 122 receives a downward stroke for the E-flat quarter note resolution. Mark measures 123-124 with clear, small wrist 'clicks.' *Do not make large forearm movements in these measures; restrict all motion to the wrist.* In contrast, make a strong forearm upward 'click' in the direction of the horns in measure 125. An alternate solution for measure 125 is to use the left hand for the horn cue while moving the right hand toward the W level for measure 126. Remain in zone 3 throughout these measures, and maintain the momentum of the tempo.

Measures 126-127-128-129

If the right hand articulated measure 125, move the baton straight down to the W level with a sharp 'click' at the conclusion of the stroke for measure 126. If the left hand articulated measure 125, the right hand should already be at or near the W level. Make a sharp 'click' at the end of the stroke. Do not *ritard* the D-flats! Maintain the rhythmic vitality of the three note unit. Stay at the W level and move through measure 127 and make the *fermata* on measure 128. Register the upward *piano* preparatory stroke to C level (in tempo) to SR, zone 1 or 2.

Measures 130-131-132-133

Use a four-beat pattern for this four-measure phrase. The right hand conducts measure 130, the left hand conducts measures 131 and 132, and the right hand conducts measure 133. Register to address each instrument or section as indicated in the PatternCube.

Measures 134-135-136-137

The right hand conducts measure 134. Use the left hand for measures 135 through 137. Register throughout, and maintain tempo.

Measure 138

The right hand begins the new phrase with the second violins.

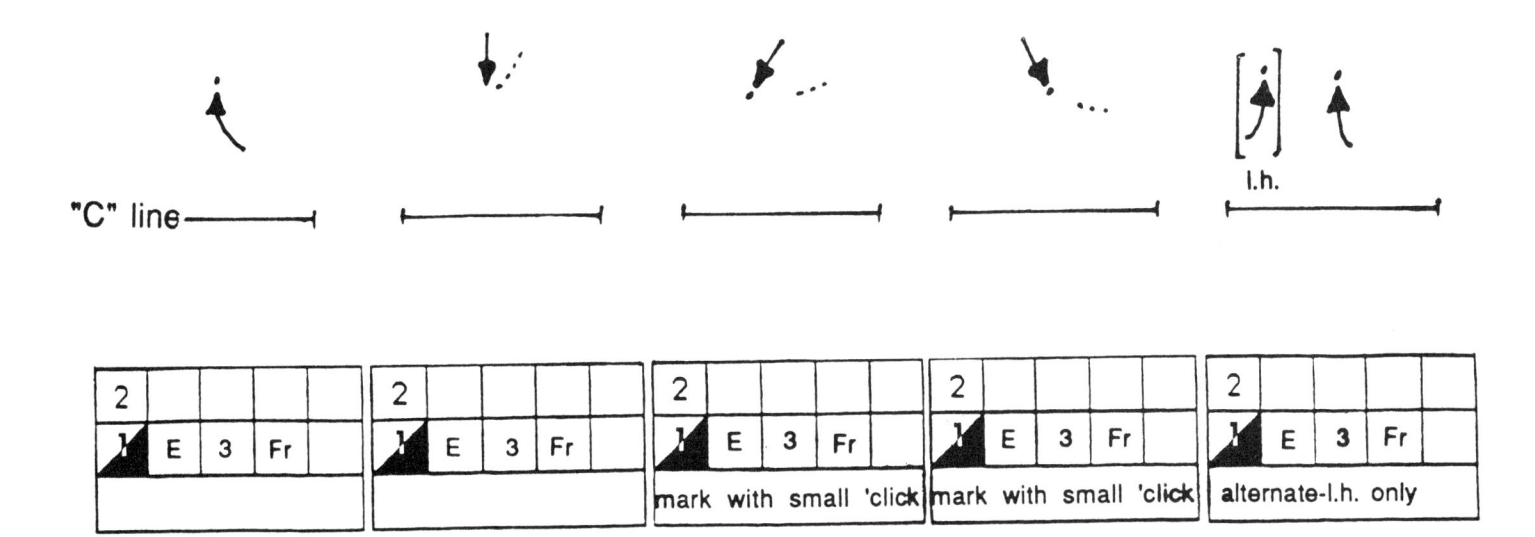

Fig. 141 **PatternCubes**

2				2				2				2				2			
♩	E	3	Fr	♩	E	3	Fr	♩	E	3	Fr	♩	E	3	Fr	♩	E	3	Fr
								mark with small 'click'				mark with small 'click'				alternate-l.h. only			

Fig. 141 **PatternCubes** (cont.)

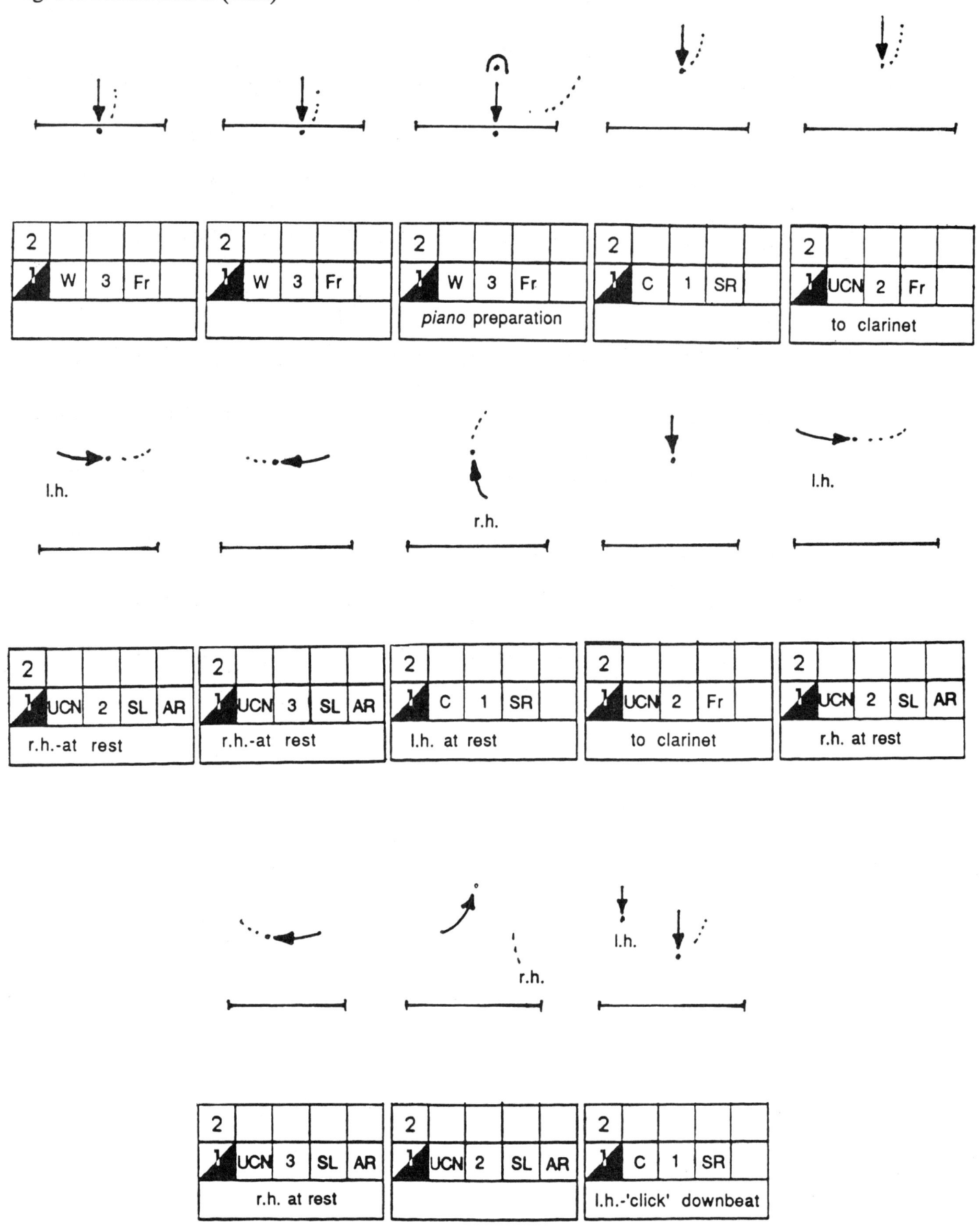

Ex. 108 Beethoven's *Fifth Symphony,* First Movement, measures 376-395

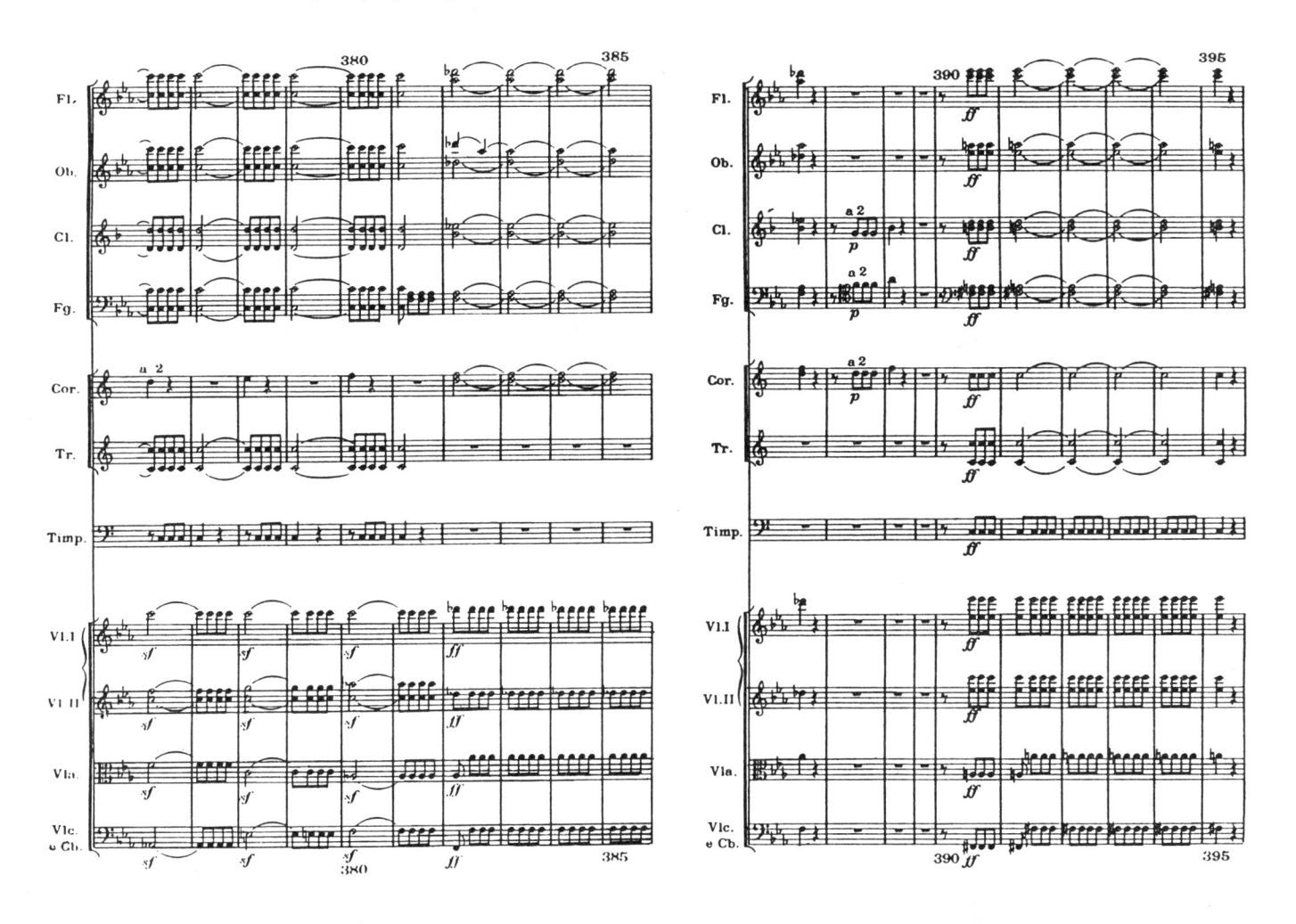

The three eighth note motive evolves into a figure of four hammered eighth notes per measure. The intensity of Beethoven's rhythmic *fortissimo* structure is broken by a sudden *piano*, followed by an uneven, short, three-bar phrase containing a measure of silence. The conductor must be prepared for this unexpected rhythmic and dynamic shift.

Visual Score Study/Baton Placement

Measures 376-381

These six measures fall naturally into 3 two-measure harmonic groups: f minor, c major, f minor. The three eighth note motive moves from one instrumental block to another, as Beethoven pits the winds, trumpets and timpani against the massed strings. In this sequence the rhythmic figures in the timpani part will dominate its instrumental group and set up the responses of the string entries.

The PatternCube uses 3 two-beat patterns for these six measures. Keep each stroke short and compact and 'click' every measure. Remain in zone 3 throughout, at E level, Fr. The stroke in measure 381 moves backward horizontally rather than upward vertically.

Measures 382-385

Beethoven shifts the three eighth note unit to four measures of repeated *fortissimo* eighth notes in the strings over a held D-flat major wind sonority. Use four short forward horizontal strokes with 'flicks,' away from and back toward the front of the body, in zone 3, E level, Fr. **Note that the baton will be in position for the forward horizontal stroke in measure 382 because of the placement of the baton in measure 381.**

Measures 386-390

These five measures begin with a two-bar sequence, starting with the conclusion of the D-flat major sonority on measure 386. Measure 387 contains the sudden, unexpected *piano* reiteration of the three eighth note motive played by the clarinets, bassoons and horns. Measures 388-390 form a three-bar-sequence. The first measure is the downbeat conclusion of the *piano* wind entrance. The second measure is silent. The third measure is a tremendous *fortissimo* explosion after the silence, and regenerates the momentum of the movement.

Conduct these five measures in a 2+3 pattern. Measure 386 will be a another forward horizontal stroke for the concluding *fortissimo* D-flat sonority. Move back to zone 1 or 2 in a short upward *piano* 'clicked' stroke for the winds in measure 387, and use the left hand, OPU, to reinforce the *piano* sonority.
The three-beat pattern begins on measure 388, the conclusion of the *piano* wind figure. Mark the second beat in the pattern, the silent measure 389, very clearly, with a small 'click' to the right. **Do not make a large stroke in this measure**, and stay in zone 1 or 2. Measure 390 is the third beat in the pattern and will have a forceful *fortissimo* upward 'click,' the arm moving forward to zone 3.

Option: For the final two measures, 389-390, **if the conductor wants to hide the oncoming *fortissimo* from the audience**: In the silent measure 389, the second measure of the three pattern, move the baton straight down to C level, and into zone 1, Fr, rather than to the right, thereby breaking the normal three-beat pattern. For the *fortissimo* measure 390 downbeat, thrust the arm straight out in a horizontal line with a 'flick,' from zone 1, C level, Fr, into zone 3. In this physical realization of measure 390, the forward movement of the baton is clearly visible to the performers on the stage, but is hidden from the audience by the body of the conductor.

Measures 391-395

Use the same forward horizontal strokes employed in measures 382-386. If the conductor chooses the option for measure 390, move the baton up to E level for measure 391.

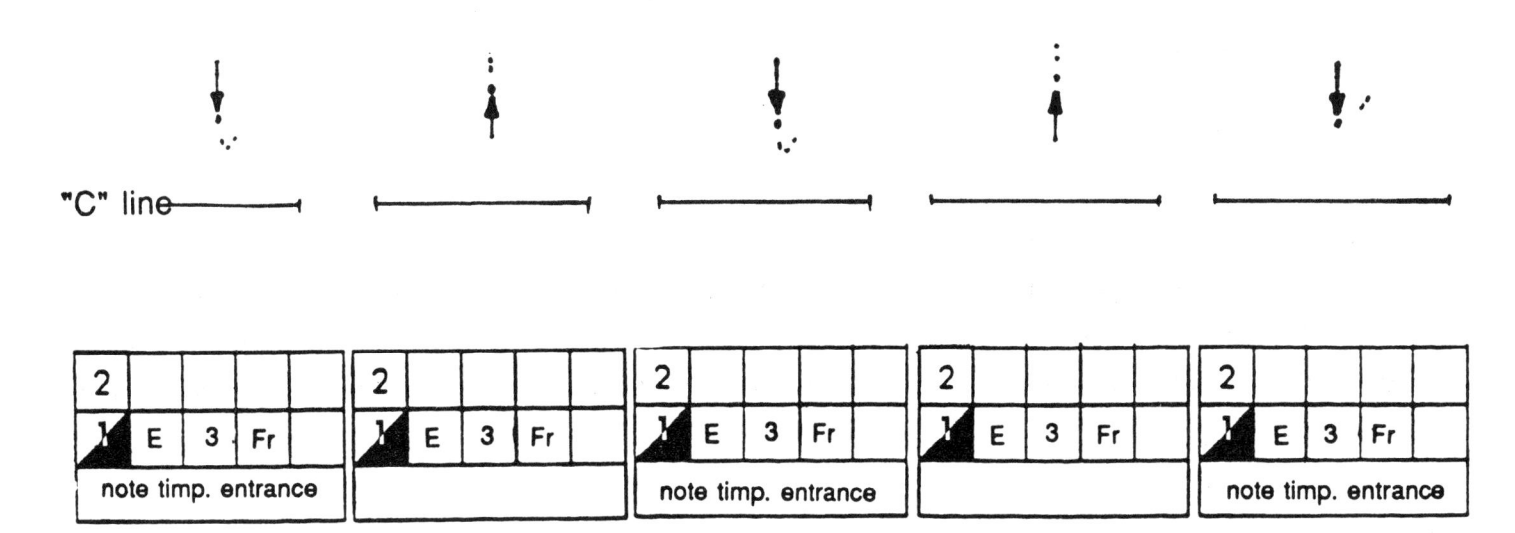

Fig. 142 **PatternCubes**

Fig. 142 **PatternCubes** (cont.)

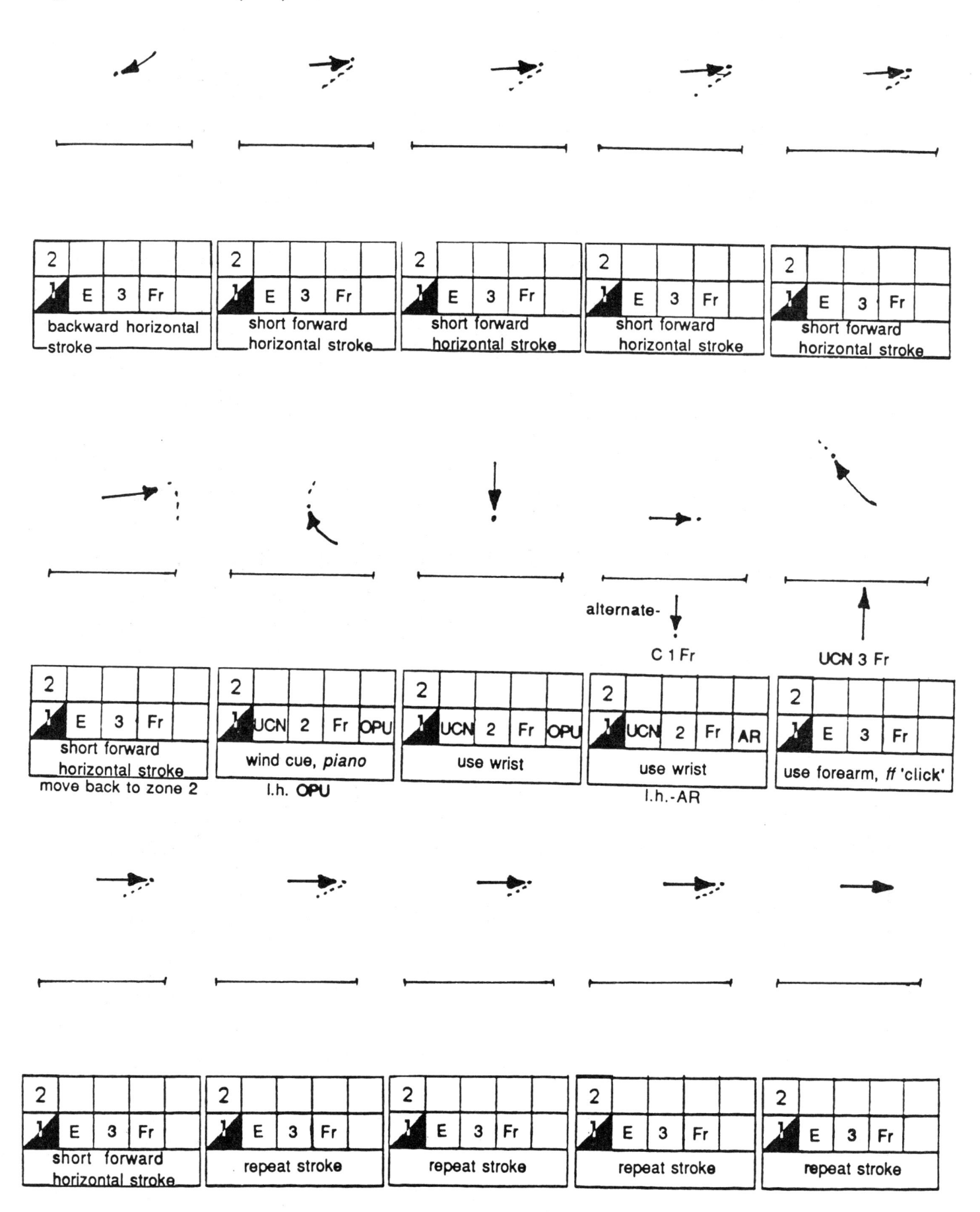

2						2						2						2						2					
1	E	3	Fr			1	E	3	Fr			1	E	3	Fr			1	E	3	Fr			1	E	3	Fr		

backward horizontal stroke | short forward horizontal stroke | short forward horizontal stroke | short forward horizontal stroke | short forward horizontal stroke

alternate- ↓ C 1 Fr   ↑ UCN 3 Fr

2					2					2					2					2				
1	E	3	Fr		1	UCN	2	Fr	OPU	1	UCN	2	Fr	OPU	1	UCN	2	Fr	AR	1	E	3	Fr	

short forward horizontal stroke, move back to zone 2 | wind cue, *piano* l.h. OPU | use wrist | use wrist l.h.-AR | use forearm, *ff* 'click'

2					2					2					2					2				
1	E	3	Fr		1	E	3	Fr		1	E	3	Fr		1	E	3	Fr		1	E	3	Fr	

short forward horizontal stroke | repeat stroke | repeat stroke | repeat stroke | repeat stroke

Ex. 109 Beethoven's *Fifth Symphony,* Second Movement, measures 1 to 31

Ex. 109 (cont.)

The opening of the second movement is an excellent example of Beethoven's awareness of string placement. He consciously moves the string sound from one area to another. The first sounds heard by the audience are played by the string sections seated <u>behind</u> the violins. It is not until measure 15 that the first sustained significant melodic material is moved to the <u>front</u> of the stage and into the violins.

The opening unison *piano dolce* line of the violas and celli demands care from the conductor on several levels: balancing the sections, awareness of unintended *crescendi* and *diminuendi*, false accents on downbeats, and above all, exact rhythmic articulation. The thirty-second note rhythms must be perfectly placed; they are often played as triplets, and attention must be paid to the one sixteenth note after the third beat in measure 5.

The metronome mark, a quarter equals 92, will allow registration to be applied throughout. The melodic materials in the first eight measures span an octave. The opening upbeat needs a clear, *piano, legato* preparation. The conductor must decide whether the first *forte* in the movement in measure 7 is a *forte* within a *piano* structure, or an independent *forte*. The conductor's decision will dictate the kind of stroke to use. (The difference will be in the weight and character of the sound and the stroke. The *forte* within a *piano* structure will be less stringent with less overall sound projection, especially if little vibrato is used.) The *piano* downbeats after *forte* indications in measures eight and ten allow the conductor to choose from among the following technical solutions:

1 - use the left hand, OPU, for the *piano* indication,
2 - withdraw the right hand from zone 2 or 3 into zone 1,
3 - combine numbers one and two,
4 - stop the movement of the right hand on the *piano* downbeat.

Note the rhythmic differences in the flute and second clarinet on the third beat in measures 14 and 19. A performing tradition of the recent past held that the clarinet player perform the final thirty-second note in the measure as though it were part of a triplet figure, thus creating a rhythmic unison with the flutist. In recent times that tradition has lost its adherents. (Measure 18 contains the same rhythmic differences between the strings and the bassoon.) The downbeat in measure 22 needs a long stroke after the short strokes in measure 21. A distinction must be made between the viola *piano* in measure 26 and the first violin *pianissimo* in the same measure. Hide the downbeat stroke in measure 29 from the audience and do not make a *fortissimo* preparatory 'click' on the third beat in measure 28. During the *pianissimo* in measure 28 conduct a clear, in tempo, third beat *pianissimo* preparatory 'click.' That small third beat stroke indication is enough for the entire orchestra to make the *fortissimo* entrance. Preceding the *fortissimo* entrance a regular, unwavering, three-beat pulse is present in every measure, beginning with the pick-up to measure 23. The surprise is in the unexpected *fortissimo*, and that surprise should not be given away with a telegraphed, large preparatory stroke from the conductor.

Do not overlook the second beat in the celli and bassi in measure 31, the conclusion of the *fortissimo* phrase.

Visual Score Study/Baton Placement

Pick-up, Measures 1-3

The *piano* opening can be effectively conducted with *legato* strokes in either zone 1 or zone 2. Zone 2 is the choice in this PatternCube. Before addressing the violas and celli, look at the bassi, an acknowledgement of their upcoming *pizzicato*. Make a *piano legato* preparatory second stroke with a 'click' for the entrance of the violas and celli on beat three. Include a *legato* 'click' on the third beat for the *pizzicato* entrance of the bassi on the following downbeat. The first eighth note in measure one, the C-natural, has a dot over it, the only articulation of its kind in the entire excerpt. Stop the movement of the baton after the downbeat stroke and make a very short rebound for the second beat. Wrist 'click' the second beat in measure 2 and note the three downward strokes in measure 3. Each of the downward strokes should be made with an outward circular wrist movement to indicate the ongoing slur. Maintain a *piano legato,* and monitor and balance. Register throughout, and use different areas within the C level space to fulfill the line.

Measures 4-7

Wrist 'click' the third beat of measure 4, as well as the third beat in measure 5, and make certain a sixteenth note is played after the third beat in the fifth measure. In measure 6 resist the temptation to make a *crescendo* on the third beat into measure 7. **In this entire opening it is critical that the thirty-second notes be played with absolute rhythmic precision, while preserving the *piano dolce* character.** Measure 7 is treated as a *forte* within a *piano* sonority. Do not make a large, accented stroke, or use the left hand as an indicator for more sound. Move into zone 3 for increased volume and lightly indicate the first two beats. On the third beat make a downward and inward upward curved stroke into zone 2 without showing a *diminuendo*. It is important to sustain the sonority level throughout or Beethoven's dynamic change on the barline will not work.

Measures 8-9

Beat one in measure 8 is a *subito piano*. (The baton arrives in zone 1 as the result of the inward curved stroke which began in the previous measure.) To reinforce the *piano* the left hand is used in the OPU position in zone 2 on the first beat. The left hand 'clicks' a *piano* cue on beat two, SL, for the entry of the first violins, while the right hand moves to SR, into zone 2, and 'clicks' a *piano* cue for the entry of the second violins. Measure 9 is again *forte* within a *piano* sonority, and the baton registers upward into zone 3. Repeat the strokes made in measure 7.

Measures 10-11

In measure 10, repeat the baton and left hand movements that were made on the downbeat of measure 8. In beats two and three the right hand 'clicks' and moves to E level and into zone 3 to address the first entrance of the woodwinds. The left hand moves into the AR position on beat two. Measure 11 is again a *subito forte* but with a new *diminuendo* marking. Move the baton back to zone 1 while conducting the oboe line, and on beat two use the left hand in the OPU position, zone 1, to reinforce the *diminuendo*.

Measures 12-15

Balance the flute and clarinet lines, and use *legato* baton strokes throughout. The third beat strokes in measures 12 and 13 do not move upward. To preserve the registration of the line, both strokes come back to the space occupied by the second stroke in the pattern. Listen for the rhythmic difference between the flute and second clarinet on the third beat in measure 14. In measure 15 move the baton to the SR position, in zone 2, C area for the second violin entrance, and on the second beat 'click' the left hand, SL for the first violin entrance.

Measures 16-19

The right hand moves to the Fr position in measure 16. In measure 17 the left hand, OPD, helps assure the *crescendo* to the *forte* in the following measure. Note the rhythmic differences in measure 18 (violins, inside violas and the first bassoon), and sustain the *forte* throughout. Do not make a *diminuendo* on the third beat! Measure 19, like measures 8 and 10, has a subito *piano* on the downbeat. Use the left hand, OPU, to reinforce the *subito piano*, and move the right hand back quickly into zone 2 from zone 3 on the downbeat. Be certain that the backward right hand movement is not made before the downbeat. The right hand 'clicks' the second beat in the measure and the left hand conducts the woodwind entrance on the third beat. The right hand is AR. Make the *crescendo* on the third beat to *mezzo piano* or *mezzo forte* by moving the left hand from zone 2 into zone 3 in the next measure. Listen for the rhythmic differences on the third beat.

Measures 20-22

The left hand conducts the first two beats in measure 20. The right hand assumes the primary time keeping duties on the third beat *forte*. Use the left hand, OPU, for the *subito piano* on the second beat in measure 21, and at the same time bring the right hand back into zone 1. Use short strokes and short rebounds for the sixteenth notes in measure 21. On the third beat move the rebound to the left to prepare for the first eighth note stroke on the downbeat of measure 22, a horizontal stroke moving to the right, Fr. The right hand 'clicks' beats two and three moving downward to the W position in preparation for measure 23. The left hand, in the Fr position, UCN Level, zone 3, 'clicks' on the second beat for the entrance of the winds on beat three.

Measures 23-26

These few measures lend themselves to several technical solutions. The following are two that are most common -- using the right hand only, and **using both hands, *in mirror fashion*,** for measures 23 and 25 to emphasize the colors of the lines. In the second solution the right hand is basically used for the woodwind line and the left hand for the first violins. Neither option covers all the details in Beethoven's scoring.

The PatternCube indicates a solution which emphasizes the lyrical aspects of the scoring and covers the rhythmic element as well. The left hand is responsible for the primary *legato dolce* lines in the winds and violins, while the right hand deals with the ongoing viola triplet rhythms as well as the celli and bass *pizzicati*.

Keep the left hand *in front of* the right hand, in zone 3, at E level, in the Fr position. The right hand will be *behind* the left hand, in zone 1, at W level, in the SR position. The left hand patterns will be made with *piano legato* strokes, while the right hand uses short *staccato* strokes without rebounds. In measure 26 the right hand remains in zone 1 and moves up to the C position from the W position on the third beat. On beat three the left hand moves back to zone 1 and into the OPS position for the *pianissimo*. The conductor must make a clear difference between the preceding *piano* and the third beat *pianissimo*.

Measures 27-31

Remain at C level, zone 1, and hardly move the baton in measure 27. Bring the second violins in on the second beat with an eye cue and a small SR stroke. In measure 28 'click' the second beat to cue the winds and move the baton up to the UCN level on beat three. For the *subito fortissimo* in measure 29, make a sudden strong forward forearm motion out to zone 3, and use the left hand fully extended in the direction of the trumpets and timpani, OPD, SL, in zone 3. Sustain the *fortissimo* throughout the measure! The first beat in measure 29 should not sound like a *sforzando* attack followed by a *diminuendo* and a *crescendo*. After a vertical downbeat in measure 30, use two horizontal SR strokes for the next two beats, and another SR horizontal stroke for the first beat in measure 31. Use a strong left hand across-the-body SR stroke for the second beat *fortissimo* in measure 31.

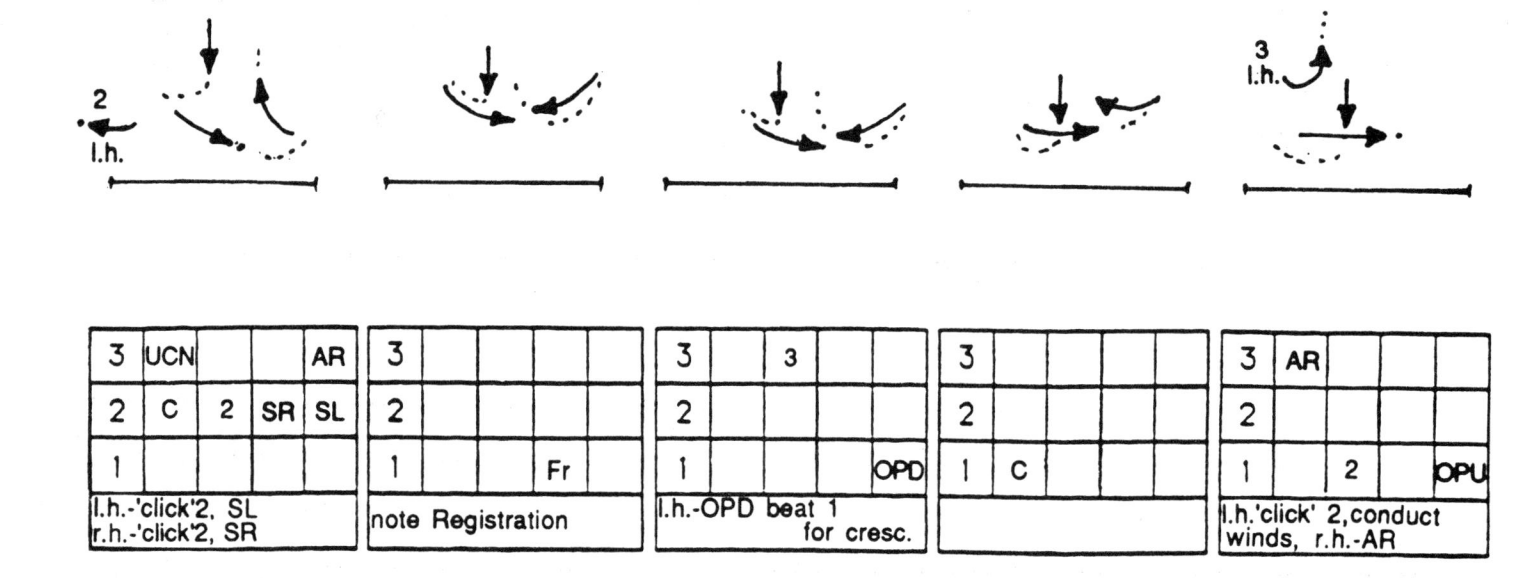

Fig. 143. **PatternCubes**

3	UCN		AR
2	C	2	SR SL
1			
l.h.-'click'2, SL r.h.-'click'2, SR			

3			
2			
1		Fr	
note Registration			

3		3	
2			
1			OPD
l.h.-OPD beat 1 for cresc.			

3			
2			
1	C		

3	AR		
2			
1		2	OPU
l.h.'click' 2, conduct winds, r.h.-AR			

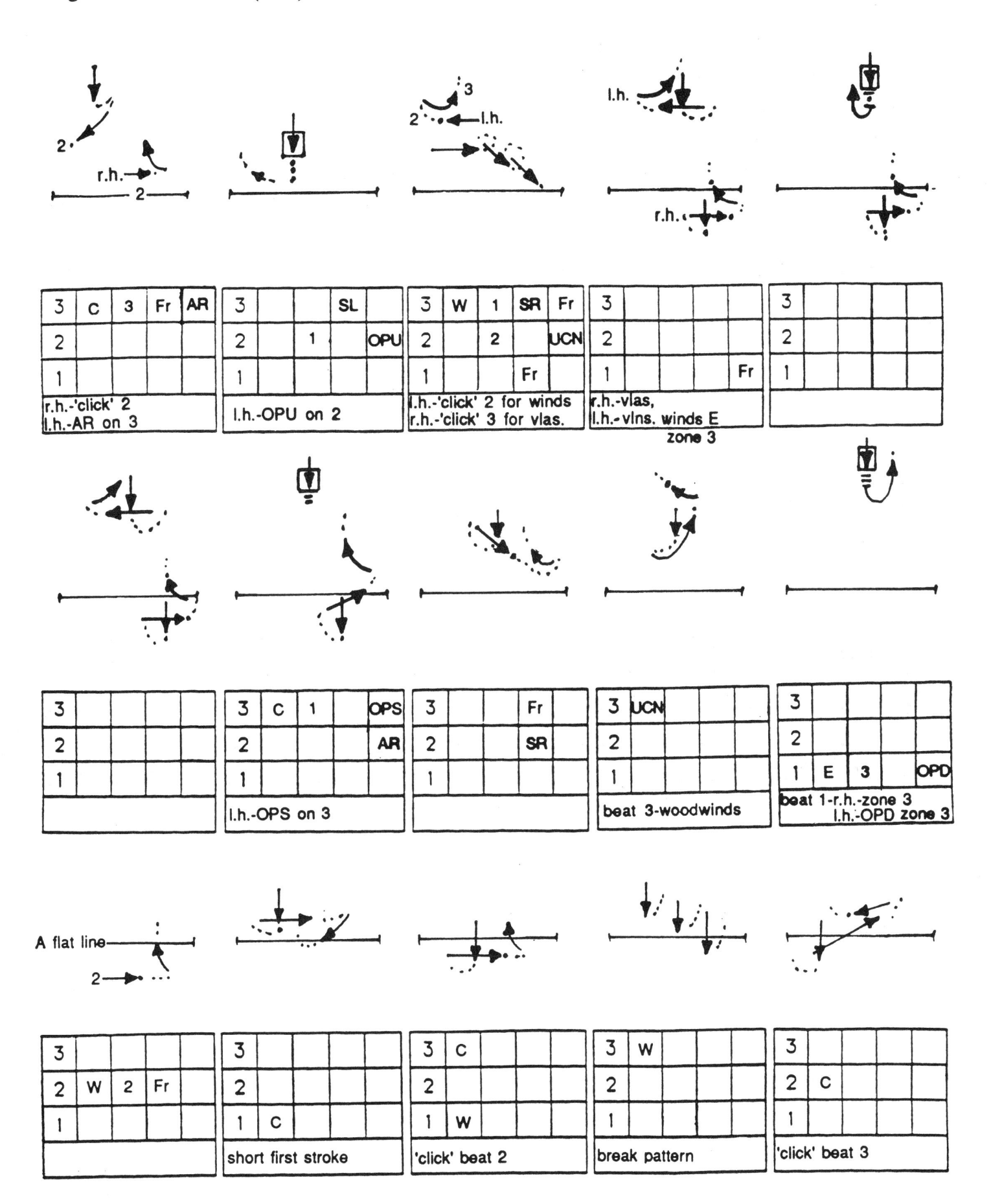

Fig. 143. **PatternCubes** (cont.)

Fig. 143. **PatternCubes** (cont.)

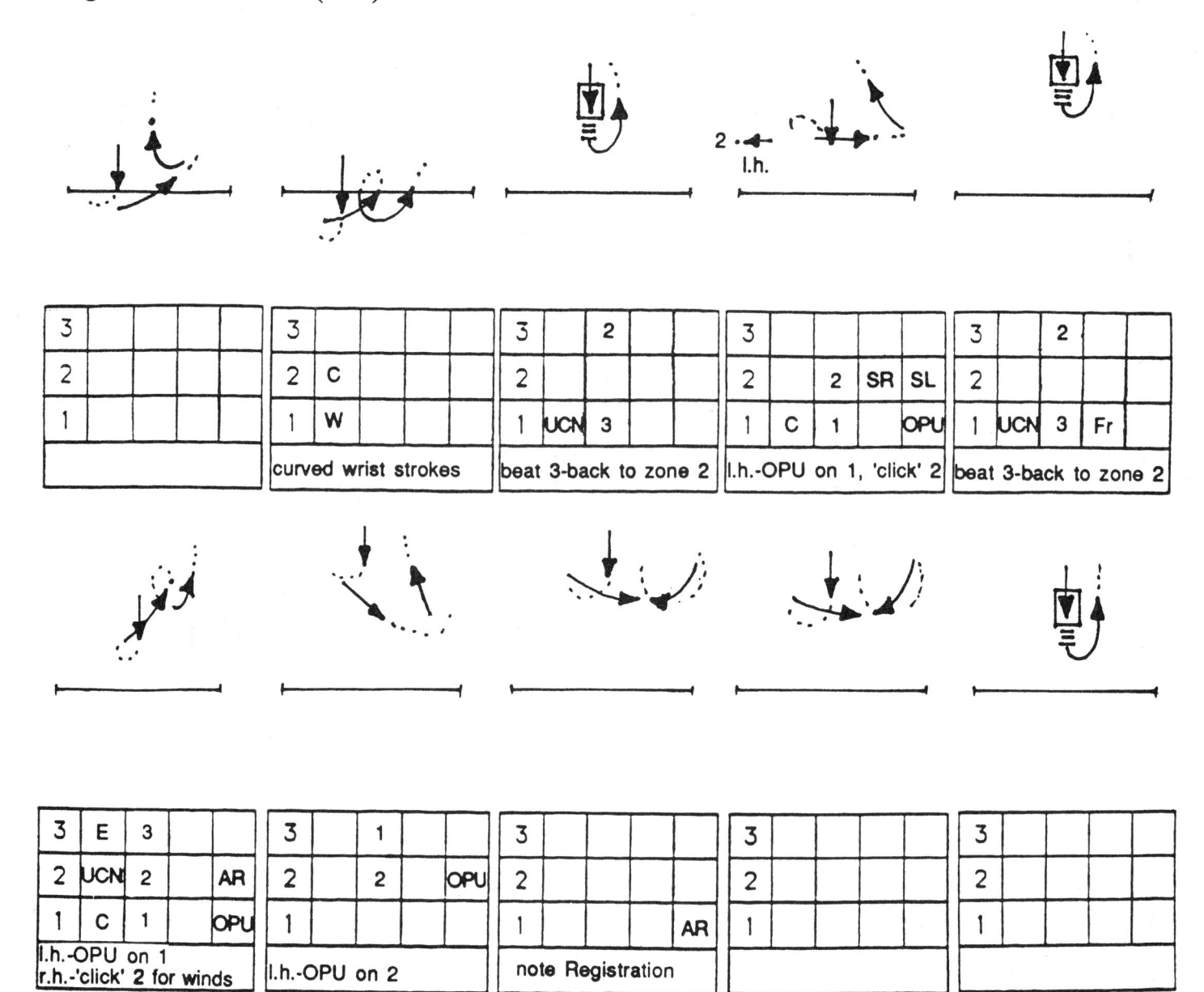

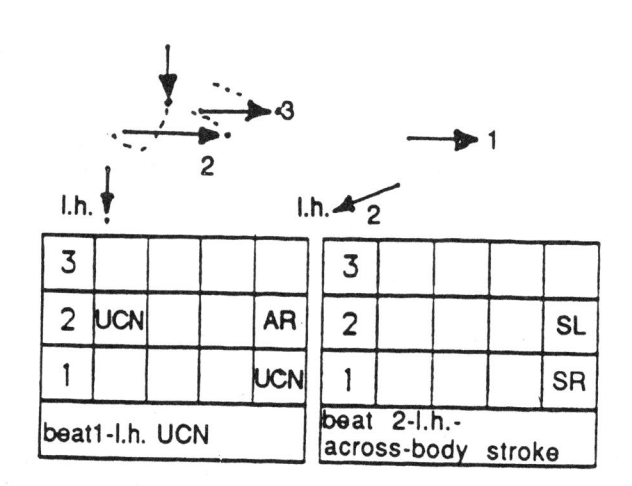

3				
2				
1				

3				
2	C			
1	W			
curved wrist strokes			

3		2		
2				
1	UCN	3		
beat 3-back to zone 2			

3				
2		2	SR	SL
1	C	1		OPU
l.h.-OPU on 1, 'click' 2				

3		2		
2				
1	UCN	3	Fr	
beat 3-back to zone 2			

3	E	3		
2	UCN	2		AR
1	C	1		OPU
l.h.-OPU on 1 r.h.-'click' 2 for winds				

3		1		
2		2		OPU
1				
l.h.-OPU on 2				

3				
2				
1				AR
note Registration			

3				
2				
1				

3				
2				
1				

3				
2	UCN			AR
1				UCN
beat1-l.h. UCN			

3				
2				SL
1				SR
beat 2-l.h.-across-body stroke				

208

Ex. 110 Beethoven's *Fifth Symphony,* Second Movement, measures 123 to 158

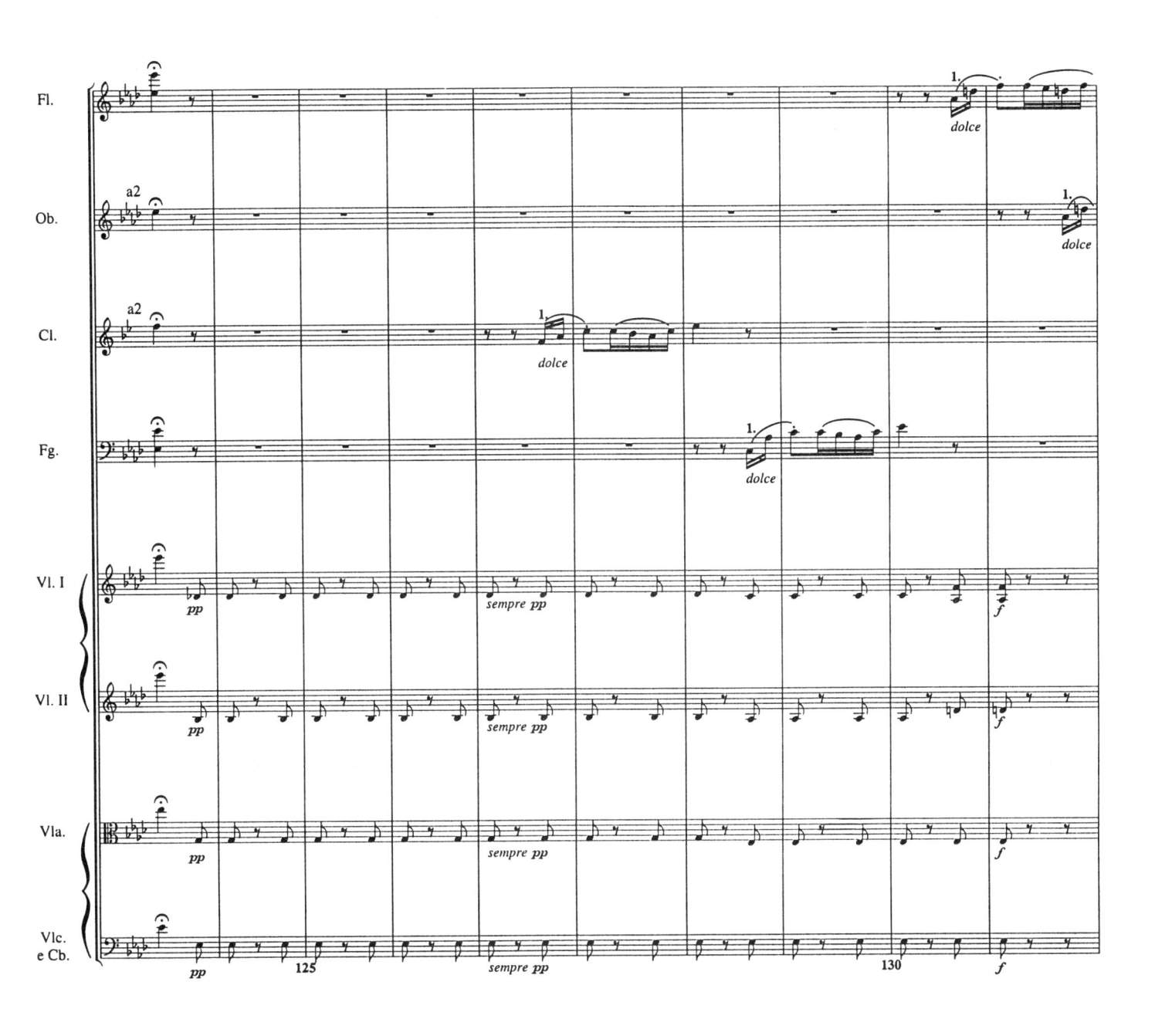

209

Ex. 110 (cont.)

Visual Score Study/Baton Placement

Measures 123-127

Sustain the *fermata* with the right hand, and use a left hand to cut-off on the second beat in measure 123. Continue to use the left hand for the string *pianissimo* accompaniment until measure 132. On beat three move the left hand back to zone 1 or 2, W level, Fr. Use very little space while maintaining the *pianissimo*, and make a very small 'click' on beat two in each of the measures. The right hand is AR until beat two of measure 127. 'Click' the second beat, zone 2, UCN, Fr, to prepare the clarinet entrance on the third beat. Beethoven provides no dynamic indication for the first four wind entrances, so the conductor must decide the sonority levels. The PatternCube assumes each of the entrances will be slightly less than a *piano*.

Measures 128-132

Note the dot over the first beat in the clarinet (the violas and celli have the same articulation in the first measure in this movement). The first beat stroke in measure 128 is a short one, followed by two *legato* strokes. (In the PatternCube the *legato* strokes are curved strokes made from the wrist.) Prepare the entrance of the solo bassoon with a 'click' on beat two in measure 129. The first bassoon note in measure 130 also has a dot over it, as does the first flute note in measure 131. *The strokes for these first beats should be short ones.* Cue the flute and oboe with second beat 'clicks' in both measures. Treat the string *forte* in measure 132 as a *forte* within a *pianissimo* texture!

Measures 133-139

Prepare the first and second clarinets in measure 133 with a *piano* 'click' on the second beat. The clarinets have dots over their first notes in measure 134, but the flute and oboe do not. (The PatternCube follows the clarinet line through measure 134 and then moves to the flute/oboe lines in measure 135.) The first note in measure 135 is a full eighth note for all the instruments. Use very *legato* registered strokes throughout, and the left hand in measures 136 and 137 for the *crescendi-diminuendi* as indicated in the PatternCube.

Measures 140-144

Instead of using the left hand for the *crescendi-diminuendi* in measures 140-142, create the dynamic shape by moving the right hand from zone 2 to zone 3 and back to zone 2 again. 'Click' the second beat in measure 142 for the upcoming *staccati*, and short *staccato* strokes in the next two measures. Make a left hand *staccato* 'click' on the third beat in measure 143 for the strings, SL, zone 2, UCN. Use very little space in the movement of the baton and left hand in measures 142-144.

Measures 145-147

The entire three-measure *crescendo* before the arrival of the *fortissimo* is entrusted to, and distributed among, six wind instruments. The *crescendo* actually stops with the entrance of the two horns, the last of the six instruments to play in this transition passage. They enter **and remain** at *forte* before the arrival of the *fortissimo* in the following measure.

Move the right hand out to zone 3 in measures 145-146 for the *crescendo*. In measure 146 the left hand 'clicks' a *forte* second beat in the direction of the horns, at E level. (The right hand is AR on beat three.) Do not allow the horns to make a further *crescendo* in measure 147. **The weight of the entire orchestra at the *fortissimo* on the third beat should overwhelm the *forte* of the two horns.** The right hand resumes the primary time keeping with a strong 'click' cue on the second beat in measure 147 for the *fortissimo* entrance of the orchestra on the third beat. At the same time the left hand, which has been occupied with the horns, 'clicks' the second beat in measure 147 at C level, zone 3, SL, for the trumpets and timpani entrance.

Measures 148-155

A traditional three-beat pattern works very well for these measures because of the upward movement of the line on the third beat. The timpani part must be carefully analyzed in this segment.

In measures 150 and 153

The *timpani strokes* are the only instrumental articulations on the first beats of these measures.

In measures 154 and 155

The timpanist's second beats in the measures are independent strokes after the rolls, and the only instrumental articulations on those beats. Beethoven has carefully scored the timpani as a final flourish in each of the melodic units in this powerful sequence. In measure 147 'click' the left hand on the second beat, zone 3, UCN, in the direction of the trumpets and timpani. Use the left hand in the OPD position in measures 149 and 152 for the first beat timpani strokes in measure 150 and 153. 'Click' the right hand on the second beat in measures 150 and 153 for the orchestral *tutti* entrances on beat three. In measures 154 and 155, use a left hand 'click' on the first beats as a preparation for the upcoming solo timpani strokes on the second beats.

Measures 156-157

For the two measure *diminuendo*, on the second beat in measure 156 move the right hand, in zone 3, back towards zone 1. At the same time move the left hand, in the OPU position in zone 3, back towards zone 1. In measure 157, 'click' the right hand on the second beat for the *piano* entrance of the first violins and violas on beat three. On the downbeat of measure 158 add a *legato* 'click' on the third beat for the string *pizzicati*.

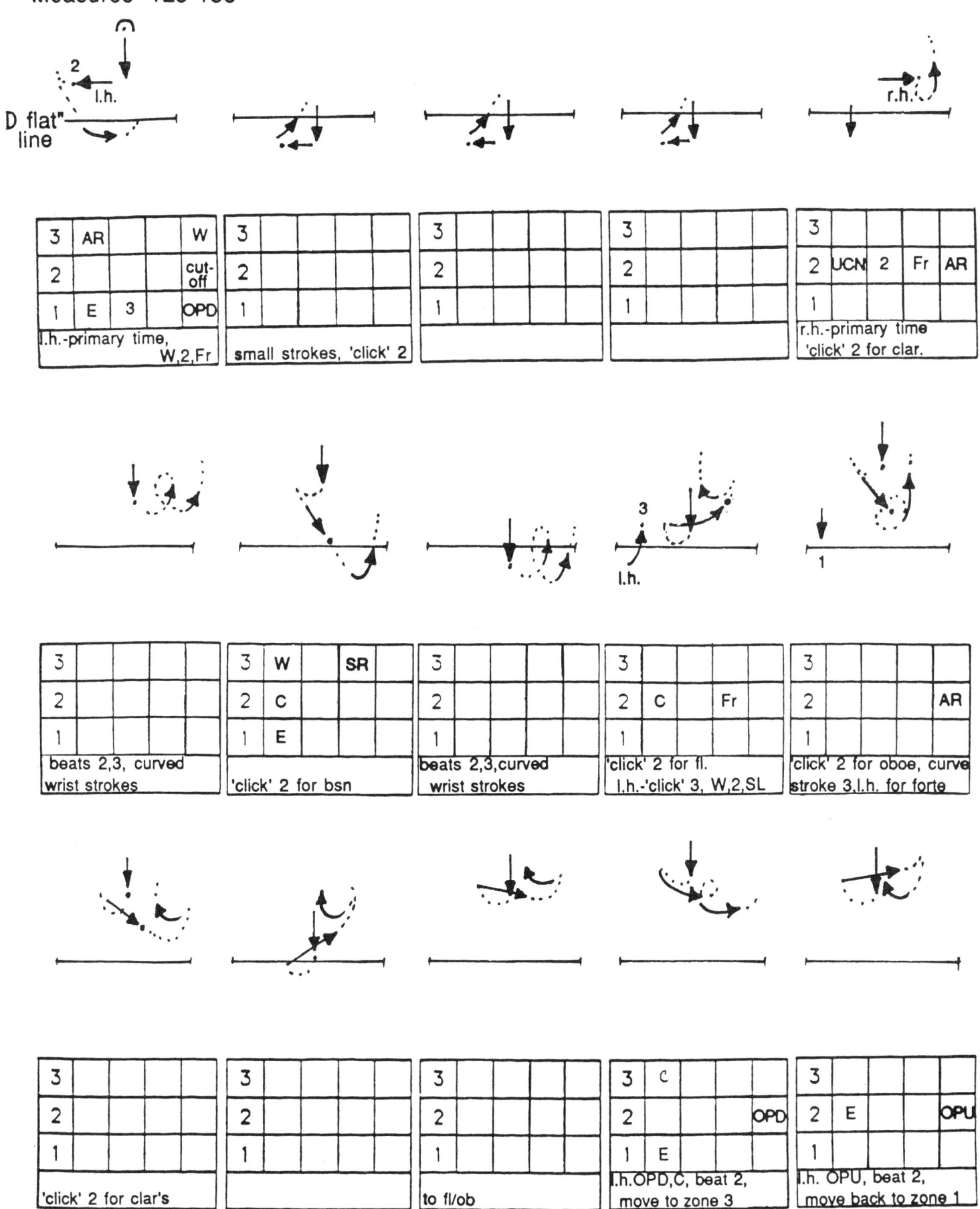

Fig. 144 PatternCubes

Beethoven Fifth Symphony, Second Movement
Measures 123-158

3	AR		W
2			cut-off
1	E	3	OPD

l.h.-primary time, W,2,Fr

3			
2			
1			

small strokes, 'click' 2

3			
2			
1			

3			
2			
1			

3				
2	UCN	2	Fr	AR
1				

r.h.-primary time
'click' 2 for clar.

3			
2			
1			

beats 2,3, curved wrist strokes

3	W		SR
2	C		
1	E		

'click' 2 for bsn

3			
2			
1			

beats 2,3, curved wrist strokes

3			
2	C		Fr
1			

'click' 2 for fl.
l.h.-'click' 3, W,2,SL

3			
2			AR
1			

'click' 2 for oboe, curve
stroke 3,l.h. for forte

3			
2			
1			

'click' 2 for clar's

3			
2			
1			

3			
2			
1			

to fl/ob

3	C		
2			OPD
1	E		

l.h.OPD,C, beat 2, move to zone 3

3			
2	E		OPU
1			

l.h. OPU, beat 2,
move back to zone 1

213

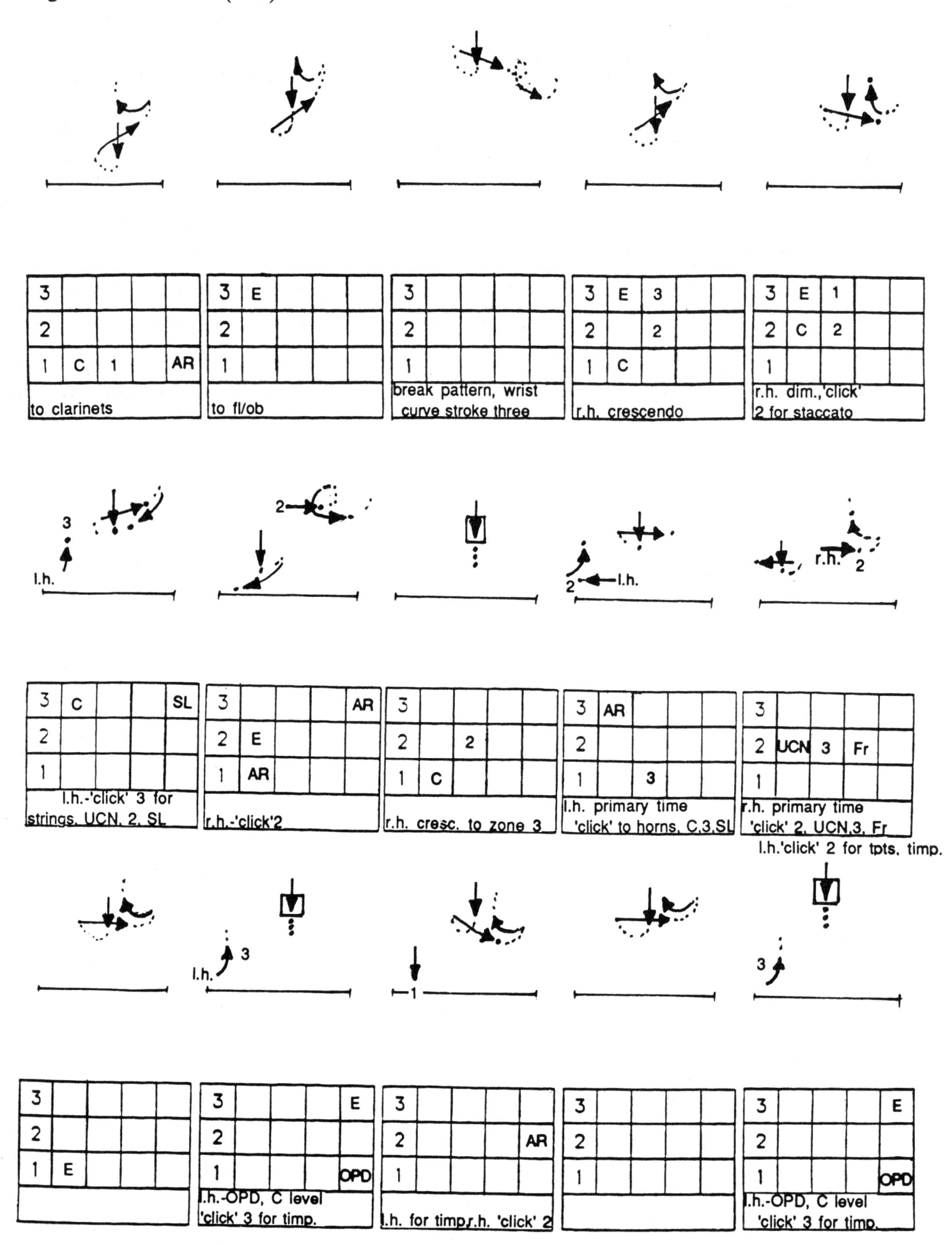

Fig. 144 **PatternCubes** (cont.)

3				
2				
1	C	1		AR

to clarinets

3	E			
2				
1				

to fl/ob

3				
2				
1				

break pattern, wrist curve stroke three

3	E	3		
2		2		
1	C			

r.h. crescendo

3	E	1		
2	C	2		
1				

r.h. dim.,'click' 2 for staccato

3	C			SL
2				
1				

l.h.-'click' 3 for strings, UCN, 2, SL

3				AR
2	E			
1	AR			

r.h.-'click' 2

3				
2		2		
1	C			

r.h. cresc. to zone 3

3	AR			
2				
1		3		

l.h. primary time 'click' to horns, C,3,SL

3				
2	UCN	3	Fr	
1				

r.h. primary time 'click' 2, UCN,3, Fr
l.h.'click' 2 for tpts, timp.

3				
2				
1	E			

3				E
2				
1				OPD

l.h.-OPD, C level 'click' 3 for timp.

3				
2				AR
1				

l.h. for timp, r.h. 'click' 2

3				
2				
1				

3				E
2				
1				OPD

l.h.-OPD, C level 'click' 3 for timp.

214

Fig. 144 **PatternCubes** (cont.)

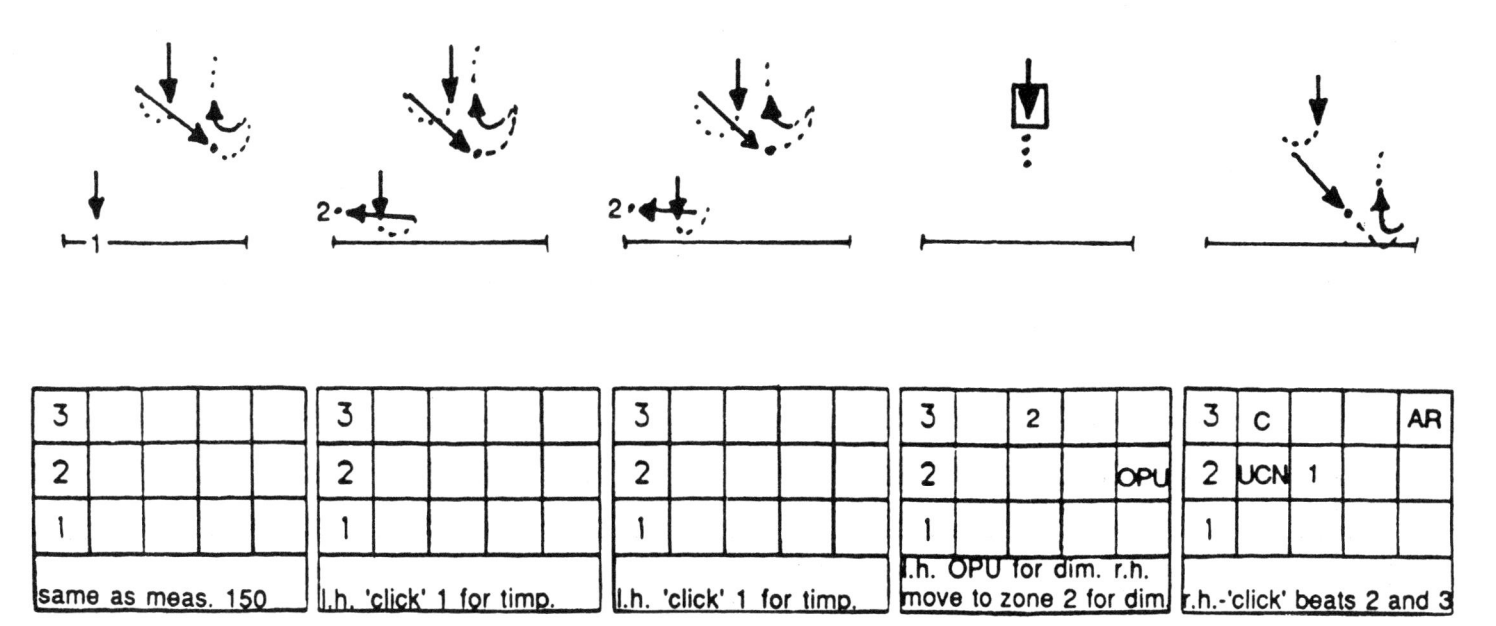

3			
2			
1			
same as meas. 150			

3			
2			
1			
l.h. 'click' 1 for timp.			

3			
2			
1			
l.h. 'click' 1 for timp.			

3	2		
2			OPU
1			
l.h. OPU for dim. r.h. move to zone 2 for dim			

3	C		AR
2	UCN	1	
1			
r.h.-'click' beats 2 and 3			

215

Ex. 111 Beethoven's *Fifth Symphony*, Third Movement, measures 1 to 20

Beethoven's metronome mark, dotted half note equals 96, indicates one baton stroke per measure. The *piano* and *pianissimo* dynamic scheme is conducted in zone 1, or from the wrist, without forearm movement, in zone 3. Note the differences in the measures which contain *fermati*. Measure 8 has a break in the sound after the second beat, while measure 18 moves directly into the horn *fortissimo*. The clarinets are in B-flat, the horns in E-flat, and the trumpets in C.

Visual Score Study/Baton Placement

This movement is generally beaten in an ongoing string of downward strokes. The PatternCube offers a different solution, *matching beat patterns to phrase structures*. While some phrase structures are easily deciphered, the opening of the third movement merits close inspection. Where does the opening phrase begin? Is it the first full measure beyond the G-natural pick-up note? The phrases arrange themselves in the following four-measure groups: 1-4, 5-8, 9-12, 13-14 (a two-measure unit), 15-18, and the horn entrance. There is an alternate possibility -- the G-natural pick-up as a part of the first measure so the phrase structure is pick-up to 3 (to make a four-measure phrase), 4-7, 8-11, 12-13 (a two-measure unit), 14-17, 18 and the horn entrance, another two measure unit.

The PatternCube opts for the latter. The entrance of the horns in measure 4 indicates the beginning of a new four measure unit, and the *fermata* on the downbeat of measure 8 is a strong arrival point and phrase indicator. Immediately after the *fermata* we have a reiteration of the materials in the first four measure unit, a confirmation of the shape of the opening phrase structure.

Pick-up to Measure 3

Conduct a four-beat pattern as indicated in the PatternCube with small *legato* strokes. Make a single *pianissimo* preparatory stroke at the W level in zone 1, Fr, and register throughout. In measure 3, cue the horns with a small 'click' of the left hand, UNC, zone 1, Fr. Remain *pianissimo* throughout. Connect to the tip of the baton!

Measures 4-7

Conduct a four-beat pattern. The left hand 'clicks' the horn entry in measure 4 and immediately moves to an OPS position to maintain the *pianissimo* for the string entrance. While the right hand 'clicks' in the direction of the bassoons for their *piano* entrances in measure 5, look at the first violins before their entrance. In measure 6 look at the bassoons and 'click' in the direction of the clarinets for their *piano* entrances in measure 7. For the *poco ritenuto* in measure 7 maintain an upward vertical stroke with two small upward wrist 'clicks' for the second and third beats in the *ritenuto* motion. Avoid a traditional three-beat pattern (with the second stroke moving to the right). It may slow the tempo beyond the *poco ritenuto* indication, and the result is an unnecessarily long *fermata*. Maintain the string *pianissimo*.

Measures 8-11

The length of the *fermata* in measure 8 is influenced by the *poco ritenuto* in measure 7. Make a slight upward motion to prepare for the downward *pianissimo* 'click.' The 'click' acts as the cut-off for the G-major sonority. It also indicates the downbeat of measure 8 again, setting the tempo for the celli and bassi entrance on the third beat of the measure. **The cut-off insures that Beethoven's slash marks after the *fermata* will be honored by creating a silence before the entrance of the celli and bassi.** Make the 'click' after the *fermata* at E or the W level. If the conductor chooses to make the 'click' at W level, move the right hand downward during the *fermata* to W level. The left hand is not needed in this measure, unless it is used to control the dynamic level. The downbeat 'click' is the beginning of a four-beat phrase pattern. Repeat the physical movement employed in the opening of the movement.

Measures 12-13

Use a two-beat pattern for these two measures. In the PatternCube, the insertion of this two-measure unit, with the *sfp* on the downbeat in measure 13, breaks up the regularity of the four-measure patterns. The *sfp* in the second measure of the unit can be thought of as a foreshadowing of the *fortissimo* horn entrance in measures 18-19. 'Click' the right hand lightly in measure twelve, and move forward to zone 2 for the *fp* in measure 13.

Measures 14-17

Use a four-beat pattern for these measures. 'Click' the left hand in measure 14 for the string entrance in measure 15. Use the right hand to prepare the wind entrances in measures 15 and 16. In measure 17 use the same technical gestures that were applied to the *poco ritenuto* in measure 7. Continue to maintain the *pianissimo* character in the strings.

Measures 18-19

Use a two-beat pattern for these two measures. Unlike measure 8, **the G major *fermata* must be held throughout measure 18**, and ceases at the sudden *a tempo fortissimo* horn attack on the next downbeat. Look at the horns during the *fermata* in measure 18, and slowly move the baton in a horizontal motion to the right. At this moment, before the horn attack in measure 19, the conductor has two options:

1) Flick' a preparatory stroke for the horns *during* the sideways horizontal movement, and make a second upward 'click' for the actual entrance of the horns. (The second 'click' is in measure 19. If the 'click' is too strong the strings or winds may stop playing!)

2) This option is possible because of the familiarity of this entrance, scored for a pair of horns. At the appropriate moment after the sideways horizontal movement make a single upward *fortissimo marcato* 'click' gesture toward the horns. The upward 'click' acts as measure 19 and ignites the tempo. Since the tempo has already been established, the two horns react to the 'click' and, in this instance, play in time without the benefit of preparation. Technically, nothing the baton does in the second option interferes with the string and wind sound until the horns enter.

The PatternCube uses a single upward 'click' after the *fermata*. The upward 'click' gesture, the second part of a two-beat pattern, frames the two measure unit, and results in a *forte* downward stroke in measure 20 emphasizing the arrival of the beginning of a new phrase.

Measure 20

The C minor string harmony supporting the horns begins another four-measure phrase.

Performance Comment

Composers do not write one-bar phrases when they compose movements to be conducted with one stroke per measure. Repeating a down/up stroke endlessly addresses the time-keeping issue, but not the relevant question of **how time is shaped** by the composer. **Combine single strokes in patterns of 2, 3 or 4 to match the phrases.**

Fig. 145 **PatternCubes**

Beethoven Fifth Symphony, Third Movement
Beginning to Measure 20

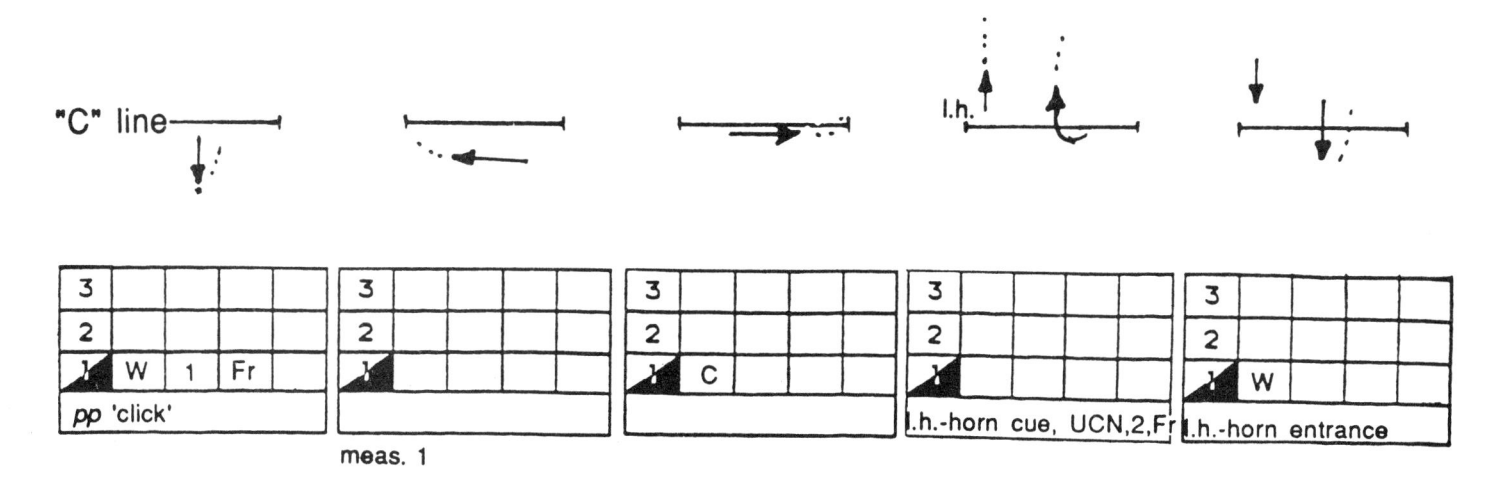

Fig. 145 **PatternCubes** (cont.)

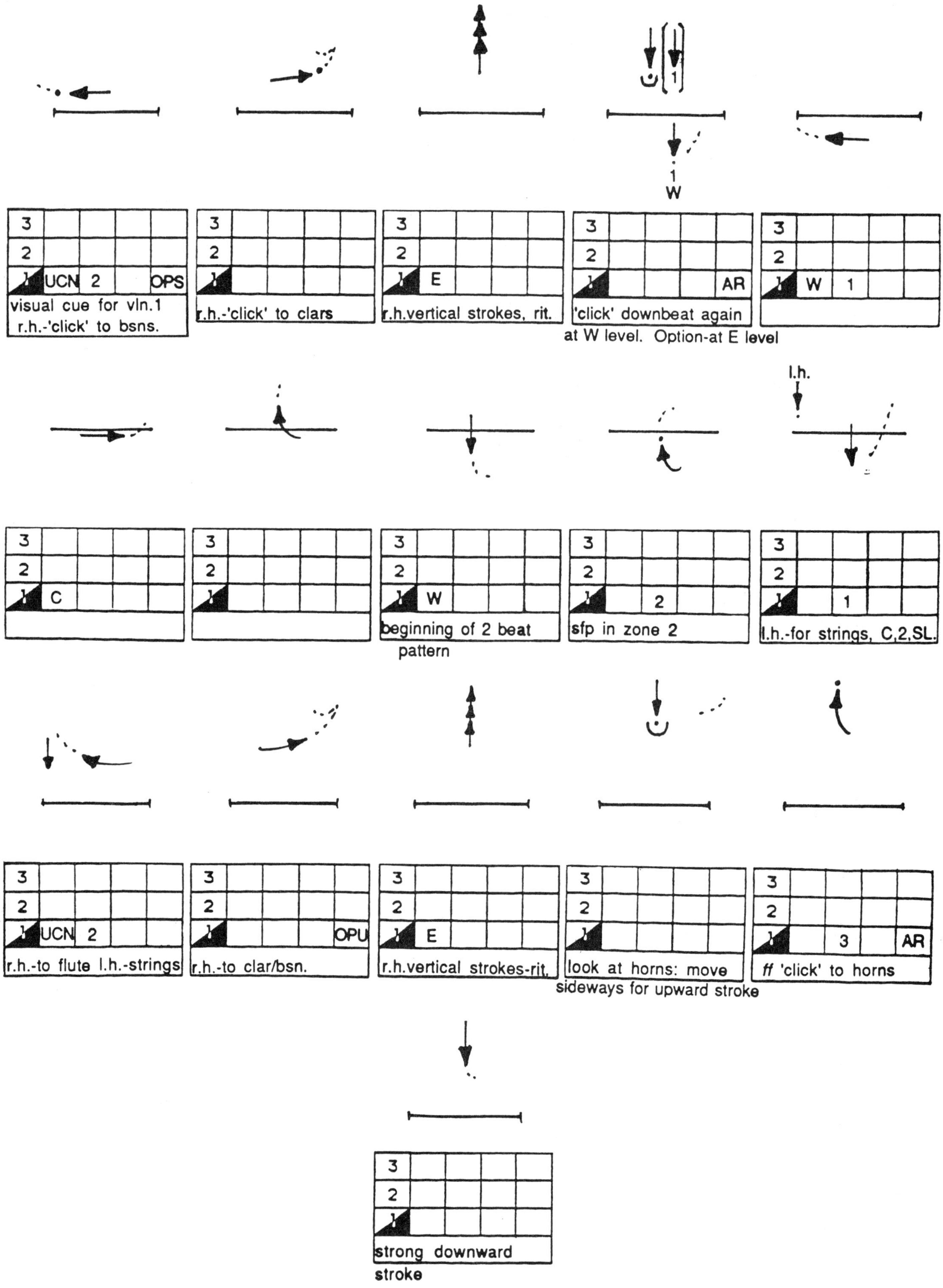

220

Ex. 112 Beethoven's *Fifth Symphony*, Third Movement, measure 336 to Fourth Movement, measure 12

Ex. 112 (cont).

Ex. 112 (cont).

A long, sustained, rhythmic *pianissimo* calm bursts into the *fortissimo* storm that announces the arrival of the fourth movement. During the *pianissimo* from measure 336 to measure 366, the conductor makes as little physical motion as possible. Registration should be used with constraint, the melodic contours etched in small baton movements.

The fourth movement arrival is powerful; every player is involved in this massive and energetic *Allegro* which Beethoven marks 84 to the half note. The conductor must respond to the exhilarating quality of the music and be prepared to keep the energy level high.

Visual Score Study/Baton Placement

Measures 336-339

Use a four-beat pattern. Direct the right hand to the timpani, below C level in zone 1. The baton strokes are small, short *pianissimo* 'clicks' for measures 336-337-338. **Do not make any large physical gestures for thirty measures!** Quietly 'click' the left hand to the first violins and bassi in measure 338, for their rhythmic entrances in the following measure. Use a *legato* stroke with a 'click' in measure 339.

Measures 340-341

Use a two-beat pattern, and right hand legato strokes.

Measures 342-343

Use a two-beat pattern, with a clear *pianissimo* 'click' for measure 342. Remain *pianissimo*. (Use the left hand for dynamic control, OPU, UCN, zone 1, SL, if necessary.)

Measures 344-345

Use a two-beat pattern.

Measures 346-347

Use a two-beat pattern.

Measures 348-349

Use a two-beat pattern.

Measures 350-353

Use a four-beat pattern. Use small *legato* strokes and register within a small space. Remain *pianissimo*.

Measures 354-357

Use a four-beat pattern. Do not make any large gestures.

Measures 358-361

Use a four-beat pattern.

Measures 362-365

Use a four-beat pattern. In measure 365 <u>look at the</u> <u>timpanist</u> to confirm that the rhythmic pattern changes to eighth notes in the next measure, and cue the bassoons for their entrances.

Measures 366-369

Cue the oboes in measure 366 for their entrances. Since this is the beginning of the *crescendo*, the conductor must decide how loud the strings, oboes, bassoons, and timpani will be at measure 370 when the horns and trumpets enter at the *piano* level - *mezzo piano, mezzo forte*? Whatever the decision is for the strings and winds, the timpanist should be no louder than the horn and trumpet *piano* at measure 370, otherwise the *crescendo* may peak too soon. In measure 369 cue the horns and trumpets with the <u>right hand</u>, look at the flutes, and use the <u>left hand</u>, OPU, for the trumpets and horns.

Measures 370-373

Move through the zones into zone 3, using larger right hand strokes and more space for the baton. Move the left hand to the OPD position, and cue the trombones in measure 373 for their *fortissimo* entrance in the fourth movement. (If the conductor cannot resist the urge to make a *ritard* in measure 373, change the string articulations from eighth notes to <u>tremelandi</u>.)

Fourth Movement-Measures 1-3

Each measure will receive two vigorous strokes. Remain in zone 3 throughout this excerpt. The baton addresses the horns, trumpets and trombones. Measure 1 receives long strokes, i.e. full value half note movement, with 'clicks.' Make a short second stroke in measure 2 for the fourth quarter eighth note. Measure 3 receives two short baton strokes. The <u>left hand</u> helps sustain the brass sonority into the second measure, and makes a short clenched fist 'click' on the second beat in measure two to prepare the fourth quarter eighth note. Register as indicated in the PatternCube.

Measures 4-5

In both measures, the stroke pattern is a long first stroke, and a short second stroke. Encourage the second violins, like the violas, to play their sixteenth notes with great energy.

Measures 6-7

Make a long stroke and a sharp 'click' short stroke for measure 6, and two short strokes for measure seven. The PatternCube adds the use of the left hand in measure 7. This is not normally done, but it influences the sound produced by the instruments in the lowest registers of the orchestra. 'Click' the left hand on the second beat in measure 7 for the celli and bassi eighth notes in measure 8. **Note the left hand stroke pattern, short-long, is the opposite of the right hand stroke pattern, long-short.** From the middle of measure 6, the horns, trumpets and trombones are rhythmic/harmonic accompaniment rather than melodic factors. Balance the sound carefully.

Measures 8-9

The left hand stroke pattern for the celli and bassi is again short-long. The pattern for the right hand is the same as in the two previous measures: long, short, short, short.

Measures 10-11-12

Measures 10 and 11 are a repeat of measures 8 and 9. In measure 12 restrict the movement to the right hand only, and use a short stroke, followed by a long second stroke. Why a long second stroke when the fourth beat contains the sixteenth note rest in the melodic material? From the opening of the movement, Beethoven has carefully avoided using a full quarter note value on the third beat in the melodic material. Unless the conductor indicates the longer second stroke, orchestras generally articulate the third beat quarter note as an eighth note.

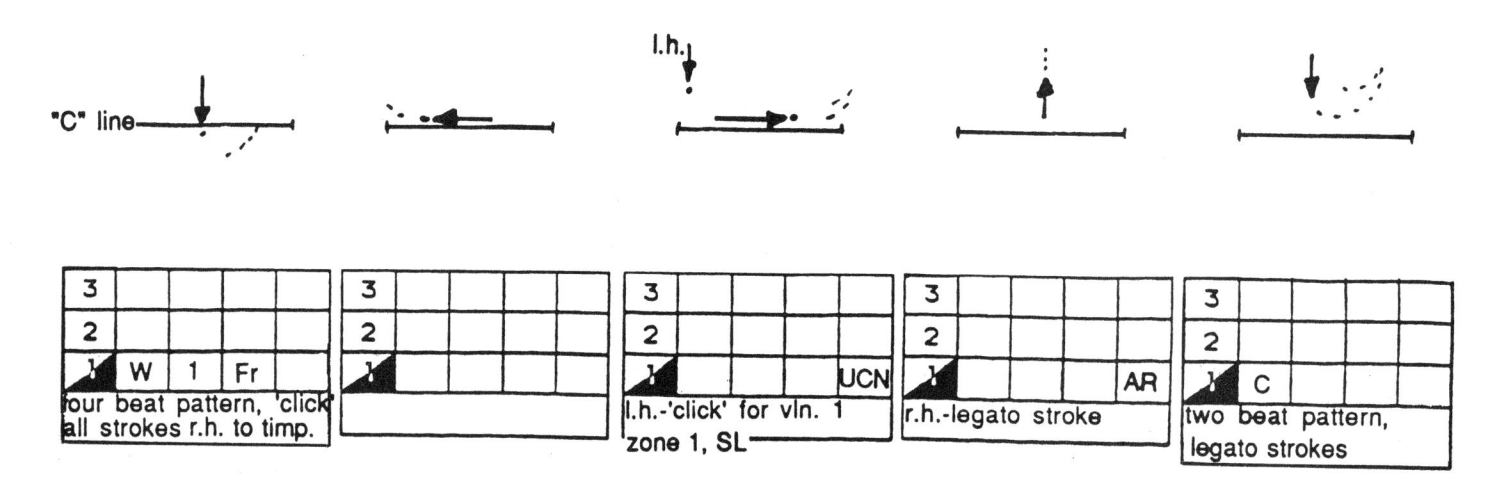

Fig. 146 **PatternCubes**

Beethoven Fifth Symphony, Third Movement, measure 336, to Fourth Movement, measure 12.

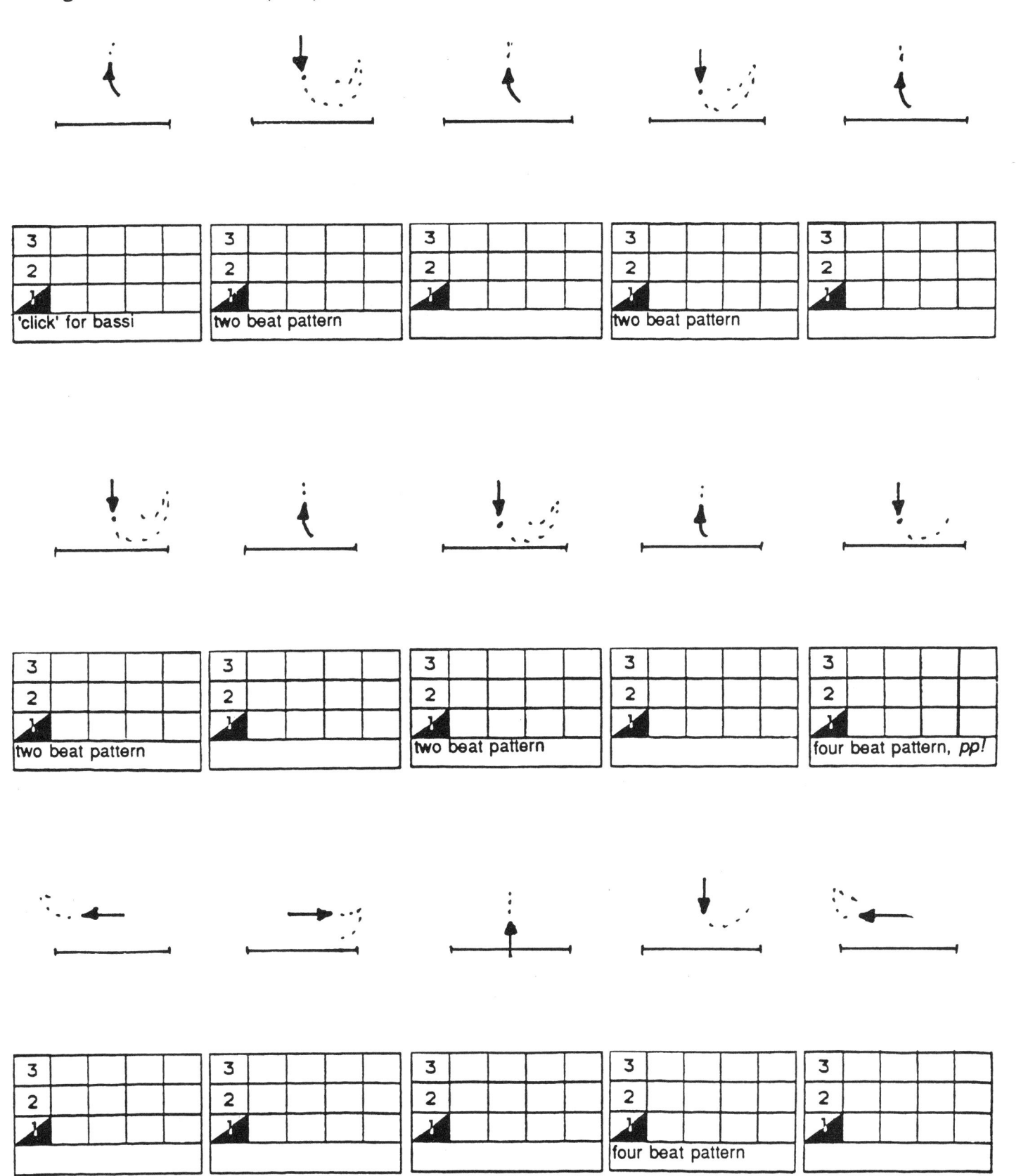

Fig. 146 **PatternCubes** (cont.)

227

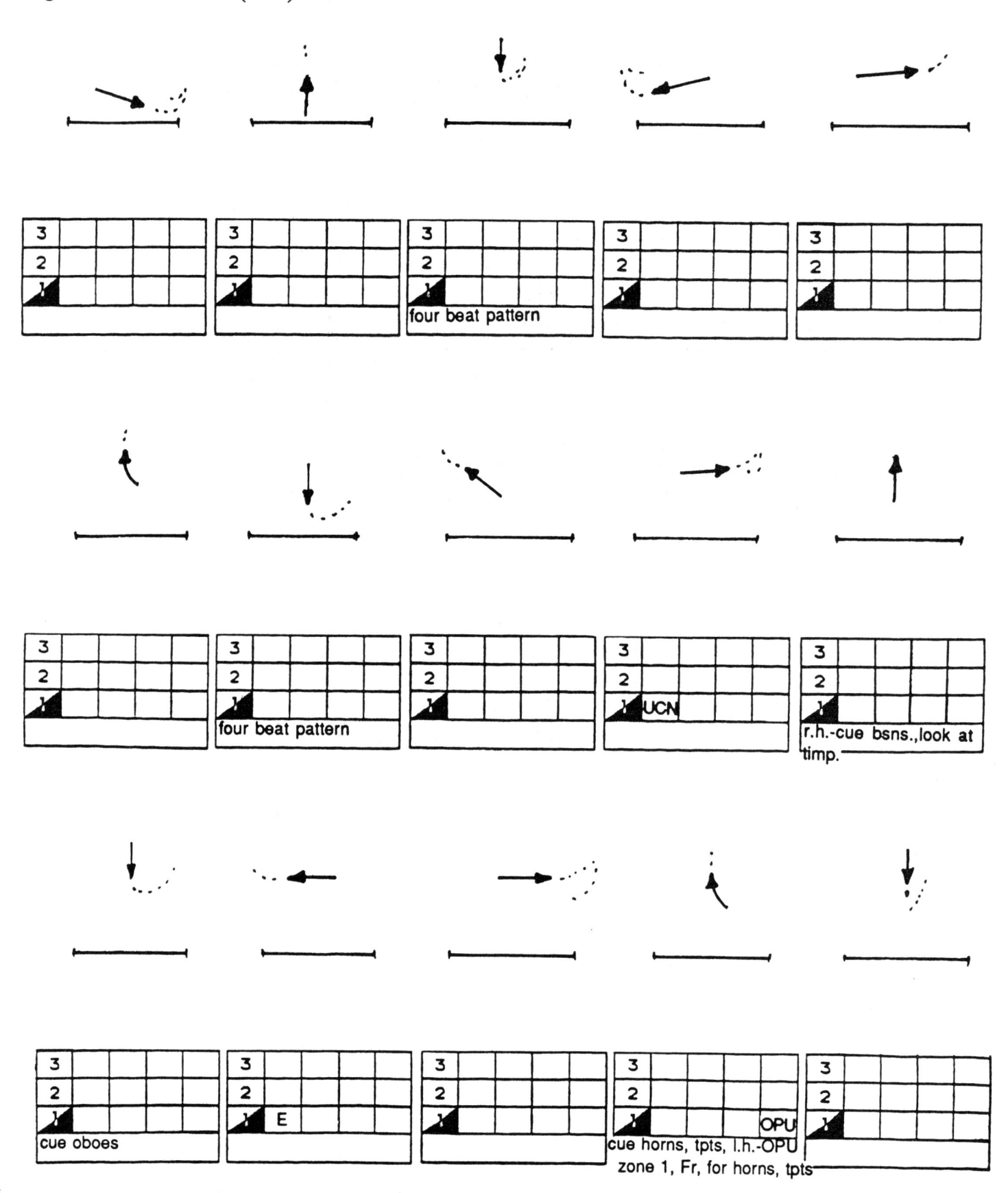

Fig. 146 **PatternCubes** (cont.)

Fig. 146 **PatternCubes** (cont.)

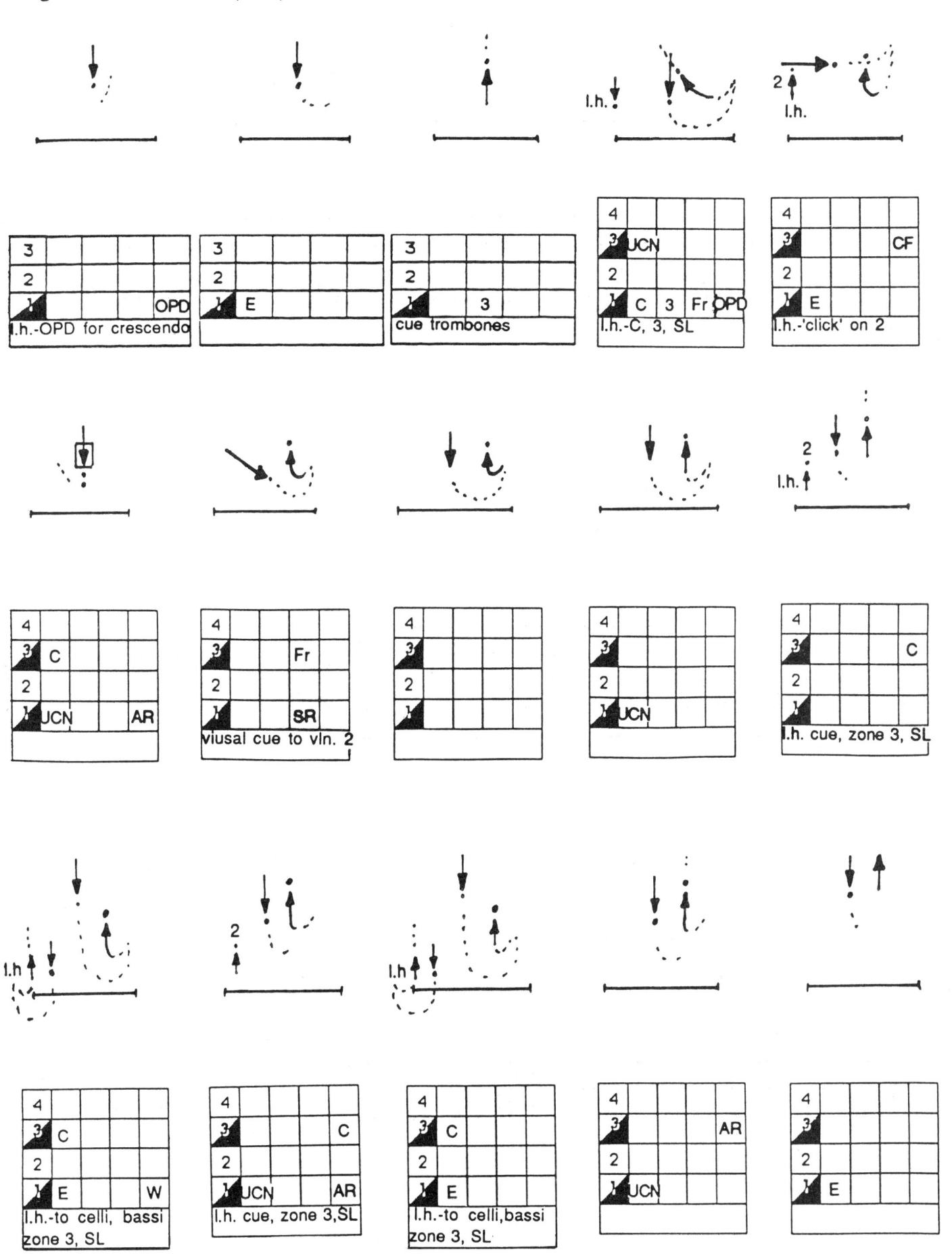

229

Ex. 113 Beethoven's *Fifth Symphony,* Fourth Movement, measures 150 to 169

Beethoven's return to the thematic material of the third movement is accomplished over a forceful nine measure G major section, when the top G-natural is sounded in a final *fortissimo* quarter note downbeat on measure 153. The 3/4 measure is marked 96 to the dotted half note, a faster metronome marking than the previous 84 to the half note. The tempo adjustment can be made in measure 152 by holding the first beat a bit longer, and then **'clicking' the preparatory second stroke in the tempo of the next measure,** 96 per dotted half note. The PatternCube adopts this method.

During the eight measure *diminuendo* from *fortissimo* to *pianissimo*, move the baton from zone 3 back into zone 1, and use less space with each passing measure. Begin with forearm strokes and conclude with wrist 'clicks.' The four-beat pattern outlines the phrase units. Attention should be paid to the articulation of all *pizzicati*--use wrist 'clicks' and the entrance of the clarinets. The clarinets, horns and trumpets are in C.

Visual Score Study/Baton Placement

Measures 150-152

With the exception of a strongly 'clicked' vertical upbeat to measure 153, use vigorous side to side *legato* horizontal strokes, with 'flicks' to sustain the sound. (As noted above, hold the first beat in measure 152 a bit longer, and then 'flick' a strong preparatory second stroke in the tempo of the next measure, i.e. 96 to the dotted half note.)

Measures 153-156

Measure 153 is both the culmination of the last section and the beginning of the long *diminuendo* bridge to measure 160. While these four measures and the following four measures could be conducted with four-beat patterns, doing so would work against the flow of the music. The stroke that is used to deliver the hammer blow in measure 153 should be used again and again with diminishing force as the echo of the reiterated sound fades to the *pianissimo* in measure 160. To help the *diminuendo* the PatternCube uses the left hand in measure 156, beginning OPU in zone 3, and moving backwards to zone 1.

Measures 157-160

Follow the PatternCube baton placements through the zones, and control the height of the strokes as measure 160 is approached. Throughout the dynamic changes, each of the strokes from 153 to 160 are short, and made with wrist 'clicks.' The rebounds are also short, with the baton moving only between beats one to two and **stopping momentarily** on beat three before moving on to the next downbeat. Prepare the *pizzicati* in measure 161 with a well articulated *pianissimo* wrist 'click' in measure 160.

Measures 161-164

The arrival of the C minor is the beginning of a series of four-measure phrases. The PatternCube uses two four-beat patterns over the next eight measures. For the sake of variety, the PatternCube uses the <u>left</u> hand for the clarinets, while the <u>right</u> hand remains in zone 1 and continues small barline 'clicks' for the string *pizzicati*. The left hand moves into zone 2, UCN, Fr, to cue the clarinets in measure 163.

Measures 165-169

Note the <u>longer stroke and the full rebound</u> for measure 165. In measure 166 make a <u>circular wrist movement</u> for two beats and then <u>stop all movement</u> on the third beat in measure 166. This *left hand articulation will account for the two-beat slur and the dot* on the third beat for the clarinets. The left hand is AR in measure 168 as the next F minor four measure phrase begins in measure 169.

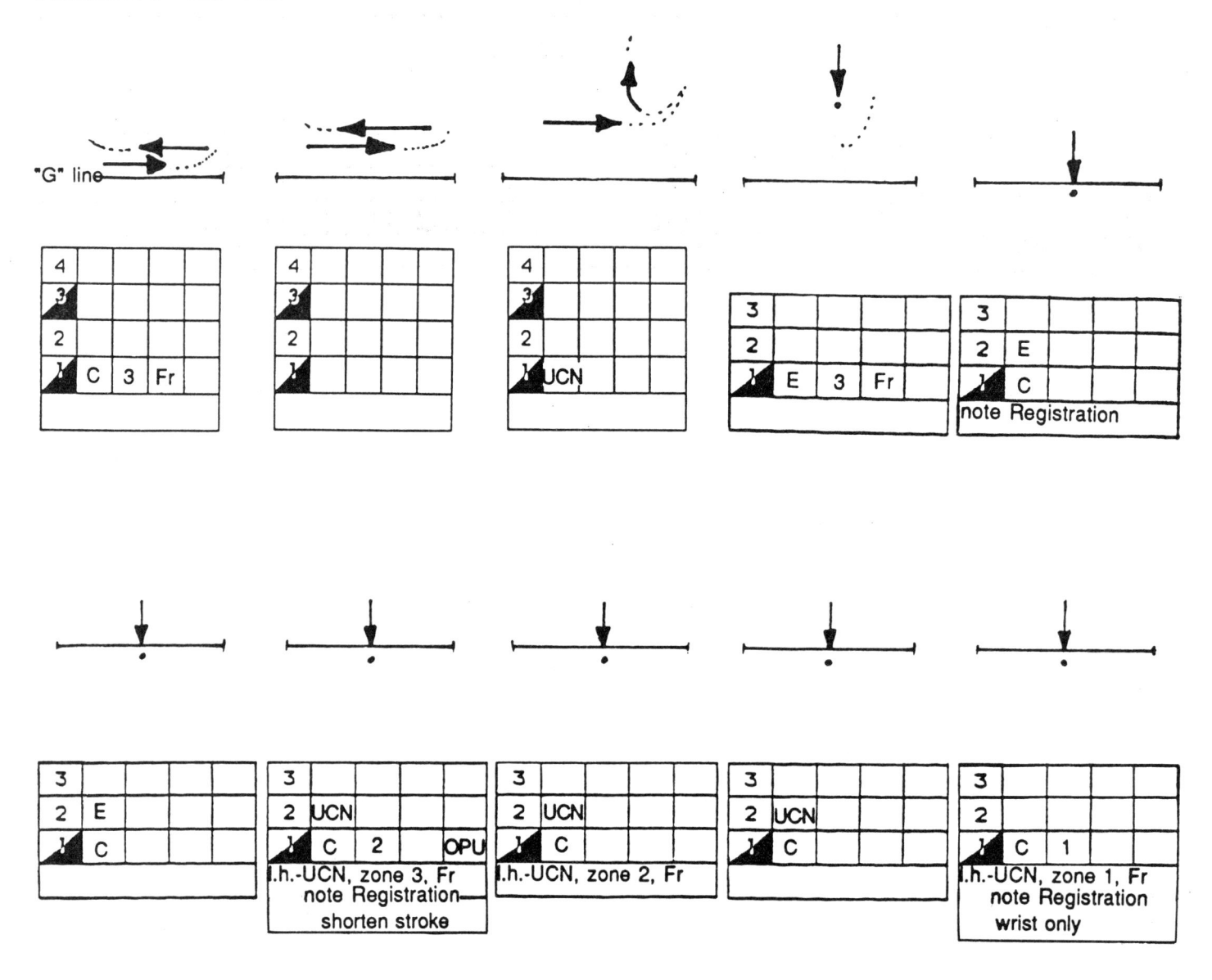

Fig. 147 **PatternCubes**

Beethoven Fifth Symphony, Fourth Movement
Measures 150-169

Fig. 147 **PatternCubes** (cont.)

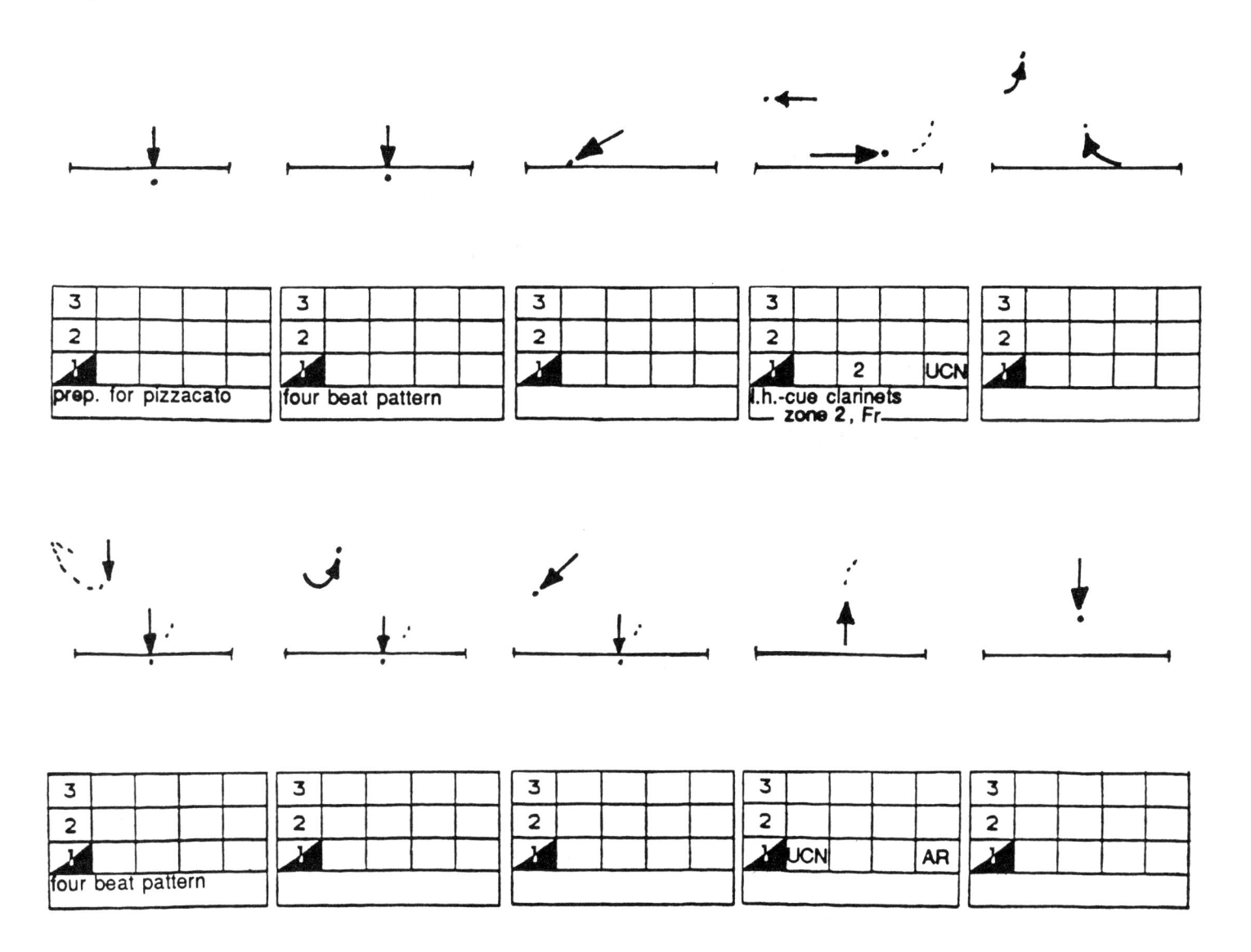

Ex. 114 Beethoven's *Fifth Symphony,* Fourth Movement, measures 350 to 371

Ex. 114 (cont.)

Beethoven's directions are explicit -- move the tempo from 84 to the half note, two beats per measure, to 112 to the whole note at the *Presto*, a nine measure span. Throughout the *accelerando*, all strokes have 'clicks' to help the winds, and later the trumpets and timpani, place their afterbeats without difficulty. The PatternCube divides the nine measures of *accelerando* into three parts, measures 353-355, 356-357, and 358 to the *Presto*, the conclusion of the *accelerando*.

The *Presto* must be conducted with one stroke per measure. From measure 362, the PatternCube uses one two-beat pattern for each two-measure group. The *forte piano* marking which defines each of the two measure groups is indicated to the players by moving the baton forward from zone 2 into zone 3, with a wrist 'click' at the end of the stroke (*fp*).

Note the use of an upward *legato* stroke for the the first and second violins in measures 363, 365, 367, 369, and 371 on the second stroke in each of the two-beat patterns. Cue the winds in measure 368 for their entry in the following measure. Follow the registration in the PatternCube.

Visual Score Study/Baton Placement

Measures 350-352

The eighth note *piano* afterbeats in the winds set the stage for the oncoming *accelerando*. Move out to zone 2 and keep the baton at E level, Fr, so that the entire orchestra, especially those not yet playing, will be able to react to what lies ahead. Use basic two-stroke patterns for the three measures. **Maintain a steady tempo.**

Measures 353-355

Measure 353 is the **beginning** of the *accelerando*. **At this moment the conductor must already know the tempo of the *Presto*, and how much forward momentum to create.** A word of caution -- do not move ahead too quickly. Keep the point of the baton visible to everyone on the stage. As the tempo quickens, the baton strokes become smaller. Sense the tip of the baton!

Measures 356-357

Make one downward vertical stroke for each measure, but indicate a second stroke in the upward vertical rebound with a small upward 'click.' (Do not move the baton to the right for beat two!) Maintain the vertical down/up one stroke motion for each measure. Continue to increase the speed of the tempo.

Measures 358-361

Four measures before the *Presto,* Beethoven fuels the forward momentum by adding the weight of the trumpets and the timpani to the ongoing *crescendo*. Use a left hand 'click,' E level, zone 3, SL, to cue the timpani on the downbeat of measure 358. Each downward stroke near the conclusion of the *accelerando* must contain 'clicks!'

Measures 362-363

Measure 362 is the arrival of the *Presto*. Use a two-beat pattern for these measures. Register <u>down to the W level</u>, and indicate the *forte piano* in measure 362 by moving the baton <u>outward</u> into zone 3 and adding a sharp wrist 'click' at the end of the stroke. The slur in measure 363 in made by the wrist with a <u>curved down/up inward motion back</u> to zone 2. The movement back to zone 2 prepares the baton for the *forte piano* in the next measure. **Keep the baton strokes light and tight, and rely on the wrist rather than the forearm for the delivery of the strokes.**

Measures 364-365, 366-367, 368-369

Use two-beat patterns for each two-measure group. Repeat the strokes in measures 362 and 363, but change the registration as indicated in the PatternCube. Cue the winds in measure 369 for their entrances in measure 370. **Maintain a strict tempo throughout the Presto.**

Measures 370-371

<u>Move up to UCN,</u> and out into zone 3 for the wind entrances. Use a two-beat pattern for these two measures and the same stroke patterns that have been used in the previous measures.

Fig. 148 **PatternCube**
Beethoven Fifth Symphony, Fourth Movement
Measures 350-371

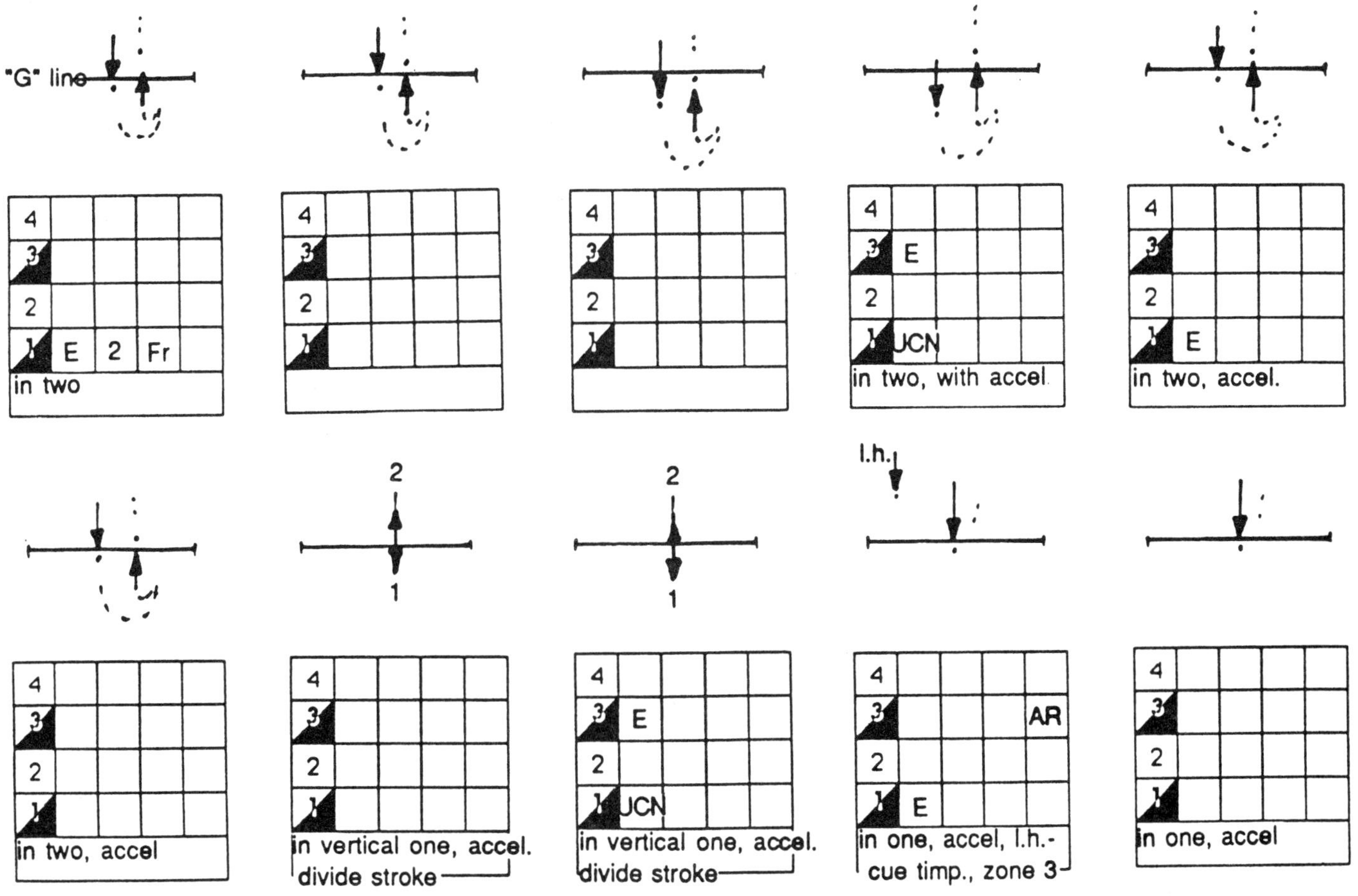

Fig. 148 **PatternCube** (cont.)

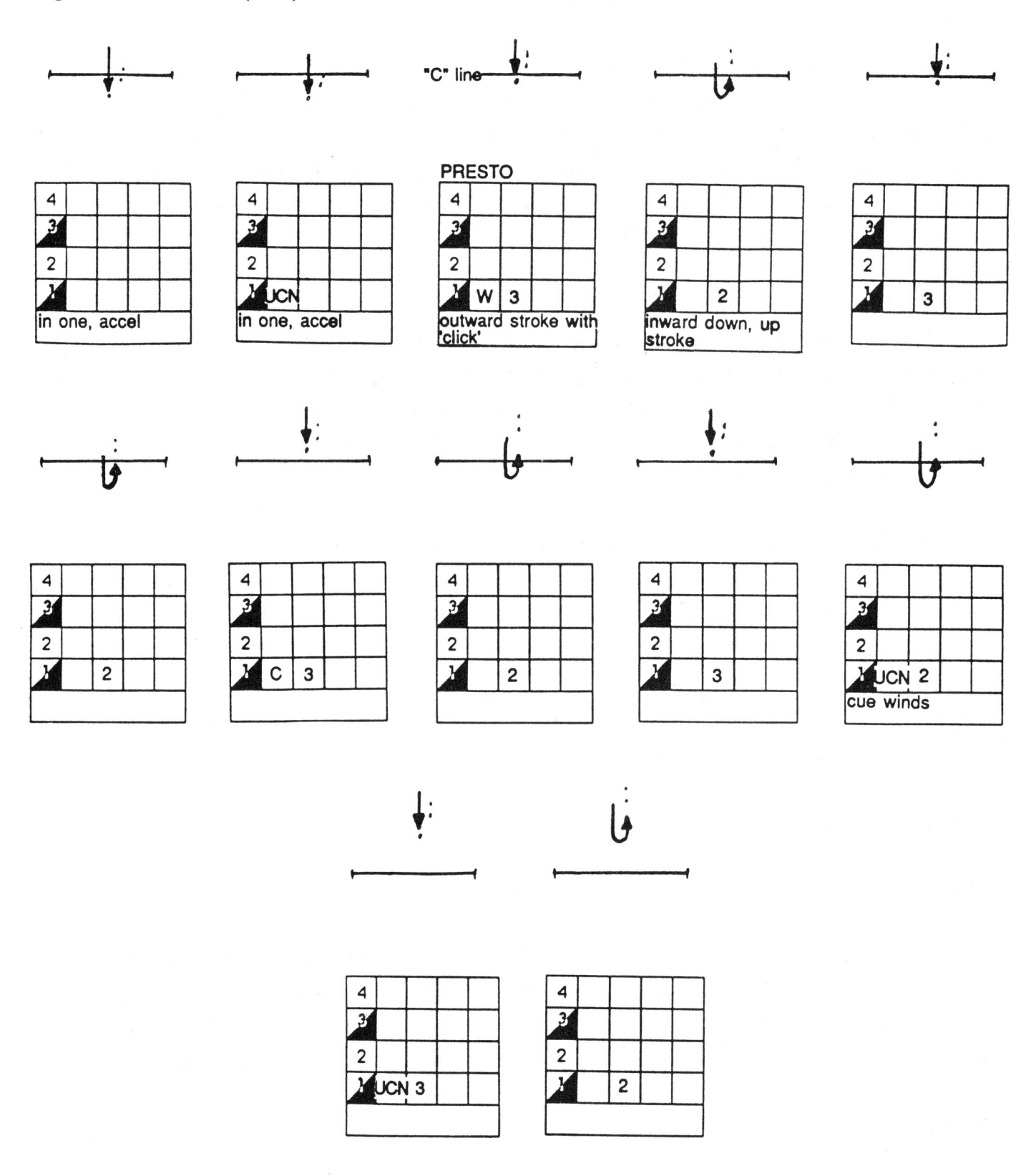

The solutions offered in the Mozart and Beethoven PatternCube excerpts will yield immediate results with most orchestras. However, the success of the following Stravinsky excerpts depends heavily on the availability of a large number of excellent performers. If key players are in need of constant attention from the conductor, the carefully detailed Pattern Cube baton movements may have to be abandoned. But if the conductor collaborates with an orchestra that is capable of meeting Stravinsky's technical challenges, she/he will quickly discover that the baton movements diagrammed in the PatternCubes will answer the musical needs of the music.

238

STRAVINSKY—*THE RITE OF SPRING,* THE SACRIFICE

After the premiere of the *Rite of Spring* on May 29, 1913, irregular movements of the baton and constantly changing rhythmic patterns became matters of importance for all conductors. Decades after the premiere, the music's supposed hostile surfaces no longer seem as formidable as in the past, but a haphazard technical approach to Stravinsky's masterpiece is not yet possible. A clear mind and quick hands in perfect coordination have been, and still are prerequisites. The following excerpts deal exclusively with Stravinsky's rhythmic constructions in the Second Part, "The Sacrifice."

Orchestration

There have been a series of editions, most notably Editions Russe-1921, Stravinsky's revision in 1947 for Boosey and Hawkes, and a reengraved Boosey and Hawkes version in 1967. There have also been corrections and revisions, and conductors planning a performance should address those problems. (Robert Craft's book "Le Sacre du Printemps: A Chronology of the Revisions," in Stravinsky: Selected Correspondence, Vol.1, ed. Robert Craft, (New York 1982), pp. 398-406, will be helpful.)

The score used for the PatternCubes is the 1967 Boosey and Hawkes edition.

Orchestra Seating

The conductor must know the exact location of the extra winds (4-4-4-4) and brass (8-4-3-2). When cues are given, direct them to specific players rather than to general areas. Strings are seated in the normal twentieth-century configuration, violins one and two to the left of the conductor, violas, celli and bassi to the right of the conductor.

For the Conductor's Consideration

Strings

The lack of sustained lyric lines, percussive stop and start playing, and constantly changing meters, all tend to work against ingrained string-playing habits. Many string players perform Stravinsky or Boulez as easily as they perform Mozart, but for those who do not, the conductor should be prepared to offer various solutions. "Could you please start with the bow on the string? Thank you." will always yield a positive result.

Timpani

Because of the forceful nature of the instrument, the one player on the stage who creates havoc with an erratic performance is the timpanist. The timpani part is almost a concerto and often used as an audition piece. If the timpanist and conductor are not together in the final pages, important musical moments will fall apart.

General Performance Note. -- This excerpt contains a large array of short notes; *pizzicati*, diamond shaped accents on eighth notes, dots over eighth notes, *secco* marks, etc. *Use the wrist as much as possible, in forte as well as fortissimo.* And throughout every excerpt continue to connect to the tip of the baton!

Ex. 115   One measure before number 104 to number 113
"Glorification of the Chosen One"

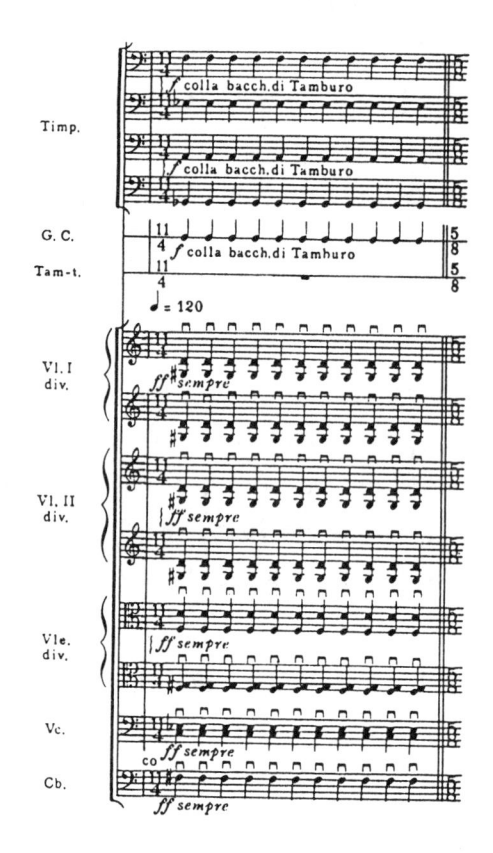

© 1921 by EDITION RUSSE DE MUSIQUE
Copyright assigned to BOOSEY & HAWKES, INC., for all countries
Used by permission

Ex. 115 (cont.)

Ex. 115 (cont.)

Ex. 115 (cont.)

Ex. 115 (cont.)

Ex. 115 (cont.)

Ex. 115 (cont.)

Ex. 115 (cont.)

Ex. 115 (cont.)

Visual Score Study/Baton Placement

The tempo, 120 and 144 to the quarter note, does not allow for exact pitch registration. The speed of the changing meters demands absolute baton clarity and exact spatial placements. The internal structures of the 5s, 7s, and 9s must be clear and delivered without hesitation. 'Clicks' are essential.

One measure before number 104

An 11/4 measure, 120 to the quarter note. Do not use a pattern in the 11/4 measure, (everyone will count to eleven), instead, use ten strong *downward* strokes, both hands in unison (*mirroring*) to reinforce the physicality of the scoring, and make a clear right hand *upward* stroke on beat 11.

The four note timpani chord needs 2 players using wood sticks. The bass drum is also played with a wood stick. Use W level, close to body, zone 1.

Number 104 to 105

The metronome marking is 144 to the quarter note. Begin securely and establish the tempo and the eighth note patterns. Cut out excess motion -- use wrist, zone 2, C and UNC levels, Fr. Show the baton to the entire orchestra, and make certain that the 2s and 3s in the patterns *do not look alike*. Maintain the speed of the baton stroke!

Measures 1-2 -- The pattern is 2+3, and not 3+2, despite the beaming of the bass part. On beat three the conductor looks at, or physically cues, timpani or winds and brass.

Performance Note -- Some conductors use the left forearm on beat 2 in the 5/8 measure for a string cue, creating hand movement on the first three beats in the measure, a lot of motion where clarity is essential. The left hand motion on beat two presupposes that the strings will not react to the right hand downbeat. That is not likely. Think of afterbeats in a 2/4 measure moving at 144 per quarter. Should the afterbeat be cued? Of course not. If the downbeat is a clear, in-tempo stroke, the afterbeat will be in its proper place.

Measure 3 -- Cue the bass drum entrance with the left hand.

Performance Note -- This 9/8 measure is often conducted in a four pattern, 2+2+2+3, which follows the bass line. However there is a tension in conducting this measure in a three pattern, with the release at number 105, that is missing when it is done in the smoother 4 pattern. Both solutions work. Maestro Pierre Monteaux, who conducted the premiere of *Le Sacre*, used a three pattern. The PatternCube uses a three pattern.

Number 105 to 106

The same musical materials were used between numbers 104 and 105, but with a different rhythmic configuration. Do not alter the pattern placements.

Measure 1 -- Use the left hand for the the bass drum downbeat. SL, zone 3, MC level.

Measure 2 -- Cue the timpani on beat 5 with the left hand. The right hand addresses the winds and brass on beats 3 and 5, Fr, in zone 3, with 2 sharp wrist 'clicks,' at the E and UNC levels.

Measure 3 -- The 3/8 bar is conducted in one.
Option -- Place a second vertical beat 'click' within the upstroke. (Do not move the baton to the right in a normal three-beat pattern.)

Number 106 to 107

A departure from the previous materials.

Measure 1 -- While their sections have played previously, trumpets 1,2 (fluttertongue), and trombones 1,2, have not yet played in this excerpt and deserve the attention of the conductor. Make a left hand cue on beat 3 for the tam-tam, the only other player who has not played in this section.

Measure 2 -- In 7/4. After beat 1 (E level for picc., flute), break the pattern. Beats 2 to 5 receive the same downward right hand strokes. The left hand encourages the *sempre forte* in top strings. (Listen for balance between timpani and bass drum; the bass drum should not cancel the timpani pitch.)

Number 107 to 108

Measure 1 -- The 3/4 meter is a one-beat extension of the materials in the first measure of no. 106.

Measure 2 -- is a repetition of the 7/4 measure in no. 106.

Number 108 to 109

All three measures are exact repetitions of measures beginning at 1 before no. 106. (The option still exists for the second 'click' stroke in the 3/8 measure.)

Number 109 to 110

Measure 1 -- This 6/8 measure is sometimes done in a *three pattern*. The PatternCube is in a *two pattern*. Note horns 5-8.

Measure 2 -- Cue the timpani on beat 3 with the <u>left</u> hand. (The right hand is free to address all sections.)

Measure 3 -- PatternCube is in a <u>three</u> pattern. (Contains an exact repetition of the first six beats in measure 1 in this sequence.)

Number 110 to 111

The materials are <u>varied</u> repetitions of what has been heard. *The timpanist must be rhythmically correct* -- cue with the <u>left</u> hand as necessary.

Number 111 to 112

Stravinsky introduces new materials.

Measure 1 -- <u>Prepare the *bass drum solo*</u>! <u>Left</u> hand cue.
<u>Performance Note</u> -- This entrance is prepared in the previous measure by eye contact.

Note piccolo and flute 2 <u>triplet</u> over the second and third beats of the measure. (<u>upward</u> 'click' on beat two.)

Measure 2 -- Address the horns with the <u>right</u> hand in zone 3, FX, register F, E, G-flat. Make *legato* strokes with <u>left</u> hand 'clicks' for the string accents.

Measures 3-4 -- A two measure repetition except for a <u>one-beat extension</u> in measure four, here a <u>4/4</u> instead of a <u>3/4</u> measure. (Horns 1-4 play in the third measure instead of horns 5-8 in measure one.) Note the <u>bass drum solo</u> in measure three.

Number 112 to 113

Measures 1-2 -- The same as in no. 111, measures 1-2.

Measure 3 -- An <u>extension of measure 2</u> with a rhythmic change for the strings. The winds are added to the strings on the second and third beats. Make a <u>left hand cut-off on beat 3</u> for the strings and winds.

Measure 4 -- Register at the W level, zone 2 (or 1) for the *mezzo-forte*.
<u>Performance Note</u> -- Timpani, bass drum -- listen for the <u>balance</u> and check the sticks, which should be light enough to match the string *pizzicati* for texture and length of sound.
The bassoon grace notes are to be played as short as possible.

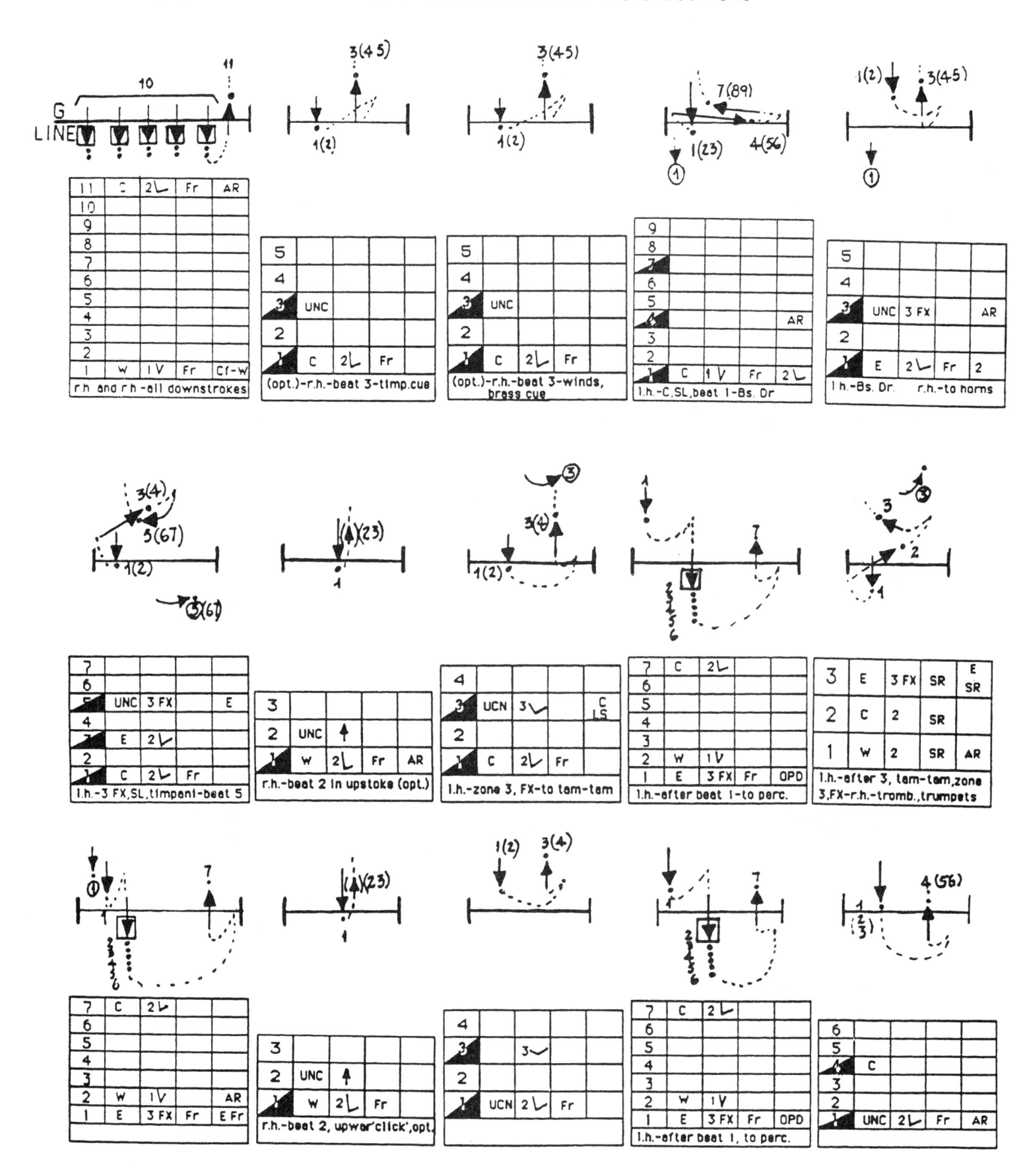

Fig. 149 PatternCubes

The Rite of Spring--Stravinsky

One Bar before Number 104--Glorification of the Chosen One

Fig. 149 **PatternCubes** (cont.)

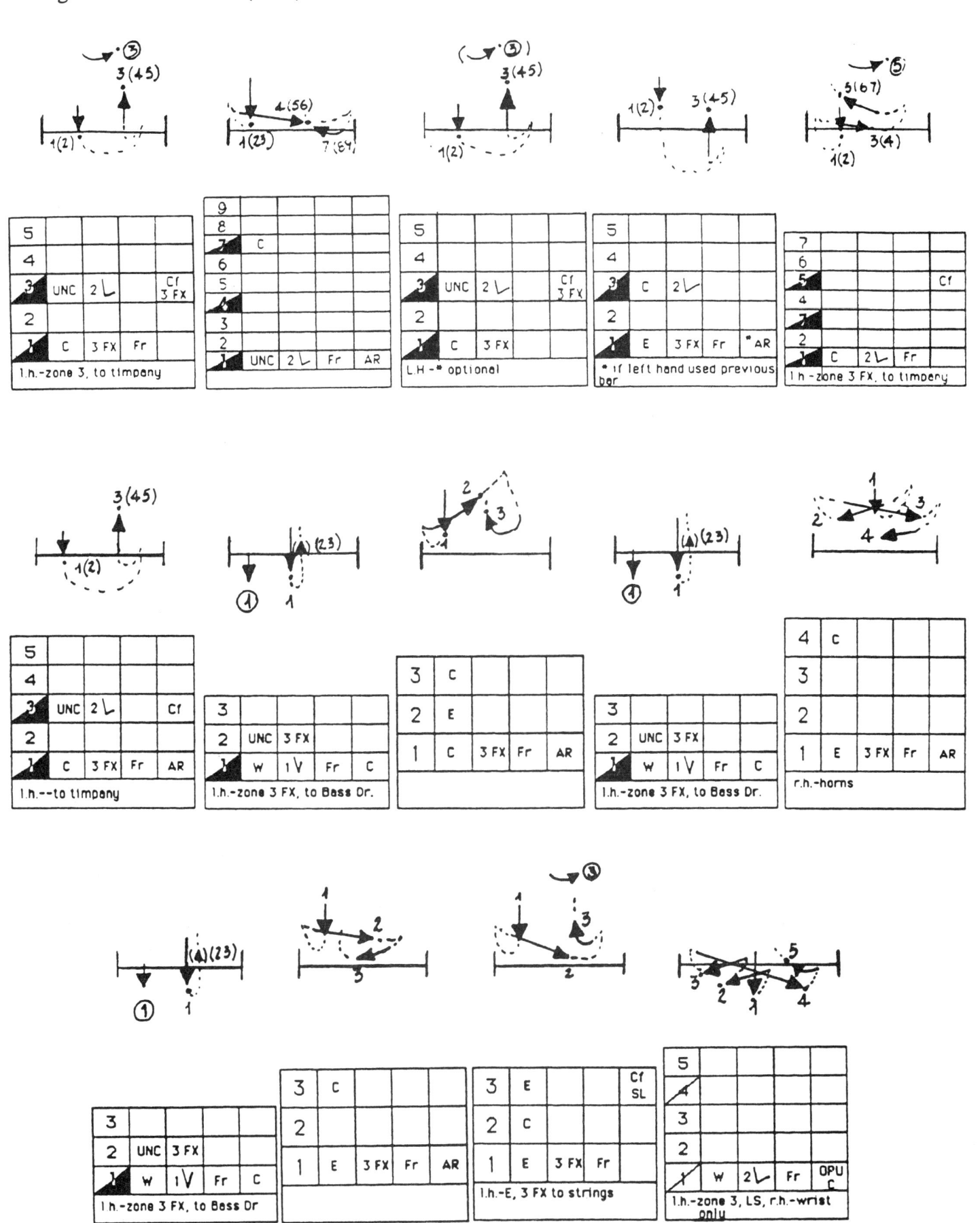

Ex. 116 One measure after number 121 to number 125

"Evocation of the Ancestors"

Ex. 116 (cont.)

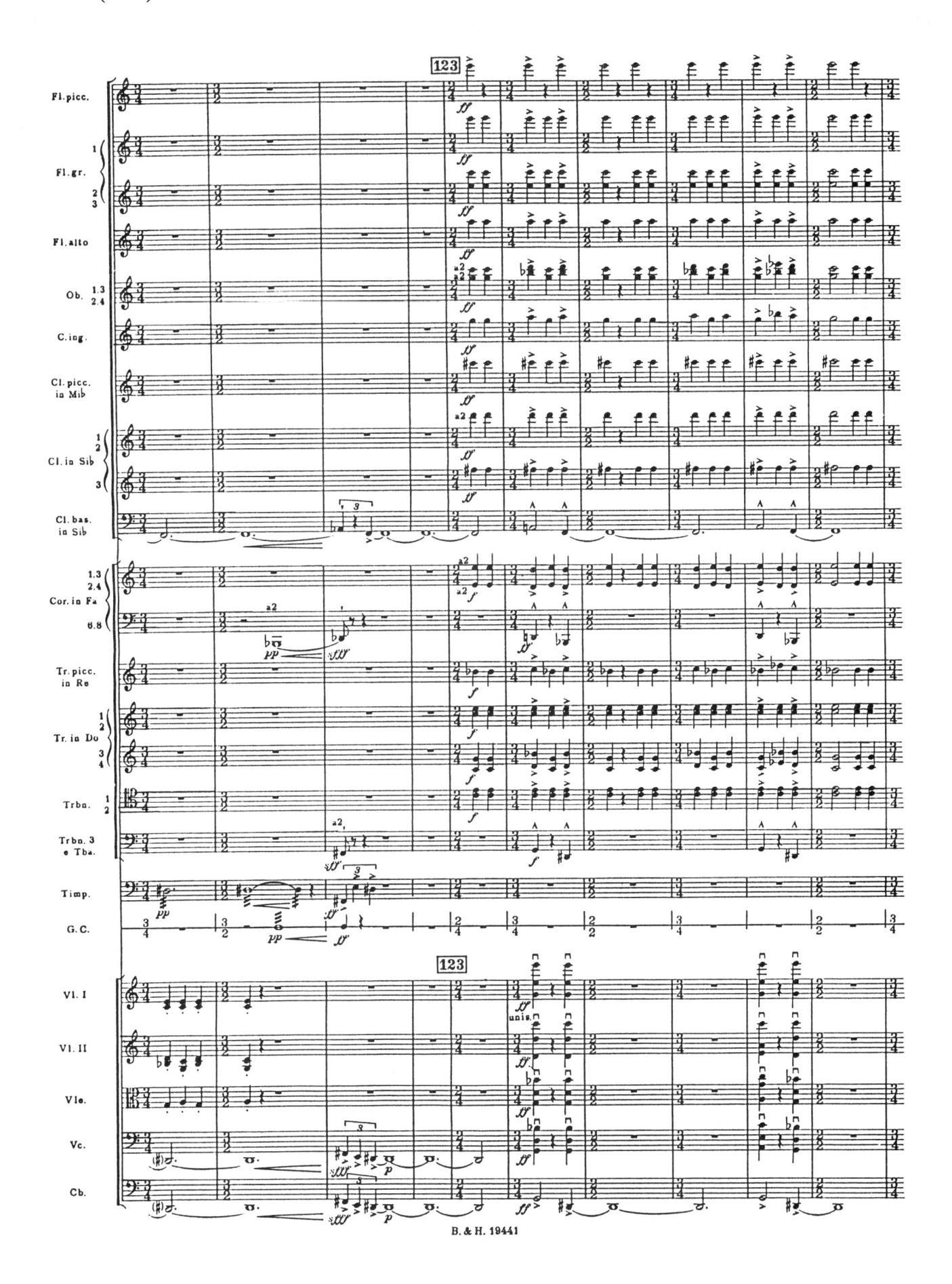

Ex. 116 (cont.)

Visual Score Study/Baton Placement

Stravinsky continues to use the same materials in a variety of rhythmic patterns. He alternates a high, bright orchestral palette (baton at E and UNC levels) with low-register dark colors (baton at W level), and utilizes the same extremes in dynamic gradations (*fortissimo*-use zone 3, to *pianissimo* or *piano*-use zones 1 or 2). The metronome is a quarter equals 144, and allows general pitch registration. All instrument transpositions as before.

Maintain the consistency of the basic unit of propulsion through the meter changes. Clean, compact, and well-placed registered strokes (wrist only with 'clicks,' or forearm only with 'clicks') will elicit rhythmically 'tight' performances.

After G.P. at Number 121 to 122

Measures 1-2 (in PatternCube) -- Timpani, bassi, celli *sffz*, W level, zone 3 FX. Mark beats 2, 3 and 1,2 in measure 2, no motion or pattern. Use left hand for *piano*-OPU. Note the sustained *fortissimo* in the bass clarinet -- eye cue only. Give a decisive upbeat preparation for the upcoming 2/2 *forte/fortissimo* measure.

Measures 3-6 -- Decide the lengths of the quarter notes. They should not be short. Address the trumpets and winds in these measures -- UCN, zone 2, Fr. measure 6, the 3/4, like measure 4, is conducted in one. Use the left hand on the first beat use for the *fortissimo* string accent. The accent on the third beat can be made by the right hand *within* the upward stroke. Momentarily stop the upward motion before three, make an upward 'click' on three, and continue downward to the next beat.

Measure 7 -- There are two dynamics on the first beat. Continue the *fortissimo* line with the right hand to the downbeat of the measure. The left hand, OPU, addresses the timpani *pianissimo* and moves to OPD for the *crescendo*. The right hand moves to the bass drum on the second beat.

Number 122 to 123

Measure 1 -- On the second beat *piano*, the left hand, OPS (fingers pointing to the side), moves to the right side at the UCN level.

Measures 2-3 -- The right hand is in zone 1, W, for the *pianissimo*. The left hand remains in place, OPU.

Measure 4 -- The timpani and bass drum are addressed by the left hand. The right hand moves through the zones for the bassi-celli *crescendi*.

Measures 5-6 -- A repeat of the two measures after the G.P. at no. 121.

Number 123 to 124

These **eight measures** are based on the five measures before no.122. They contain a series of ongoing quarter notes with one exception, the one half note three measures before 124. Make certain the length of that wind and brass articulation is a full half note! The left hand articulates the string chords on the downbeats of measures 2, 5, and 7, and, as before, the right hand can exercise the third beat option in those measures.

Number 124 to 125

This is a repeat of the **four measures** beginning from the second bar of number 122.

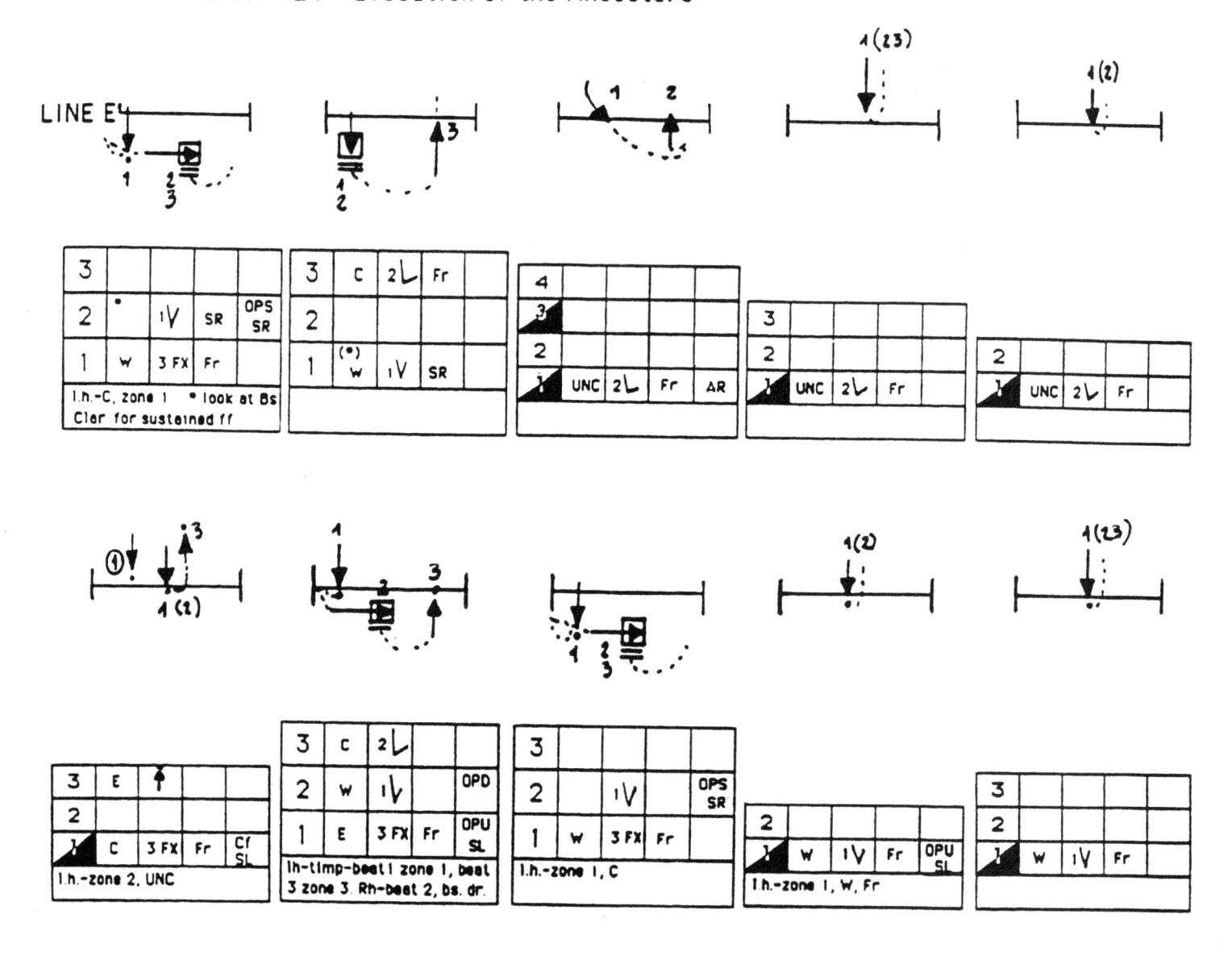

Fig. 150 **PatternCubes**

The Rite of Spring--Stravinsky

One Bar after 121--Evocation of the Ancestors

Fig. 150 **PatternCubes** (cont.)

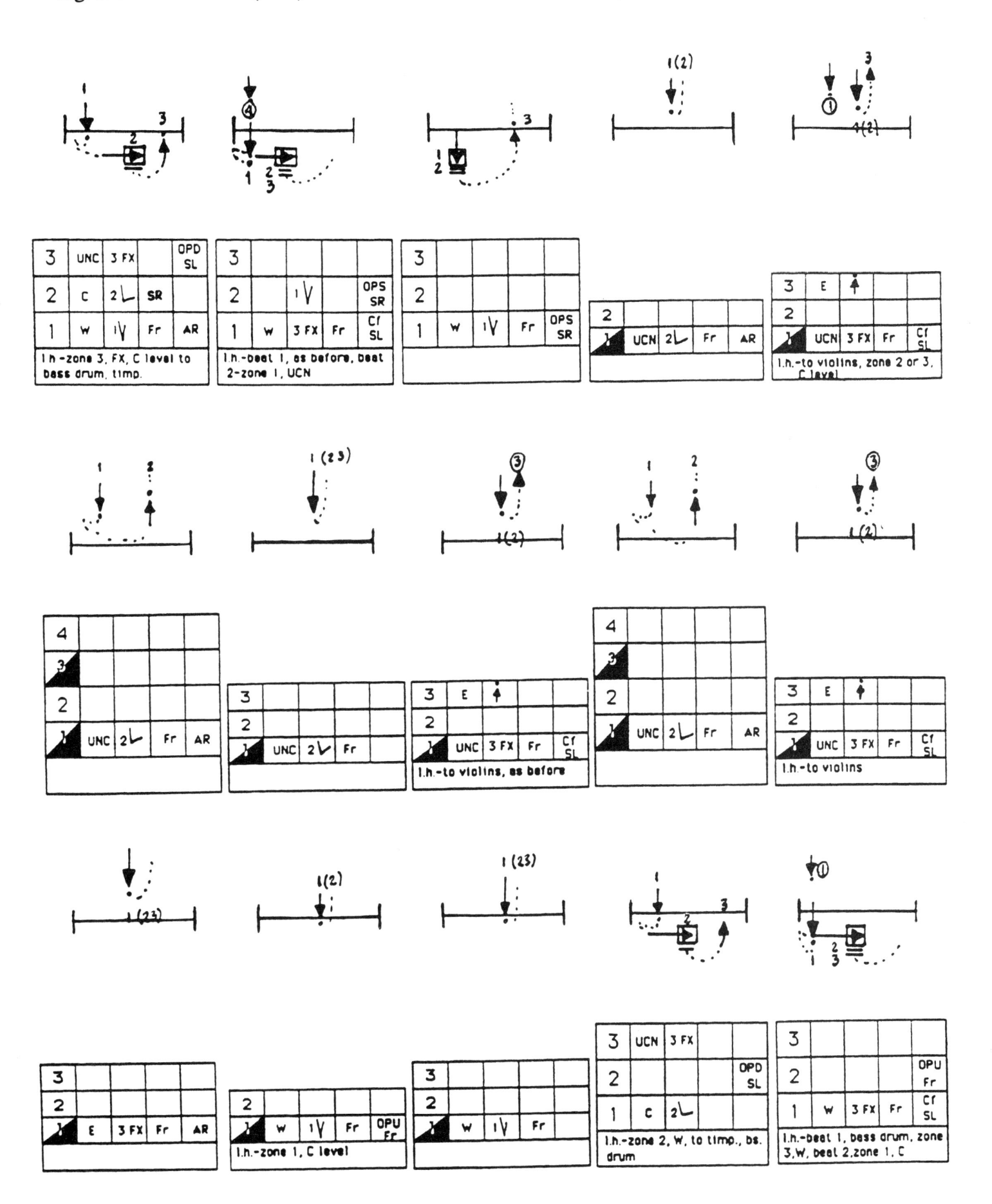

Ex. 117 Number 142 to Number 149

"Sacrificial Dance (The Chosen One)"

Ex. 117 (cont.)

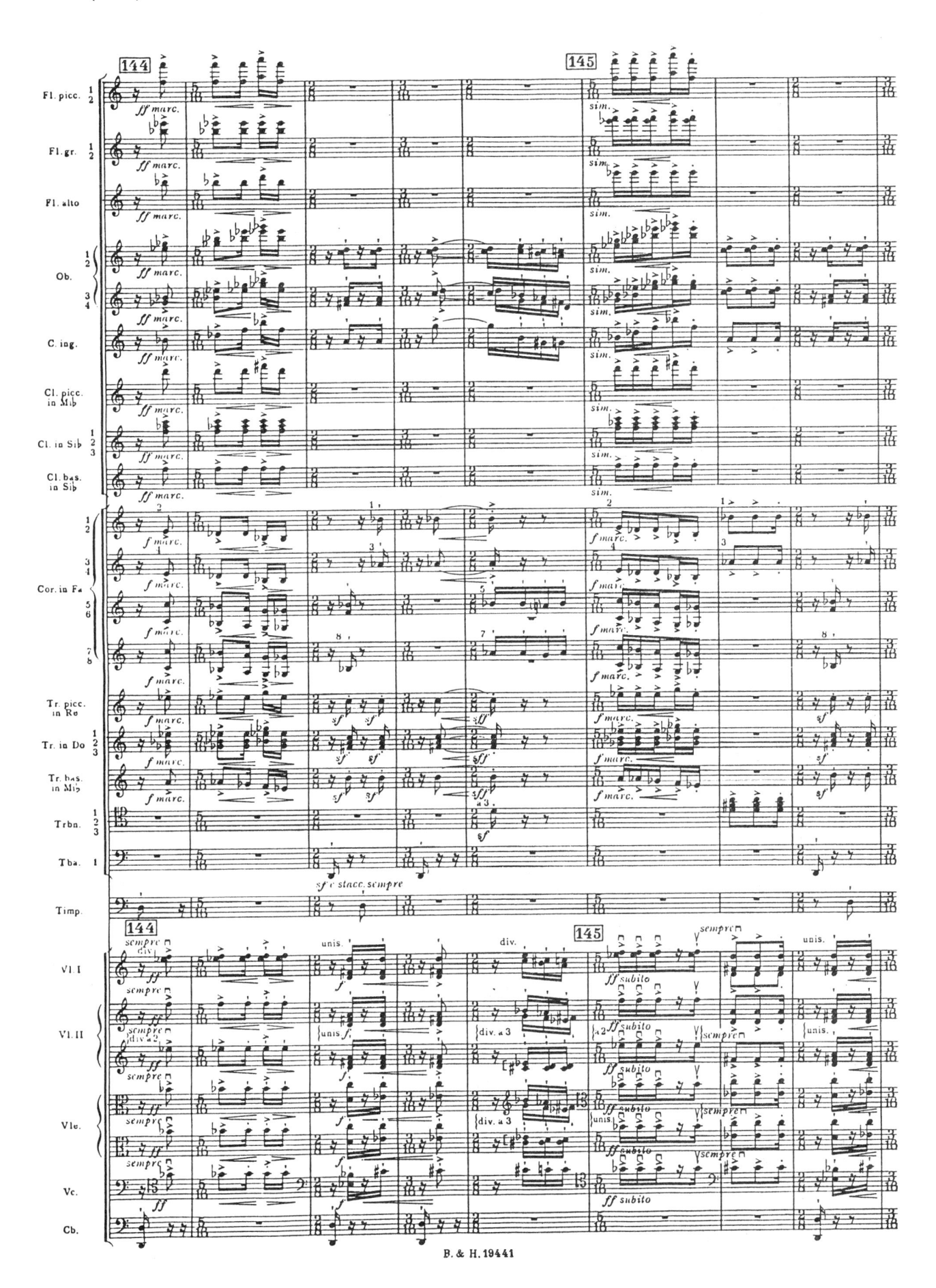

Ex. 117 (cont.)

Ex. 117 (cont.)

Visual Score Study/Baton Placement

The "Sacrificial Dance" **looks** daunting. It contains numerous 2/16, 3/16 and 5/16 measures, moves quickly, and is sprinkled with unexpected sixteenth note rests. Is the music really so different? Are there any familiar signposts to help the conductor? Let us **remove the visual barrier and alter the *physical* appearance** of the music, by changing the meters in the first five measures to read—3/4, 2/4, 3/4, 3/4, 2/2 (cut-time), instead of 3/16, 2/16, 3/16, 3/16, 2/8. The sixteenth note rests become quarter note rests. The metronome marking of 126 remains unchanged, and is now applied to the half note instead of the eighth note -- the *2/4 and 3/4* will be beaten in *one* and the *2/2 (cut-time)* in *two*. The music will *sound* exactly the same, but the *visual* aspect is not nearly as dense, or complicated looking.

Ex. 118

Eighth note equals 126

Ex. 119

Half note equals 126

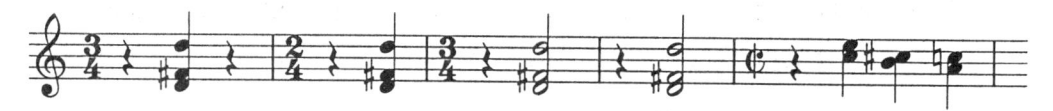

Compared to the 1967 Boosey and Hawkes, the rewritten version looks relatively tame. On closer examination the music in the 1967 version is *not* as difficult as it *looks*.

Continue the search for the familiar by adding a vocal text to Stravinsky's sound patterns. Add the word 'oom' for all the downbeats, and the word 'pah' for the remaining beats in each measure.

Ex.120

oom pah   oom pah(pah) oom pah(pah)   oom pah pah pah

The vocal version of Stravinsky will sound like—*oom-pah, oom-pah-(pah), oom-pah-(pah), oom-pah-pah-pah*. The words make Stravinsky's music sound suspiciously like two measures of a waltz surrounded by one and a half measures of a march. It is not, but a rhythmic connection with the familiar has been made, and technical needs can be addressed in a more coherent context.

Set the metronome at 96, use the PatternCube diagrams, and sing and beat the "oom-pah" text. Increase the speed of the tempo until the goal of 126, or more, is reached. When Stravinsky's metronome mark is reached, sing the original pitches instead of the "oom-pahs." The rhythmic series that is the essence of the "Sacrificial Dance" has been learned.

Number 142 to 143

Measure 1 -- This 3/16 measure is conducted in one -- beat one needs a sharp, short *staccato* stroke in order to initiate the string attack on the second beat. Use zone 1, C level. Make the short hold on 3 and *do not move the baton* until the in-tempo upbeat is made for measure 2.

Measure 2 -- This 2/16 measure is conducted in one.
Performance Note -- A reminder -- since all 2/16 and 3/16 bars are beaten in one, the heights of the 2s and 3s must differ. Make a short stroke for the wind entrance, in zone 2, UNC. Use wrist 'clicks' as much as possible throughout!

Measure 3 -- The left hand addresses the timpani, *secco*, in zone 3, C level. The conductor will get full-length eighth notes if the strokes in the 3/16 measures are higher than the strokes in the 2/16 measures.

Measure 4 -- Cue the trombones with the right hand, SR, zone 2 or 3, MC.

Measure 5 plus measure 1 of number 143, are combined **to make one 3/8 measure,** conducted in 3.
Performance Note -- Combining measures does not disrupt the flow of the music, and has the advantage of the orchestra seeing a pattern of three amidst all the downstrokes for each of the 2/16 and 3/16 measures. Do not combine measures if a set rhythmic pattern is disrupted. That is not the case at no. 143, nor in any of the combinations that follow.

Use the right hand for the trumpets on beat one in zone 3, E level. Move to the bassi on beat three, W, zone 3, SR. The left hand makes the downbeat for the violins, SL.

Number 143 to 144

Measures 1-2-3 -- These are measures 2, 3, and 4 of no. 142 with a slightly different texture. Conduct as before, but substitute a trombone cue in the second measure for the timpani cue.

Measure 4 -- This is the original measure 5 of no. 142. Conduct this measure in two. It will *not* be combined with the following bar. Cue the trumpets on beat one.

Measure 5 -- With the exception of horns 5 and 7, this is a repeat of the first measure in no. 143. Beat one for the bassi is an across-the-body stroke, SR, W, zone 3, FX.

Number 144 to 145

Measure 1 -- Use the left hand for the timpani on beat one. Note the string *fortissimo*.

Measure 2 -- There is a tutti *crescendo* to beat four, and a *diminuendo* for the next two beats. The right hand addresses the trumpets and moves from zone 2 to 3, and the left hand helps with the dynamics -- OPD for the first three beats, OPU for the last two beats.

Measure 3 -- Left hand timpani cue on beat 2. Note the string *crescendo*.

Measure 4 -- Indicate the *crescendo* for the trumpets and horns with the left hand, and within the stroke move up (C level to E level), and out (zone 2 to zone 3). Make a short left hand wrist 'click' on the next downbeat for the strings.

Measure 5 -- What is the dynamic for the strings before the *subito fortissimo*? It must be less than the *fortissimo*, so the strings are marked *forte* again after their *crescendo*.

Number 145 to 146

Measure 1 -- The strings play a *subito fortissimo*. Use the left hand to reinforce the violin dynamic. Note that all other instruments except the horns have a *crescendo*. Is that a mistake in the score?

Measure 2 -- The right hand should address the trombones, SR.

Measures 3-4, and Measures 5-6--Combine to form two patterns which contain three strokes each -- 2 +2 +3. The orchestra sees two large pattern units before moving to no.146.

Original measure 3 -- Cue the timpani with the left hand.

Original measure 4 -- Make the *crescendi* for the trumpets and winds within the stroke as before, in measure 4, no. 144.

Numbers 146-147-148

Performance Note -- Stravinsky writes a constant sixteenth note pattern which is divided between two instrumental units in irregular rhythmic configurations.

Timpani, bass and tuba form one group, and the strings, oboes, English horn and horns 5 and 7 form the other group. The timpani is the predominant instrument as it outlines the meter changes moving into no. 148.

Number 146

Measures 1-2 -- The right hand addresses the timpanist.
Note: All sixteenths must be short, and eighth notes must be given full value!

Measure 3 -- The left hand 'clicks' beat one for the violins, SL.

Number 147

Measures 1-2 -- These measures are the <u>reverse</u> of first two measures of no. 146; 3+2 instead of 2+3.

Measure 3 -- In the first three measures of no. 147, the conductor's baton and the sticks of the timpanist <u>must be as one</u>.

Measures 4-5 -- Combine into one 3/8 bar.
In original measure 5 the trumpet, trombone and wind cue should be made with the <u>right</u> hand; therefore the timpani stroke on the downbeat of the bar can be given by the <u>left</u> hand.

Number 148

Measure 1 -- 'Click' 3 in the upward stroke for the strings.

Measure 2 -- Make the <u>rebound to the left</u> in preparation for the next measure.

Measure 3 -- Make an <u>across-the-body stroke</u> to the right for the winds and brass after beat one. Use the left hand for the timpani on beat 2.

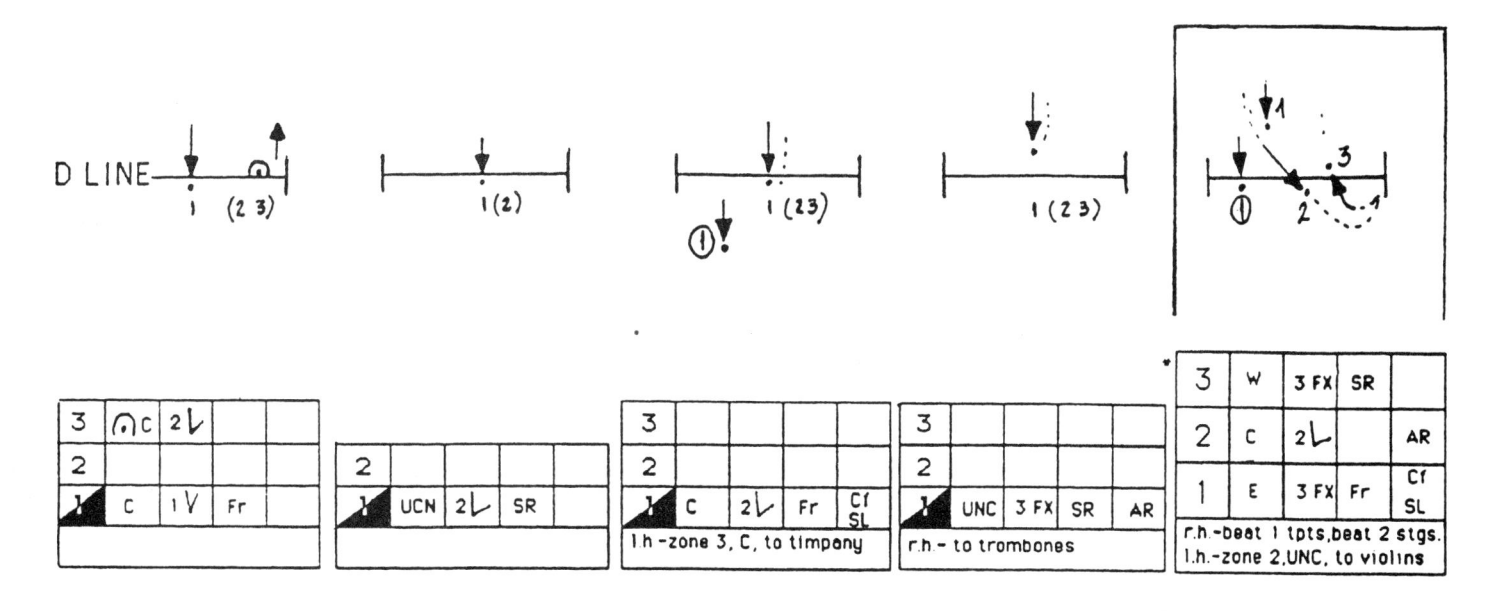

Fig. 151 **PatternCubes**

The Rite of Spring--Stravinsky

Bar Number 142 --Sacrificial Dance (The Chosen One)

267

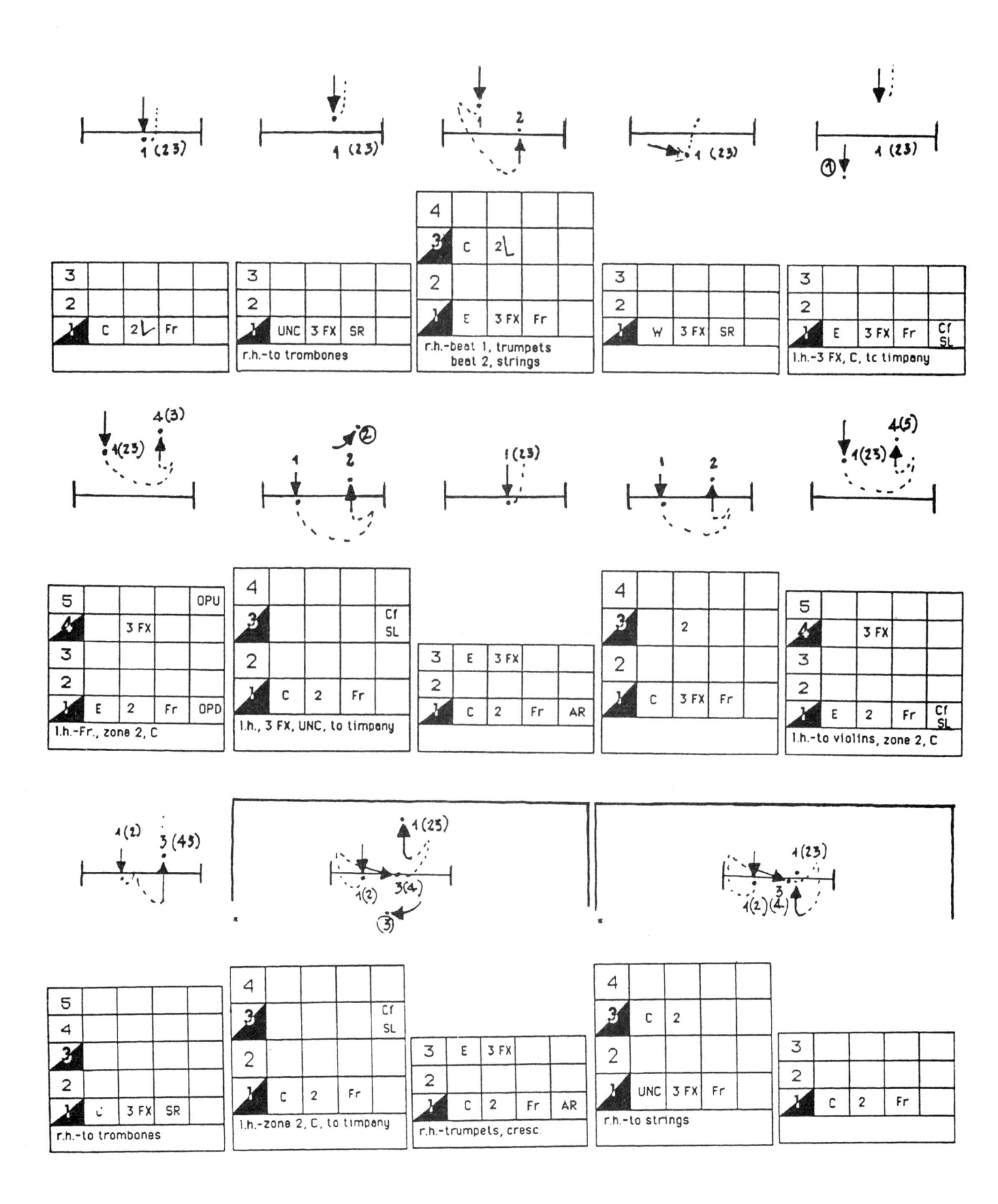

Fig. 151 **PatternCubes** (cont.)

268

Fig. 151 **PatternCubes** (cont.)

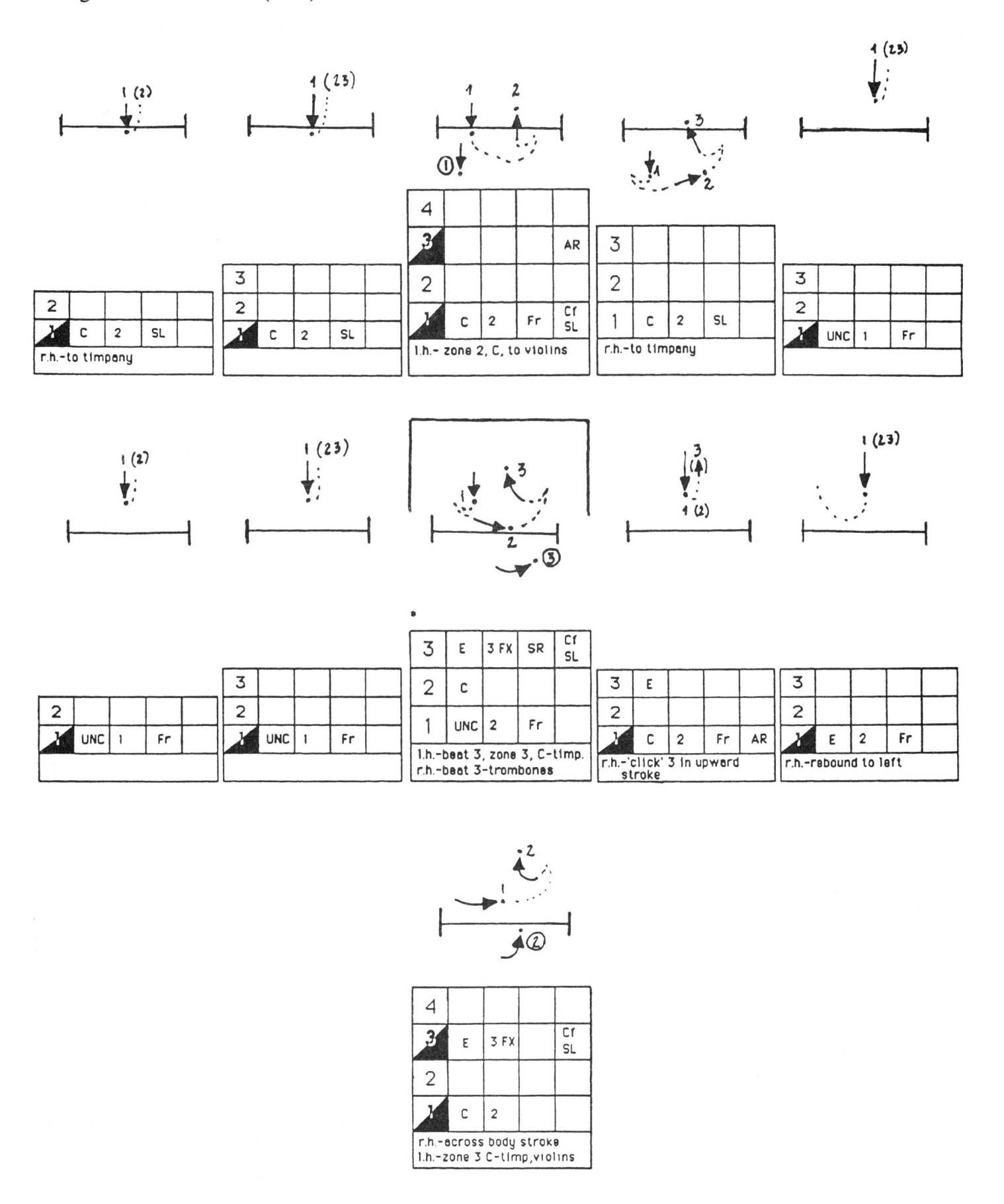

269

Ex. 121 measure number 186 to the end

"Sacrificial Dance, The Chosen One"

© 1921 by EDITION RUSSE DE MUSIQUE
Copyright assigned to BOOSEY & HAWKES, INC., for all countries
Used by permission

Ex. 121 (cont.)

Ex. 121 (cont.)

Ex. 121 (cont.)

Ex. 121 (cont.)

Ex. 121 (cont.)

Ex. 121 (cont.)

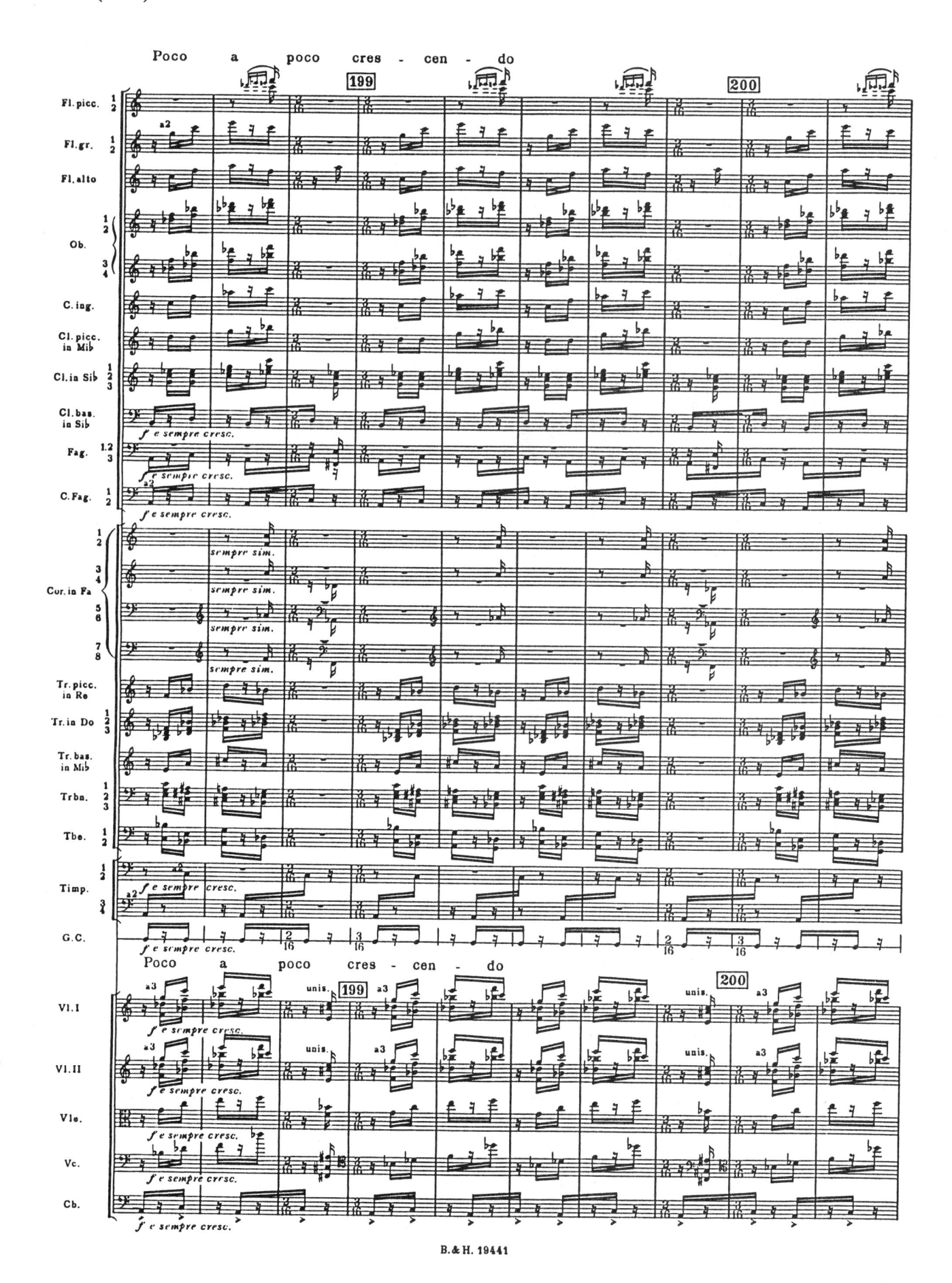

Ex. 121 (cont.)

The composer fills every pulse of every measure with sixteenth notes from no. 186 until two measures before the conclusion of the work. While the movement is constant, it is disjointed. The sixteenths are often distributed *between* various sections of the orchestra, and the interplay between orchestral blocks of sonority are scored over constantly changing meters.

Stravinsky's final charge to the finish line will benefit greatly from all the techniques that have been employed in the previous excerpts -- short, concise strokes of differing heights, use of wrist and forearm 'clicks,' and a constant pulse throughout all the meter changes, plus a constant sense of connecting to the tip of the baton.

Note: *Combined* measures are bracketed in Ex. 121

Visual Score Study/Baton Placement

Eighth note equals 126. Pitch registration possibilities are limited.

Number 186 to 188.

The two contrasting instrumental rhythmic groups are: trombones, tubas, bass trumpet, bassoons, contra-bassoon, bassi and bass drum in group one, and violins, violas and celli in group two. These units repeat the same materials for eleven bars, but in different sequential patterns.

Measure 1 -- Use downward strokes of differing heights. The dynamic is only *forte*. Beat 3 moves in the direction of the bassi and tubas. The right arm is at SR, W, zone 3, FX.

Measures 2, 3 -- Combine into one 3/8 bar.

Original measure 2 -- Address the bass drum with the left hand, SL.

Original measure 3 -- Cue the trombones with the right hand, SR. Rebound to the left.

Measure 4 -- (Cue the bass drum with the right hand, SL.)

Number 187

Measure 1 -- A repeat of no.186 without the first beat sonority.

Measure 2 -- A repeat of original measure two of no. 186.

Measure 3 -- A repeat of no. 187

Measure 4, Number 188 -- Combine these two bars into one 3/8 bar.

These measures are a repeat of measures 2 and 3 after no. 186.

Original measure 4 -- Cue the bass drum with the <u>left</u> hand (SL).

Number 188

Measure 1 -- The <u>right</u> hand moves to the trombones on beat three of the combined measure (SR).

Measure 2 -- The bass drum cue with the left hand is <u>optional</u>.

Measure 3 -- On beat 3 -- cue the bass drum with the <u>left</u> hand

Number 189 to 190

The trumpet and horn figure in the 5/16 bar, 3 after no. 189, is a new rhythmic element, <u>an entire bar of un-broken sixteenth notes within one group of instruments.</u>

Timpani is added to bassi as rhythmic units are <u>reconstructed</u>. The strings repeat their figures an octave higher, 2 after no. 189, with added afterbeats for horns as well as strings (189).

Number 189

Measure 1 -- Once again the timpanist, *mezzo-forte* only, outlines the meter. Use the <u>right hand</u>, C level, in zone 2, for the timpani. (Left hand third beat *crescendo* for the timpani, SL, optional.)

Measure 2 -- The strings are an octave higher than previously in measure 2 of no. 186

Measure 3 -- Use the right hand in zone 3, C to UNC for the trumpets and horns. Keep hand in position for measure 5 for the same instruments.

Measure 4 -- The <u>left</u> hand gives the primary pulse for the timpani.

Measure 5 -- The <u>right</u> hand is already in position for the trumpets and the horns.

Number 190

The string patterns are reconstituted. The afterbeats at no. 190 are fully harmonized, with an octave jump. The flutes and clarinets are added to horns 1 and 2. One after no.190, the pattern is again moved an octave higher. Oboes and bassoons are added to horns 1 and 2. **A bass drum note is added to the timpani pattern.** (The composer has reconstructed the two rhythmic units which he introduced at no. 186.)

Number 190

Measure 1 -- The orchestra plays at a *forte* level. The left hand for the timpani *crescendo* is optional.

Measure 2 -- Use the left hand to cue the bass drum, marked *mezzo-forte*.

Measures 3-4 -- A repeat of measures 1 and 2. The timpani *crescendo* is *poco a poco*.

Number 191

There is a *crescendo* for flutes, clarinets, horns.
(Note: Is the same *crescendo* missing for the oboes and bassoons?)

Measure 1 -- A repeat of no. 190

Measures 2-3 -- Combine into one 3/8 bar.

Original measure 3 -- Move the right hand to address the bassi, SR, in zone 2, C or UNC level.

Measure 4, no. 192 -- Combine into one 3/8 bar.

Number 192

Measure 1 -- A tutti *fortissimo crescendo* after the downbeat. The left hand addresses the bass drum, SL, and the right hand moves to the trumpets, in zone 3, FX, UNC.

Performance Note -- This combination of measures breaks up the first of a series of 2/16 plus 3/16 patterns. Based on the score these measures should not be combined. *However the arrival of the measure 2 downbeat after no. 192 has a far greater impact when it comes from the third beat of the 3/8 combination, than it has coming from the first beat of a 2/16 measure.* Stravinsky's measure structure works, and can and should be used. For those who would like to experiment, the PatternCube offers the 3/8 combination.

Measure 2 -- Note the *mezzo-forte* or *meno-forte* on beat 3, and use the left hand, OPU, in zone 2, Fr. The right hand moves back into zone 1 on the third beat.

Measures 3-4 -- The dynamic is *mezzo-forte/forte*, so remain in zone 1. Note the **rhythmic pattern for the timpani**.

Measure 5 -- A dynamic change to *subito fortissimo* and *crescendo*. Use the left hand for the bass drum, SL, zone 3, C level.

Measure 6 -- A repeat of measure 2. The left hand is in the OPU position. Performance Note -- measures 5 and 6 can be conducted as a one 6/16 measure, conducted in 2.)

Number 193 to 195 is the quiet before the final storm.

Number 193

Measures 1-2, 3-4 -- The left hand assumes the responsibility for the primary pulse -- zone 1, C, Fr. These are repeats of measures 3 and 4 of no. 192, except the horns are now marked *piano*.

Measures 5, 6 -- These two measures can be combined and conducted as 6/16, in 2.

Number 194

Measures 1-2 -- A repeat of measures 1 and 2 of no. 193

Measures 3-4 -- These measures can be combined as one measure of 6/16.

Measure 5 -- This 2/16 measure is technically important because no. 195 comes as a *jolt to the audience*. While the left hand completes its primary pulse duties, the right hand is in the middle of the body, C area, zone 1, hidden from the audience.

Number 195

Measure 1 -- The right hand makes a short forearm straight line outward stroke on beat 1, and returns toward the body on beat 2.

Measure 2 -- The right hand makes the same kind of stroke, but a longer rebound. The left hand is in the OPU position for the *mezzo forte/forte*.

Measures 3-4 -- Repeat of measures 5 and 6 of no. 193. (These measures can be combined into one 6/16 measure, and conducted in 2.)

Number 196

Measures 1-2 -- Repeat of no. 195, but do *not* use the left hand, OPU, in measure 1.

Measure 3 -- Use the normal down stroke of the left hand for the bass drum.

Measure 4 -- Use the left hand, OPU, on beat 3, for the dynamic change.

Number 197

Measure 1 -- The string dynamic remains *meno forte* until 3 measures after no. 198.

Measure 2 -- The first piccolo entrance in this section needs a right hand cue, E level, zone 2 or 3, Fr. Note the dynamics for the horns-*sff*.

Measures 3-4-5 -- Despite the meter changes, the bass drum and timpani pulse remains regular over these measures into no. 198.

Performance Note -- Some conductors have rescored the 3+3+2 sequence into one 4/8 bar. The displacement of these bar lines, the beginning of the final surge towards the end of the piece, generally flattens the tension that is inherent in the irregular metric structure. The PatternCube adheres to Stravinsky's original meters.

Measure 5 -- Use wrist only for this 2/16 and the following measure.

Number 198

Measure 1 -- Make a right hand wrist stroke with the rebound moving to the left. The left hand accounts for the bass drum.

Measure 2 -- A right hand across-the-body stroke to the right. The left hand is OPU on beat 3.

Measures 3-4 -- The beginning of a *poco a poco crescendo* to no. 201. Repeat of measures 3 and 4 from no. 197.

Measure 5 -- A repeat of 1 measure before no. 198.

Number 199

Measures 2-3-4 -- The *crescendo* continues. These measures are a repeat of measures 2, 3, and 4 of no. 198.

Measure 5 -- A repeat of 1 before no. 199. Use the wrist.

Number 200

Measures 1-2 -- Continue the *crescendo*, but *do not get faster*. Change the right hand beat pattern to a down/up 2 pattern over the two measures, a stroke for each measure.

Measures 3-4 -- A repeat of measures 1 and 2.

Measure 5 -- A repeat of 1 measure before no. 200.

Number 201

Measure 1--The left hand moves to the bass drum in zone 3, SL. The right hand addresses the trumpets and the other brass instruments.

Measure 2 -- The right hand makes a sharp 'click' on beat 1 in zone 3. Beat 2 is made in zone 1, a preparation for the flute *piano* on beat 3. On beat 2 the left hand shows the OPU position to the first violins, SL.

Measure 3 -- *Do not make any movements for the first 2 beats in the measure.* On beat 3, the right hand makes a sharp upward 'click' stopped stroke in E level, zone 3, FX.

Final measure -- Make an emphatic downward left hand stroke, in zone 1, at the W level.

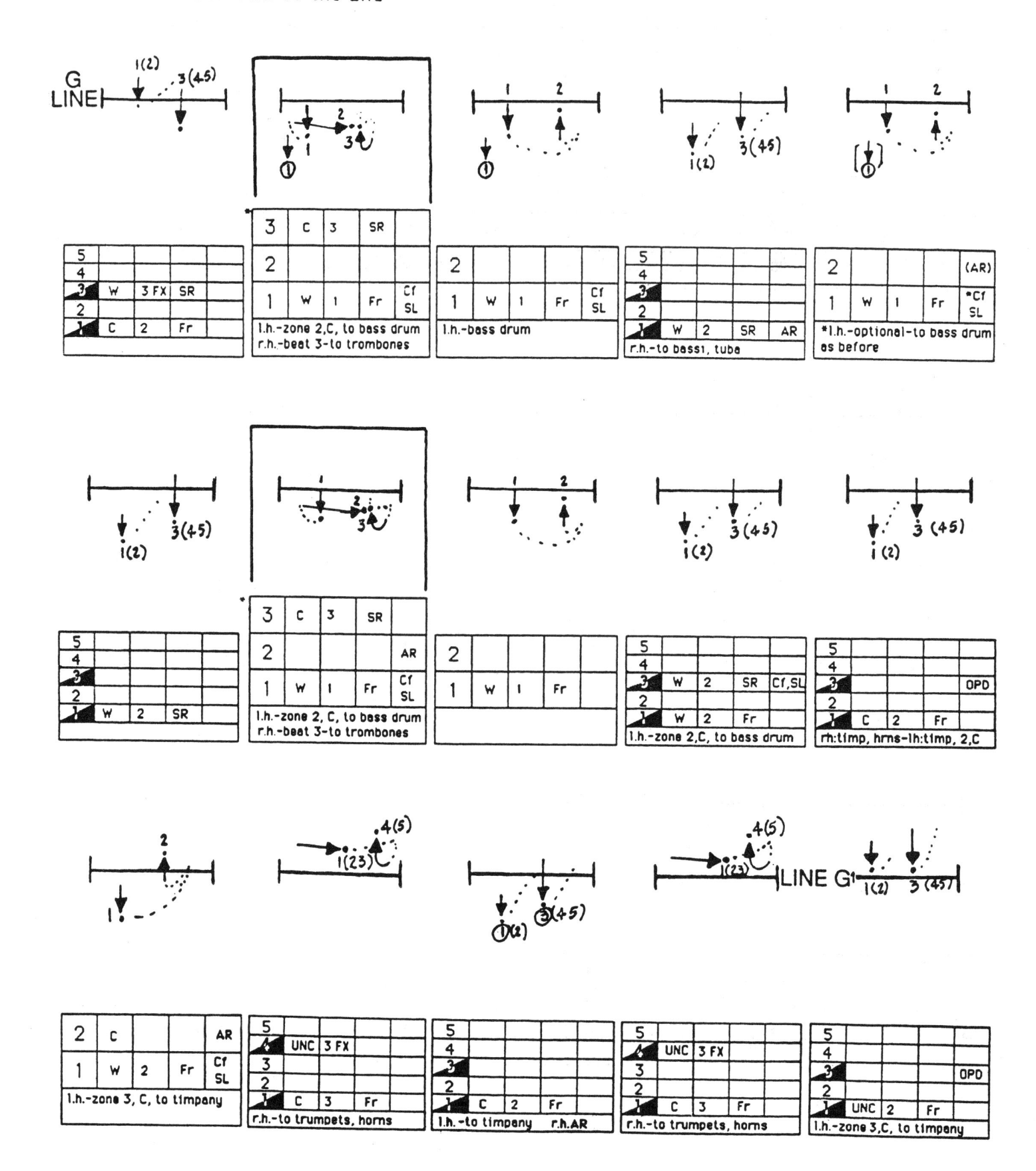

Fig. 152 PatternCubes

The Rite of Spring--Stravinsky

Bar Number 186 to the End

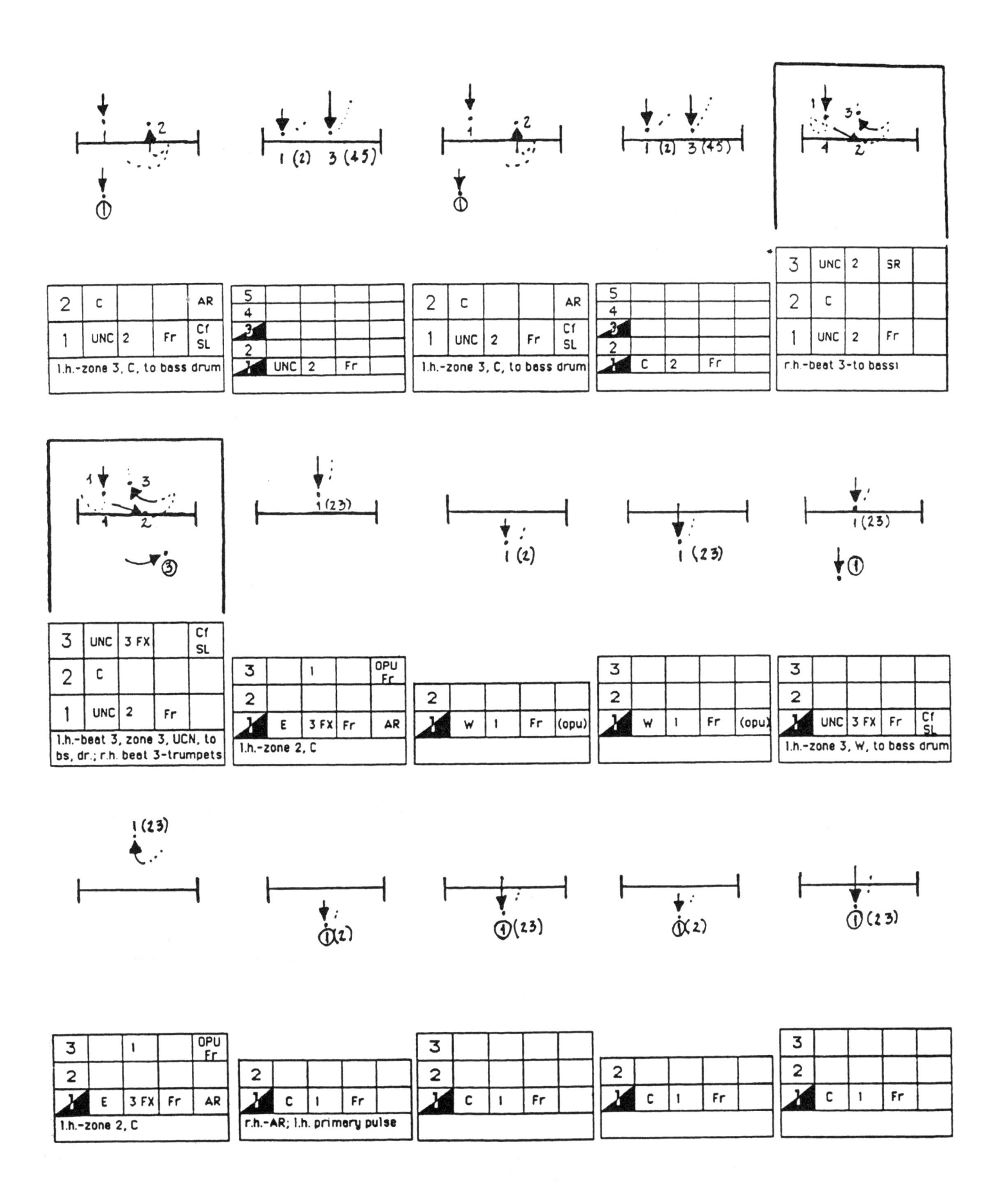

Fig. 152 **PatternCubes** (cont.)

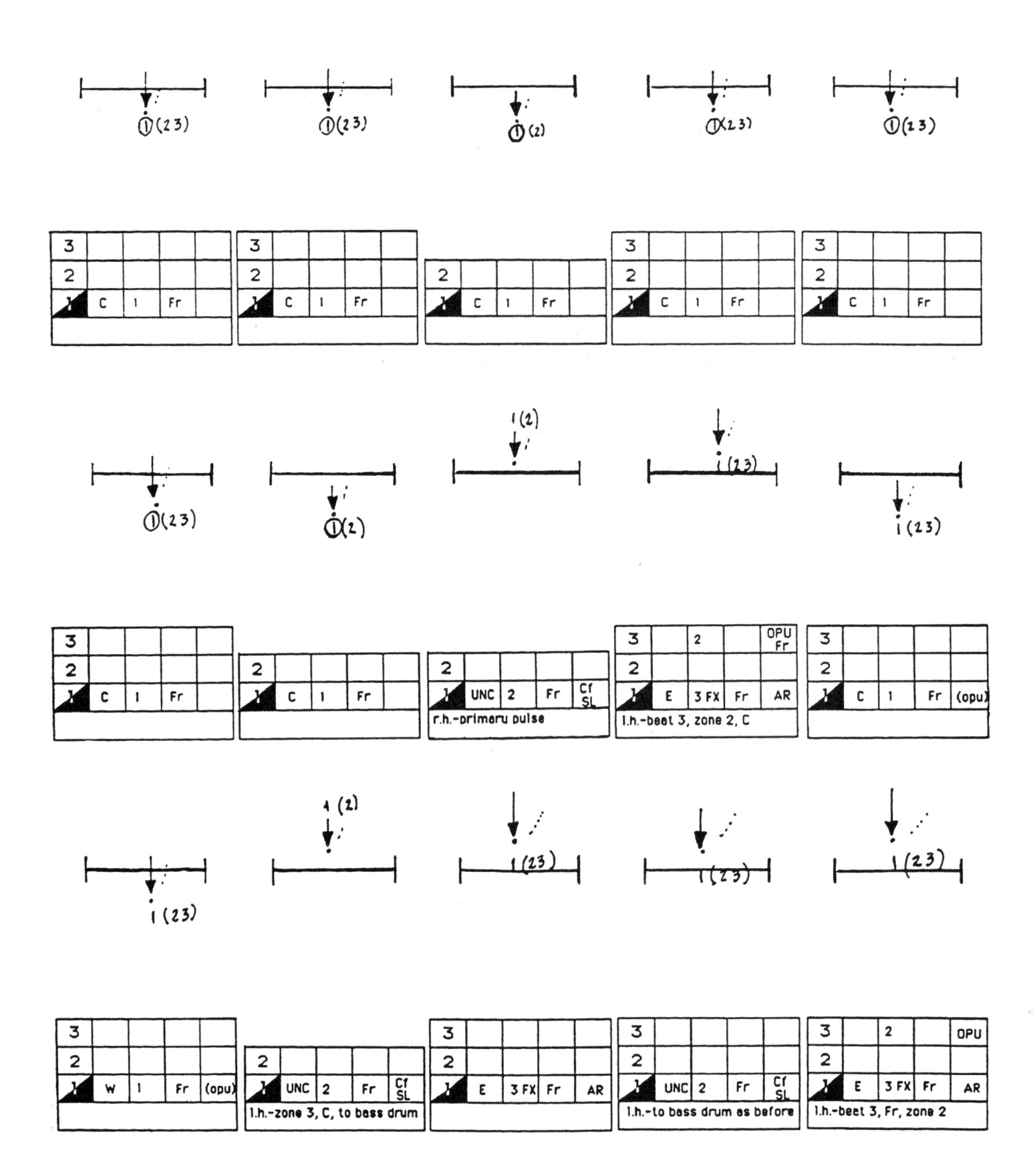

Fig. 152 **PatternCubes** (cont.)

286

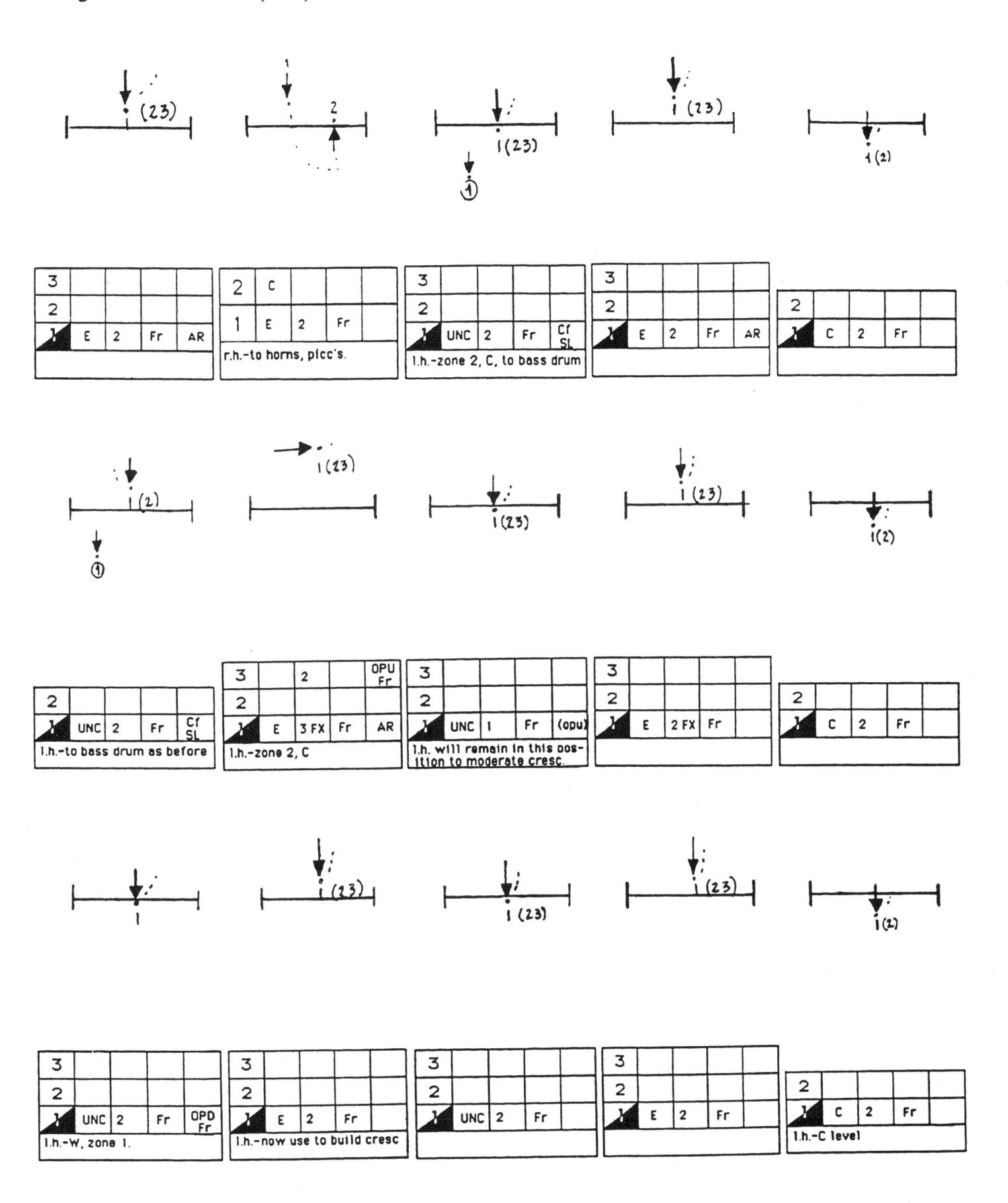

Fig. 152 **PatternCubes** (cont.)

Fig. 152 **PatternCubes** (cont.)

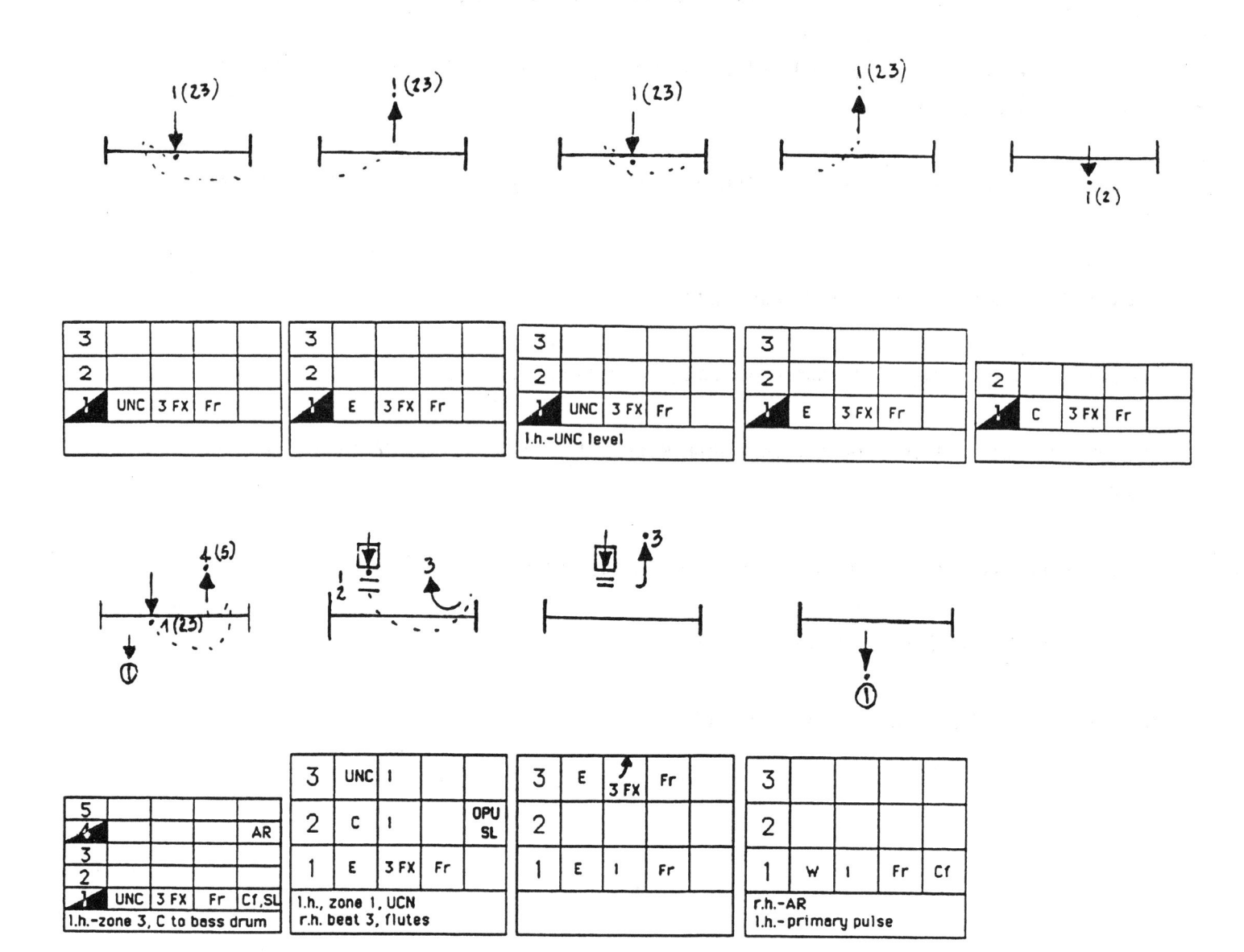

BIBLIOGRAPHY

Blom, Eric. *Syncopation.* Grove's Dictionary of Music and Musicians, 5th ed., vol. 8. New York: St. Martin's Press, Inc., 1954.

Galkin, Eliott W. *A History of Orchestral Conducting in Theory and Practice.* New York: Pendragon Press, 1988.

Harvard Dictionary of Music, s.v. "breath mark."

Random House Unabridged Dictionary, 2nd ed., s.v. "art form & music."

Schenker, Heinrich. "Konzertdirigenten." 1894. Reprint. *Heinrich Schenker als Essayist und Kritiker* (1990): 81-82.

Schunemann, Georg. *Geschichte des Dirigierens.* Leipzig: Brietkopf und Hartel, 1913.

Speyer, Rudolf Cahn. *Handbuch des Dirigierens.* Leipzig: Brietkopf und Hartel, 1919.

Strauss, Richard. *Capriccio.* Berlin: Oertel, 1942.